CW01429721

CERVANTES THE POET

Cervantes the Poet travels from the court of Isabel de Valois to Rome, Naples, Palermo, Algiers, and Madrid's *barrio de las letras*. Recovering Cervantes' nearly forty-year literary career before the publication of *Don Quijote*, Gabrielle Ponce-Hegenauer demonstrates the cultural, literary, and theoretical significance of Cervantes' status as a late-sixteenth-century itinerant poet. This study recovers the generative literary milieus and cultural practices of Spain's most famous novelist in order to posit a new theory of the modern novel as an organic transformation of lyric practices native to the late sixteenth century and Cervantes' own literary outlook.

GABRIELLE PONCE-HEGENAUER is Associate Professor of Letters and Associate Professor of Feminist, Gender, and Sexuality Studies at Wesleyan University.

CERVANTES THE POET

The Don Quijote*, Poetic Practice, and the Conception of the First Modern Novel*

GABRIELLE PONCE-HEGENAUER
Wesleyan University

CAMBRIDGE
UNIVERSITY PRESS

University Printing House, Cambridge CB2 8BS, United Kingdom

One Liberty Plaza, 20th Floor, New York, NY 10006, USA

477 Williamstown Road, Port Melbourne, VIC 3207, Australia

314–321, 3rd Floor, Plot 3, Splendor Forum, Jasola District Centre, New Delhi – 110025, India

103 Penang Road, #05–06/07, Visioncrest Commercial, Singapore 238467

Cambridge University Press is part of the University of Cambridge.

It furthers the University's mission by disseminating knowledge in the pursuit of education, learning, and research at the highest international levels of excellence.

www.cambridge.org
Information on this title: www.cambridge.org/9781316517390
DOI: 10.1017/9781009041119

First published 2023

A catalogue record for this publication is available from the British Library.

Library of Congress Cataloging-in-Publication Data
NAMES: Ponce-Hegenauer, Gabrielle, author.
TITLE: Cervantes the poet : the Don Quijote, poetic practice, and the conception of the first modern / Gabrielle Ponce-Hegenauer.
DESCRIPTION: Cambridge, United Kingdom ; New York, NY : Cambridge University Press, 2023. | Includes bibliographical references and index.
IDENTIFIERS: LCCN 2022023845 (print) | LCCN 2022023846 (ebook) | ISBN 9781316517390 (hardback) | ISBN 9781009045414 (paperback) | ISBN 9781009041119 (ebook)
SUBJECTS: LCSH: Cervantes Saavedra, Miguel de, 1547–1616 – Technique. | Poetics. | Quixote, Don (Fictitious character) – In literature. | LCGFT: Literary criticism.
CLASSIFICATION: LCC PQ6356 .P66 2023 (print) | LCC PQ6356 (ebook) | DDC 863/.3–dc23/eng/20220817
LC record available at https://lccn.loc.gov/2022023845
LC ebook record available at https://lccn.loc.gov/2022023846

ISBN 978-1-316-51739-0 Hardback

Pero, para la carga de un poeta,
siempre ligera, cualquier bestia puede
llevarla, pues carece de maleta

Viaje del Parnaso
(1614)

Contents

Figures

Acknowledgments

This project began during my first semester as a doctoral student in Harry Sieber's seminar on the *Don Quijote* in the Rare Books Room of the Peabody Library. Since that time, I have benefited from the generosity of countless individuals and organizations. I wish to extend my gratitude to the librarians and staff of the following libraries and archives: Biblioteca Nacional (Madrid, Spain), Biblioteca de la Real Academia de Historia (Madrid, Spain), British Library (London, UK), Vatican Library (Vatican City, Italy), Biblioteca dei Lincei (Rome, Italy), Biblioteca Nazionale (Rome, Italy), Biblioteca Santa Scholastica (Subiaco, Italy), Bibliothèque Nationale de France, Richeleau (Paris, France), National Library (St. Petersburg, Russia), Biblioteca centrale della Regione Siciliana (Palermo, Sicily), Biblioteca Comunale di Palermo (Sicily), Biblioteca Nazionale (Naples, Italy). A special thanks to Gabriela Lo Presti and the erudite ladies of the reading room at the Biblioteca centrale della Regione Siciliana, Palermo, and to Madame Natalia Elagina of the National Library of Russia, St. Petersburg. I also wish to express my gratitude to my editor, Emily Hockley, who took an immediate interest in and supported this project from the beginning, and throughout the many challenges of the pandemic, and to the staff of Cambridge University Press for the many hours and much hard work that went into this publication.

For insights and assistance of every kind, I wish to thank Betsy Wright, Rodrigo Cacho-Casal, Felipe Valencia, Marsha Collins, Felipe Pereda, Karla Mallette, Geoffrey Parker, Fernando Bouza, Manuel Colas Gil, Giuseppe Grilli, Alessandro Serio, Chris Celenza, Eugenio Ruffini, Jim Coleman, Denis J.-J. Robichaud, Sara Castro-Klarén, Sue Waterman, Michael Armstrong-Roche, Marco Arezu, Jeff Rider, Michael Meere, Phil Wagoner, Maria Ospina, Hirsh Sawany, Valeria López Fadul, Courtney Weiss Smith, Suzy Taraba, Lori Nussdorfer, and the many members of the Wesleyan Renaissance Seminar. For discussions of incredible breadth and invaluable collaboration which have informed and improved upon many features of this project, I wish to thank my colleagues in the College of Letters at Wesleyan University: Charlie Barber Joe Fitzpatrick, Daniel Smyth, Jesse Torgerson, Tushar Irani, Typhaine Leservot, Uli Plass, Ethan Kleinberg, Kari Weil, and Khachig Tölölyan. For their instrumental feedback and generous support of this project, I wish to thank the anonymous reviewers who took the time out of their own lives to review this work prior to publication, despite the many challenges of the pandemic. This project would not have been possible without several grants from the Charles Singleton Center for the Study of Early and Pre-Modern Europe, the Millicent Mercer Johnson Pre-Doctoral Rome Prize Fellowship from the American Academy in Rome, the Johns Hopkins University Dean's Teaching Fellowship, and a Faculty Fellowship in the Center for the Humanities at Wesleyan University.

My debt to the idyllic fields of contemplation both in and around Gilman Hall at The Johns Hopkins University is ineffable, and my poor *ingenio* is hardly up to the task of thanking the many people who populated my intellectual imagination during my time in Baltimore. Thank you to Earle Havens, who first hired me in Special Collections when I was still an MFA student in the Writing Seminars Department, and who hired me again as a Teaching Assistant in his Museums and Archives winter-intersession study abroad course, an opportunity that allowed me to make my first consultation of ms. Egerton 2062 at the British Library. To Paul Espinosa of the Peabody Library, who oversaw much of my work in the Rare Books Room and whose support was a great boon. To Bill Egginton, for taking charge of a *Festschrift* issue of the *MLN* in honor of Harry Sieber in which "Lyric and Empire" (2021) appeared. To Eduardo Gonzalez, who welcomed me into his seminar on the contemporary novel in Spanish when I was still an MFA student, who introduced me to the Department of German & Romance Languages & Literatures, and who shepherded me to the first of many gatherings of the Humanities Center which took place in the home of Dick Macksey (invaluable intellectual opportunities from which I greatly benefited), for his theoretical dynamism, and his warmth and goodwill for the graduate student body. To Richard Kagan, for teaching me to decipher a *b* from a *v* from a *u*, and all things paleographical, archival, and convivial. To Walter Stephens, whose support from the very outset of this project opened many windows and doors and made possible research that would otherwise have gone unrealized, for his curiosity, enthusiasm, and genuine encouragement. To Harry Sieber, my dissertation advisor, whose *agudo ingenio*, inestimable erudition, endless patience, and exemplary integrity cannot be repaid, a true mentor. Without his guidance and support this project would not have been realized.

Hundreds of years ago, amidst every kind of violence and fanaticism (ideologies from which many never entirely freed themselves), a number of individuals chose (however imperfectly) to dedicate considerable time and effort to the writing of imaginative literature. These authors may be dead in the biological and theoretical sense, but I have spent such a great deal of time with these literary artifacts, texts which have changed who I am and the course of my life, that I would be remiss not to acknowledge the power of poiesis here.

To Cervantes, the poet, and his peers, the deceased and the imaginary, thank you.

Note on Abbreviations, Translations, and Terms

For the sake of simplicity, I have abbreviated "the *Don Quijote*" (text) as **the *DQ*** and "don Quijote" (character) as **dQ**. For the *DQ* I have retained Leo Spitzer's use of the definite article. For dQ I have preferred the Spanish lowercase "don" to differentiate text from character. Alonso Quijano appears as **AQ**. For eponymous titles such as *La Diana*, *El pastor de Fílida*, and *La Galatea*, I have dropped the definite article in Spanish and retained it in English (i.e. **the *Diana***).

Unless otherwise noted, all translations are my own. At the risk of infelicitous renderings I have attempted to stay close to the original text, often retaining Latin roots and preferring a scholarly over a poetic emphasis. Words such as ***ingenio*** which must acquire meaning through the usages discussed in this text, are left in the original.

For the purposes of this study, I differentiate **Lyric**, a type of non-narrative poetry which privileges the interiority of the speaker, from **Poetry**, a stand-in for literature at large, from **Verse**, as a format that Poetry can take (the metric in prosimetrics), from **Poiesis**, as making.

Romance, sometimes called the Byzantine Romance, should not be confused with the English "Romances of Chivalry," which are *libros de caballeria* in the Spanish or with the Spanish ***romance***, a narrative-ballad associated with folk traditions which was "modernized" by poets such as Lope de Vega, Liñán de Riaza, and Cervantes in the 1580s, or **Romantic** in the nineteenth-century literary sense, or with **romantic** in as a synonym for erotic or amorous.

For the sake of space, all bibliographic references occur in their entirety in their first mention in the notes and subsequently as short titles. There is no bibliography.

INTRODUCTION

The Unknown History of the Conception of the Don Quijote

> Folly, where the values of another age, another art, another morality are put into question, and also, where all the forms, even the most distant, of the human imagination, are mixed up, troubled, and strangely compromised by one another in a common chimera.[1]

Writing at the perigee of what could be called the modern era (mid-fifteenth century–mid-twentieth century), Michel Foucault historicized madness in civilization as a "nouvelle incarnation du mal" that came to replace the socio-cultural role of leprosy – a periphery that denotes a center – between the fourteenth and seventeenth centuries as leprosy was eradicated from Europe.[2] A "nouvelle incarnation de l'homme," Cervantes' *DQ* situated the first modern novelistic character at that "obscure limit, indeterminate but constant, that passes between those who are fools and those who are not."[3] Through the use of an original protagonist, in the *DQ* Cervantes placed the periphery at the center of the modern novelistic plot. As Lukàcs observed, the modern European novel as a literary genre is generated by a protagonist who occupies a fundamental

[1] "Folie, où sont mises en question les valeurs d'un autre âge, d'un autre art, d'une autre morale, mais où se reflètent aussi, brouillées et troublées, étrangement compromises les unes par les autres dans une chimère commune, toutes les formes, même les plus distantes, de l'imagination humaine," (M. Foucault, Histoire de la folie . l'.ge classique, Paris : Gallimard, 1972, 57).

[2] "c'est le sens de cette exclusion, l'importance dans le groupe social de cette figure insistante et redoutable qu'on n'écarte pas sans avoir tracé autour d'elle un cercle sacré" (M. Foucault, *Historie de la folie à l'âge classique*, Paris: Gallimard, 1972, 18–66, esp. 18–21). Foucault's analysis is more complicated and includes the figures of venereal disease and death. When he resituates the errant fool of the *Narrenschiff* from the periphery of the social milieu to its center, the interior functions as another periphery, an exiled core, the interiorization of death: "Dans la littérature savante également, la Folie est au travail, au cocur même de la raison et de la vérité" (*ibid.*,29).

[3] "limite obscure, indécise, mais constante qui passe entre les fous et ceux qui ne le sont pas" (M. Foucault, *Folie, langage, littérature*, eds. H.-P. Fruchaud, D. Lorenzini, and J. Revel, Paris: J. Vrin, 2019, 89). On madness in the *DQ:* (C.B. Johnson, *Madness and Lust: A Psychoanalytic Approach to DQ*, Berkeley: University of California Press, 1983). For Cervantes' intersection with early modern humoral theory via Huarte de San Juan's *Examen de ingenios*: (O. Green, "El ingenioso hidalgo," *Hispanic Review*, 1957, vol. XXV, 171–193).

divide between interior and exterior. For Cervantes, this was not a simple movement of inversion. In the *DQ* the boundary between folly and reason, drawn by the limits of language itself, destabilizes the gesture of putting the outside in or turning the inside out.[4] There is little question that this unsettling revolves around the mad knight errant, dQ. But this study shifts the focus away from the Knight of the Lions to his maker. Not to Cide Hamete Benengeli, nor to the archivists of La Mancha, not even to the translator or the unwieldly narrator. This study is interested in AQ, a modern author, the author of dQ. He is a special kind of maker caught up in a special kind of making: poiesis. This study of poetic practice and the conception of the first modern European novel is interested in AQ, the poet, and in the poet who made him, Miguel de Cervantes.

Hero or fool? is the question that society asks of the poet, and finally the question that the poet must ask of themselves.[5] At once poet and pseudonym (AQ and dQ), Cervantes' most infamous literary character takes up the limits of language, again and again, as the site of articulation by way of which the intimate lyric interior attempts to become legible within the socialized history of a human life.[6] While the modern European novel has habitually been studied and theorized as a version of the classical literary genre of epic poetry, this study seeks to demonstrate that the modern European novel—what makes it possible and what makes possible its dialectic with madness—is actually a form of lyric poetry which problematizes the role of the human interior within the social whole or "common chimera."[7]

[4] For the continuation of this theme in contemporary thought: (eds. O. Custer, P. Deutscher, and S. Haddad, *Foucault/Derrida Fifty Years Later*, New York: New Directions, 2016). As Lynne Huffer observes in the same volume, "It would be more appropriate, Foucault writes, to approach the [*History of Madness*] as a study of 'the structure of experience': not a linguistic structure, but a *historical* one 'whose seat is,' paradoxically, at that structure's 'margins [*confins*]' (HMP xxxii/192). This 'experience,' Foucault suggests, does not reside *outside* of history (it 'is,' after all, 'history through and through'), but on the very border that tells us what history is, the very border that constitutes the experience of madness as limit, exclusion, or confinement (as the original French '*confins*' suggests). . . . And that 'structure of experience' is historical in a specifically Foucauldian, archival sense: not as a historical totality, but as a 'precarious' (AK 17/29) seat on the border of time that Foucault calls 'this blank space from which I speak' (AK 17/29)" ("Looking Back at *History of Madness*," in eds. O. Custer, P. Deutscher, and S. Haddad, *Foucault/Derrida*, 25–27).

[5] (J. Allen, *DQ, Hero or Fool?*, University of Florida Press, 1969, vol. I–II).

[6] As Foucault observed, "Cervantès, c'est la littérature même dans la littérature" (Foucault, *Folie, langage*, 91). Mary Gaylord on the *Galatea* has written, "Cervantes here makes the central issue of pastoral art not sentiment but the way that sentiment can be expressed" (M. Gaylord, "The Language of Limits and the Limits of Language: The Crisis of Poetry in *La Galatea*," *MLN.*, n.2, 1982, vol. XCVII, 254–271).

[7] In *Theory of the Novel*, Lukács comes very close to the lyric as modern novelistic fiction, especially when his analysis is focused on the *DQ*, but he consistently misidentifies this as an epic impulse: "The epic and the novel, these two major forms of great epic literature, differ from one another not by their authors' fundamental intentions but by the given historico-philosophical realities with which the

At the same time that madness took up an exiled center within the domains of reason and truth in European thought, the *figura of the poet* went underground.[8] Once central to the structure of court patronage, during the final decades of the sixteenth century the practice of lyric poetry began to disappear from spheres of socio-political power.[9] Coincident with the rise of proto-capitalism, religious extremism, urban economic sprawl, and the growing efficacy of the Cartesian *cogito*, over the course of the seventeenth and eighteenth centuries the gradual devaluation of the lyric human interior, as an exiled space of unreason, recast the *figura of the poet* as madman, a figure whose very *raison d'être* was viewed as folly.[10] At the

authors were confronted. The novel is the epic of an age in which the extensive totality of life is no longer directly given, in which the immanence of meaning in life has become a problem, yet which still thinks in terms of totality" (G. Lukács, *Theory of the Novel: A historico-philosophical essay on the forms of great epic literature*, trans. Bostock, Cambridge: MIT Press, 1987, 54–56). While Bakhtin severed poetry from the heteroglossia of the novel, lyric practice in sixteenth-century Spain was utterly heteroglot, aptly though unwittingly described in the following comment: "The word, breaking through to its own meaning and its own expression across an environment full of alien words and variously evaluating accents, harmonizing with some of the elements in this environment and striking a dissonance with others, is able, in this dialogized process, to shape its own stylistic profile. Such is the *image in artistic prose* and the image of *novelistic prose* in particular" (M. Bakhtin, *The Dialogic Imagination*, M. Holquist and C. Emerson (trans. and eds.), University of Texas Press, 1981, 277–278, emphasis in original). I treat lyric as a force of heterogeneity within the hegemonic language of empire (G. Ponce-Hegenauer, "Lyric and Empire," *MLN*, 136.2, 2001, 423–440). For poiesis and the novel in Cervantes: (A. Cascardi, "'Orphic Fictions': Poesía and Poiesis in Cervantes," in eds. A. Cascardi and L. Middlebrook, *Poiesis and Modernity in the Old and New Worlds*, Vanderbilt University Press, 2012, 19–42; 20); (A. Cascardi, *The Subject of Modernity*, Cambridge University Press, 1992, 72–124).

8 "La dénonciation de la folie devient la forme générale de la critique . . . Il n'est plus simplement, dans les marges, la silhouette ridicule et familière: il prend place au centre du théâtre, comme le détenteur de la vérité . . .. Dans la littérature savante également, la Folie est au travail, au coeur même de la raison et de la vérité" (Foucault, *Historie de la folie*, 29).

"Ainsi ont-ils tous les deux, au bord extérieur de notre culture et au plus proche de ses partages essentiels, cette situation «à la limite» – posture marginale et silhouette profondément archaïque–où leurs paroles trouvent sans cesse leur pouvoir d'étrangeté et la ressource de leur contestation" (M. Foucault, *Les mots et les choses. Une archéologie des sciences humaines*, Paris: Gallimard, 1966, 63–64).

9 Many nobles were patrons and poets. It is not my intention to uphold the aristocracy as an ideal alternative to proto-capitalism and imperial expansion. The distinction is that under the aristocratic order the poet was legible within cultural discourse as a reasonable actor.

10 The backlash occurs in the nineteenth century with Romanticism, which, in its resistance, reified the *figura of the poet* as madman. "It could be said that the tears of sympathy shed by birds, brooks, and flowers in Heinrich Heine's garden as the young poet sat reading *Don Quixote* aloud symbolize a new epoch for Cervantes' masterpiece, an epoch in which the reader's reaction to the work has been conditioned by his own awareness that he, just like the demented knight-errant, is a homeless wanderer, lost somewhere between the world as he would like it to be and the world as he knows it to be" (A. Forcione, *Cervantes, Aristotle, and the Persiles*, Princeton University Press, 1970, 7). As shall be seen, the tension between lyric sempiternity and narrative emplotment will be conversant with the Romantic view of the *DQ* which Close registers within the "Perspectivist movement" (A. Close, *The Romantic 'DQ': A Critical History of the Romantic Tradition in 'Quijote' Criticism*, Cambridge University Press, 2010, 218–220). For *DQ* and the modern subject: (Cascardi, *Subject of Modernity*, 72–124).

same time, lyric life did not disappear from the spheres of human experience and its cultures. In literature the lyric entered the space of novelistic fiction in the form of an indeterminate human interior whose internal–external dynamism generated novel plots. While not all novelistic protagonists are as explicitly mad as in the Cervantine model, this creative tension between the poetic and the prosaic, between unreason and reason, lies at the heart of the novel as genre. Interior and exterior, it is also a dialectic between lyric temporality (sempiternity) and the historical time of narrative. This slow transition from lyric to novel began midway through the sixteenth century with the pastoral prosimetric works of Sannazaro, Montemayor, Gálvez de Montalvo, and Cervantes; in these, the *figura of the poet* was progressively transformed into the modern character of the novel.[11]

In his 1915 *Theory of the Novel,* Gyorgy Lukács inferred this lyric struggle in modern novelistic fiction as a rift between the interior and the exterior, which he called *transcendental homelessness,* particularly in his analysis of the *DQ*. But he consistently misidentified lyric struggle as epic impulse.[12] In epic the hero's many conflicts never threaten his own status as an exemplar within his own particular social order. When Odysseus descends to Hades, it is not the inner hell of Robert Lowell, but a collectively recognized underworld.[13] When dQ enters the Cave of Montesinos, he goes alone as a sole witness to "the other side."[14] In epic, the hero may be a negative or positive exemplar, but he is never peripheral to that "obscure limit". In lyric, the "I" of the speaker is only ever-at-stake. Beginning in Queen Mab's dream world of vision and the ineffability of sempiternal interior experience, the lyric of the sixteenth century begins on the other

11 *L'Arcadia* (1504); *La Diana* (1559); *El pastor de Fílida* (1582); *La Galatea* (1585), respectively. See also Lope de Vega's *Arcadia* (1598).

12 "Since Lukács defines the novel as the outward reflection of a cultural totality whose substance has been lost but whose forms have remained more or less intact, he sees the problem posed by disenchantment as the reintegration of the internal and external aspects of experience, of substance and form, of *Wesen* and *Leben*" (Cascardi, *Subject of Modernity*, 73–74). For lyric and novel in eighteenth-century English prose: (G. Starr, *Lyric Generations: Poetry and the Novel in the Long Eighteenth-Century*, Baltimore: Johns Hopkins University Press, 2004, 8).

13 "A car radio bleats, / 'Love, O careless Love . . .. ' I hear / my ill-spirit sob in each blood cell, / as if my hand were at its throat . . . / I myself am hell; nobody's here– . . . " (R. Lowell, "Skunk Hour", in *New Selected Poems*, Farrar, Straus and Giroux, 2017, 82–83). Lowell, of course, is drawing on Milton's Satan, "Which way I fly is Hell; myself am Hell" (*Paradise Lost*, Book IV, line 75).

14 As a lyric in prose, Joyce's *Ulysses* repeatedly falls out of language. For the "other side": (G. Ponce-Hegenauer, "La muerte de Aldonza Lorenzo," *Anuario de Estudios Cervantinos: La muerte en Cervantes*, XVII, (2021), 83–96).

side of language (which is always historical) with the ineffable.[15] It is significant that Foucault also situated the rift between image and text at this early modern juncture.[16] From Cervantes' AQ to Defoe's *Robinson Crusoe* to Flaubert's *Madame Bovary*, these eponymously titled exemplars of modern novelistic fiction all tell the story of the lyric interior as an order other than the one it is meant to engage.[17] Formally speaking, the modern novel as a literary genre concerns itself with that "obscure, indeterminate, and constant limit" between individual interiority and shared communal history, which Leo Spitzer called "linguistic perspectivism," and which is the content and the action of lyric poetry.[18]

That the first modern novel, the *DQ*, was born of sixteenth-century poetry has been known for some time. As early as 1924, Ramón Menéndez Pidal had intervened in discussions initiated by Adolfo Castro on the *Entremés de los romances*, as a source text for the premises of the *DQ*.[19] The anonymous interlude, which pertains largely to chapters 4, 5, and 7 of

[15] Recently, the lyric as genre has come in for considerable debate in English literary criticism. The debate returns to contention over generic form as either historical or transhistorical. While the answer is likely both, both sides of the current polemic are inflected by nineteenth-century understandings of poetry. For an intervention into the debate: (S. Burt, "What Is This Thing Called Lyric?," *Modern Philology*, 113.3, 2016, 422–440). For the transhistorical: (J. Culler, *Theory of the Lyric*, Harvard University Press, 2015). For historical poetics: (V. Jackson and Y. Prins, *The Lyric Theory Reader: A Critical Anthology*. Baltimore: Johns Hopkins University Press, 2014) and (V. Jackson, "Lyric," in ed. R. Greene, *Princeton Encyclopedia of Poetry and Poetics*, Princeton University Press, 2012, 826–834). The present study attends to the historical particularities of sixteenth-century poetic practices, and in so doing questions any understanding of the lyric as limited to nineteenth-century and/or English literary practices. For poetry writ large: (Aristotle, *Poetics*, trans. and ed. R. Janko, Indianapolis: Hackett, 1987, 51b1–51b15). For *poiesis* and Cervantes: (Cascardi, "'Orphic Fictions'").

[16] "Entre le verbe et l'image, entre ce qui est figuré par le langage et ce qui est dit par la plastique, la belle unité commence à se dénouer; une seule et même signification e leur est pas immédiatement commune. Et s'il est vrai que l'Image a encore la vocation de *dire*, de transmettre quelque chose de consubstantiel au langage, il faut bien reconnaître que, déjà, elle ne dit plus la même chose" (Foucault, *Historie de la folie*, 33).

"De là sans doute, dans la culture occidentale moderne, le face à face de la poésie et de la folie. Mais ce n'est plus le vieux thème platonicien du délire inspiré. C'est la marque d'une nouvelle expérience du langage et des choses" (Foucault, *Les mots*, 63).

[17] "Il est le joueur déréglé du Même et de l'Autre" (Foucault, *Les mots*, 63).

[18] (L. Spitzer, "Linguistic Perspectivism in the *DQ*," in *Linguistics and Literary History: Essays in Stylistics*, New York: Russel & Russel, 1962, 41–85). On the epistemological stakes of perspectivism: (A. Cascardi, "Perspectivism and the Conflict of Values in *DQ*," *Romance Quarterly*, 34.2, 1987, 165–178). The play of proper names in the *DQ* discussed by Spitzer is something that Cervantes took from the play of pseudonyms in the practice of Pastoral Petrarchism.

[19] (R. Menéndez Pidal, *Un aspecto en la elaboración del Quijote*, Madrid: Cuadernos Literarios, 1924). The Spanish *romance* (a narrative verse ballad often of folk or quasi-folk tradition) should not be confused with the prose fiction genre of the Romance or Byzantine Romance which found early modern inspiration in the rediscovery (1534) and translation of Heliodorus' *Aethiopica*. Nor should it be confused with the English term: Romances of chivalry.

the first part of the *DQ*, has seen considerable debate over the identity of the author (Cervantes and Lope de Vega, among others) and the primacy of the source (whether the *DQ* draws on the *Entrémes* or vice versa).[20] While it is curious to consider the possibility of Cervantes and Lope de Vega intertwined in yet another story, given the commonalities between the *Galatea* and the *Dorotea* discussed in Chapter 5, this study makes no pretense of determining either the author or the primacy of the *Entremés*. More importantly, the shared premise takes the reader so little way into Cervantes' *DQ* that it would be imprudent to suggest that the modern novel is generated from the interlude. What is interesting here is that the *Entremés de los romances* was not comprised of *libros de caballeria* (romances of chivalry) but of *romances* (narrative ballads). The *romance* was a type of narrative poetry written in verse. Its origins were medieval and folk, but during the 1580s, its revival was brought about by an erudite group of poets known as *los modernos*, which included Cervantes, Lope de Vega, Liñán de Riaza, and many of their peers.[21] Just as *romances* inspired Lope's new theatre (such as *El caballero de Olmedo*), Cervantes may have drawn upon, authored, or inspired the *Entremes de los romances*. Many of the stories from *libros de caballería* which dQ recalls in the early chapters are in fact taken from popular *romances*. Casually then, one could conjecture that the *DQ* came from a theatrical interlude which itself came from (narrative) poems. This, however, does not answer the question of lyric poetry and the modern novel but rather attests to the shared thematic or topographical content across various genres of poetry in sixteenth-century Castile. The interlude constructed out of ballads may provide the content of the burlesque, but it does not transform the burlesque into a novel. *Cervantes the Poet: The* Don Quijote*, Poetic Practice, and the Conception of the First Modern Novel* attends to the practice of lyric poetry and the *figura of the poet* in the culture of Pastoral Petrarchism during the 1560s, 1570s, and 1580s in the Habsburg territories, Europe, and the Mediterranean in order to examine the conception of the first modern novel through the early works of Cervantes. This poetry developed the lyric subjectivity of the speaker both in the *rime sparse* of individual verse poems and within the fabric of prosimetric narrative fiction. From this introduction of lyric subjectivity into narrative fiction, the modern novel was organically conceived.

[20] (G. Stagg, "*DQ* and the 'Entremés de los romances': A Retrospective," *Cervantes*, 22.2, 2002, 129–50).

[21] (Lope de Vega, *Romances de juventud*, ed. A. Sánchez Jiménez, Madrid: Cátedra, 2015); (A. Carreño, *El Romancero Lírico de Lope de Vega*, Madrid: Gredos, 1979, 28).

As a modern poet, Cervantes was the first among many to make famous the history of a lyric life in prose. But he was not only a poet of modern prose fiction. He was also, and primarily, a poet of the sixteenth century who lived through the foreclosure of his own lyric practice within the poetics of Pastoral Petrarchism.[22] This form of Petrarchism, writ within literary conceptions of classical Arcadia in which poets assigned pastoral pseudonyms to themselves and to their beloveds, produced new poetic figurations of the Petrarchan lover and beloved within a highly conventionalized and idyllic state of nature, which Cervantes in the *Galatea* refers to as a *tercia naturaleza*, and which Elias Rivers has called the "pastoral paradox of natural art."[23] While Petrarchism has often been dismissed as

[22] For Petrarchism: (W. Kennedy, *Petrarchism at Work: Contextual Economies in the Age of Shakespeare*, Cornell University Press, 2016); (I. Torres, *Love Poetry in the Spanish Golden Age: Eros, Eris and Empire*, Tamesis, 2013); (A. Ramachandran, "Tasso's Petrarch: The Lyric Means to Epic Ends," *MLN*, n.1, 2007, vol. CXXII, 186–208); (M. Lefèvre, *Una poesia per l'Imperio. Lingua, editorial e tipologie del petrarchismo tra Spagna e Italia nell'epoca di Carlo V.*, Rome: Vecchiarelli, 2006); (G. Braden, *Petrarchan Love and the Continental Renaissance*, Yale University Press, 1999); (H. Dubrow, *Echoes of Desire: English Petrarchism and Its Counterdiscourses*, Cornell University Press, 1995); (I. Navarrete, *Orphans of Petrarch: Poetry and Theory in the Spanish Renaissance*, Berkeley: University of California Press, 1994); (R. Greene, *Post-Petrarchism: Origins and Innovations of the Western Lyric Sequence*, Princeton University Press, 1991); (A. Cruz, *Imitación y Transformación: El Petrarquismo en la Poesía de Boscán y Garcilaso de la Vega*, Amsterdam: John Benjamins Publishing Company, 1988); (M. Waller, *Petrarch's Poetics and Literary History*, Amherst: University of Massachusetts Press, 1980); (A. Deyermond, *The Petrarchan Sources of La Celestina*, Oxford University Press, 1961); (S. Vento, *Petrarchismo y concettismo in Antonio Veneziano e gli spiriti della lirica amorosa italiana: richerche e studi*, Rome: E. Leoscher, 1917).

Literature on the pastoral – Antique, Renaissance, Spanish – is broad. T. Rosenmeyer (*The Green Cabinet: Theocritus and the European Pastoral Lyric*, University of California Press, 1969) developed a long historical scope dating to Theocritus, while W. Empson (*Some Versions of the Pastoral*, New York: New Directions, 1974) leaned toward a decidedly theoretical, English, and Marxist investigation. R. Poggioli (*The Oaten Flute: Essays On Pastoral Poetry and the Pastoral Ideal*, Harvard University Press, 1975) provided a firmly biblical and essentializing analysis of vast historical scope. A comparative analysis by P. Alpers (*What is Pastoral?*, University of Chicago Press, 1996) takes good account of Spanish literary history. M. Collins (*Imagining Arcadia in Renaissance Romance*, Routledge, 2016) examines the blending of romance with arcadian fictions in the sixteenth century. See also: (M. Scalabrini and D. Stimilli, "Pastoral Postures: Some Renaissance Versions of Pastoral," *Bibliothèque d'Huamnisme et Renaissance*, t.71.1, 2009, 35–60); (G. Velli, "'Tityrus redivivus': The Rebirth of Vergilian Pastoral from Dante to Sannazaro (and Tasso)," in eds. D.J. Dutschke, P.M. Forni, F. Grazzini, B.R. Lawton, and L.S. White, *Forme e parole: Studi in memoria di Fredi Chiappelli*, Rome: Bulzoni, 1991, 67–79, esp. 68–72); (W. Kennedy, *Jacopo Sannazaro and the Uses of Pastoral*, Lebanon: University Press of New England, 1983, 29); (J. Spargo, *Virgil the Necromancer: Studies in Virgilian Legends*, Harvard University Press, 1934); (N. Lindheim, *The Virgilian Pastoral Tradition: From the Renaissance to the Modern Era*, Pittsburgh: Duquesne University Press, 2005). The definitive study for Spanish pastoral remains: (J.B. Avalle-Arce, *La Novela Pastoril Española*, Madrid: Ediciones Istmo, 1974).

[23] "Aquí se ve en cualquiera sazón del año andar la risueña primavera con la hermosa Venus en hábito subcinto y amoroso, y Céfiro que la acompaña, con la madre Flora delante, esparciendo a manos llenas varias y odoríferas flores. Y la industria de sus moradores ha hecho tanto, que la naturaleza, encorporada con el arte, es hecha artífice y connatural del arte, y de entrambas a dos se ha hecho una

a collection of uninspired and recycled tropes, images, motifs, and verse forms, within the mid-sixteenth-century practice of Pastoral Petrarchism, the immediate particularities of each poet's lived experience (real or feigned) reinvigorated literary form with the *novedades* of contemporary life. The *figura of the poet*, Petrarch, became for Cervantes and his peers a model by which to sketch their own literary lives and afterlives. From Petrarch's lady Laura to Montemayor's Diana, Gálvez de Montalvo's Fílida, Cervantes' Silena, AQ's Aldonza Lorenzo, and dQ's Dulcinea, the path to an immortal life in letters ran by way of the beloved.

Whether blunt satire or tragic irony, the thematic of the Cervantine oeuvre has typically been reduced to the *burlas y veras* of picaresque prose fiction, another genre to which the modern novel has been attributed.[24] Dubbed *ingenio lego*, Cervantes has come to be known as a master of Spanish Realism. As such, the forty-year literary career that he cultivated as a pastoral poet prior to the publication of the *DQ* (Part 1, 1605) rests on the other side of Lethe in formations of Golden Age literary history. Situated at the transition from the Renaissance to the Baroque: (the pitfalls of periodization notwithstanding), most of Cervantes' literary career occupied a curious midway point in the '*siglo' de oro*, which is generally taken to run from the poetry of Garcilaso in the early sixteenth century to the works of Calderón de la Barca and Juana Inés de la Cruz in the late seventeenth. While Foucault, and more recently Rodrigo Cacho Casal, have been careful to distinguish between the hidden secrets of signs in Renaissance texts and their arbitrary play in those of the "Classical" and Baroque, subsequent readings of Cervantes' *DQ* and Velázquez's *Las Meninas* have tended to collapse this complex period of transition, a transition in the very understanding of meaning and madness, into a single conceptual plane.[25]

tercia naturaleza, a la cual no sabré dar nombre" (M. de Cervantes, *Galatea*, ed. J.B. Avalle-Arce, Madrid: Espasa-Calpe, 1961, vol. II, 170; all citations of the *Galatea* are given from this edition, unless otherwise noted). For art and nature in Arcadia: (E. Rivers, "The Pastoral Paradox of Natural Art," in *Talking and Text: Essays on the Literature of Golden Age Spain*, Newark: Juan de la Cuesta, 2009, 83–101).

24 (F. Rico, *The Spanish Picaresque Novel and the Point of View*, trans. H. Sieber and C. Davis, Cambridge University Press, 1969, 28).

25 Recently, Cacho Casal has glossed Foucault's thought within early modern Spanish literature: "El Renacimiento aspira a la unidad y la armonía cultural para alcanzar la verdad oculta, y es por ello que en esta época tienen tanto predicamento también otras ramas del saber que pueden considerarse pseudociencias caracterizadas por una pretensión totalizadora: la magia, la alquimia, la quiromancia, la fisiognomía, la astrología, la mnemotecnia .... Hasta el Renacimiento la doctrina analógica es la que predomina en el pensamiento europeo, que ve el universo y sus partes como un tejido entrelazado de relaciones ontológicas tan sutiles como profundas .... Todo nuevo paradigma cultural y epistemológico se impone y se asienta en un determinado momento histórico en oposición al que lo precedió. *En este sentido, el Barroco supone una respuesta, a veces polémica, a algunos de los ideales del Renacimiento y su forma de percibir y analizar el mundo. Sin embargo, este*

Cervantes' literature is about literature. Velázquez's painting is about painting. This compression of the internal machinations in Renaissance and Baroque Iberian culture, and Cervantes' novel within it, into a single era continues to obscure the lyric origins of modernity's favorite and most mysterious poet: Cervantes.

Housed in the Museo del Prado, Velázquez's portrait of *El bufón don Juan de Austria* (oil on canvas, 210 cm × 123 cm, ca. 1632), completed some sixteen years after Cervantes' death, offers an alternative and unlikely metonymy in miniature for the trajectory of his literary career and its first period of posthumous reception.[26] Velázquez's painting of a jester – whose satiric identity was modeled on the illegitimate and ill-fated step-brother of Philip II, the "hero" of the Battle of Lepanto, Don Juan de Austria (1545–1578) – active in the court of Philip IV (r. 1621–1640), illustrates the transformation of early modern Spanish poetics metonymically from Don Juan de Austria in the court of Isabel de Valois (1560–1568) to *el bufón don Juan* in the court of Philip IV (1560–1632).[27] Like a worn-out rhapsode, Velázquez's *bufón* looks out from his theatrical attire, the iconography of *armas* in which he is cloaked and which forms the backdrop of his portrait, as if to convey his exhaustion with the scene. Like AQ *el Bueno* come home to die at the close of the *DQ II*, the weary visage of the *bufón* points beyond the figure of the jest toward the lyric life of the actor himself. What kind of life could this have been? This palace scene, as is known, would have been enveloped in the practices of a hyperbolic religious fanaticism which sought to collapse the ontology of representation

tipo de esquematismos no siempre resultan eficaces para explicar momentos de transición como el que se vive entre mediados del siglo XVI y comienzos del XVII" (R. Cacho Casal, *La esfera del ingenio: las silvas de Quevedo y la tradición europea*, Madrid: Biblioteca Nueva, 2012, 37–41, emphasis mine). For a summary of this view: (A. Close, *Romantic Approach to dQ*, 220). See also: (R. El Saffar, *Distance and Control in DQ: A Study in Narrative Technique*, Chapel Hill: University of North Carolina Press, 1975, 19).

26 (J. Portús Pérez, "Velázquez, pintor de historia. Competencia, superación y conciencia creativa," in *Fábulas de Velázquez: Mitología e Historia Sagrada en el Siglo de Oro*, ed. Portús Pérez, 2007, 14–71; 47, 67, 328)

27 "el bufón don Juan de Austria, que recibió ese apodo del héroe de la batalla de Lepanto, y que trabajó al servicio de la corte entre 1624 y 1654. Velázquez, como en muchos de sus cuadros a lo largo de toda su carrera, juega con la paradoja narrativa, en la que era un auténtico maestro. Nos presenta a un bufón vestido como el héroe que le dio nombre (1545–1578), y extrema el contraste entre su expresión atemorizada y huidiza y el entorno bélico del que se rodea: su traje militar, el bastón de mando o las armas, pertrechos y armaduras que se esparcen por el suelo. Al fondo, se presenta de manera prodigiosa una batalla naval que es alusión inequívoca a Lepanto, y que por su valentía y soltura revela lo mucho que aprendió el maestro español de la pintura de Tiziano. . . . *en esta obra, a través de la paradoja, está proponiendo al espectador un juego sutil e inteligente sobre los límites entre la realidad y la ficción, entre la identidad individual y la identidad histórica o social*" (Portús Pérez, *Fábulas de Velázquez*, 328, emphasis mine).

and represented into a single phenomenon.[28] The political paranoia of palace life in the 1630s would have imbued this military burlesque with a degree of uncomfortable reality. "If folly leads everyone into a blindness where each is lost, the fool, to the contrary, calls each to their truth."[29]

Like a riddle of reason, his self-denial, submerged in the madness of his socio-religious and political moment, renders the *bufón* a figure of truth whose gaze questions the viewer's very place in a shared chimera. This candor that Velázquez details in the eyes of his subject arrests the viewer in a confrontation with an incredulous actor who has quit his own scene. Lyrically speaking, what is at stake in Velázquez's portrait is neither a tragic nostalgia for the age of Don Juan nor the satiric comedy of an unhinged Baroque court, but rather the figure of an actor at the crossroads of human immediacy and authorial distance, history and allegory, mimesis and poiesis, for whom the semiotics of his attire are called into question by the corporeal gesture of his visage. His sorrowful countenance introduces a human immediacy to the core of his theatrical burlesque and therefore throws the dialectic between reason and folly into question.

Cervantes the Poet: The Don Quijote, *Poetic Practice, and the Conception of the First Modern Novel* takes seriously the body of poetic work produced prior to the publication of the *DQ* through a recontextualization of that work within the various circles of poetic practice in which and for whom Cervantes wrote.[30] While both philological and theoretical studies of Cervantes tend to cast him as a novelist of the seventeenth-century Spanish Baroque, this study resituates the author of the *DQ* within the very milieu of the original Don Juan (just two years his senior) and the poetics of Pastoral Petrarchism patronized by Isabel de Valois and in other European courts during the second half of the sixteenth century.[31] Miguel

[28] (F. Pereda, "Cultures de la représentation dans l'Espagne de la Réforme catholique," *Perspective: Actualité en histoire de l'art*, n.2, 2009, 287–300) for Velázquez's crucifix paintings and the collapse of represented and representation in the reign of Philip IV.

[29] (Foucault, *Historie de la folie*, 29).

[30] There is an obvious temptation to understand sixteenth-century poetic practice and the makings of the modern novel by way of the theories of literature proposed within nineteenth-century German Romanticism. However, this study takes the eighteenth-century English satirist and nineteenth-century German Romantic points of view as indicative of the dialectics that the *DQ* inspires. As such, the productive work to follow on this study would be to attempt to understand nineteenth-century German Romanticism by way of the paradigms of sixteenth-century Pastoral Petrarchism, rather than the other way around. For a cogent and precise (if not also limited) look at German Romanticism: (P. Lacoue-Labarthe and J-L Nancy, *The Literary Absolute*, trans. P. Barnard and C. Lester, State University of New York Press, 1988).

[31] Don Juan de Austria should not be confused with the literary Don Juan of Tirso de Molina (*El burlador de Sevilla*, 1616–1630), Lord Byron (*Don Juan*, 1819–1824), José Zorrilla (*Don Juan Tenorio*, 1844), George Bernard Shaw (*Man and Superman*, 1905), etc.

Fig. 0.1 *El bufón don Juan de Austria* (ca. 1632), Diego Rodríguez de Silva y Velázquez, oil on canvas, 210 cm × 123 cm, ©Madrid, Museo Nacional del Prado

de Cervantes Cortinas (Saavedra was a pseudonym) was fifty-seven years old when the first part of the *DQ* went to print in January of 1605. He was sixty-eight when Part II was published late in 1615. After completing his Byzantine Romance, the *Persiles y Sigismunda*, he died on April 22, 1616, a day prior to Shakespeare. This study of the nearly forty-year literary career (1567–1605) that Cervantes cultivated as a poet and pastoral novelist seeks to resituate the author of the first modern European novel at several crossroads in his conception of modern fiction. Most of the authors who pertained to the circles of poets with and for whom he wrote during the decades of the 1560s, 1570s, and 1580s – Jorge de Montemayor, Diego Hurtado de Mendoza, Francisco de Figueroa, Pedro Laínez, Luis Gálvez de Montalvo, Antonio Veneziano, Pedro de Padilla, Gabriel López Maldonado, Luis de Vergara, Pedro Liñán de Riaza, Félix Lope de Vega, Luis de Góngora, and others – were lyric poets practiced in Pastoral Petrarchism. While Cervantes did not live to see the court of Philip IV and its *bufón*, his literary career ran a striking distance from the court of Isabel de Valois and Philip II (in which he was a contemporary of don Juan) to that of Philip III and the Duke of Lerma (ca. 1567–1616).

Where studies in literary context have frequently focused on a single political moment, language, and culture (that of Philip III), this study allows for Cervantes' early texts, or sets of texts, to indicate particular sites of poetic production that often complicate traditional notions of nation, temporality, and influence (complications friendly to Barbara Fuchs' notion of imperium studies).[32] Relying primarily on sixteenth-century manuscript collections of poetry, paratextual materials of sixteenth-century printings of original works and translations, and archival correspondence between poets and patrons, this study gives shape to a period of literary development in early modern poetics as generative of the conception of the first modern novel.[33] Bringing together the many poets with and for whom Cervantes wrote, this book posits an alternative literary continuum on the terms expressed in these texts.[34] Cervantes' early poetry for Isabel de Valois (Habsburg court, 1560s), his poetry for Bartolomeo Ruffino di Chiambery and Antonio Veneziano (Italian territories and Algiers, 1570s), and his early encomiastic poetry and pastoral prosimetrum (Madrid, 1580s) each supply a unique context and literary community which together may be considered within the larger scope of Pastoral

32 (B. Fuchs, "Another Turn for Transnationalism: Empire, Nation, and Imperium in Early Modern Studies," *PMLA*, 130.2, 2015, 412–418).

33 For practices shared with the history of the book and cultural history: (J.B. Avalle-Arce, "*La Galatea*: The Novelistic Crucible," *Cervantes*, 8, 1988, 7–15); (P. Burke, *The Fortunes of the* Courtier*: The European Reception of Castiglione's* Cortegiano, Cambridge: Polity Press, 1995); (S. Byrne, *Ficino in Spain*, University of Toronto Press, 2015).

34 In addition to Castilian and other Iberian dialects, Sicilian was an ancient poetic lexicon operative within the Habsburg territories whose literary history is often minimized both in Italian (Tuscan) and Spanish (Castilian) studies of early modern poetic practice.

Petrarchism as the primary mode of poetic practice in Spain and its Mediterranean territories during the second half of the sixteenth century. Countering the authorial figuration of Cervantes as a nationalist, realist novelist of the Spanish empire, this study brings to light the history of Cervantes as a Mediterranean poet of diverse lexical and cultural variety within the "transnational" practice of Pastoral Petrarchism.[35]

That Cervantes' status as a poet of the sixteenth century has been somewhat belied should come as little surprise. The history of derisive comments on the topic date to the author's own self-deprecative asides in the front matter and body of several of his texts.[36] Early in the seventeenth century, increasingly venomous rivalries with Lope de Vega and Quevedo tended to cast him to the periphery of the circles of younger poets who reached the heights of their careers during the final decade of Cervantes' life. This somewhat marginalized status was visible in Cervantes' late narrative poem the *Viaje del Parnaso* (1614), a work that in many ways updated the lyric outlook given in the "Canto de Calíope" in Book VI of the *Galatea* (1585) some thirty years earlier. However, to take these disingenuous asides and spurious attacks at face value would be to ignore Cervantes' reputed status as a poet, evident in the decision of López de Hoyos to publish him as the featured poet of the 1569 exequies for Isabel, in Antonio Veneziano's decision to transcribe and include Cervantes' 1579 *octavas* in his own autograph manuscript collection of poetry, and in the laudatory sonnet of Gálvez de Montalvo, amongst others, in the 1585 publication of the *Galatea*. López de Hoyos was the official court chronicler in 1569. In 1579 Veneziano was poet laureate of Palermo; his ransom from Algiers had been paid by the city. In 1585 Gálvez de Montalvo, himself a lauded poet and pastoral novelist, was in the service of Philip II's favored minister, the Roman nobleman Ascanio Colonna (likely patron of the *Academia Imitatoria*, to whom the *Galatea* was dedicated). When in the early 1580s Cervantes returned to Madrid to lament the state of the eclogue in Spain in the prologue to the *Galatea*, his dismay at the fallen status of the

[35] (Fuchs, "Another Turn for Transnationalism," 412). I have retained the use of "transnational" here; however, it should be taken in light of Fuchs' conception of "imperium studies."

[36] "Two prevalent notions interfere with our disposition to read *La Galatea* as primarily a defense of poetry. Cervantes himself promoted both of these conceptions, which have become persistent axioms in Cervantes' criticism. One is the idea of the 'failure' of *La Galatea*, suggested in the prologue ... and in the famous judgment voiced in the *escrutinio* of *DQ* ... The other is the portrait of Cervantes as 'failed poet' ... The prologue of the *Ocho comedias y ocho entremeses* reports the book dealer's blunt verdict: 'de la prosa se podría esperar mucho, pero del verso nada'" (Gaylord, "Language of Limits," 256). See also: (J.M. Blecua, "La poesía lírica de Cervantes," in *Sobre poesía de la edad de oro*, ed. J.M. Blecua, Madrid: Gredos, 1970, 161–195; 161–162).

poet underscored his position as an established poet at that time.[37] As celebration and commemoration, the *Galatea* gave voice to a lyric culture soon to be swept from the pages of literary history. The final festivity of the text remembers the already deceased Meliso (pastoral pseudonym for Diego Hurtado de Mendoza). A master of a literary lexicon in decline, with the exception of a few *rime sparse*, between 1589 and 1605 Cervantes disappeared from lyric culture.

It was during this period of errant silence that Cervantes as a poet of Pastoral Petrarchism began to reimagine the tropes and forms of his literary formation within a new prose fiction.[38] Some of his earliest *novelas*, which Francisco Rico has dated to the decade of the 1590s, attempt to do just that.[39] It should not be forgotten that most of Cervantes' protagonists, who appear in the many prose works that he published during the first decades of the seventeenth century, continue to express their inmost narrative drives in lyric verse. Although "retired" in the prosaic life of the novelist, Cervantes did not abandon the *figura of the poet.*[40] During the final decade of the sixteenth century the lyric went underground in the work of Cervantes. When in the opening decade of the seventeenth century the lyric reemerged in his prose work, it took the shape of a divided figure, AQ/dQ, poet and pseudonym, modern madman. Safely grounded in the quotidian topography of contemporary prose, the *DQ* situated the mad modern poet at the heart of the modern subject, a mysterious and exiled center, an unknown core, around whose folly human existence organized its reason and its truth linguistically. If in the *DQ* Cervantes offered his reader an insight into the interior of the madman, he was able to do so because he knew the *figura of the poet.* A thinly veiled restaging of the pastoral prosimetrum in chivalric garb, the lyric underpinnings at work in the narrative structure of the *DQ* would have been immediately recognizable to his literary contemporaries had not most of them already been dead by 1605. By the time the *DQ I* went to print, Montemayor, Hurtado de

[37] In 1584 Philip II officially retired to El Escorial.

[38] "Entre 1590 y 1600 parece que Cervantes mismo sufrió una crisis espiritual, literaria y social, después de la cual no le bastaban ya los ideales clásicos que representaba la poesía garcilasiana" (E. Rivers, "Cervantes y Garcilaso," in *Homenaje a José Manuel Blecua*, ed. M. L. Atares, et al., Madrid: Gredos, 1983, 565–570; 570). While I agree with Rivers on the importance of this transitionary period, this study argues that Cervantes does not abandon Renaissance poetry, but dramatizes its place within the prosification of modernity. From poetry to prose: (Cascardi, "'Orphic Fictions'").

[39] (F. Rico, "Sobre la cronología de las novelas de Cervantes," in eds. Couderc and Pellistrandi, *Por discreto y por amigo, Mélanges offerts à Jean Canavaggio*, Madrid: Casa de Velázquez, 2005, 159–165).

[40] My use of "retired" is somewhat cheeky. Cervantes traveled widely as a grain commissioner for the Spanish Armada during the final decade of the sixteenth century, a job which twice landed him in a debtor's prison.

Mendoza, Figueroa, Laínez, Gálvez de Montalvo, Veneziano, and Padilla had all died. Only the youngest generation of Pastoral Petrarchists, Pedro Liñán de Riaza, Félix Lope de Vega, and Luis de Góngora, survived – a generation which Cervantes never successfully joined. This is the second, and perhaps more significant, reason that Cervantes' status as a poet has so far been brushed over, if not outright denied. Contemporary reading practices in literary criticism are still determined by the very shift in the *figura of the poet* that rendered Pastoral Petrarchism obsolete and turned lyric practice into folly, the very shift which the *DQ* dramatizes. To get inside the forbidden center of a text composed by a Renaissance poet for a Baroque world – a center around which Cervantes drew the *cercle sacré* of madness – we will have either to occupy the site of madness or to recover the literary lexicon that the novel puts into action. In terms of "linguistic perspectivism," this is the same thing.[41]

While Cervantes' status as a poet and the importance of the Spanish pastoral have been marginalized, several of the most distinguished scholars to have treated the Cervantine oeuvre have made overtures in the direction of such a revaluation.[42] On April 9, 1945, in a letter to Ramón Menéndez Pidal, Américo Castro lamented the way in which scholarship had overlooked the pastoral in Cervantes' oeuvre as a key to the author's work.[43] In 1947 Alberto Blecua, following an exhibition at the National Library of Madrid, advocated for a reconsideration of Cervantes as poet in "La poesía lírica de Cervantes."[44] The quadricentennial of the publication of the *Galatea* also led to significant contributions to scholarship on Cervantes' early pastoral prosimetrum, championed by Juan Bautista Avalle-Arce.[45] In 1974 and 2016 collections of Cervantes' poetry appeared in substantial critical editions.[46] Recent attention to early modern Spanish poetry has

41 (Spitzter, "Linguistic Perspectivism").

42 (F. Romo Feito, "Cervantes ante la palabra lírica': el Quijote," *Anales Cervantinos*, 5.44, 2012, vol. XLIV, 133–158); (F. Ynduráin, "La poesía de Cervantes: aproximaciones," in *Edad de Oro*, Madrid: Departamento de Literatura Española, Universidad Autónoma de Madrid, 1985, vol. IV, 211–235).

43 "El Cervantes estaré [sic] muy en contacto con lo pastoril hasta estos años últimos. Es la clave literaria en este caso. No sé [sic] nadie haya considerado lo pastoril sino como una 'moda' artificiosa, con lo qual la historia se vuelve impenetrable" (BNE, *El Cid y Ramón Menéndez Pidal*, exhibit, August 2019, transcription mine). Many thanks to Betsy Wright for alerting me to this.

44 (Blecua, "La poesía lírica").

45 (ed. J.B. Avalle-Arce, *La Galatea de Cervantes cuatrocientos años después: Cervantes y lo pastoril*, Newark: Juan de la Cuesta, 1985).

46 (M. de Cervantes, *Poesías completas*, ed. V. Gaos, Madrid: Castalia, 1974, vol. I–II); (M. de Cervantes, *Poesías*, ed. A. Sáez, Madrid: Cátedra, 2016; all citations of Cervantes' poetry are given from this edition unless otherwise noted).

seen article contributions from Felipe Valencia, Leah Middlebrook, and Marsha Collins.[47] However, the culture of Pastoral Petrarchism, Cervantes' status within it, and the decisive role that this forgotten literary history played in the conception of the first modern European novel remains to be studied. This book explores the rich linguistic fabrics of late sixteenth-century poetic practice in order to understand how lyric subjectivity became the generative force for novelistic plots in the *DQ* as modern literary genre. It recovers the role of erotic subjectivity in the practices of the pastoral courts which fostered the literary becoming of Miguel de Cervantes, and shows how lyric subjectivity produced narrative emplotment in the modern novel: a formal mode of infinite diversity.

Chapter 1 recovers the pastoral precedents for the culture that directly precipitated Cervantes' first poems within the court of Isabel de Valois (Queen of Spain, 1560–1568), where literary art forms and forms of cultural practice became intertwined in complex mimetic processes. From Theocritus, Vergil, Horace, Ovid, Petrarch, Boccaccio, Poliziano, Sannazaro to Garcilaso de la Vega, Juan Boscán, and Jorge de Montemayor, the retreat of the pastoral was understood to be a device employed to encode and allegorize the private life and lived experience of the court which made poiesis possible.[48] Drawing on archival records (*relaciones*) of life in the court (Biblioteca de la Real Academia de Historia, Madrid), the remarkable diary kept by one of the queen's ladies-in-waiting (National Library of St. Petersburg), as well as histories of her reign, this chapter explores how the frequent and often improvisational imitation of various literary genres, including the romance of chivalry, by members of the court, was caught up in the erotic entanglements that became the content of pastoral literature.[49] At the confluence of literary allegory and contemporary history, through the exchange of *motes* in the *terrero*, the palace became pastoral.

[47] (M. Collins, "Lauso, a Portrait of the Poet," in *Cervantes's La Galatea, Symposium: A Quarterly Journal in Modern Literatures*, 72.3, 2018, 138–148); (L. Middlebrook, "Poetry and the Persiles: Cervantes' Orphic Mode," *eHumanista/Cervantes*, 5, 2017); (F. Valencia, "No se puede reducir a continuado término': Cervantes and the Poetic Persona," *Calíope*, 2016, vol. XXI, 89–106).

[48] For the tension between *erlebnis* and *poiesis* in Lope de Vega: (A. Trueblood, *Experience and Artistic Expression in Lope de Vega: The Making of La Dorotea*, Harvard University Press, 1974).

[49] (DC. Dubrowsky Collection, Western Manuscripts, National Library of St. Petersburg, *Memoire pour le reine*, Abt. 97, 1560); (F. Rodríguez Marín, "La Fílida de Gálvez de Montalvo," in ed. W.R. de Villa-Urrutia, *Discursos leídos ante la Real Academia de la Historia*, Madrid: Revista de Arch., Bibl. y Museos, 1927, 5–54); (A. Amezúa y Mayo, *Una reina de España de la intimidad, Isabel de Valois, 1560–1568*, Madrid: Discursos leídos ante la Real Academia de Historia,1944); (A. Amezúa y Mayo, *Isabel de Valois. Reina de España (1546–1568)*, vol. III, Madrid: Gráficas Ultra, 1949).

Chapter 2 treats the early Italianate verse poetry that Cervantes wrote for Isabel in 1567 and 1568, when the poet was around twenty years old, as serious works composed within the cultural and literary context of their making. In his first sonnet, Cervantes' speaker develops a conceptual play between the speaking-*ingenio* and the lofty-lady through the use of an exalted apostrophe, a key feature of Pastoral Petrarchism that would inflect the subsequent decades of the author's literary career.[50] The only known copy of this sonnet was preserved in a late sixteenth- and early seventeenth-century manuscript collection of predominantly pastoral and erotic lyric and narrative poetry pertaining to the Habsburg court, now housed in the Bibliothèque Nationale de France, Richelieu.[51] This chapter examines and draws upon the manuscript collection as a whole in order to reconstruct the literary world in which and for whom Cervantes wrote, as it was understood by the early modern compiler, a primary source on readership, reception, and genre. Ms. Espagnole 373 also recontextualizes the poetry that Cervantes composed the following year, in 1568, to mark the untimely death of Isabel on October 3.[52] This chapter considers Cervantes' relationship to Giulio Acquaviva while the papal legate was present in the Habsburg court in the fall of 1568, his journey to Rome, and the Sigura affair.[53]

Chapter 3 explores how over the course of the sixteenth century an exemplary amorous biography, a type of *vita poetica* or literary hagiography, was attributed to *el divino* Francesco Petrarca such that *imitatio* applied not only to the figures and tropes of the *Trionfi* and *Canzoniere*, but also to the *figura of the poet* itself as a model or exemplar for the life of the poet.[54] Over a period of roughly two centuries (1374–1575), Petrarch's lasting fame took on the form of vernacular literary immortality against the

50 For a recent and serious treatment of *conceptismo*: (Cacho Casal, *La esfera del ingenio*).

51 (BNF, ms. Espagnole 373, Département des manuscrits, Bibliothèque nationale de France, Richelieu). Catalogued as ms. 602 by A. Morel-Fatio (*Catalogue des manuscrits espagnols et des manuscrits portugais, Bibliothèque Nationale, Département des Manuscrits*, Paris: Imprimerie Nationale, 1892, 218–225).

52 (López de Hoyos, *Historia y Relación Verdadera de la Enfermedad, Felicísimo Tránsito, Y Suntuosas Exequias Fúnebres de la Serenísima Reina de España Doña Isabel de Valois* . . ., Madrid: Pierres Cosin, 1569). The poetry is not reprinted in the modern facsimile: (López de Hoyos, *Historia y Relación Verdadera*, fasc., Madrid: Ábaco, 1976).

53 This study updates and revises earlier scholarship by A. Morel-Fatio ("Cervantes et les cardinaux Aquaviva et Colonna," *Bulletin Hispanique*, 8.3, 1906, 247–256).

54 (M. Arezu and D. Marno, "Figura" in ed. R. Greene, *Princeton Encyclopedia of Poetry and Poetics*, Princeton University Press, 2012, 485–486); (R. Barthes, "The Death of the Author" [1967], in ed. J. Faubion, *The Rustle of Language*, trans. R. Howard, University of California Press, 1989, 49–55; (M. Foucault, "What is an Author?" [1969], in *Aesthetics, Method, and Epistemology*, trans. R. Hurley et al., New York: The New Press, 1997, vol. II, 205–222).

backdrop of ancient authors such as Homer and Vergil. From the 1535 alleged rediscovery of Laura's grave and Alessandro Piccolomini's 1540 pilgrimage to Petrarch's tomb, to the various sixteenth-century translations of Petrarch's poetry into other vernaculars, as well as commentaries on Petrarch made by lyric poets in the front matter to publications, in manuscript poems, and in pastoral fiction, the literary afterlife of the *figura of the poet* took shape. This chapter reconstructs the *figura of the poet*, Petrarch, as it was imagined, articulated, imitated, and reinvented by sixteenth-century poets writing in Castilian.[55] By the middle of the sixteenth century the Castilianized *ingenio* (*ingenium*) had come to define the *figura of the poet*.[56] This chapter works to elaborate on a lacuna (between Garcilaso and Góngora) of roughly sixty years which is not only crucial to an informed understanding of Cervantes' work but which is also much needed in studies of early modern poetics.

Chapter 4 resituates the Pastoral Petrarchism of Cervantes and his peers within the erotic philosophy of the sixteenth century, particularly in Judah Abravanel's *Dialoghi d'Amore* ([Leone Ebreo], Rome, 1535).[57] That Cervantes was a deep reader of Abravanel is evident in his mention of the philosopher in the prologue to the *DQ I*. Less remarked upon, but far more foundational, was Abravanel's influence on Tirsi and Lenio's debate on love in Book IV of the *Galatea*.[58] By 1569, Cervantes was serving in the court of the young Neapolitan nobleman Giulio Acquaviva in Rome, where Vicenzo Orsini's gardens at Bomarzo were one of many private pastoral courts cultivated by various Italian noblemen throughout the region.[59] Within pastoral poetics, the beloved, as the embodiment of beauty, was often conceived of as the *summa belleza* or *summum bonum* in the natural world (an encounter with the formal by way of the sensuous). In light of Abravanel's influence on early modern poetics, this chapter

[55] I draw upon translations such as that of Salmon Usque (*De los sonetos*, 1569 Venice printing), as well as an unpublished manuscript by Trenado de Allyon, which contains an approbation by Cervantes' close friend Juan Rufo, author of *La Austriada* (1584), housed in the British National library (Ms. Egerton 2062, ca. 1595).

[56] This understanding of the *ingenio* shares something with Cacho Casal's study of the term in the Spanish Baroque (*La esfera del ingenio*), but pertains to an earlier period.

[57] (J. Abravanel, *Los diálogos de amor de maestre Leon Abarbanel Médico y Filósofo de nuevo traducidos en lengua castellana, y dirigidos ala Majestad del Rey Filippo*, Venice, 1568). (J. Nelson Novoa, "Leone Ebreo's *Dialoghi* d'amore as a Pivotal Document of Jewish-Christian Relations in Renaissance Rome," in eds. I. Zinguer, A. Melamed, Z. Shalev, *Hebraic Aspects of the Renaissance, Sources and Encounters*, Leiden: Brill, 2011, 62–79).

[58] (F. López Estrada, "La influencia italiana en *La Galatea* de Cervnates," *Comparative Literature*, 1952, vol. IV, 161–169).

[59] (A. Alessi and S. Frommel, eds., *Bomarzo: il Sacro Bosco*, Milan: Electa architettura, 2009).

studies Cervantes' *octavas* for the Sicilian poet and fellow captive Antonio Veneziano that Cervantes wrote from solitary confinement in Algiers and sent to Veneziano in 1579 in response to Veneziano's own songbook, the *Celia*. They survive in Veneziano's autograph manuscript (Biblioteca centrale della Regione Siciliana, Palermo) along with Veneziano's sonnet response. This chapter concludes with Cervantes' earliest dramaturgical works, the *Trato de Argel* (likely composed in Algiers or shortly upon his return to Madrid, ca. 1575–1582), in which Cervantes developed the concept of "love as faith" within the confluence of Islamic and Christian beliefs in which erotic faith transposed the religious.[60] Through attention to this voicing of lyric subjectivity by the *summa belleza*, the *Trato de Argel* evidences early figurations of the intersubjectivity and female desire necessary for character formation in Cervantes' subsequent fiction, such as in the *Galatea*.

Chapter 5 reconstructs the site of production for Cervantes' prosimetric pastoral novel, the *Galatea* (1585), and investigates the way in which Cervantes disguised himself and members of his own literary milieu as shepherd-poets under pastoral pseudonyms in his text. It employs paratextual sources (front matter, dedications, prologues, and laudatory sonnets) to reconstruct the "urban-pastoral" milieu to which Cervantes returned in 1580. Drawing on early manuscript annotations (ms. 2.856, Biblioteca Nacional, Madrid) that identify Cervantes as the "Lauso" of the *Galatea*, in conjunction with earlier scholarship on the *Galatea* as a *roman à clef*, this chapter proposes an additional decoding of the prose work through attention to the use of biographical names (and their pseudonyms) for poets associated with the river Tajo in the "Canto de Calíope" (Book VI of the *Galatea*).[61] With the decline of literary circles in both royal and private noble courts, literary life migrated from the Alcázar to the *barrio de las letras*. In addition to the established poets of Isabel's reign – Figueroa, Laínez, Gálvez de Montalvo, Gómez de Tapia, and Cervantes – several new poets – López Maldonado, Pedro de Padilla, Vargas Manrique, Liñán de Riaza, Juan Rufo Gutiérrez, Lope de Vega, and Luis de Góngora – joined this milieu of "urban pastoralists." The encomiastic poetry that Cervantes

[60] (J. Canavaggio, *Cervantès dramaturge: un Théâtre à naître*, Paris: Presses universitaires de France, 1977).

[61] (R. Schevill and A. Bonilla, "Introduction," in M. de Cervantes, *Galatea*, Madrid: Gráficas Reunidas, 1914); (G. Stagg, "'A Matter of Masks: *La Galatea*," in *Hispanic Studies in Honor of Joseph Manson*, Oxford University Press, 1972, 255–267); (G. Stagg, "The Composition and Revision of *La Galatea*," *Cervantes*, 1994, vol. XIV, 9–24); (Gaylord, "The Language of Limits," 254–271); (Avalle-Arce, "The Novelistic Crucible").

wrote at this time participates in literary attitudes amongst a network of authors working in Madrid contemporary to Cervantes' composition of the *Galatea*, in which the *figura of the poet* became a literary character. These ingenious shepherds of the *Galatea* were also "gathered together" in the *"logos" amoenus* of the opening leaves of López Maldonado's *Cancionero* (Madrid) of 1586.

The final chapter, Chapter 6, examines the force of lyric subjectivity as narrative emplotment in the *Galatea*. At the confluence of verse and prose, allegory and history, mimesis and poiesis, this chapter treats the *Galatea* and other contemporary works, beginning with the 1582 transition from verse to prose in Pedro de Padilla's *Églogas pastoriles* (Seville). While the *Galatea* has frequently been dismissed in scholarship as a partially formed and immature work, or reinterpreted through standard approaches to the *DQ*, this chapter studies the chronotopic dynamism of Cervantes' first prose fiction through the narrative emplotment of Lauso's lyric interior. It is attuned to the sophisticated narrative architecture of an unprecedented capacity to juggle multiple lyric temporalities within a single narrative landscape.[62] The *Galatea* lent novelistic immediacy to the timeless retreat of the pastoral through the use of lyric subjectivity. As a meditation on the nature of love and lyric subjectivity inherent in Pastoral Petrarchism, the *Galatea* transformed the *figura of the poet* into the modern literary character, a transformation that was most fully developed in Lauso. As a *roman à clef*, the *Galatea* not only pertained to the *fábulas* of Cervantes' literary milieu, but also wove a tapestry of narrativized lyric intersubjectivity necessary to the conception of the first modern novel.[63]

In closing, the Coda engages prior theories of the novel which have unwittingly touched on lyric subjectivity as the motor of the genesis of modern fiction qua the *DQ*. It returns to Leo Spitzer's seminal article "Linguistic Perspectivism in the *DQ*" (1948), in which negotiation of lexicons also invokes Mikhail Bakhtin's understanding of heteroglossia and polysemy in the *Dialogic Imagination* (1930s and 1940s, published 1975), and Lukács' understanding of a rift between interiority and exteriority as transcendental homelessness in the *Theory of the Novel* (1915).[64] While several of the insights

[62] (R. El Saffar, "*La Galatea*: The Integrity of the Unintegrated Text," in ed. M. Criado de Val, *Cervantes: su Obra y su Mundo*, Madrid: EDI-6, 1981, 345–353); (S. Polchow, "The Embryonic Manifestation of Cervantes's Narrative Genius," *Hispanica*, 2010, vol. XCIII, 165–176).

[63] For "fabula": (S. Covarrubias, *Tesoro de la lengua castellana o española*, eds. F.C.R. Maldonado and M. Camarero, Madrid: Castalia, 1995, 531); (S. Covarrubias Horozco, *Tesoro della lengua castellana o española*, Madrid: Luis Sánchez, 1611, 393v).

[64] That Luckács later distanced himself (1962) from this early work will not prejudice the present study against his insights into theories of the genre.

in their work hold true, their observations often unwittingly point toward the lyric, rather than epic, features of the novel as a modern literary genre. Their insights show that novelistic fiction is everywhere impossible without the lyric subjectivity at work in the practice of sixteenth-century Pastoral Petrarchism, in particular in the *Galatea*. In his conception of the modern novel, Cervantes preserves lyric subjectivity as narrative emplotment through the transformation of the *figura of the poet* into the modern madman AQ/dQ. This *figura of the poet* as modern madman is not particular to the *DQ* but in fact inhabits the "center" of the modern subject.[65] As such, the *DQ* allows us to consider the foundational division of the modern subject: reason and madness. For some time now, subjectivity and the modern subject have come in for considerable criticism. Most formulations and critiques of the modern subject implicitly retain the Cartesian tendency toward the erasure and evacuation of lived, emotive, and affective experience. The lyric subjectivity of the *figura of the poet*, and perhaps lyric subjectivity at large, is not a subjectivity of erasure but of integration, an embodied and affected "I" whose chronotopic dynamism reveals the heterogeneity at work in even the most "totalizing" of narratives. In consonance with postmodern and postcolonial critiques of the sov(reign)ty of the modern subject as the subject of reason, the Coda considers the efficacy of the subject of unreason as an ethical and as a productive actor within us.

[65] There is no space to treat the question of a "center." In the Q&A subsequent to the delivery of "Structure, Sign, and Play" at the 1966 Sciences of Man conference (Johns Hopkins University), Derrida does not (by his own account) do away with the "center" of the subject, but he does suggest than it is other than the identity (Reason) previously afforded to it. Read in this way, postmodern critique is not the overthrow of the subject of modernity but its fractured hyperbole.

CHAPTER I

Mimesis in the Court of Gentlewomen: The Pastoral Fabric of Everyday Life

On the morning of May 16, 1560, some forty-four kilometers south of Madrid, Isabel de Valois appeared in the gardens of the royal residence at Aranjuez, dressed and ready for an outing in the countryside. It was not yet 8 o'clock and the fifteen-year-old queen had arrived only the previous afternoon, in time to join her new husband, Philip II (thirty-two years old), her sister-in-law, Princess Juana de Austria (twenty-four years old), her brother-in-law, Don Juan de Austria (thirteen years old), and her son-in-law, to whom she had previously been betrothed, Prince Carlos (fourteen years old) for an intimate and, no doubt, youthful dinner.[1] The rustic honeymoon, which the couple would repeat annually, was to be filled with bucolic outings, Arcadian games, and the art of the hunt, of which Philip, Juana, and soon Isabel were avid *aficionados*. On that first morning in Aranjuez, Isabel was joined by Juana, herself an early riser, Mademoiselle Bourbon, another unnamed lady of Juana's entourage, and an unnamed lady-in-waiting to the queen who had accompanied Isabel from France in January of that year. The five young women were attended by their *mayordomo mayor* (high steward), Don Fadrique Enríquez de Guzmán, Count of Alba de Liste.[2] Having set out on horseback, the group soon came

[1] Philip II (b. May 21, 1527); Juana of Austria (b. June 24, 1535); Juan of Austria (b. February 27, 1547); Prince Carlos (b. July 8, 1545). (National Library of St. Petersburg, Dubrowsky Collection, anonymous, *Mémoire pour le reine*, Abt. 97, n.18, 58r-73v; 64r). The *Mémoire* is sixteen folios with modern numeration from 58r to 73v. The last folio (73r & 73v) is blank, except for the following note approximately 5 cm from the top-right margin: "1560." On the far-right margin of the center page with landscape alignment is the following text: "Memoire pour la raine [sic] | maire du roy" (73v). Following M. le Comte Hector de la Ferrière (*Deux Années de Mission a Saint-Pétersbourg, Manuscrits, Lettres et Documents Historiques Sortis de France en 1789*, Paris: Imprimerie Impériale, 1868) and Amezúa y Mayo's (*Isabel de Valois*, Madrid: Gráficas Ultra, 1949, vol. I–III), I have personally consulted the original diary. All transcriptions are my own. Because Ferrière's modernization is now dated, I have chosen to give exact transcriptions without editorial alterations. I was recently made aware of another partial transcription contained in the 1841 edition of Limoge's papers but I have not yet been able to consult this text.

[2] The high steward of Isabel's household should not be confused with Fernando Álvarez de Toledo y Pimental, Duke of Alba de Tormes, Grandee of Spain, who was charged with Philip's household.

upon a wooden footbridge that linked two of the poplar-lined paths in the royal grounds. There they met an elderly peasant, mounted on a donkey, carrying *pastes de poisson* for sale. Delighted with the idea of a rustic breakfast, Isabel and her companions purchased a handful of the *empanadas* and began a picnic, retreating to a small brook in order to scoop up sips of fresh water with their bare hands. Continuing on, they discovered a harnessed wagon and, led by the new queen, climbed atop. In picturesque fashion the four noble personages rode through the forest (presumably they hitched their horses to the wagon), accompanied by the two anonymous ladies, who rode together on an old mule. At the end of a long path, they found a herd of cattle grazing in an open prairie amongst a *force* of goats. Isabel and Juana, thrilled with the idea of drinking fresh milk from the cows, and undeterred by the absence of utensils, decided upon Isabel's bonnet as the most likely substitution for a milk pitcher. Having tasted the fresh milk, they began to dip the bread they carried with them into the bonnet, delighting in the authenticity of the rustic life.[3]

This episode may evoke the *petit trianon* of Marie Antoinette (1755–1793) and its place in the historical imagination. But the playmaking of Isabel and her intimates refers to an earlier formative period of the 1560s, in which pastoral practices were taking shape within the everyday fabric of European court life and its literatures. Coming into fashion across the European continent, pastoral play was a practice that Isabel brought with her from her mother's court in France. In fact, Marie Antoinette's dairy farm, some two centuries later, was modeled on plans that survived from the court of Catherine de' Médici (1519–1589), great-granddaughter of Lorenzo *il Magnifico*, queen of France, and mother of Isabel.[4] It was also a practice that the Habsburg princess, Juana of Austria, had cultivated during her regency court at Valladolid (1554–59), the period and place that is thought to have inspired Jorge de Montemayor's pastoral novel, the *Diana* (1559). At the outset of the sixteenth century, there were only scattered precedents for a classical Arcadia in European court practices, but by its close a noble household without an Arcadian garden was nearly unimaginable.[5] When Isabel traveled to Toledo via Guadalajara in 1560, the pastoral was coming

[3] (Anonymous, *Mémoire*, 64r–64v).

[4] (M. Martin, *Dairy Queens: The Politics of Pastoral Architecture from Catherine De' Medici to Marie-Antoinette*, Harvard University Press, 2011). When he related this scene from the early reign of Isabel de Valois (1560–1568) to the Real Academia de Historia in Madrid, Amezúa y Mayo invoked Marie Antoinette (*Una reina de España en la intimidad*, 1944).

[5] In Iberia, pastoral practices date to the Islamic caliphate in medieval Córdoba and the corresponding gardens at Madinat al-Zahra.

into vogue, and doing so amongst young erudite women and men across the European continent, readers of Sannazaro, Castiglione, and Montemayor.[6]

This chapter recovers the pastoral precedents for the culture that directly precipitated Cervantes' first works as a poet by situating pastoral practices in the court of Isabel de Valois (queen of Spain, 1560–1568) as part of a larger cultural phenomenon in the Mediterranean and throughout continental Europe in which literary art forms and forms of cultural practice became intertwined in complex mimetic processes. From classical and Italian models to the earliest Castilian poets of the pastoral, it was understood that the retreat of the pastoral was a device employed to encode and allegorize private life and lived experience such that that experience was made to pass through a formalizing process from mimesis to poiesis.[7] Neither raw emotional expression nor removed aesthetic design, imitation was entangled in the figurative processes of poetry and experience. Lyrical and episodic, allegorical and historical, by the middle of the sixteenth century, pastoral play in court culture had become a primary mode of making sense of intimate human experiences in early modern Europe. This was the cultural *"logos" amoenus* of Cervantes' literary beginnings.

While literary works bore the traces of lived experience, cultural practice was inflected by the very poetries it produced. In the case of Montemayor's *Diana*, pastoral literature inaugurated forms of reverse mimesis in which the content of fiction came to determine the ways in which members of the court acted out and understood their own experiences. The frequent and often improvisational imitation of various literary genres, including the romance of chivalry, by members of the court exposed the ways in which mimetic play was often caught up in the various amorous escapades and scandals that became the content of pastoral literature.[8] Meanwhile, within the pages of pastoral fiction, it was taken for granted that when shepherds spoke of their interior lives, they did so in highly formalized lyric verse. Out of the confluence of literary allegory and contemporary history, the novelistic character emerged at the site of original lyric verse interpolated into

[6] Young women played a role in the development of the pastoral in key instances, such as Clarice Orsini in Poliziano's *Orfeo*, Isabella d'Este in Ariosto's *La tragedia di Tisbe*, and Lucrezia and Eleonora d'Este in Tasso's *Aminta*.

[7] For *erlebnis* and *poiesis*: (Trueblood, *Experience and Artistic Expression*). Lope de Vega's *Dorotea*, the subject of Trueblood's study, while published in 1632, concerns the decade of the 1580s and the poetic milieu of Cervantes' *Galatea* (1585). (Avalle-Arce, *La novela pastoril española*); (G. Teskey, *Allegory and Violence*, Cornell University Press, 1996).

[8] (Anonymous, *Mémoire*); (Rodríguez Marín, "La Fílida de Gálvez"); (Amezúa y Mayo, *Una reina de España*); (Amezúa y Mayo, *Isabel de Valois*, 1949).

highly symbolic narrative prose: herein lay the erotic *novedades* of quotidian contemporary life. In this context, early shepherd-poets such as Diego Hurtado de Mendoza, Francisco de Figueroa, and Pedro Laínez had an exemplary influence on the young poet Miguel de Cervantes. While several scholars have remarked *en passant* on the autobiographical underpinnings of the pastoral, this chapter delves more deeply into the explicit coincidence of cultural and poetic practice in Cervantes' poetic formation.[9]

The anonymous young chronicler responsible for the preservation of the episode related above was the author of a now partially lost *mémoire* of Isabel's first days in the Spanish court. Kept at the behest of Isabel's mother, Catherine de' Médici, the anonymous chronicler interrupts the history of the Spanish Golden Age to point out a lacuna that stretches between the posthumous publication of Garcilaso de la Vega's Italianate verse (1543) and the new poetry of Góngora and Quevedo (first decade of the seventeenth century), a period of roughly sixty years.[10] An amateur historian endowed with incredible candor, she interjects the cultural and literary context of Cervantes' poetry into the standard narrative of literary history and its lacunae.

> Madame ne voulant faillir continuer au discours, que j'ai vous envoyé par mons.r. de Rambouillet, Je reprendrai au xxix. jour d'avril, pour vous dire . . .
>
> (Madame, not wanting to fail to continue in the discourse that I sent to you by way of Monsieur Rambouillet, I pick up again on the 29th day of April, in order to tell you . . .)[11]

The fragment begins here. How old could our historian have been? The Spanish queen herself had turned fifteen at the start of that month. The requisite age for a lady-in-waiting was sixteen, but it is known, as in the case of Magdalena Girón, that frequently this was not enforced. Doubtless barely a teenager, the young court chronicler eschews the studied genuflection of her humanist peers. She says nothing of the feeble inadequacy of her *ingenio* or *esprit* to produce a text suitable for the consumption of her

[9] See Chapter 5 for full bibliography on the pastoral as *roman à clef.*

[10] Navarette briefly mentions Herrera independent of his cultural moment. The example ignores the Madrileño court (Navarette, *Orphans of Petrarch*).

[11] "DISCOUREUR, / DISCOURIR, / DISCOURS . . . On dit, *Faire courir un livre, une lettre, un manifeste,* pour dire, Le faire voir à plusieurs personnes . . . On dit aussi, *Faire courir la voix,* pour dire, Demander les avis à ceux qui composent une assemblée. . . . DISCOURS. f. n. Propos, assemblage de paroles pour expliquer ce que l'on pense . . ." (*Le Dictionnaire de l'Académie françois*, Paris, 1694, 335, 268 and 269, 271). The "discourse" sent by way of Monsieur Rambouillet has, to my knowledge, been lost.

patroness, nor does she genuflect before the ineffability of her subject matter. Neither feigned humility nor poetic bravado inflect or distort the contents of her narrative. If, at times, she verges on banality, the near total absence of style and the mundanity of her list-like syntax underscores the privileging of candor over embellishment. She reports, in earnest, to one of the most powerful women in Europe, as an eyewitness whose testimony depends on veracity, not verisimilitude. Her intention is to chronicle the contemporary history of Isabel's intimate quotidian life at court. If and where she fails, the failure is all the more interesting for its pretense. Where the repeated formulae of *s'habille*, *après*, and *jusques* structure the many details of Isabel's dress and pastimes, and where the narrator makes no overtures about investing her text with the pleasures of narrative structure, the literary topography of this cultural history shines through and Isabel's court comes to life. As in the pastoral conceit of speaking simply, we trust her because she does not engage in artifice. Her historical merit has won her few admirers. Nearly consumed by the fires of the Bastille and the Abbey de Saint-Germain-des-Prés in July 1789, the now partial record of her work was taken to St. Petersburg by the bibliophile Pierre Dubrovsky the secretary to the Russian ambassador. Transcribed in an appendix by Comte Hector de la Ferrière in 1867, she is cited, but not consulted, by Amezúa y Mayo in the 1940s, and *après* the *mémoire* disappears from the pages of history. We have no record of who she was or what happened to her. She was never granted an audience with Cervantes, as far as is known. And yet the journal of 1560, written just seven years prior to the first sonnet that Cervantes would compose for Isabel, is a direct window onto the court she inaugurated first in Toledo and then in Madrid.

That Isabel cultivated pastoral practices in her court upon her arrival in Spain is of literary significance. In the episode related above, the reader may unearth a correlation between the cart on which the four persons rode and the burgeoning of early theatre from the medieval carts used to process *auto sacramentales* through villages for Corpus Christi. Indeed, both queen and princess enjoyed the pastoral farces of the itinerant Lope de Rueda as private court entertainment during the 1560s.[12] But on that first May morning in Aranjuez, all the world was not yet a stage. The improvisation of pastoral play reported in this episode was of another generic garb. In particular, what characterized this remarkable episode in the life of the

[12] (Anonymous, *Mémoire*, 60v). We may speculate whether the Spanish comedian who performed for Isabel and Juana alongside a group of nuns during their visit to a nearby convent was the famed traveling bard (Lope Rueda) who was later invited to give private performances at court.

young queen was not its theatricality, but its improvisational innocence. In her enthusiasm, Isabel all but forgets about her unlikely chronicler, who is left to follow on the back of a mule. Of the theatre, Matthew Potolsky has written, "[it] is incomplete, almost unimaginable, without an audience."[13] Without an audience and the fourth wall that the theatre creates, the boundaries between life and fiction, history and allegory, mimesis and poiesis blurred into a liminal space which was repeatedly taken up by pastoral literature. The inevitability of becoming at which one played later became a leitmotif in Cervantes' many fictions.[14] While none of the royal persons involved in the amateur play-making of Isabel's first morning at Aranjuez suffered a quixotic fall into their fictions, the thin and porous boundary that separated lived experience from poetic figuration, that "obscure limit, indeterminate, but constant that passes between those who are fools and those who are not," was occupied by a complex web of mimetic processes throughout this period.[15] Literary works were not merely a source of entertainment: they became the subject matter, inspiration, and lexicons by which imaginative landscapes were interwoven with the pastoral fabric of everyday life at court. The pastoral became its own quotidian discourse. We cannot know the fluttering of Isabel's imagination in these moments. Was it a *bonnet* or a *milk pitcher*?

~

While pastoral poetry in Iberia dates to, at least, the royal gardens at Madinat al-Zahra, with the invention of moveable typeset in the middle of the fifteenth century and Aldus Manutius' recovery of Greek and Latin authors, printed by the Aldine Press in Venice from 1495, the classical and late medieval precedents of pastoral literature – Theocritus, Longus, Horace, Vergil, Ovid, Dante, Petrarch, Boccaccio – began to circulate *en masse* throughout the continent.[16] New pastoral models – Poliziano, Sannazaro, Garcilaso, Marot, Wyatt – emerged in vernacular

[13] (M. Potolsky, *Mimesis*, New York: Routledge, 2006, 74). The literature on enthusiasm (ενθουσιασμός) in the Early Modern is extensive. For a new approach with thorough treatment of previous scholarship: W. Miller, *The Enthusiast* (forthcoming from Cornell University Press).

[14] As with Timbrio of the *Galatea*, "to play" was also "to become."

[15] "limite obscure, indécise, mais constante qui passe entre les fous et ceux qui ne le sont pas" (Foucault, *Folie, langage, littérature*, 89).

[16] For Madinat al-Zahra: (M.R. Menocal, J.D. Dodds, A. Krasner Balbale, *The Arts of Intimacy: Christians, Jews, and Muslims in the Making of Castilian Culture*, Yale University Press, 2008, 59–60). "The first ed. of the Greek text was printed by Bonus Accorsius in Milan, ca. 1480, the second ed. by Aldus in Venice, 1495. The first Latin translation of Theocritus's idylls ... was made by Martino Filetico ca. 1454–1455 and printed in Rome by Eucarius Silber, ca. 1482" (Scalabrini and Stimilli, "Pastoral Postures," 36, n.7). For Petrarchism and the Pastoral, see n.22 of the Introduction.

poetry. Under the patronage of Lorenzo *il Magnifico*, Marsilio Ficino's Florentine academy found its philosophical precedent in the idyllic setting of Plato's *Phaedrus*.[17] From this first of pastoral circles sprung Poliziano's *Orfeo*.[18] Lorenzo himself authored pastoral poetry in the Petrarchan style during the final quarter of the fifteenth century. Intertwined with Renaissance Neoplatonism from the outset, sixteenth-century pastoral literature was pregnant with philosophical content.[19] Works such as Mario Equicola's *Libro de natura de amore* (1525), Judah Abravanel's (Leone Ebreo) *Dialoghi d'Amore* (1535), and Tullia D'Aragona's *Dialogo della infinità d'amore* (1547) elucidated erotic experience, poetic practice, and pastoral literature. Abravanel's synthetic work of Renaissance Platonism, which drew upon Platonic, Neoplatonic, Jewish mystical and Kabbalistic, Islamic, and Hermetic sources, became the conceptual foundation for the practice of pastoral poetics.[20] Over the course of the sixteenth century, erotic philosophy followed Ficino's sizable contribution to the translation and commentary of classical and late-antique Greek texts into Latin and Tuscan. As Richard Cody has observed in his study of Neoplatonism and the pastoral in Tasso and Shakespeare,

> To the literature of passion Tasso brings the Renaissance Italian trick of sublimation, a variation on the *dolce stil nuovo* and Petrarchism: romantic myth transposed to conscious art. . . . Such a combination is feasible and even powerful because both the courtly myth and the myth of the shepherd imply a communion of the pure. . . . This is the fascination of pastoral, the secret that makes it the poetry of poetry – that it is not to be understood unless one grants that it is more than mere literature.[21]

[17] (E. Wind, *Pagan Mysteries in the Renaissance*, Yale University Press, 1958, 183); (D.J.-J. Robichaud, *Plato's Persona: Marsilio Ficino, Renaissance Humanism, and Platonic Traditions*, University of Pennsylvania Press, 2018, 122–19); (Byrne, *Ficino in Spain*); (T. Reeser, *Setting Plato Straight: Translating Ancient Sexuality in the Renaissance*, University of Chicago Press, 2015).

[18] (M.L. Doglio, "Mito, metamorfosi, emblema dalla 'Favola di Orfeo' del Poliziano alla 'Festa de lauro'," *Lettere Italiane*, 1977, vol. XXIX, 148–170).

[19] (Alpers, *What is Pastoral?*). "Indeed, it is as if the revelatory motifs at the heart of the hermeneutic endeavor to which allegory gives rise have been converted into factual, novelistic elements" (F. Lavocat, "Playing Shepherd: Allegory, Fiction, Reality of Pastoral Games," in eds. M. Skoie and S. Bjórnstad Velázquez, *Pastoral and the Humanities: Arcadia Re-Inscribed*, Exeter: Bristol Phoenix Press, 2006, 65–77; 71).

[20] The French translation was dedicated to Isabel's mother, Catherine. (J. Abravanel [Hébreu], *Philosophie d'Amour de M. Leone Hébreu, Traduite d'Italien en Françoise, par le Seigneur du Parc Champenois*, Lyon: Guil. Rouille, 1551). See the sonnet contained in the front matter for reading practices at that time (2r).

[21] (R. Cody, *The Landscape of the Mind: Pastoralism and Platonic Theory in Tasso's* Aminta *and Shakespeare's Early Comedies*, Oxford: Clarendon Press, 1969, 60–61).

Cody's insights inform the complex forms of mimesis at work in the melding of the chivalric, the erotic, and the poetic in pastoral culture and its literatures in mid-sixteenth-century Spain. In the cultural practice of the court of Isabel, remnants of the courtly myth were a historical reality encoded within the myth of the Arcadian shepherd-poet, sometimes in quixotic ways.

In 1504, the publication of Jacopo Sannazaro's *Arcadia* (composed in the 1480s and 1490s) opened a space for the prosimetric pastoral in European vernacular literature.[22] Sannazaro was an avid reader of Theocritus, Vergil (who was said to have composed his own eclogues at a swimming hole on the outskirts of Naples), and Boccaccio. He was also an accomplished Petrarchan poet, as evidenced in his sonnets and *canzoni.*[23] From Theocritus to Vergil to Sannazaro, the pastoral represented a going out, a setting apart, an escape from the complexities of courtly, urban, and social experience in favor of the simplicity of an idyllic natural world, perhaps paradoxically used for the purpose of the contemplation and representation of that urban experience.[24] That nature and its articulation were available as literary art only to those of minor and greater gentry is one of the features of pastoral fiction that rendered it a mode ripe with encoding rather than revelation. The very terms of social hierarchy that it sought to escape were frequently its condition of possibility and its content.

Sannazaro's *Arcadia* unfolded over the course of twelve prose chapters, each of which was accompanied by an eclogue in verse at its close. Voicing some twenty characters (depending on how one counts the cowherds), this prosimetric eclogue gave lyric voice and narrative context to the amorous and elegiac dramas of an idyllic world over which Pan presided. This situated the lyric at the center of literary and cultural practice for the duration of the sixteenth century. When Sannazaro encoded his Neapolitan circle as shepherds in the *Arcadia*, he gave full force to the pastoral novel or eclogue *à clef* that would endure at least until D'Urfé's *L'Astrée* (1607 and 1627) in France. As William Kennedy has observed,

> Biographically the characterizations of Barcinio and Summonzio and their action entail situations that evoke ones attending the publication of the *Arcadia*. Barcinio's name refers to Cariteo of Barcellona, called 'Barcinio' in Chapter II, while 'Summonzio' of course refers to Pietro Summonte, the author's friend and editor who rescued the text from its pirated printings.[25]

[22] In his *Fabrica*, under "Egloga," Alunno writes: "Egloga. Lat. val Regimento, elettione, Scelta. SAN. Raccontare le rozze Egloge da natural vena uscite," paying witness to Sannazaro's creation of a Renaissance paradigm (F. Alunno, *Fabrica del mondo*, Venice, 4th printing, 1562, 14r).

[23] (Kennedy, *Uses of Pastoral*, 37). [24] (Rosenmeyer, *The Green Cabinet*).

[25] (Kennedy, *Uses of Pastoral*, 102).

Throughout the sixteenth century, Garcilaso's *Eclogues* (ca. 1520s), Montemayor's *Diana* (1559), Tasso's *Aminta* (1573), Cervantes' *Galatea* (1585), Campiglia's *Flori* (1588), Guarini's *Il pastor fido* (1589), Sidney's *Arcadia* (ca. 1580), and Lope de Vega's *Arcadia* (1598) all reconceived of this model at the intersection of private history and classical allegory, each in their own particular way.[26]

The Renaissance pastoral was informed not only by classical precedents but also by the thirteenth and fourteenth-century works of Petrarch and Boccaccio, and, less pronouncedly, Dante. When, in 1548, Francesco Alunno completed his lexicography, humbly titled *Della fabrica del mondo*, he based his text on usage found in a select number of poets: Petrarch, Dante, Boccaccio, Ariosto, Sannazaro, Vergil, Alunno himself, Bembo, and "Other Authors." These authors appeared in the list of source abbreviations that Alunno gave in the front matter to his text. Petrarch was the primary source author, but Boccaccio's pastoral work also served as a significant source for Alunno's lexicography, singled out by title in the "Abbreviature dell'opera": *Il ninfale d'Ameto*, *Il filocolo* (a romance taken from Chaucer), *Laberinto d'Amore*, and the *Elegia di Madonna Fiammetta* all played a crucial role.[27] As a composite of linguistic authority, Alunno's text made clear that by the middle of the sixteenth century pastoral poetry threaded the fabric of a living vernacular language, an active participant in Bembo's ambitions for eloquence and the *questione della lingua*.[28] This "world-making" of Alunno's *fabrica* was constructed from a pastoral poetic lexicon.[29]

[26] I have included both prosimetric and dramaturgical works here because the pastoral was loosely biographical in both. The standard approach to the *roman à clef* can be found in studies of seventeenth-century France. The usage of this literary device in Spain predates such scholarship, but it shares the basic contours: "*Roman à clef*, a French term meaning 'novel with a key', refers to fictional works in which actual people or events can be identified by a knowing reader, typically a member of a coterie" (M. Boyde, "The Modernist Roman à Clef and Cultural Secrets, or I Know That You Know That I Know That You Know," *Australian Literary Studies*, 24.3–4, 2009, 155–166; 156).

[27] For Boccaccio's pastoral: (P.M. Forni in G. Boccaccio, *Ninfale fiesolano*, ed. P.M. Forni, Milan: Mursia Press, 1991).

[28] In Alunno's text, poetry (the eclogue, in particular) appeared in the section "Cielo" (Alunno, *Fabrica del mondo*, 10r).

[29] My use here indicates that the place of lyric practice in the formation of early modern lexicons played a determinant role in world making: poetic practice (praxis) as *poiesis*. "When in 1651 Andrew Marvell mused, 'Tis not, what once it was, the world,' he was speaking for at least two generations of Europeans … the poet articulates one of the most profound intellectual shifts of early modern Europe: the definition of 'the world' as a new category encompassing a previously unknown intellectual expanse and holding new imaginative power. For the poet and his contemporaries, the crumbling of old systems of explanation had left the concept vague and undefined. No longer did a golden chain connect 'this pendant world' to

ABBREVIATVRE DELL'OPERA.

Auttori citati nell'opera.		AM.	Ameto.	Vol.	Volgare.
PET.	Petrarca.	PH.	Philocolo.	Sin.	Singulare.
DAN.	Dante.	LA.	Labirinto.	Plu.	Plurale.
BOC.	Boccaccio.	FI.	Fiammetta,	Maſ.	Maſculino.
ARI.	Arioſto,	EP.	Epiſtola conf.	Fe&.	Feminino.
SAN.	Sannazaro.	VI.	Viſione amo.	Soſt.	Soſtantiuo.
VIR.	Virgilio.	LA.	Latino.	Adie.	Adiettiuo.
ALV.	Alunno.	Gr.	Greco.	Aduer.	Aduerbio.
T.	Tale auttore.	Pr.	Prouenzale.	Dim.	Diminutiuo.
BEM.	Bembo.	As.	Aſolani	Vo.	Voce, o Vocabolo.
Gli altri ſono tutti diſtinti.		Meta.	Metaphora.		

Fig. 1.1 *Della fabrica del mondo di M. Francesco Alunno da Ferrara. Nella quale si contengono le voci di Dante, del Petrarca, del Boccaccio, & d'altri buoni autori, mediante le quali si possono scrivendo esprimere tutti i concetti dell'uomo di qualunque cosa creata.* Francesco Alunno. Venice, 1562, 4th printing, front matter. (PDM)

Two decades prior to Alunno's *fabrica*, the Castilian works of Garcilaso and Boscán linked Petrarchism and pastoralism in Spanish vernacular poetry through the use of pastoral pseudonyms in erotic verse. This taste for pastoral literature developed within the Habsburg court of the Empress Isabella of Portugal when Garcilaso de la Vega and Juan Boscán, who had spent time in Naples and its literary environs such as the Accademia Pontaniana during the years following the publication of Sannazaro's *Arcadia*, undertook their Italianate lyric project. This highly artificial simplicity, what Elias Rivers has called the "pastoral paradox of natural art," found a ready home in the lyric friendship of Boscán and Garcilaso.[30] By setting his eclogues on the banks of the Tajo, Garcilaso also introduced a vision of a pagan Iberian past, the renaissance of an ancient Arcadia, within the Castilian landscape.[31] In the

Heaven ... leaving the idea of 'the world' itself desperately in need of redefinition, re-imagination, and renewal ... it therefore emphasizes the importance of *poiesis* – artful making – as a means of eliminating contingency and making sense of the pieces," (A. Ramachandran, *The Worldmakers: Global Imagining in Early Modern Europe*, University of Chicago Press, 2015, 5 and 8).

30 (Rivers, "The Pastoral Paradox of Natural Art," 83).

31 "The tradition of the pastoral mode was alien to this type of contrast, and its portrayal separates Garcilaso from his predecessors. Yet it brings him closer to those later writers who departed from the milder pastoral à la Sannazaro ... who created worlds of violence in the midst of an Arcadian setting:

court of Charles V in Toledo Boscán and Garcilaso also cultivated a close friendship with Baldassare Castiglione. At the prompting of Garcilaso, and in conjunction with its author, Boscán brought out a Castilian translation of *Il Cortegiano* (*El Cortesano*), which became a primer for pastoral and palace etiquette, Neoplatonic discourse, and Petrarchan poetry.[32] As Peter Burke has observed, "At least twelve and perhaps as many as sixteen editions of his translation had been published by the end of the sixteenth century (three of them in Antwerp)."[33]

This period also marked the early years of the court poet and ambassador Diego Hurtado de Mendoza, whom Cervantes later immortalized in the pages of the *Galatea* (1585) under the pseudonym of Meliso. While neither Boscán nor Garcilaso undertook the prosimetric genre of pastoral fiction, together they dignified an Italianate tradition for Castilian poets throughout the sixteenth and seventeenth centuries. Garcilaso's poetry, as pastoral as it was Petrarchan, formalized the Castilianized Arcadia as a *locus amoenus* of amorous suffering. Along with Montemayor, Garcilaso's Pastoral Petrarchism remained the Castilian model for pastoral poetics well into the seventeenth century and the *conceptismo* of Francisco Quevedo.[34]

In 1559 the publication of Jorge de Montemayor's pastoral novel, the *Diana*, sparked the vogue for pastoral poetics across Europe, one of the most imaginative literary decades in sixteenth-century Spain.[35] Owing to Montemayor's experience as choirboy and cantor in the courts of the Princesses Juana and María, the *Diana*, a self-identified lyrical autobiography, implicated the personages and pastimes of the royal court, likely

Montemayor in the *Diana*, Sir Philip Sidney in the *Arcadia*, and Cervantes in the *Galatea*" (Poggioli, *The Oaten Flute*, 109).

32 "[T]he courtly ideal was spread over much of Europe by the poetry of the troubadours and by the 'courtly romance' (*roman Courtois*), a story written about knights, for knights, and not infrequently by knights (the examples of Wolfram von Eschenbach and Sir Thomas Malory, among others, show that the 'literature as knight' was not an unrealistic ideal). This new literary genre reveals fusion, or more exactly, the unstable mixture of chivalry with courtesy, the values of the battlefield with those of the court .... In Italy, for example, the fusion of *cavalleria* and *cortesia* may be illustrated from Ludovico Ariosto's rewriting of the story of Roland in his epic poem *Orlando Furioso*, first published in 1516 .... In Spain, romances of chivalry seem to have been particularly popular in the early sixteenth century, with at least 157 editions between 1501 and 1550" (Burke, *The Fortunes of the Courtier*, 14–17).

33 (Burke, *The Fortunes of the Courtier*, 62–63).

34 See Quevedo's "Amor constante." In Cervantes' *Licenciado vidriera* (1613), Tomás Rodaja is said to have sojourned in Italy with a copy of Garcilaso's poetry "*sin comento*" and an "*Horas de nuestra señora*," showing once again that the Christian norm may have been that faith was a matter of love, but for the Petrarchan Pastoral poet, *erotic love was a matter of faith*.

35 For pastoral prose texts: (H. Rennert, *The Spanish Pastoral Romances*, Philadelphia, 1912). For the *Diana* across Europe and England: (Alpers, *What is Pastoral?*, 35).

from Juana's regency in Valladolid.[36] Montemayor's *Cancionero* of 1554 was dedicated to the princess and her Portuguese husband, Prince Juan Manuel. A Portuguese poet by origin, Montemayor also translated the works of the fifteenth-century Catalan Petrarchist Ausias March into Castilian, thus "civilizing" the scope of the Castilian language, its burgeoning literary canons, and poetic lexicons. The *Diana* developed the manner and scale by which imaginative, particularly pastoral, literature was cultivated within the Habsburg court by poets and prose authors writing in Castilian at that time. Because few historical sources on cultural practices in the regency court of Juana have been brought to light, it is not possible to study the full biographical extent of Montemayor's work.[37] But it is reasonable to conjecture that the palace of the *sabia Felicia* referred to Juanas regency court. The palace paintings which give way to the "Canto de Orfeo" in Montemayor's fiction resemble the tour of a "hall of realms" to which Juana introduced Isabel in the activities chronicled in the anonymous *Mémoire* of 1560.[38] That the *Diana* was autobiographical was something that the Portuguese author and Habsburg courtier stated at the opening of his text:

> Y de aquí comienza el primero libro y en los demás hallarán muy diversas hystorias, de casos que verdaderamente an sucedido, aunque van disfraçados debaxo de nombres y estilo pastoril.
>
> (And from here where begins the first book, and in the others they will find different histories, of cases that truly have happened, although they go about disguised beneath the pastoral names and style.)[39]

This quality of the pastoral, which Avalle-Arce understood as the ability of the "created-I" to "pensarse en función del mito (think itself according to the function of myth)" lent to a mode otherwise steeped in inherited tropes the qualities of immediacy, contingency, and improvisation associated with court *nouvelles* or *novedades*.[40] Just one year prior to Isabel's installation in the Alcazar of Toledo (1560) the pastoral vogue was set in motion in Spain.

[36] For Montemayor's service to Princess Juana and Princess María, see introductions to (J. de Montemayor, *Los siete libros de la Diana*, ed. Francisco López Estrada, Madrid: Espasa-Calpe 1970); (J. de Montemayor, *Poesía completa*, ed. J.B. Avalle-Arce, Madrid: Biblioteca Castro, 1996). All modern citations of the *Diana* from this 1970 edition by López Estrada unless otherwise noted.

[37] For Juana's court: (A.J. Cruz, "Juana of Austria: Patron of the Arts and Regent of Spain, 1554-1559," in eds. A.J. Cruz and M. Suzuki, *The Rule of Women in Early Modern Europe*, University of Illinois Press, 2009).

[38] (Anonymous, *Mémoire*, 71r). [39] (Montemayor, *Diana*, 1970, 7).

[40] The full citation is of relevance. It should be noted that Avalle-Arce's use of the word "gesto" in the third sentence would have picked up the sixteenth-century valence of "the visage or the face" as given in Covarrubias, in addition to the modern valence of "gesture." "En primer lugar, la elección de la pastoril como vehículo de la expresión del yo creado implica el pensarse en función del mito.

As if to inaugurate this new cultural mode, the coincidence of the publication of the *Diana* with the marriage of Isabel paved the way for poets and courtiers, queens and ladies, to engage in forms of mimetic play drawn directly from imaginative prose and poetry. As Cervantes' poetic mentor Pedro Laínez – courtier and *camarero* (chamber man) to Prince Carlos during the 1560s – wrote in his sonnet to Montemayor:

> En cargo te es España, pues le diste
> al obra, que con ella le ganaste,
> a mal grado del tiempo, un nombre eterno.
> Y a ti, Montemayor, pues solo fuiste
> el que tan alto bien comunicaste
> que sacas dél renombre sempiterno.
>
> (Spain is in your charge, well, you gave it
> such a work, that with it you won
> from the poor decline of time, an eternal name.
> And to you, Montemayor, well, you alone were
> he that communicated such a lofty good
> that you win for yourself an eternal renown.)[41]

For the court poets of the 1560s, Montemayor conditioned the way in which mimesis underwent poiesis as literary art changed the way in which love was conceptualized, mythologized, and experienced within the court. His ability to secure an afterlife in letters, as noted by Laínez, also placed him within the ranks of Petrarch and Garcilaso as an immortal poet. In the 1560s the courtly shepherd-poets Diego Hurtado de Mendoza (1503–1575), Francisco de Figueroa (ca. 1536–1540–ca. 1588–1591), Pedro Laínez (ca. 1538–1584), Luis Gálvez de Montalvo (ca. 1547–1591), Luis Gómez de Tapia (ca. 1545–1547–unknown), and Miguel de Cervantes (1547–1616)

O mejor dicho, la validez pasa a ser más que literaria para entrarse en las zonas de las posturas vitales. El gesto – como en el mundo de dQ – es aquí lo valedero, pues se basta para conferir a estas obras una nueva categoría histórica – humana, ya que no artística. La posibilidad – realidad de que el escritor se piense como pastor debe dar el golpe de gracia a la opinión de aquellos que todavía ven la pastoril como un género falso" (Avalle-Arce, *La novela pastoril*, 143). For the sociological aspects of the pastoral in Spain: (J. Irigoyen-García, *The Spanish Arcadia: Sheep Herding, Pastoral Discourse, and Ethnicity in Early Modern Spain*, University of Toronto Press, 2014, 27). For the study of gender in Spanish pastoral literature: (R. Hernández-Pecorario, *Bucolic Metaphors: History, Subjectivity, and Gender in the Early Modern Spanish Pastoral*, Chapel Hill: University of North Carolina Press, 2006, 27–28).

[41] (P. Laínez, "A [Jorge de] Montemayor," in ed. J. de Entrambasaguas, *Obras*, Madrid: Consejo Superior de Investigaciones Científicas, 1951, vol. I–II; vol. II, 233–234).

followed these models in becoming the lyric lovers of Spain.[42] By way of the pastoral, the shepherd-poets of the 1560s reformulated Petrarchan suffering into a poetics of erotic pursuit and encomiastic capture of the beloved as the *summa belleza* within the Arcadian world.[43] As Francisco de Figueroa wrote:

Tomó Naturaleza
en su mano un pincel,
y quiso hacer perfecta una figura:
mostrando su destreza
en ella, mostró aquel
extremo de belleza . . .

(Nature took
in hand a paint brush,
and wanted to make a perfect *figura*:
showing its skill
in this, it showed that
extreme of beauty . . .)[44]

In keeping with readings and interpretations of Plato's *Symposium* and Plotinus' *Enneads*, the lady was often referred to as the *summa belleza* (supreme or absolute beauty), a phrase which shared its meaning with *summum bonum*.[45] This ideal was said by poets to be physically embodied in the beloved. Encomiastic poetry became a metaphysical laud to the formal perfection which was shown through her gaze. This modification, from the beauty of her visage to her gaze, gave rise to a rich metaphysics of intersubjectivity in which the lover was pierced by the divinity of the beloved.[46] In the Arcadian landscape of pastoral poetics, Nature's figuration of the beautiful lady probed ideas of immanence where the formally ideal and sensually real

[42] (Laínez, *Obras*, vol. 1, 11); (F. de Figueroa, *Poesía*, ed. M. López Suárez, Madrid: Cátedra, 1989, 15 and 43); (L. Gálvez de Montalvo, *El pastor de Fílida*, ed. J. Arribas Rebollo, Valencia: Albatros-Hispanófila, 2006, 19–20). For Gómez de Tapia: (F. Rodríguez Marín, *Pedro Espinosa, Estudio biográfico, bibliográfico y crítico*, La Real Academia Española, 1907, 31–34, n.1); (M. Méndez Bejarano, *Diccionario de escritores, maestros y oradores naturales de Sevilla y su actual provincial*, Seville: A. Guichot, 1922, 257–258).

[43] For an exemplary example of encomiastic capture in the seventeenth century: Juana Inés de la Cruz, "Sonnet 165."

[44] (Figueroa, *Poesía*, 117). "DESTREZA. La agilidad con que se hace alguna cosa, atribuyéndolo a la mano diestra. *Vide* diestra" (Covarrubias, *Tesoro*, 1995, 421). Covarrubias' entry on "destreza" underscores that Nature is conceived of as acting on the Platonic good by virtue of the association with the "destra" (Italian) or right hand.

[45] For the beloved in the context of mid-sixteenth-century Neoplatonism, see Chapter 4.

[46] The concept of being pierced by the Other can be found in Emmanuel Lévinas' *Totality and Infinity: An Essay On Exteriority* (trans. A. Lingis, Pittsburgh: Duquesne University Press, 1969); however, Lévinas does not extend the concept to an erotic context, nor an immanent framework.

became one. This was a transposition of the transcendental to the immanent in the face of Counter-Reformation censorship, which often went undetected in literary garb. The conceit of ineffability was a key feature of this poetry.

~

The marriage of Isabel and Philip in 1560 and the transposition of the court to Madrid in 1561 centralized the Habsburg culture cultivated there. When Philip permanently established the Habsburg court in Madrid in 1561, he wrested the empire away from strongholds of the Castilian aristocracy in Toledo and Valladolid. In 1561 the *villa* of Madrid was a mere backwater. By the time Philip II retired to El Escorial in early 1584, the city had become a capital.[47] As with that of Magsimino and Sigismunda in the *Persiles*, Philip's third marriage to Isabel de Valois (1545–1568) should never have taken place. Isabel was betrothed to Philip's son by Maria Manuela, Prince Carlos; the two *infantas* were born just three months apart. But during negotiations for the Treaty of Cateau-Cambrésis (April 3, 1559), the recently widowed Philip, whose marriage to Mary Tudor had been childless, proposed taking Isabel as his wife. Isabel's aunt, Marguerite de Valois, sister of Henry II of France, who may have been Philip's original intended, was given to the Duke of Savoy. As Duchess of Savoy, this "Minerva" of the French court would become one of Europe's foremost patronesses of letters. Bartolomeo Ruffino di Chiambery's *Sopra la desolation della Goletta e forte di Tunisi* (1577), for which Cervantes composed two laudatory sonnets in Algiers, was dedicated to her husband.[48] Following the treaty, Philip's concord with Henry II was short lived. Isabel's father died unexpectedly from a jousting accident during festivities following his daughter's marriage-by-proxy at Notre Dame Cathedral in June 1559. But for the duration of Isabel's brief tenure (1560–68), the queen mother of France, Catherine de' Médici, maintained a frequent and supportive correspondence with the king of Spain.[49] Isabel, the seal of the treaty, was perceived as a harbinger of

[47] (C.W. Sieber, *The Invention of a Capital: Philip II and the First Reform of Madrid*, doctoral dissertation, Baltimore: Johns Hopkins University Press, 1985); (M.J. del Río Barredo and Peter Burke, *Madrid, Urbs Regia: La Capital Ceremonial De La Monarquía Católica*, Madrid: Marcial Pons, 2000); (J. Martínez Millán (ed.), *La corte de Felipe II*, Madrid: Alianza, 1994); (G. Parker, *The Imprudent King: A New Life of Philip II*, Yale University Press, 2014).

[48] (Amezúa y Mayo, *Isabel de Valois*, vol. I, 24).

[49] There is no space here to treat the rich portfolio of letters from Philip II to Catherine de' Medici (now housed in the National Library of St. Petersburg, Western Manuscripts, Dubrowsky Collection, Abt. 15).

peace in Europe. As will be seen in Cervantes' early poetry, she was *flor de la paz* and a *summum bonum.*

To a large degree, this has been the extent of Isabel's role in history. Having departed for Spain too young to have captured the imagination of most French historians, the eight-year reign of a teenage French queen has held little clout with Spanish historians, Amezúa y Mayo and Rodríguez Marín notwithstanding.[50] This oversight is felt in cultural histories and literary histories (and their corresponding theories) of early modern Spain, where the logic of empire frequently regards poetry and its patronesses as derivative of (or only justified in) political processes.[51] While still a girl, Isabel had been fully immersed in the imaginative culture of her mother's court. Catherine's learned ladies in waiting were renowned for their mastery of both Greek and Latin.[52] Her aunt Marguerite, *Minerva of France*, was a virtuosa of Greek, Latin, and Italian. Hellenists such as Jacques Amyot (translator of Heliodorus' *Æthiopica*, Longus' *Daphnis et Chloë* and other works), poets of the *La Pléiade* such as Joachim du Bellay, and the first French translator of Judah Abravanel's *Dialoghi d'Amore* (*Philosophie D'Amour de M. Léon Hébreu*, 1551), Parc Champenois, populated the circles of Isabel's childhood.[53] It is likely that Abravanel's dialogues were known in Isabel's Spanish court, both in French and Italian, long before the publication of the first Spanish translation in 1568. The *Heptameron* of Isabel's great-aunt, Marguerite de Navarre, had been published posthumously in 1558.

Isabel's pronounced taste for poetry began during her youth, when Pierre de Ronsard, "prince of poets," served as official court poet in France – a function similar to the one that the young Cervantes would

50 All subsequent scholarship on Isabel's time, such as the work of (M.J. Rodríguez Salgado, "«Una princesa perfecta» Casa y vida de la reina Isabel de Valois (1559–1568) Segunda parte," *Cuadernos de Historia Moderna*, 28, 2008, 71–98); (M. García Barranco, "'La casa de la reina en tiempos de Isabel de Valois," *Chronica Nova*, 29, 2002, 85–107); (A. Pérez de Tudela Gabaldón, "La entrada en Madrid de la reina Isabel de Valois en 1560," *Torre de los Lujanes: Boletín de la Real Sociedad Económica Matritense de Amigos del País*, 35, 1998, 141–166) relies on the research of Amezúa y Mayo.

51 (L. Middlebrook, *Imperial Lyric: New Poetry and New Subjects in Early Modern Spain*, University Park: Pennsylvania State University Press, 2009).

52 (Amezúa y Mayo, *Isabel de Valois*, vol. I, 26).

53 "Aquel retorno al paganismo que el Renacimiento trae consigo en ninguna Corte de Europa se advierta y campea tanto como en la francesa . . . justas, naumaquias y cabalgatas, bailes y comedias, en las que los príncipes y princesas de sangre real y más linajudas y hermosas damas de la Corte representan las farsas del Ariosto y de los poetas italianos . . . Pero que caracteriza sobre todo aquella sociedad francesa de los Valois es una vitalidad inaudita, un poderoso dinamismo . . . la constante presencia en ella de helenistas como Amyot y de poetas como Du Bellay y Ronsard contribuyeron, a no dudarlo, a que se desarrollasen y avivaran sus prendas nativas, su precoz inteligencia, su felicísima memoria, su amor de las artes bellas, singularmente a la poesía, de cuyos libros gusto por extremo" (Amezúa y Mayo, *Isabel de Valois*, vol. I, 4–5 and 20).

later fulfill with his elegiac poetry for the young queen. While it is known that Isabel, Juana, don Juan, and perhaps Prince Carlos employed a number of poets in their households, records of this have been lost. This would have been the most obvious place of employment for the teenage Miguel de Cervantes, pupil of López de Hoyos' *estudio de la villa*, in which he wrote the featured elegiac poetry for the printing of Isabel's funeral exequies in 1568. But the possibility and the clarification it would lend is purely conjectural without the recovery of these documents. In a poem that Ronsard composed to commemorate one of her mother's festivities, the mythology of the pastoral took hold within the imaginative world of the young princess through a depiction of Isabel and her sisters as the Three Graces, a figuration that since Ficino's academy in late fifteenth-century Florence had been understood as an allegory of Venus.[54] This melding of poetic allusion with the improvisational attitude of cultural practice was cultivated in the Valois court and fostered by Juana and Isabel in Spain. The pleasures of the dairy farm, evident in the playful sojourn of Isabel and Juana that first morning at Aranjuez, and its revelation of a complex intertwining of literary trope and cultural practice, were inspired by the inventions of her mother's court.[55] Later, Vicenzo Orsini's "little wood" at Bomarzo, which Cervantes may have known during his time in Rome, likewise tended this confluence of literary trope, ingenious invention, pastoral quotidian, and natural landscape.

There is no space here to reconstruct the rich festivities that took place for the marriage of Isabel and Philip, by proxy, at Notre Dame Cathedral in Paris on June 22, 1559, where Fernando Álvarez de Toledo, second Duke of Alba, stood in for Philip at the ceremony. But the various welcoming ceremonies for Isabel in Spain are indicative of the Habsburg *locus amoenus* she found there. When she arrived at Roncevalles on January 6, 1560, it was rumored that Philip came disguised amongst a group of masked *caballeros* to witness her entrance into Spain. During the fall of 1559, Philip had arranged for Don Íñigo López de Mendoza, fourth Duke of Infantado, to orchestrate a welcoming party for Isabel. She was formally received at Pamplona by the Duke of Infantado, his son, grandsons, the Countess of Ureña, her daughters, the Cardinal of Burgos, and an entourage of an estimated four thousand. On January 28, 1560, the greeting party

[54] On the Three Graces and Venus: (Wind, *Pagan Mysteries*, 41–43).
For Ronsard's verses: (Amezúa y Mayo, *Isabel de Valois*, vol. I, 23–26).

[55] As Meredith Martin has observed, there was an "established tradition of dairy construction within the French royal and elite gardens that began in the sixteenth century with Catherine de' Medici in the court in Fontainebleau" (*Dairy Queens*, 4).

established Isabel within the Palace of the Infantado, near the banks of the Henares River, where she was introduced to the princess Juana, co-host of the Spanish marriage festivities. Isabel and Philip met for the first time on February 2.

As co-organizer of the festivities at the Palace of the Infantado, Juana brought to life the pastoral culture familiar to her court.[56] The triumphal arches filled with lyric verse and allegorical emblems accompanied an artificial forest of oak trees that ran from the bank of the Torreón del Alamín to the Puerta del Mercado in Guadalajara. These pastoral *tableaux vivants* were populated with rabbits, deer, and birds – the artificial forest was said to have been so natural that the trees were thought to be real.[57] For Isabel's reception in Toledo on February 12, the citizens erected a giant figure of Bacchus over the hospital from whom a font of wine flowed freely, a large Venus from whose breasts flowed fonts of fresh water, and a variety of allegorical statues, which included the river Tajo. The statues were painted *a lo Romano*, in keeping with newly recovered archeological knowledge of ancient Greek statuary.[58] There were four triumphal arches, designed by Alvar Gómeze, replete with painted figures, allegories, and short poems. The streets were said to have been filled with minstrels, choirs of children, gypsies, and nymphs. "Harbinger of peace," Isabel entered on a white horse accompanied by the Cardinal of Burgos and the Almirante of Castile. Philip rode masked alongside the Duke of Alba. As in Guadalajara, the streets were decorated with artificial forests and images of birds, and Arcadian figures which brought the pastoral to life in these widely attended festivities. From February 1560 to May 1561 the royal residence remained in Toledo. During that time, pastoral festivities both within the Alcázar and during visits to Aranjuez became a ready feature of everyday court life.[59] In

56 In the inventory taken at Juana's death several copies of the *Diana* were found in her possession (Cruz, "Juana of Austria," 103–122).

57 (Amezúa y Mayo, *Isabel de Valois*, vol. I, 118). On *tableaux vivants*: (J.R. Mulryne, "4. Festivals in Valois France," in *Treasures in Full: Renaissance Festival Books*, British Library: Online Resource, 2019, www.bl.uk/treasures/festivalbooks/valois.html). Referenced in: (R. Strong, *Art and Power: Renaissance Festivals 1450–1650*, Woodbridge: The Boydell Press, 1984, esp. ch. 3); (R.J. Knecht, "Court Festivals as Political Spectacle: The Example of Sixteenth-Century France," in eds. J.R Mulryne, H. Watanabe O'Kelley, and M. Shrewing, *'Europa Triumphans' : Court and Civic Festivals in Early Modern Europe*, Aldershot: Ashgate, 2004, 19–31); (M. Chatenet, *La Cour de France au XVIe siècle*, Paris: Picard, 2000); (W. McAllister Johnson, *The Royal Tour of France by Charles IX and Catherine de Medici, 1564–6*, University of Toronto Press, 1979).

58 Jean-Luc Godard made reference to this practice at the opening of his 1962 film *Le Mépris*. For a contemporary American context: (M. Talbot, "Color Blind: The Myth of Whiteness in Classical Sculpture," *The New Yorker*, 2018).

59 In fact, Isabel spent most of her days during the autumn of 1560 not in the Alcázar of Toledo but in the Huerta del Capiscol on the left bank of the river Tajo, cultivated by Don García Manrique: "la

Toledo, Isabel spent her time in leisurely play along the banks of the Tajo, events later translated into literary life by Gálvez de Montalvo in *El pastor de Fílida* (1582).

Under the fourteen-year-old queen, the palace became pastoral. Pastoral culture thrived in the Habsburg court, in which the mimetic distinction between art and nature blurred, and where even the most private of actions could be immortalized for posterity once guised in Arcadian dress.[60] In palace life the various tropes and figures of imaginative texts – pastoral and lyric poetries, romances of chivalry, sentimental novels, byzantine romances, "*morisco*" romances, theatrical eclogues and farces – provided imaginative codes for the serious play of Isabel and Juana, and the hundreds, if not thousands, of individuals involved in quotidian court life. Of these literatures, pastoral verse and prose became the cultural discourse of the day. This was evident in the exchange of palace epistles and *motes*, often in the form of prohibited *billetes*. At the time of her marriage to Philip II, the etiquette of the Habsburg court was so strict that the king dismissed several of Isabel's French ladies-in-waiting upon their arrival in Toledo. The French women were replaced with Spanish ladies raised under the strict discipline of the Habsburg court (the indomitable spirit of the Princess of Eboli notwithstanding).[61] In spite of the rigorous Burgundian etiquette, Isabel's court successfully reinvented a Petrarchan erotics, which depended on restriction and longing. Theirs was a necessary encoding, an art of concealment within the veiled hierarchies and nuanced intricacies of one of the most elaborate and rigid protocols of the period.

Motes, wrote Amezúa y Mayo, "were like a poetic duel between courtier and lady," a delightful rhetorical device akin to a Shakespearean quip, a source of unprecedented entertainment and unforeseen conflict in the Habsburg court. *Motes* were whispered quietly or passed on scraps of paper

Reina come y descansa allí a la sombra de una ramada que se ha levantado en la huerta para defenderla del sol, entretenida con los juegos de naipes y en otras diversiones" (Amezúa y Mayo, *Isabel de Valois*, vol. I, 197).

60 "Aún en España la propia *Diana* de Montemayor se informa en parte sobre la anécdota vivida, si bien es la expresión del mito la que le confiere validez extra-personal. En casi todas las otras novelas pastoriles españoles ocurre algo semejante" (Avalle-Arce, *La Novela Pastoril*, 141–142). And: "The pastoral romance did not take the form in which we know it until Jorge de Montemayor's *Diana* (1559), which derives from Sannazaro, but in which the prose narration dominates and the poems appear embedded in it .... The number and variety of pastoral narratives in European literature of the sixteenth century ... emphatically show that Renaissance pastoral, far from being simply transnational, everywhere reflects cultural histories and interests that belong to specific languages and political-social entities" (Alpers, *What is Pastoral?*, 67 and 348). Religious poetry, such as that of Fray Luis de León, also drew heavily on the image of the shepherd. However, this should not be confused with the vogue for Pastoral Petrarchism.

61 (M. Fernández Álvarez, *La princesa de Éboli*, Madrid: España, 2009).

in the *terrero* (central courtyard) of the Alcázar. Largely understood as frivolous flirtation devices, these passing exchanges led to intrigues and scandals which saw gentlemen exiled to Flanders and ladies to the nunnery. Small barks with rather large bites, they entered the content of pastoral fiction. These witticisms often took the form of a call and response or question and answer. Two-line (never more than four) quips, they were highly conceptual in nature. *Motes* hinged on the art of saying something clever, witty, or difficult with simplicity, clarity, and concision, in verse, and without appearing to have made much of an effort.[62] This easy spontaneity was inspired by Castiglione's ideal of *sprezzatura*.[63] The improvisation of *motes*, off-the-cuff remarks of easy ingenuity, drew upon astute engagement with tropes and commonplaces and underscored the literary inheritance at play in each linguistic event. *Motes* could be privately directed to a single lady or gentleman, or intended for court consumption. They were glossed by various participants as a point of departure for the *pláticas* on amorous philosophy (Abravanel and Castiglione) and the *alabanza de aldea* (Guevara) which were favorite pastimes in court life.[64] The same *motes* and their corresponding *glosas* and *pláticas* brought together several shepherds in the pages of pastoral fiction, who, gathered around a fountain or small clearing, passed their time in the pastoral discourse of the palace.

Motes were understood as a form of lyric poetry in which ladies and gentlemen exercised the power of their *ingenios* for the reworking of literary culture into concise, lyrical, spontaneous representations of their own interior lives. They adapted tropes and timed them to particular contexts that bridged the public and the private.[65] The examples recorded in manuscript reveal a variety of expression, ranging from the grave to the jocular, the tender to the burlesque, the hopeless to the impassioned, all of which hinge on an early propensity for *conceptismo*, in which the allegorical figures of seas, rocks, shipwrecks, squalls, and doors, and the rhetorical devices of antithesis and chiasmus were employed. In this truncated Petrarchism the spirit of invention was not to be found in the trope itself (always a literary inheritence), but in the way in which that trope was playfully reconceived of anew in fresh and

62 "... y aunque ponga el arte en lo que se dice y cómo se dice, ha de estar tan encubierto, que no parezca que costó cuidado" (Rodríguez Marín, *La Fílida de Gálvez*, 23–26).

63 For *sprezzatura*: (Burke, *The Fortunes of the Courtier*, 52–53).

64 See the *Galatea*, Books III and VI, for verse glosses of *motes*. See *DQ* II: 28 for dQ's own comments on the same.

65 (Amezúa y Mayo, Una reina de España, 41). The sense of timing (*Kairos*, καιρός) would later emerge in the lyric genesis of novelistic plots. For *Kairos* in the Early Modern: J. Paul, "The Use of Kairos in Renaissance Political Philosophy," *Renaissance Quarterly*, 2014, 67.1, 43–78.

ingenious ways. As *mimetic play*,the *mote* rendered imitation a matter of contingency, from whence the new consistently emerged in acts of literary and cultural poiesis. This involved participants in situations which put the lyric interiority of the participant at stake. The result was an intimate literature of immediacy which directly involved the private lives of courtiers and ladies within an allegorized linguistic field, a discourse which they shaped and by which they themselves were shaped. Deadly clever, amorous declarations, passed in whispers or on scraps of paper, the *motes* of the *terrero* were a key feature of pastoral life in the court.

One of the leading practitioners of the art of the *mote* was the young Magdalena Girón (1545–?), lady-in-waiting to Isabel and daughter of the fourth Count of Ureña. Her literary afterlife may be found in the eponymous heroine of Gálvez de Montalvo's *El pastor de Fílida*.[66] Her mother, the widowed Countess María de la Cueva y Toledo, who had served in the court of the Empress Isabel (Philip II's mother), was chosen by Philip II to be *camarera mayor* of Isabel's private household. Magdalena's sister was also a lady-in-waiting to Isabel. Though firm in her refusal of the various *galanes* with whom she entered into verbal-joust, this "mistress of the *mote*" revealed the humor and erudition of a discrete but flirtatious court.

Don Juan Pacheco a Madalena Girón

¿Qué muda en mudar fortuna
quien no muda voluntad?

(What do they move in moving fortune / they who do not move the will?)

Respuesta:

Que alguna vez sea segura
la fortuna, aunque imposible.

(That sometimes fortune may be certain, / although impossible.)[67]

These imaginative practices were augmented by the arts of music and dance. The amorous verse set to music by Miguel de Fuellana in 1554, of

[66] Her brother, Pedro, fifth Count of Ureña, became the first Duke of Osuna, and later served as Viceroy of Naples.

[67] "*Don Diego de Acuña a Madalena Girón* // Quien está sin esperanza, / partido le es el destierro. // Respuesta: / No la tiene por perdida/ quien sabe tornar por si. // Don Luis Quijada a Madalena Girón // ¿Que puede haber tras mentir, / sino sólo haber mentido? // Respuesta: // Que aunque diga la verdad, / no se crea. // *Don Enrique de Guzmán a Madalena Girón* // ¿Qué espera de su verdad / remedio podrá tener? // Respuesta: // Que si la verdad es grande, / remedio podrá tener" (Rodríguez Marín, *La Fílida de Gálvez*, 27).

which Isabel and Juana were both patrons and participants, cultivated the use of various musical instruments at court, which also appear in pastoral fiction as accompaniments to each shepherd's lyric song. In the *Libro de musica para vihuela, intitulado Orphenica Lyra* (Seville, 1554) poetic and musical culture were intertwined within the soundscape of Pastoral Petrarchism. According to Amezúa y Mayo, Isabel brought six vihuela players and a bagpiper with her from France. Upon her arrival in Toledo in 1560, the bagpiper was replaced by a flautist. Isabel's aunt, Marguerite of Savoy, also sent her a laud player during her first year in Toledo. All of these musicians fell under the direction of Miguel de Fuellana and were constantly employed in performances for the young queen.[68] Not all of the *motes* that originated in the court were attributed to their authors, as in the case of Magdalena de Girón's *motes*. The rigidity of court etiquette required that most court discourse circulate anonymously, or under pseudonyms drawn from classical Arcadia and the romances of chivalry.[69] Magdalena de Bobadilla (a shepherdess in *El pastor de Fílida*) was known to have entertained an epistolary correspondence with Don Juan de Silva, the future Count of Portalegre, in which they took the pseudonyms of the "saudosa Corisandra" and the "caballero don Florestán" from the romances of chivalry.[70] Forty years before AQ's imitation of Amadís' penance in the Peña Pobre in the Sierra Morena, this serious play was alive and well within the royal palace.[71] Pedro Laínez's poem "Enviando a Filis un Amadís en Toscano (Sending to Fili an Amadís in Tuscan)" reveals the extent to which the knight errant had become an ideal of erotic devotion within pastoral court culture during the 1560s.

Del famoso Amadís la insigne historia
nos muestra la alta fama que ha dejado
de leal amador; y cuanta gloria
se le debe al que es firme enamorado;
pues en el siglo nuestro su memoria
no menos viva está que en el pasado.

(Of the famous Amadís the excellent history

[68] (Amezúa y Mayo, *Una reina de España*, 37–40). While Pastor Comín reads the Cervantine oeuvre well, he pays little attention to the pastoral as the predominant source and character of music throughout Cervantes' work (J.J. Pastor Comín, *Loco, trovador y cortesano. Bases materiales de la expresión musical en Cervantes*, Vigo: Academia del Hispanismo, 2009).

[69] "Otras veces usaban ellas y ellos, nombres de las damas y los galanes que figuran en los libros de caballerías" (Rodríguez Marín, *La Fílida de Gálvez*, 25).

[70] (Rodríguez Marín, *La Fílida de Gálvez*, 22).

[71] (M. de Cervantes, *DQ*, ed. Francisco Rico, Barcelona: Crítica, 1999, II: 25–26, esp. 275) All citations from this edition unless otherwise noted.

shows us the lofty fame he left behind
as a loyal lover; and how much glory
is owed to he who is steadfastly enamored;
well, his memory is no less alive
in our century than in the past.)[72]

Had Cervantes recalled Laínez's reference to an Amadís in Tuscan with dQ's invocation of Orlando in the Sierra Morena?[73] Or was this behind dQ's diatribe against translation in the bookshop of Barcelona? Both knight and shepherd exemplified the ideal of courtly love and it was by way of erotic discourse that the two figures frequently coincided in literary and cultural practice, as in dQ's encounter with the posthumous poetry of Grisóstomo in the pastoral episode in the first part.[74] A taste for the chivalric romance extended to the queen herself, who in 1563 paid 121 *reales* for seven romances of chivalry and in 1564 requested the purchase of *Los cuatro libros de Amadís de Gaula* in French.[75] The dedication of Jerónimo de Contrera's *Selva de aventuras* to Isabel in 1565 is testimony to how readily the young queen's literary preferences inflected poetic practice and printing at court.[76]

During the 1560s the dissolution of the mimetic boundary was everywhere at work in quotidian court life. Young ladies who, jesting at the rigid etiquette, signed their scraps of paper as "soror Magdalena" or "soror Eufrasi" sometimes risked monastic incarceration in a nunnery, well illustrating that play-making could easily result in becoming. Don Diego

72 (Laínez, *Obras*, vol. II, 251).

73 "Por otra parte, veo que Amadís de Gaula, sin perder el juicio y sin hacer locura, alcanzó tanta fama de enamorado como el que más, porque lo que hizo, según su historia, no fue más de que por verse desdeñado de su señora Oriana, que le había mandado que no pareciese ante su presencia hasta que fuese su voluntad, de que se retiró a la Peña Pobre en compañía de un ermitaño" (Cervantes, *DQ*, I: 26, 291).

74 "No hemos de olvidar que la temática pastoril y la ficción caballeresca fueron de la mano en numerosas ocasiones .... en los espectáculos cortesanos, por ejemplo, las representaciones caballerescas y pastoriles compartían en ocasiones un mismo espacio dramático ... también en las fiestas y justas poéticas ... asimismo, las críticas de los moralistas a la literatura de ficción hablaban indistintamente de los libros del *Amadís* y los de *La Diana* .... es sabido que Feliciano de Silva introdujo numerosos elementos pastoriles en varias de sus obras antes de la aparición de *La Diana*" (J.J. Martín Romero, "La temática pastoral en los libros de caballerías de la época de Felipe II," *NRFH*, 2009, vol. LVII, 563–605; 565). This is also evident in the palace of the duke and duchess (Cervantes, *DQ*, II: 41, 964).

75 (Amezúa y Mayo, *Isabel de Valois*, vol. I, 247).

76 Printed in the 1565 edition was a lengthy dedication authored by none other than the printer, Claudes Bornat, to Isabel de Valois, in which he describes and situates the thematics of the text within the Renaissance inheritance of classical texts (Bornat, in: Jerónimo de Contreras, *Selva de Aventuras*, Barcelona: Claudes Bornat, 1565, unpaginated [4v]). The frontmatter of the 1565 printing also included a sonnet to Isabel whose final tercet declared,

"En esta Selva por deporte lea
mirando, los conceptos que hallare
y alegrará su ingenio Peregrino" (unpaginated [6r]).

Hurtado de Mendoza's "Sátira contra las damas de palacio" attests to the way in which the diversion of *motes* and "hablar por cartapacio" involved in this *play-making* could end in real scandal and the seclusion of the lady in a convent.[77] This was exactly the case with Magdalena de Guzmán, another lady-in-waiting to Isabel. In late 1566 or early 1567, the first son of the Duke of Alba, Don Fadrique de Toledo, Marquis de Coria, secretly promised marriage to Magdalena. In 1557 the heir to the dukedom of Alba had suffered the death of his first wife, Guiomar de Aragón. She was daughter to the Duke of Segorbe, Alfonso de Aragón y Portugal, to whom in 1562 Diego Ramírez Pagán dedicated his *Floresta de varia poesía*, which included elegiac verses for Doña Guiomar, as well as Don Fadrique's personal – and Petrarchan – elegy.[78] By the second half of the 1560s, presumably while they were both residing in the palace, Don Fadrique became close to Doña Magdalena. As in the books of chivalry, the unsanctioned marriage had been secretly consummated on the word of the bride and groom. But the union quickly dissolved. After Magdalena complained to Philip, she was banished from court and cloistered within her own house. On February 12, 1567, she was confined within the Convent of Santa Fe in Toledo. Don Fadrique was sent to serve in Oran for ten years. A decade later, in 1578, Magdalena was still petitioning the king, from her monastic incarceration, to reprieve her sentence and enforce the marriage which had been promised. The Great Duke of Alba was able to convince Philip to allow his son to return from Oran in order to serve with him in Flanders, but royal favor did not last. At Magdalena's request, between June and September 1578, Philip reopened the case and temporarily held Don Fadrique under arrest in Tordesillas. Don Fadrique escaped and, with the permission of his father, secretly married Doña María de Toledo. For the offense, Philip locked Don Fadrique in the Castle of the Mota and the Great Duke of Alba in the Castle of Uceda. The most influential minister in Spain, Philip's master general, the Great Duke of Alba, had fallen from favor as a result of these events. Doña María was sent to the Convent of San Leonardo in Alba de Tormes. Both ladies (Magdalena de Gúzman and María de Toledo) appeared in the *Canto de Erión* in Gálvez de Montalvo's pastoral novel *El pastor de Fílida*.

Throughout the 1560s, the gallant duels of the romances of chivalry were not limited to the pages of books or palace epistles. Discord regarding

[77] (D. Hurtado de Mendoza, *Poesía completa*, ed. J. Ignacio Díez Fernández, Seville: Fundación José Manuel Lara, 2007, 213–220).

[78] (D. Ramírez Pagán, *Floresta de varia poesía*, ed. A. Pérez Gómez, Barcelona: Selecciones Bibliófilas, 1950, vol. I, 57).

verses which had passed between Don Diego de Leyva and Don Diego Hurtado de Mendoza led to a duel within the royal palace in 1568, for which both were exiled from court. Ms. 3670 of the Biblioteca Nacional (Madrid) records Leyva's versified lament and Hurtado de Mendoza's cutting poetic reply, both written within a discourse that blends fact and literary artifice in cultural practice. Giving up palace life, Leyva writes:

Ni quiero musiquear
en el terrero a tal hora
que en ella óigame señora
cuanto La quiero decir ~~hablar~~

(Nor do I want to make music[79]
in the *terrero* at such an hour,
when in it, lady, you listen to
everything I want to say ~~to speak~~ to you)[80]

Similarly, decades earlier, Garcilaso de la Vega's assistance in a secret marriage that had not been sanctioned by the emperor (Charles) led to his exile on the Danube.

In addition to the use of *motes*, residents of the palace created their own forms of entertainment. In 1564 Isabel and Juana inaugurated a game of enigmas to be played between them with a band of seven ladies each. The game involved the construction of living emblems or *tableaus* (*invenciones*) that depicted highly allusive scenes which the queen and the princess had constructed out of the symbolic figures, tropes, and motifs of imaginative literature. At this time, a printed emblem, like those contained in Andrea Alciato's (1492–1550) *Emblemi* (1531), consisted of an image and a small piece of verse that illuminated it.[81] Each *invención* (or *cuadro*) created an allegorical representation that, in keeping with the dynamic play of word and image natural to the genre of emblem books, was intended to elicit a certain piece of rhymed wisdom, a *sentencia*. Both Isabel and Juana, enthusiasts of card games, wagered upon their respective teams. The Queen offered the prize of a writing desk valued at 1,500 *ducados*. The princess, not to be outdone, put forth a small chest filled with silks, jewels

[79] Neither Covarrubias, the *Diccionario de Autoridades*, nor the *RAE* record entries for "musiquear" or "musicar".

[80] I have retained the revision of "hablar" to "decir" as it appears in the manuscript (BNE, ms. 3670, 45r).

[81] For emblem books, in particular Alciato: (A. Alciato, *Il libro degli emblemi secondo le edizioni del 1531 e del 1534*, ed. Mino Gabriele, Milan: Adelphi, 2009); (M. Bath, *Speaking Pictures: English Emblem Books and Renaissance Culture*, London: Longman, 1994); (P. Daly, *The Emblem in Early Modern Europe: Contributions to the Theory of the Emblem*, New York: Ashgate, 2014).

and perfumes that was valued at 2,500 *ducados*. The contest consisted of eleven *invenciones* – life-sized *tableaux vivants* designed by the queen and princess. The *invenciones* were depicted on large set pieces by live actors drawn from the ladies-in-waiting and other members of the *cámaras* of the queen and princess.

The aim of the game was to decipher the hidden meaning which each *invención* was meant to represent. With a linguistic dexterity similar to that required by the *mote*, the players elicited the wisdom or *sentencia* (accompanying text) that corresponded to each *invención*. It was as much a contest of readership as of authorship. In this inventive form of active reading, the proximity of both queen and princess to the forms of mimesis and poiesis involved in the production of highly allusive texts underscored the way in which both reader and writer "put on" the *disfraces* of imaginative literature during the creative and interpretive processes. Contrary to Bakhtin's conception of poetry as monological, the lyric discourse of the sixteenth century was intertwined with the dialogical processes of quotidian court life. Not constrained to the palace, lyric heteroglossia (a mixture of new vernaculars and folk dialects) was pervasive in oral and written culture. As orchestrators of mimetic play, the erudite and imaginative ladies anticipated dQ in the palace of the duke and duchess by nearly fifty years. The fifth *invención*, which I paraphrase here from the Spanish, illustrates the rich texture of these improvised works.[82] The choice of the name, Laura, for the shepherdess indubitably invoked Petrarch's beloved lady, and anticipated Merlin and the enchanted Dulcinea in the Cave of Montesinos (*DQ*, II: 22–23). As presider over the enchanted cave, she also anticipated *La morada de los celos*.

The fifth *invención* was designed by Princess Juana. It involved an enchanted cave surrounded by two large rocks. The author of the *relación* attests that the stones (presumably some sort of plaster) "eran tan hermosas que parecían naturales (so lovely that they seemed natural)." In the cave there was an enchanted shepherdess, and from the cave eight dragons "tan espantables que parecían estar vivas (so frightening that they seemed alive)" emerged toward the participants. Next to these were four sorcerers and four sorceresses with flaming candles and books in their hands. When the queen entered, the dragons began to "dar silvos," beat their wings and breathe fire from their mouths. The sorcerers and sorceresses gestured wildly to indicate that the enchantment of the

[82] (Amezúa y Mayo, *Una reina de España*, 35–40), in consultation with the manuscript: (Salazar, *Las invenciones que sacaron la reina y la princesa año de mil y quinientos y sesenta y cuatro fueron desta manera*, Biblioteca de la Real Academia de la Historia, *Salazar*, L/1, fols. 24–27).

dragons was complete. Then the shepherdess, Laura, began to gently sing. She delivered a small speech that told the queen to choose a dragon, and that whichever dragon the queen chose would be free from the enchantment.[83]

When Isabel entered the space of the game, she entered the space of anachronism, one that Harry Sieber, after Frank Kermode's discussion of *aevum*, has called the "literary time" of the *cueva de Montesinos*.[84] Literary time also keys the temporality of the Arcadia of pastoral poetry, which Cervantes referred to as a *tercia naturaleza* in the *Galatea*.[85] When Isabel stepped into the game, mimesis and poiesis, fiction and experience, temporal and eternal, poetics and practice blurred. Life and its discourses began to unfold within mimetically received and poetically indeterminate forms of play. In designing and erecting the *tableau vivant*, Juana invited Isabel into the living space of her linguistic imagination, which dQ would later do time and time again throughout his many sallies and encounters. To participate in the game without a predetermined *papel* (part or role) was to enact the novelistic (rather than the theatrical or the historical), wherein speech and action derived from the contingency of moving parts at the intersection of interiority and exteriority. In this space of contingency, tropes and words were not copied but reformed into immediate innovations.[86] The *mimetic play* of the court opened language at the site of invention where literary anachronism became the condition of possibility for making sense. Intelligibility, communicability, and meaning depended on Juana's ability to refashion literary inheritance into a new *invención*, and it

[83] (Amezúa y Mayo, *Una reina de España*, 35–40) and (Salazar, *Las invenciones*, L/1, fols. 24–27). For the corresponding scene in the palace of the Duke and Duchess: (Cervantes, *DQ*, 1999, II: 35, esp. 921).

[84] "The sense of an ending is complete and irrevocable in fiction and in life. However, it points to freedom from time, a freedom DQ glimpsed momentarily, and then only in his dreams. The severing of the ties of human temporality is an escape into an eternal *durée* – the Divine present – as Cervantes indicates several times in the novel .... Let us suppose that literary time stands between *temps* and *durée*, that it shares characteristics of both but consists of neither .... [T]he *temps* is *chronos* (passing time), the *durée* is *kairos* (the duration of fulfillment; critical time; the time of death, of the unconscious). Kermode describes literary time with the term *aevum*, 'a third order of duration, distinct from time and eternity ... participating in both the temporal and the eternal. It does not abolish time or spatialize it; it co-exists with time, and is a mode in which things can be perpetual without being eternal .... *Aevum*, you might say, is the time order of novels.' .... Cervantes is playing with these outer edges of *aevum* where both the eternal and the temporal intermingle" (H. Sieber, "Literary Time in the Cueva de Montesinos," *MLN*, 1971, vol. LXXXVI, 268–273; 268).

[85] For my comments on literary time in the *Galatea*: (G.P. Ponce-Hegenauer, "Lyric and Empire," *MLN*, 136.2, 2021, 423–440).

[86] For a critical account of postmodern language games: (Cascardi, *Subject of Modernity*, 286).

depended on Isabel's ability to engage the reordered meaning into a new cultural event, the *tableau vivant*. I do not mean to suggest that Isabel took the enchantment of the shepherdess Laura with the full quixotic *furore* that befell dQ. But both Isabel and Juana played their game sincerely. In entering the space of the game, forms of fiction and forms of life were intertwined in a process of becoming, a transformation of mimesis into poiesis, an untimely text.[87]

What is significant in this pastoral period which fostered the earliest poetry of Cervantes is the acute awareness of the blurring of these boundaries as poetic technique and as discursive cultural practice. It is often suggested that dQ is a character out of time, a figure who harkens back to a medieval reality which might have welcomed him. He himself refers back further, to the myth of the Golden Age. In the court of Isabel, one discovers that his anachronism was not as distant as it may seem. What he lacked was not a bygone chivalric society but a literary topography in which to lodge his highly aestheticized discourse. During the 1560s, the historical realities of mimetic play gave rise to poetic invention. The question of engagement with an as yet unwritten present, in which poetic and historical boundaries blurred, was everywhere present in the court of the young queen, as it was in the pastoral literatures inspired there.[88] This mimetic play brought the poetic discourse to dialogic life within pastoral poetry as a thinly veiled account of courtly love.

[87] In his study of play in Cervantes, Scham builds on Huzinga's understanding of games: "The ordering demarcation of play, and its freedom from both obligation (to participate) and utility (to produce) are fundamental principles . . . a game is an agreed-upon fiction, an experience created by a particular structure: 'It is an activity which proceeds within certain limits of time and space, in a visible order, according to the rules freely accepted, and outside the sphere of necessity or material utility'" (M. Scham, *Lector Ludens: The Representation of Games and Play in Cervantes*, University of Toronto Press, 2014, 8 and 132). The *invenciones* of Isabel and Juana reveal the breakdown of the game once the participants are caught up in immediate mimetic processes.

[88] Shortly after the pastoral escapade of May 16, 1560, Madamisela Chesnau, lady to Isabel, disguised as a nun, leapt to her death from a tower in the Alcázar in Toledo, convinced that she would be executed for her Reformation sympathies (Anonymous, *Mémoire*, 59v–60r).

CHAPTER 2

Exalted Apostrophes: Cervantes in the Court of Isabel de Valois

From the outset of her reign in 1560, the court of Isabel de Valois fostered a literary *locus amoenus* informed by the legacy of the first Spanish pastoral novel, Jorge de Montemayor's *Diana* (1559). In this culture of mimetic play, pastoral poetry was understood to encode intimate experience in an artificial process of *poiesis* in which poets employed pseudonyms for themselves and their contemporaries. In the case of Gálvez de Montalvo's *El pastor de Fílida* (1582), this decorous *disfraz* encoded the author's experience as a minor courtier during the first three years of Isabel's reign. Along with the court poetry of Figueroa, Laínez, Gómez de Tapia and others, his pastoral prosimetrum sets the stage for Cervantes' earliest verse poetry (1567 and 1568). Pastoral court poetry inspired future mimetic play in its cultural afterlife, as has been seen in the case of the *motes* in the *terrero* and the palace *invenciones* in Chapter 1. This reworking of an inherited topography of figures, tropes, and conceits reorganized formal expectations, and outcomes in plot, by intermingling literary techniques with the immediate *novedades* of contemporary life, what Isabel repeatedly refers to as "nouvelles de cette compagnie" in her letters to her mother and her brother.[1] This shaping of a shared *heteroglossia* conditioned the way in which lived experience was conceptualized and understood at the level of the lyric individual. This was the power of pastoral literature, whether in verse or prose: it could shape linguistically the (lyric) interiority of the individual author by virtue of a multidimensional discourse contingent on ongoing practice, a process that writ lyric subjectivity at the intersection of (ineffable) immediacy and (intelligible) authorial distance. Neither raw emotionality nor controlled performativity, these organic morphologies in lyric art and cultural practice gave rise to novelistic becomings in the early modern world. In the case of the pastoral prosimetrum, the form invited

[1] National Library of St. Petersburg, Western Manuscripts, Dubrovsky Collection, Abt. 15, n.37, n.69. n.70, n.81, n.84, n.88, n.107.

the expression of lyric interiority into the narrative thematic through the interpolation of lyric verse into prose fiction.[2] The emergence of diverse individuations within the formulaic dress of poetic garb gave way to an inventive space where experience and myth shared the site of *poiesis*, on and off the page.[3]

This chapter recovers the pastoral poetics intimately connected to the life of Isabel's court. From *El pastor de Fílida*, to Gómez de Tapia's eclogue for the birth of Isabel's first daughter, Isabel Clara Eugenia (1566), to the poetry of Hurtado de Mendoza, Francisco de Figueroa, and Pedro Laínez contained in mss. Espagnole 373 (BNF), this chapter recontextualizes Cervantes' first years as a poet.[4] From this early period, five of Cervantes' poems remain: two sonnets, a *redondilla* (or *copla real*), a lyric of eight *quintillas*, and a lengthy elegy in *terza rima*.[5] While this Italianate poetry, composed when he was just twenty years old for Isabel de Valois, has been undertreated in scholarship, this chapter pays particular attention to the use of apostrophe and formal modes of address.[6] In Cervantes' first sonnet, the architecture of conceptual play between the speaking-*ingenio* and the lauded lady is developed through the use of an exalted apostrophe, a key feature of the Pastoral Petrarchism that would inflect the subsequent decades of the author's literary career.[7] The only known version of this sonnet is contained in an early seventeenth-century manuscript collection of predominantly pastoral and erotic lyric

[2] By "narrative thematic," I mean the collective concerns of the story (syuzhet) as opposed to the individual concerns of lyric (expression). The juxtaposition between narrative and lyric is one not only of content, but also of temporality.

[3] I will return to the figure of the author and historically situate lyric interiority as it was understood within poetic practice during the sixteenth century in Chapter 3.

[4] (Morel-Fatio, *Catalogue*, n.602); (L. Astrana Marín, *Vida ejemplar y heroica de Miguel de Cervantes Saavedra*, Madrid: Instituto Editorial Reus, 1948–1953, vol. VII; vol. II, 157).

[5] (Cervantes, *Poesías completas*, vol. II, 325–335). For original: (López de Hoyos, *Historia y relación verdadera*); various copies in the BNE.

[6] For Cervantes' poetry: (M. Menéndez Pelayo, "Cervantes considerado como poeta," in ed. E. Sánchez Reyes, *Estudios y discursos de crítica histórica y literaria, I.*, Santander: Aldus, 1941, 257–268); (A. de Castro, "Cervantes ¿fue o no poeta?," in *Poetas líricos de los siglos XVI y XVII*, A. de Castro, Madrid: Atlas, 1951, vol. IX-XIII); (Florit, "Algunos comentarios sobre la poesía de Cervantes," 262–275); (Elias Rivers, "Cervantes' Journey to Parnassus," *MLN*, n.2, 1970, vol. LXXXV, 243–248); (Blecua, "La poesía lírica de Cervantes," 1970); (A. Lewis Galanes, "Cervantes: el poeta en su tiempo," in ed. M. Criado de Val, *Cervantes, Su obra y su mundo*, Madrid: Edi-6, 1981, 159–178); (Ynduráin, "La poesía de Cervantes," 1985); (E.D. Lokos, *The Solitary Journey: Cervantes's Voyage to Parnassus*, New York: Peter Lang, 1991); (José Domínguez Caparrós, *Métrica de Cervantes*, Alcalá de Henares: Centro de Estudios Cervantinos, 2002); (Valencia, "No se puede reducir," 2016); (Middlebrook, "Poetry and the Persiles," 2017). For apostrophe and public address: (J. Culler, *The Pursuit of Signs: Semiotics, Literature, Deconstruction*, London: Routledge and Kegal, 1981); (Culler, *Theory of the Lyric*, 2015); (J. Sider, *Parting Words: Victorian Poetry and Public Address*, University of Virginia Press, 2018).

[7] For *conceptismo*: (Casal, *La esfera del ingenio*, 2012).

poetry pertaining to the Habsburg court, now housed in the Bibliothèque Nationale de France, Richelieu. This chapter studies the manuscript as a whole to learn how Cervantes' sonnet was understood in its own time by the compiler. As a primary source on readership and reception, the manuscript contextualizes the 1567 sonnet and, by implication, the poetry that Cervantes composed the following year, 1568, for the untimely death of Isabel (on October 3). These elegiac poems, occasioned by her funeral exequies, were included by the court chronicler, López de Hoyos, in the commemorative volume *Hystoria y relación verdadera* (1569), one of few works printed in Madrid during its first decade as a capital. This chapter briefly considers Cervantes' relationship to Giulio Acquaviva while the papal legate was present in the Habsburg court in the fall of 1568, Cervantes' journey to Rome, possibly with Acquaviva, and the Sigura affair.[8] Cervantes' use of the word *ingenio* in his first sonnet of 1567 is brought into relation with the last sonnet of his life, inserted late in Book IV of *Los trabajos de Persiles y Sigismunda* (post. pub. 1617), a rewriting of the form which evinces the consistencies and transformations in Cervantes' career as a poet (1567–1616).

~

The court poet, Luis Gálvez de Montalvo, interpolated his amorous experience with Magdalena Girón (Fílida) during the 1560s into a sophisticated expression of Neoplatonic love as the fictional shepherd Siralvo in his pastoral prosimetrum *El pastor de Fílida* (pub. 1582). In addition to his own interiority, he gave creative voice to the lyrical trajectories of several contemporaries, including his patron, court poets, and his beloved. This ability to reconceive and give poetic life to the lyric interiority of contemporaries in an allegorical discourse was crucial to the conception of novelistic fiction in mid- and late sixteenth-century Spain. Just three years after the belated publication of the *Fílida* (1582), Gálvez de Montalvo contributed one of the laudatory sonnets included in the front matter to the pastoral prosimetrum of his close friend Cervantes (*Galatea*, 1585).[9] As a literary record of the early years of Isabel's reign (1560–1563), the *Fílida* is an important source on the primacy of pastoral poetry at play in Cervantes' first site of literary production.

[8] (Morel-Fatio, "Cervantes et les cardinaux," 1906).

[9] Nearly twenty years after his 1567 sonnet for Isabel, Cervantes' *Galatea* was a commemoration of and a re-initiation into the culture of pastoral poetry in which he began as it continued in the 1580s. Gálvez de Montalvo's sonnet welcomed Cervantes back to the "fold" from which he had departed after he left Spain for Rome in late 1568 or early 1569.

In the service of the Infantados, Gálvez de Montalvo would have been familiar with the poetic traditions of the day – the *scuola siciliana*, the *dolce stil nuovo*, Dante, Petrarch, Boccaccio, the Marquis de Santillana (a Mendoza), Garcilaso, and Montemayor – by the time he reached his adolescence and had his first meeting with Magdalena Girón (the *Fílida* of his poetry). Following a common practice, Gálvez de Montalvo encoded Enrique de Mendoza y Aragón as the shepherd Mendino, and Enrique's grandfather, Don Íñigo López de Mendoza, fourth Duke of Infantado (Mendiano), in his work.[10] At the time of Isabel's marriage to Philip II, the Mendoza of Infantado were one of the oldest, most powerful, and most learned families in Spain.[11] In 1560 they hosted the welcoming party for Isabel at the Palace of Infantado in Guadalajara, where Gálvez de Montalvo lived and was educated.[12] The 1560 marriage festivities at the Palace of the Infantado occasioned Gálvez de Montalvo's meeting with Magdalena Girón (Fílida), later "mistress of the *mote*."[13] At the written request of Philip II, in 1559 Magdalena's widowed mother,

[10] "Es evidente que... Gálvez de Montalvo usa de nombre y disfraz pastoril para introducir personajes reales. Algunos son nobles principales, contemporáneos al autor, como el mismo Mendino que esconde a don Enrique de Mendoza y Aragón" (Arribas Rebollo in: Gálvez de Montalvo, *El pastor de Fílida*, 2006, 31). Don Enrique was the brother of the fifth Duke of Infantado, Don Íñigo López de Mendoza, son of Don Diego Hurtado de Mendoza, Count of Saldaña and Marquis of Cañete, and grandson of the fourth Duke of Infantado (homonym of his grandson).

[11] "Don IV Duque de este título, dueño y cabeza de una de las casas más antiguas, nobles y opulentas de España, había nacido en 1493; tenía, pues, a la sazón [de las bodas] sesenta y seis años; alto de cuerpo, airoso de presencia, hermoso de rostro y aspecto grave, era por extremo culto y ansioso de saber, y continuando la gloriosa tradición literaria de la casa de Santillana, no sólo empleaba largas horas en el estudio de los buenos libros y magníficos códices heredados de sus mayores, que él también acrecentó, sino que además llevó la imprenta a Guadalajara para sacar a luz en un precioso volumen el fruto de su bien empleada ociosidad" (Amezúa y Mayo, *Isabel de Valois*, 1949, vol. I, 95). (Gálvez de Montalvo, *El pastor de Fílida*, 2006, 115).

[12] "Su educación, a juzgar por su obra, parece que fue refinada; bien pudo nutrirse de la excelente biblioteca de los Duques del Infantado, aunque debido a su incendio sea ahora ésta difícil de reconstruir. Gálvez de Montalvo fue un hombre de su tiempo: cortesano y aristocrática refinado, caballero aventurero y galán, inclinado al servicio militar y dotado al mismo tiempo de una exquisita sensibilidad poética y gusto por la lectura ... Sirvió a la Casa de los Duques del Infantado" (Arribas Rebollo in: Gálvez de Montalvo, *El pastor de Fílida*, 2006, 19, n.1).

As in the case of Mateo Vázquez in the household of Ovando, or of Figueroa in the home of Morales, private education in a noble or royal household was of a higher caliber, a tradition developed by the Empress Isabel earlier in the century (Gonzalo Sánchez-Molero, José Luis, *La epístola a Mateo Vázquez: historia de una polémica literaria en torno a Cervantes*, Alcalá de Henares: Centro de Estudios Cervantinos, 2010, 188–189). For Figueroa and Morales: (Figueroa, *Poesía*, 1989, 19). It is reasonable to consider whether López de Hoyos' *estudio della villa* was of this nature, as the maestro was official court chronicler when he published Cervantes' earliest poems.

[13] "doña Magdalena Girón es *la Fílida de Gálvez de Montalvo*, resumiendo de camino lo que he logrado saber acera de *el Gálvez de Montalvo de la Fílida*, no pastor, ciertamente–como observó el Cura al hacer el escrutinio en la librería de dQ–, 'sino muy discreto cortesano', cuyo libro debía guardarse 'como joya preciosa'" (Rodríguez Marín, *La Fílida de Gálvez de Montalvo*, 39).

María de la Cueva, her brother Pedro, then Count of Ureña, and Magdalena traveled to the frontiers of Spain to meet with and receive Isabel's entourage at Pamplona.[14] Gálvez de Montalvo was roughly thirteen years old at the time of the festivities, just a year younger than the new queen. The Countess, Doña María, was named *camarera mayor* of Isabel's household. Magdalena, at times favored by Prince Carlos, became one of her ladies-in-waiting.[15] Magdalena, like Isabel, was fourteen years old at the time of the marriage festivities, just a year older than Gálvez de Montalvo (about four to five years older than Dante at his first sighting of Beatrice).

El pastor de Fílida opens on the shores of the river Tajo, presumably at the court in Toledo. The pseudonymic work of the text was to gloss the historical and mythopoetic subject simultaneously:

> Cuando de más apuestos y lucidos pastores florecía el Tajo, morada antigua de las sagradas musas, vino a su celebrada ribera el caudaloso Mendino, nieto del gran rabadán Mendiano, con cuya llegada el claro río ensoberbeció sus corrientes, los altos montes de luz y gloria se vistieron, el fértil campo renovó su casi perdida hermosura; pues los pastores de él, incitados de aquella sobrenatural virtud, de manera siguieron sus pisadas que, envidioso Ebro, confuso Tormes, Pisuerga y Guadalquivir admirados, inclinaron sus cabezas, y hinchadas urnas manaron con un silencio admirable. Sólo el felice Tajo resonaba, y lo mejor de su son era Mendino, cuya ausencia sintió de suerte Henares, su nativo río, que con sus ojos acrecentó tributo a las arenas de oro.
>
> (When the Tagus, ancient dwelling of the sacred muses, bloomed with the most handsome and splendid shepherds, the mighty Mendino,[16] grandson of the head shepherd[17] Mendiano, came to its celebrated bank, with whose arrival the clear river made proud its currents, the lofty mountains dressed themselves in light and glory, the fertile countryside renewed its almost lost beauty; well, his shepherds, inspired by [his] supernatural virtue, followed in his footsteps in such a manner that the envious Ebro, the troubled Tormes, admiring Pisguera, and Guadalquivir inclined their heads, and pompous urns poured with an admirable silence. Only the happy Tagus resounded,

[14] (Rodríguez Marín, *La Fílida de Gálvez de Montalvo*, 15–16).

[15] "Y una de las españolas que entraron al servicio de doña Isabel fué doña Magdalena Girón, la cual perteneció a su cámara aun antes de cumplir los diez y seis años, edad mínima con que se solía obtener tan honroso empleo" (Rodríguez Marín, *La Fílida de Gálvez de Montalvo*, 16–18).

[16] "Caudaloso," or "mighty," was used both for men of great estates and for great rivers (Covarrubias, *Tesoro*, 1995, 287).

[17] "RABADÁN. El mayoral, que es sobrestante a todos los hatos del Ganado de un señor; y púdose decir del nombre griego. . .Algunos quieren decir que es hebreo. . .El padre Guadix dice que vale como el gran pastor o el señor de las ovejas, en la lengua arábiga," (Covarrubias, *Tesoro*, 1995, 847).

and the best of its sound was Mendino, for whose absence, Henares, his native river, felt lucky since by his eyes tribute to its sands of gold increased.)[18]

The geography of this pastoral world should be the source of some confusion and it requires further explication. The Palace of the Infantado was not set on the banks of the Tagus (where Mendino has come). The nearest river to Guadalajara is the river Henares (which feels his absence). The Tagus most likely refers to the city of Toledo, home to Isabel's court until the 1561 transfer to Madrid. When Gálvez de Montalvo writes that Mendino, grandson of Mendiano, arrived at the Tagus from the Henares, he is telling his reader that Enrique de Mendoza, grandson of the fourth Duke of Infantado, arrived at the city of Toledo from Guadalajara. In keeping with the precedent set by Garcilaso in his Eclogue II, the rivers of Spain, and the mention of funeral urns, were often used as metonymies for noble families.[19] Arribas Rebollo concludes that the mention of other rivers – Pisuerga, Guadalquivir, and Ebro – were employed by Gálvez de Montalvo to refer to other noble families present in Toledo during the marriage festivities – Manrique de Lara, Medina Sidonia, and Luna.[20] The novel opens with the marriage festivities which took place in Toledo (on the Tagus) for the installation of the royal couple in the Alcázar ten days after Isabel's arrival in Guadalajara. Nearly the entirety of the novel takes place on the Tagus over the course of three years, indicating that the river served as a metonym for the court (both in Toledo and in Madrid, perhaps also in Aranjuez). When the novel begins, the shepherd Siralvo (Gálvez de Montalvo) has already fallen in love with Fílida (Magdalena Girón), presumably on the banks of the Henares during the marriage festivities at Guadalajara in February 1560.

Because Don Íñigo, who is mentioned at the opening of the novel as Mendiano, died in 1566, the three-year span of the novel is likely set between 1560 and 1566, long before the first printing of the work in 1582. The royal families encoded at the outset of the work indicate an occasioned gathering, such as the marriage festivities in Toledo in February of 1560. As the Mendoza of Infantado held one of the highest stations in the court of Philip II, it is likely that the Mendoza were housed in the Alcázar in Toledo. In the novel, Siralvo (Gálvez de Montalvo), the page of the

[18] (Gálvez de Montalvo, *El pastor de Fílida*, 2006, 113–114).

[19] "Garcilaso usa de estas metonimias asociadas (urna y río Tormes) para expresar figurativamente la heroicidad del linaje y el lugar de señorío del mismo" (Arribas Rebollo in Gálvez de Montalvo, *El pastor de Fílida*, 2006, 114).

[20] (Gálvez de Montalvo, *El pastor de Fílida*, 2006, 114–115).

Mendino (Enrique de Mendoza), is sent to deliver Mendino's love letter to his beloved, Elisa (also of the same noble station as Mendino). By way of his secret errands in the palace, Siralvo is enmeshed in the highly nuanced inner machinations of quotidian court life. Mocked by Hurtado de Mendoza in his own *sátira contra las damas del palacio* of the same period, the *billetes* in the *Fílida* demonstrate that these amorous epistles and their messengers were pervasive in palace life.

Siralvo's role reinforces the difficulty for Gálvez de Montalvo of pursuing Magdalena under the strict etiquette of the *cámara* of Isabel.[21] The etiquette set out for the ladies-in-waiting of the queen was strict, though rarely successful.[22] The text pays close attention to rights of access and the hierarchies of court life.[23] Mendino was "siempre acompañados de la mayor nobleza de la pastoría (always accompanied by the highest nobility of the shepherd-community)" and the poor Siralvo struggles to meet with Fílida because they are not of the same station or gender.[24] The shepherds who meet to play games, partake in *pláticas* (discourses or philosophical dialogues), and enjoy poetry contests, return to the "amparo de nobles mayorales (refuge of the noble overseers)."[25] In the court of Isabel, Gálvez de Montalvo enjoyed proximity to Magdalena, but as a lower hidalgo he would not have had direct access to her, as with Siralvo and Fílida.

> Andaba [Siralvo] furiosamente herido de los amores de Fílida. Fílida, que por lo menos en hermosura era llamada sin par, y en suerte no la tenía. Y como los días, con la ocupación del ganado y el recelo de Vandalio y sus pastores (adonde Fílida estaba), no le daban lugar a procurar verla ni oírla . . .
>
> (He [Siralvo] went about furiously wounded by the loves of Fílida. Fílida, who at the least was in beauty called peerless, though of luck she had

[21] It is this same manner of courtship, both of palace life and pastoral poetics, that dQ resurrects in the *billete* that he pens to Dulcinea as the Amadís of the Sierra Morena in DQ I:23.

[22] "la custodia y vigilancia que las Instrucciones de Palacio encomendaban a la Guarda mayor de damas, muchas jóvenes todas, lindas, de las más linajudas familias, grandes partidos, que diríamos hoy, ¿quién podía impedir que el amor se filtrase al través de puertas, rejas y tocas para hacer de las suyas? Porque aunque las curiosísimas e inéditas Instrucciones . . . extremasen todas las severidades y rigores para evitarlo, con muy copiosas y meditadas reglas, por más que encomendasen a la Guarda mayor de damas que tuviera «mucha vigilancia, recato y cuydado con su buen recaudo», obligándolas a asistir de continuo en la cámara de la reina, mandando cerrar sus ventanas y echar candados en ellas «cuando así pareciere», visitando de improviso sus aposentos, para sorprenderlas, a más del constante acecho de la portería llamada de damas, de la prohibición de recibir billetes, recados y vistas de fuera, así como el salir de Palacio, no siendo por enfermedad y acompañada de la Guarda mayor, y menos aún hacer noche fuera de él «sino con gran ocasión y licencia de la Reina» . . ." (Amezúa y Mayo, *Isabel de Valois*, 1949, vol. I, 160–161, emphasis mine).

[23] For class in the pastoral: (Hernández-Pecoraro, *Bucolic Metaphors*, 2006, 27–28).

[24] (Gálvez de Montalvo, *El pastor de Fílida*, 2006, 116).

[25] (Gálvez de Montalvo, *El pastor de Fílida*, 2006, 124).

> none. And as the days, with the occupation of the flock and [because of] the suspicion of Vandalio and his shepherds (where Fílida was), did not give him the opportunity to procure either to see or to hear her . . .)[26]

Vandalio was the pseudonym for Magdalena's elder brother Pedro, Count of Ureña and, after 1562, first Duke of Osuna.[27] Though highly visible to Siralvo, Fílida also lived under the oversight of the *guardia mayor*, and with the suspicions of her elder brother, *sus pastores*, and her mother, acting *camarera mayor* of Isabel's household. In referring to Fílida as unlucky, presumably because she cannot free herself to meet with Siralvo, the passage implies that the love was requited but forbidden.

While Fílida occupies most of Siralvo's lyric energies, theirs is not the only lyrical plot at stake in the *Fílida*. The tragic love and loss that his patron, Mendino, suffered with Elisa (heretofore unidentified) spanned three and a half years, the timespan of the first part of the novel. Part 1 concludes with the tragic death of Elisa. In 1563, three years after the marriage festivities of Isabel and Philip, Ana Florencia de la Cerda Bernemicort (b. 1540, wife of Enrique de Mendoza from 1560, and daughter of Ana de Bernemicort and Fernando de la Cerda y Silva, *sumiller de corps* of Charles V) died.[28] From the opening in Toledo in 1560 with Mendino's courtship of Elisa to the untimely death of Elisa three years later, in 1563, the timeline of the novel coincides with the amorous intrigues of both poet and patron that began in January 1560.[29] The text was closer to

[26] (Gálvez de Montalvo, *El pastor de Fílida*, 2006, 131).

[27] "Como en *La Galatea*, bajo los nombres pastoriles se ocultan personajes reales de la alta sociedad en que Gálvez de Montalvo vivía. Algunos son fáciles de identificar, como los mencionados, y otros; por ejemplo, *Campiano* es el doctor Francisco de Campuzano; *Bandalión*, Felipe II; *Livio*, el príncipe don Carlos; *Arsia*, doña Mariana de Garcetas, persiguiendo a la cual rodó el príncipe en Alcalá, como se dijo, por una escalera el 19 de Abril de 1562; *Uranio*, el conde de Ureña; *Vandalio*, el duque de Osuna; *Nerea*, Luisa de Sigea, según estas palabras: «la sin igual discreción de *Nerea*, acostumbrada a vencer en versos a los más celebrados poetas del Tajo», y *Arciolo*, Ercilla, por lo que dice en un pasaje: «el celebrado *Arciolo*, que con tan heroica vena canta del Arauco los famosos hechos y vitorias. » Todo lo principal de la novela es autobiográfico. El pastor *Siralvo*, protagonista, va narrando, punto por punto, sus amores con *Fílida*, concorde con lo que conocemos de doña Magdalena Girón" (Astrana Marín, *Vida ejemplar*, 1951, vol. III, 224).

[28] Enrique de Mendoza was not the first son of Don Diego de Mendoza y Aragón and second sons were not prioritized in noble archives unless the primogenitor met with untimely death. From the *Historia de la Casa de Silva* (Madrid: 1685, 564–565), it is clear that the two were married sometime between 1558 and 1560. The marriage was concluded in 1563, presumably upon the death of Ana Florencia. The marriage was without issue. Biographical data for Ana is extremely limited.

[29] While Ana Florencia did not pertain to Isabel's household, she could easily have pertained to that of Juana de Austria or, simply by way of her noble station, to any number of households in Toledo with access to the court. As her father served as *sumillier de corps* to Charles V, she likely pertained to court life in Toledo before Isabel's arrival in 1560. In the novel, it is clear that she is not one of Isabel's ladies-in-waiting as she is not restricted from excursions in the same way as is Siralvo's beloved

private chronicle than to allegory. He mythologized experience in his fiction.

Returning to the anonymous chronicler and keeper of the *Memoire pour la reine*, it is clear that Gálvez de Montalvo's shepherds were engaged in the same courtly pastimes as the queen and members of her entourage. The author of the *Memoire* frequently reports that Isabel would retire to "deviser" with the Princess Juana and various other interlocutors.[30] The *Fílida* evidences that a primary form of discourse in quotidian court life – from page to queen – was lyric poetry, a feature both historical and literary which transforms Bakhtin's understanding of poetry, as a (monological) thing apart, into a primary mode of discourse. Playing at jacks and cards were favored forms of recreation.[31] These daily goings-on of court life are represented in the pages of Gálvez de Montalvo's pastoral fiction.[32] Following the happy union of the ill-fated couple, Mendino and Elisa, in Part I, the reader is told:

> para cualquier género de ejercicio había en la ribera bastantísima compañía. En fuerza y maña: Mendino [Enrique de Mendoza], Castalio [don Luis Hurtado de Mendoza], Cardenio, y Coridón. En la divina alteza de la poesía: Arciolo [Alonso de Ercilla y Zúñiga], Tirsi [Francisco de Figueroa], Campiano [Dr. Francisco Campuzano], y Siralvo [Gálvez de Montalvo]. En la música y canto: con la hermosa Belisa, Sasio, Matunto, Filardo y Arsinio;
>
> (for any type of recreation[33] there was plenty of company on the riverbank. In strength and skill: Mendino [Enrique de Mendoza], Castalio [don Luis Hurtado de Mendoza], Cardenio, y Coridón. In the divine nobility of poetry: Arciolo [Alonso de Ercilla y Zúñiga], Tirsi [Francisco de Figueroa], Campiano

Fílida. While Mayans (1792) and Arribas Rebollo (2006) interpret the novel and the persons encoded within it as pertaining to the late 1570s (the court of Ann of Austria), Rodríguez Marín's attention to details which reveal a pertinence to the earlier years of the 1560s under Isabel de Valois is compelling. The unanimous identification of Mendino as Enrique de Mendoza y Aragón grounds the central timeline of the text and underscores the efficacy of Rodríguez Marín's scholarship.

30 "DEVISER. v. n. S'entretenir familierement. Il eft bas. *Ils devifoient enfemble. ils s'amufoient à devifer*" (*Le Dictionnaire de l'Académie françois*, 1694, 324).

31 (DC, *Memoire*, Abt. 97, n.18, Friday, May 10, 1560, 61r–61v).

32 "el venerable Sileno le tomó la lira con que los tañia, y colgandola de la ancha rama, que de una gran encina sobre ellos pendía, mandó que Arsindo tocase nueva señal, a cuya bocina los pastores y pastoras se fueron dividiendo por el ameno valle: y sobre humildes mesas, cual de cortado tronco, y cual de la fresca y menuda yerba, gastaron las rústicas viandas que traían. Lo mismo hicieron el viejo Sileno y los gallardos cuatro pastores que le acompañaban con el Rabadan Alfesibeo, y todos seis al cabo de su breve comida, que fue al pie de una fuente que salía de una viva peña, poco distante de la alta pira, enderezaron a la parte que la pastora Belisa de los más hábiles y nobles pastores de nuestro Tajo estaba acompañada, y con gran cortesía les pidieron que mudasen lugar, porque la fuente de la peña estaba más fresca, y el sitio más acomodado" (Gálvez de Montalvo, *El pastor de Fílida*, 2006, [Book II] 166).

33 (Covarrubias, *Tesoro*, 1995, 450).

[Dr. Francisco Campuzano], and Siralvo [Gálvez de Montalvo]. In music and song: with the beautiful Belisa, Sasio, Matunto, Filardo and Arsinio;)[34]

While not all of these pseudonyms have been identified, some are indicated in the translation by their historical names in brackets.[35] If pseudonymic practice was an intrinsic part of pastoral poiesis, it is not the case that the *Fílida* is simply a chronicle of the court in the way that Isabel's anonymous chronicler takes down quotidian events in her *Mémoire*. It would be reductive to say that Gálvez de Montalvo had simply encoded the private lives of the court within an Arcadian landscape. The *Fílida* was as much an Arcadian allegorization of the intimate histories of contemporary life as it was a meditation on erotic experience writ according to Renaissance Neoplatonism in lyric art. Through discursive improvisation in the interstice between chronicle and allegory, pastoral poetics reconceptualized intimate human experience. It translated the quotidian into poetry, altered the meaning of experience itself, and novelized an inherited style.

Because the erotic was a serious thematic in philosophical discourse at that time, the amorous life of the poet and his peers served as the content for philosophical inquiry in the incubated space of pastoral fiction. Interwoven with narrative discourse, the poet's "communal autobiography" in the lyric mode became a complex space of entanglement that intertwined the emotional with the affective, the metaphysical with the physical, and the transcendent with the immanent in a quotidian *poiesis*. In this way, the beloved as *summa belleza* became the embodiment of the *summum bonum*, a realization of the ideal form. Of his beloved Fílida, Siralvo sings:

Al revolver de vuestra luz serena
se alegran monte y valle, llano y cumbre.
La triste noche de tinieblas llena
halla su día en vuestra clara lumbre.
Sois, ojos, vida y muerte, gloria y pena;

[34] (Gálvez de Montalvo, *El pastor de Fílida*, 2006, 132, square brackets mine).

[35] "Algunos personajes son nobles de rango algo inferior a estos primeros, otros son poetas contemporáneos y aun amigos del autor, y hay aún otros que son sirvientes y pastores. Y de ese modo Gálvez de Montalvo jerarquiza una ficción pastoril, reflejo de una sociedad cortesana, que sufre experiencias amorosas universales en casos particulares de amor" (Arribas Rebollo in: Gálvez de Montalvo, *El pastor de Fílida*, 2006, 31). While the musicians and singers are not identified, the poets Benito Caldera (Batto), Pedro Laínez (Damón), Gregorio Silvestre (Silvano), and Luis Camoes (Licio) populate the banks of the Tajo. Prince Carlos (Livio), who fell in Alcalá while chasing Doña Mariana de Garcetas (Arsia), and the events of his fall are included in the novel. The Marquis of Coria (Coriano), Fadrique Álvarez de Toledo y Enríquez de Guzmán, appears in reference to Gálvez de Montalvo's own father (Montano): (Rodríguez Marín, *La Fílida de Gálvez de Montalvo*, 41–44). Rodríguez Marín identified Coriano as the Marquis of Coria. The identification of the Marquis of Coria as Fadrique Álvarez de Toledo is mine.

el bien es natural, el mal costumbre.
No más, ojos, no más, que es agraviaros.
Sola el alma os alabe con amores.

(At the stirring of your serene light
hill and valley, plain and peak rejoice.
The sad night full of darkness
finds its day in your clear fire.
You are, eyes, life and death, glory and pain;
the good is natural, the bad is custom.
No more, eyes, no more, [oh] that it is to offend you.
Only the soul praises you with loves.)[36]

Here, in Gálvez de Montalvo's Pastoral Petrarchism, the trope of the beloved as the sun places her as the center and animating force around whom the natural world revolves.[37] She is not only a light-giver, but an emanating life-giver. Part-cosmological, part-theological, it is the force of her eyes – the window to the soul, or in this case, the cause – to whom the lyric apostrophe is addressed. By way of the gaze, the erotic other becomes a micro-universe or *pequeño mundo*.[38] In this way, the poetry of Gálvez de Montalvo renewed Petrarchan commonplaces within the Pastoral poetics that he shared with Figueroa, Laínez, and the young Cervantes. The narrative of the *Fílida* sets the stage for deep character development in which we come to know Siralvo's lyric interiority as a key feature of the story or plot (the exteriorized action). This is not only the case with Siralvo. Gálvez de Montalvo heightened the private histories and lyric expressions of his contemporaries to a highly aestheticized literary art as novelistic plot. In so doing, Gálvez de Montalvo's pastoral fiction develops the private aspect of human experience, which soon became the generative force for novelistic character formation, modeled on but independent of their prior figurations in histories and romances. The lyric interiority of the novelistic character, and the way in which the lyrical human life organically generated new plots, set the novel, as a literary genre of "modernity," apart from precursors in the romance and the picaresque.

Gálvez de Montalvo was not the only member of Cervantes' first literary milieu to encode quotidian life at court within pastoral poetics. While little information about the poet Gómez de Tapia has survived,

[36] (Gálvez de Montalvo, *El pastor de Fílida*, 2006, 185).

[37] The figure of the divine beloved as the *summa belleza* and "luz serena" is more fully explored with Judah Abravanel's *Dialogues of Love* in Chapter 4.

[38] (F. Rico, *El sueño del humanismo (De Petrarca a Erasmo)*, Madrid: Alianza, 1993); (Cacho-Casal, *La esfera del ingenio*, 2012).

during the 1560s (and later in the 1580s) the poet touched upon the same circles in which Cervantes wrote.[39] Gómez de Tapia's *Égloga Pastoril en que se describe el Bosque de Aranjuez, y el Nacimiento de la Serenísima Infanta Doña Isabel de España* commemorated pastoral festivities held at Aranjuez for the birth of Isabel's first daughter, Isabel Clara Eugenia, in 1566.[40] Like Gálvez de Montalvo's *Fílida*, Gómez de Tapia's *Égloga* was not printed until 1582, when it appeared as an appendage to Gonzalo Argote de Molina's updating of Alfonso El Sabio's *Libro de la montería* (Seville: Andrea Pescioni), dedicated to Philip II.[41] The *Égloga* followed Chapter 47 of Argote de Molina's "Descripción del Bosque y Casa Real del Prado," which resituated Alfonso's *Libro* within the contemporary practices of Philip II's court – a transposition from the "medieval" to the "renaissance" landscape on a par with AQ's interpolation of dQ into late sixteenth-century Castile. Gómez de Tapia's *Égloga* preserves the pastoral play of court practice as the primary site of production for Gálvez de Montalvo's *Fílida* and Cervantes' first poems. In seventy-six octaves, the poem employs mythical allusions (Zephiro, Daphne and Apollo, Venus and Adonis), an amorous exchange between the shepherdess Daphne and the shepherd Virgilio, and Arcadian descriptions of the royal family and a company of noblemen, pages, poets, entertainers, and guests. In 1582, fifteen years after the birthday festivities for Isabel Clara Eugenia, Argote de Molina framed its printing as an accurate representation of cultural practices that his *Discurso de la montería* was intended to describe and preserve. The *Égloga* was included as an historical source on the pastoral fabric of everyday life in the court in which Gómez de Tapia depicts the following scene in his account of festivities at Aranjuez in 1566:

> De bello Bosque, y de la huerta amena
> la fama y de la casa peregrina
> del Ártico al Antártico resuena
> y hasta a donde el rostro el Sol inclina,
> de gente esta la estancia siempre llena
> que de apartada parte y de vecina,

[39] Like Cervantes' *Galatea* (1585), Gómez de Tapia's translation of Camoes' *La Lusiada* (1580) was dedicated to Ascanio Colonna.

[40] (Alfonso XI, *Libro de la montería*, ed. Gonzalo Argote de Molina, Seville: Andrea Pesconi, 1582, 22r–25v).

[41] "me pareció hacer un breve discurso, de la forma que al presente se usa en la Montería, y en los officios de la Casa Real de España, tocantes al ministerio della: con la memoria de algunos sucessos y exemplos, que a las personas Reales han acaecido en este exercicio" (Argote de Molina, *Libro de la Monteria*, 1582, [unpaginated] 2r).

DE LA MONTERIA. 22

ño de Alonso Sanchez Cuello Pintor famoso de su Magestad. Los de las letras M I., son de Maestre Luca, Pintor Flamenco, todos de los mejores y mas celebrados Pintores deste tiẽpo. Vee se por baxo destos retratos, dos de Stanislao Enano de su Magestad, de quien se a hecho memoria eneste libro, Y quatro al temple, de las Villas de Valladolid, y Madrid, y de las Ciudades de Londres, y Napoles, con ocho tablas de Pintura de las jornadas que el Emperador Carlo quinto nuestro señor, hizo en Alemania, de mano de Ioan de la Barua longa, Flamenco, a quien dieron este nombre, porque tenia la Barua de vna vara y media de largo.

De aqui se van a los aposentos de los Reyes. Y a estos sigue el aposento de la Camarera, que esta pintado al fresco, de mano de Bezerra, natural de Baeça, cuyo Pinzel ygualó a los mejores Pintores destos tiempos, y de mano de Ioan Baptista Bergamasco, y Romulo Italianos, donde se vee la historia de Perseo, con muchas Tarjas a lo Romano, de admirable pintura sobre Estuco.

EGLOGA PASTORIL

En que se descriue el Bosque de Aranjuez, y el Nascimiento de la Serenissima Infanta Doña Ysabel de España.

Compuesto por Don Gomez de Tapia Granadino.

EN lo mejor dela felice España
do el rio Tajo tercia su corrida,
y con sus cristalinas aguas baña
la tierra entre las tierras escogida,
esta vna vega de belleza estraña
toda de verde yerua entretexida,
donde natura y arte en competencia
lo vltimo, pusieron de potencia.

Aqui jamas nubloso velo encubre
dl siẽpre claro cielo el rostro hermoso,
aqui el Thesoro de su luz descubre
con nueuo resplandor el Sol lustroso,
no se conosce aqui desnudo Octubre
perpetuamente es Mayo deleytoso,
aqui el templado Zefiro se anida
y a quantos vienen à anidar combida.

En medio deste nueuo Parayso
vn ancha huerta esta ẽ quadro traçada
de rojo y odorifero Narciso
y blanco Lirio a trechos esmaltada,
en torno todo esta con tal auiso
dela Nimpha a quien Pã siguio cercada
que puesto que alos pies haga reparo
alos ojos permite entrar de claro.

Los arboles de hojas siempre llenos
de vn blando y fresco viẽto meneados
el dulce murmurar de los Amenos
arroyos, de Cristales variados
los Ruyseñores por los verdes senos
de los ramosos arboles sentados
que siempre estan cantando dulcemẽte
ya ay nueuo parayso en Occidente.

Esta de verde Yedra y de hojosas
Nuezas, aque la huerta entretexida
y por do puedẽ mil purpureas rosas
parece que procuran la salida,
en torno estan Portales de sabrosas
Parras, que entre si guardã tal medida
que ninguna endistancia ni en altura
excede, y es perpetua su verdura.

De

Fig. 2.1 Gómez de Tapia, *Égloga Pastoril*, Argote de Molina, *Libro de la Montería*, 1582, 22r–23v. Imágenes procedentes de los fondos de la Biblioteca Nacional de España

cual de oscuro linaje, cual de claro,
a ver concurren el milagro raro.

Aquí concurren todos los pastores
por la vecina tierra derramados
mientras del alto cielo los ardores
vedan el pasto tierno a los ganados,
dellos cuentan a veces sus amores
sobre la verde Yedra reclinados,
otros mil juegos rústicos probando
están las largas horas engañando.

Las bellas Ninfas del lugar dichoso,
están de tal manera enamoradas
que dejan por el bosque deleitoso
muchos y largos ratos sus moradas,
las Náyades olviden el reposo
de las amenas fuentes y mezcladas
andan en dulces corros con las Dríadas
Oreadas, Napeas, y Amadriadas.

Entre otros muchos días que vinieron
y por el Bosque y Huerto se holgaron
un día señalado concurrieron
que por solemne fiesta celebraron
de varias flores multitud cogieron
y sus rubias cabezas coronaron
al claro Tajo, a paso largo llegan,
y que sus Ninfas les envíe, le ruegan.

(Of beautiful Wood and pleasant garden,
the fame, and of the pilgrimed house
from the Artic to the Antarctic resounds
and even to where the Sun inclines its face,
this country retreat is always full of people
who from far away and from neighboring places,
of obscure and of clear lineage,
come together to see the rare miracle.

Here they come together all the shepherds
spilt forth from nearby lands,
while the burning rays from the high heaven
prohibit the flocks from the tender pasture,
of them they recount at times their loves,
reclined over the green Ivy,
others play a thousand rustic games
cheating the long hours.

The beautiful Nymphs of this happy place
are enamored in such a manner
that they leave their flocks about the delightful wood
for many and long periods,
the Naiads forget the repose
of the pleasant fountains, and mixed together
they go about in sweet choirs with the Dryads,
Oreads, Napaeaes, and Hamadryads.

Among many other days that they came –
and were found in the Wood and the Garden,
on a designated day they came together
and celebrated a solemn *fiesta*,
and chose a multitude of the various flowers,
and crowned their blond heads –
to the clear Tagus. With great strides they arrive,
and plead that [the river] send them its Nymphs.)[42]

The presence of nobility and lower *hidalgos* ("of obscure and clear lineage") underscores how pervasive pastoral court culture became, as also evidenced in the anonymous *Memoire*, which reports Isabel's visits to nearby villages and the invitation of villagers to evening dances at the palace in Aranjuez. In both documents, these festivities drew visitors of all stations and ranks, and from various regions into the pastoral play at court. Given Cervantes' 1567 sonnet celebrating the birth of Isabel's second daughter, Catalina Micaela, it is reasonable to believe that the young poet, Miguel de Cervantes Cortinas, may have been present in Aranjuez for occasions such as the one that Gómez de Tapia celebrates in 1566.[43] The "rare miracle," of course, was Isabel Clara Eugenia. According to Amezúa y Mayo, the festivities for her birth lasted for at least fifteen days, replete with ladies disguised as nymphs and shepherdesses in imaginative forms of entertainment.[44] When Cervantes' 1567 sonnet is read in relation to Gálvez de Montalvo's *Fílida*, Gómez de Tapia's *Égloga*, and the pastoral practices detailed in Chapter 1, the lyrical culture of Pastoral Petrarchism takes shape as the primary context for the poetic beginnings of the author of the *DQ*.

[42] (Argote de Molina, *Libro de la Monteria*, 1582, 22r–23v).

[43] While Astrana Marín does not definitively place the Cervantes family in Madrid until January 1567, Cervantes could already have been in service, likely as a page, to any number of noblemen who pertained to the royal court. The Dukes of Sessa were long-standing patrons of the Cervantes family as far back as the author's grandfather, and contemporaneously of his uncle, Andrés. The third Duke of Sessa authored a letter of commendation on Cervantes' behalf during his period as a soldier-poet in Italy, 1571–1580 (*Vida ejemplar*, 1948–1951, vols. II–III).

[44] (Amezúa y Mayo, *Isabel de Valois*, 1949, vol. II, 392).

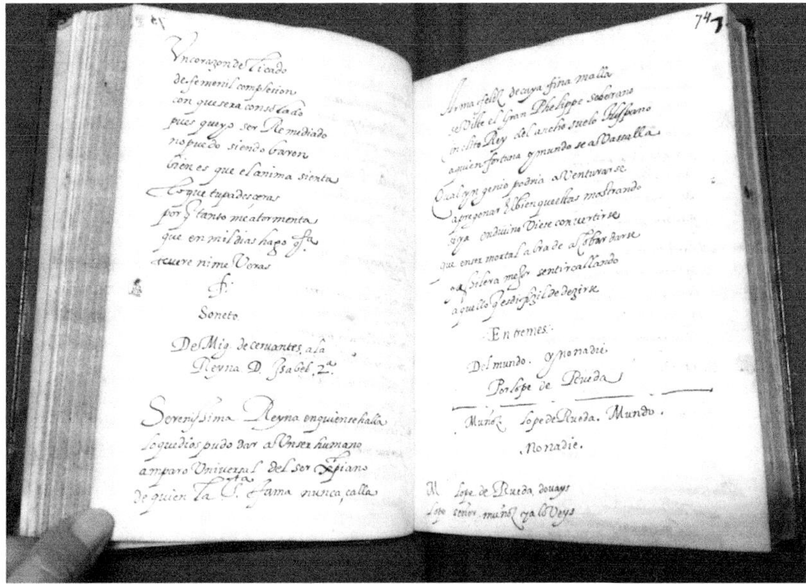

Fig. 2.2 Cervantes, "Serenísima Reina," ms. Espagnole 373, 73v–74r, Bibliothèque Nationale de France

In 1567, the twenty-year-old poet celebrated his own feast day by writing his first sonnet to the queen.

> Serenísima reina, en quien se halla
> lo que Dios pudo dar a un ser humano;
> amparo universal del ser cristiano
> de quien la santa fama nunca calla;
> arma feliz, de cuya fina malla
> se viste el gran Felipe soberano,
> ínclito rey del ancho suelo hispano,
> a quien Fortuna y Mundo se avasalla:
> ¿cuál ingenio podría aventurarse
> a pregonar el bien que estás mostrando,
> si ya en divino viese convertirse?
> Que, en ser mortal, habrá de acobardarse
> y así le va mejor sentir callando
> aquello que es difícil de decirse.

> (Most serene queen, in whom is found
> all that God could give to a human being;
> universal shield of the Christian being

about whom the saintly fame is never quiet;
happy arm, in whose fine chain mail
the great sovereign Philip is dressed,
illustrious king of the wide Hispanic soil,
to whom Fortune and World are subjugated:
  What *ingenio* could venture
to extol the good you are showing,
if you are already seen to be converted into a thing divine?
  Such a mortal being will have to cower
and thus [such praise] is better felt by falling silent
in that which is difficult to be spoken.)[45]

Long before Cervantes took the lyric conceit of the divine lady to its full hyperbolic figuration as Dulcinea of the *Quijote*, his poetry for Isabel de Valois employed the same Neoplatonic and Petrarchistic conceits of the divine lady as *summa belleza* and *summum bonum* which collapsed the queen's two bodies (natural and politic) into the poetry of a single immanent figure.[46] The first quatrain identifies the subject of the poem, Isabel, the queen as perfect mortal. The second quatrain modifies the subject: the queen is figured as an idealized demi-goddess. The *volta*, at the first tercet, complicates the theme: Can the poet articulate such divinity? In asking the question, the poet alters the subject yet again and the queen is transformed from idealized lady to ineffable divinity. The final tercet confirms the transformation by answering the question through an act of negation: the poet succumbs to his sense of ineffability. Silence. The failure of poetic language before ineffability was not new to literature. Augustine's *Confessions*, the lyric tradition of the Islamic world, the *scuola siciliana*, the *dolce stil nuovo*, Dante, the troubadours, Petrarch, Ficino's Neoplatonism, and the poetry of Figueroa and Laínez had engaged the same paradox of articulating ineffability. In another poem from Gálvez de Montalvo's *Fílida*, the shepherd-poet Siralvo had declared:

  Rostro divino, que de entrambos fuiste
sacado en condición y en hermosura,
pues tiemblo y ardo el punto que te veo.

[45] In consultation with the manuscript record of this poem (BNF, ms. Español 373, fol. 73–74), I have kept the transcription given in the following edition of Cervantes' poetry: (Cervantes, *Poesías*, 2016, 135).

[46] "The state of superhuman, 'absolute perfection' of this royal *persona ficta* is so to speak the result of a fiction within a fiction" (E.H. Kantorowicz, *The King's Two Bodies: A Study in Medieval Political Theology*, Princeton University Press, [1957] 1985, 5). The retention of this medieval conception of kingship in Habsburg Spain is mingled with the divinization of the beloved throughout encomiastic poetry.

(Divine visage, that was drawn both
in condition (inner state) and in beauty (outer state),
well I tremble and I burn in the event of seeing you.)[47]

A few decades later in England, Sir Philip Sidney would attest that "his right badge is worn but in the heart." Rhetorically, the conceit of Cervantes' sonnet turned on a locutionary speech act: in the moment that the speaking *ingenio* realizes the ineffability of the lady, the poem comes to a close. The expression of the proposition is actualized by the speaker's speechlessness. Language succeeds in its own failure. A sort of negative onomatopoeia, the conclusion of the poem makes the sound of silence. The lady, in becoming divine, conditions the outcome of the sonnet just as the outcome of the poem affects her divinity.

Through the use of apostrophe, Cervantes' ecstatic encomium destabilized the division between the public and the private. Resituated within the public and political arena, the divine lady became purveyor not only of nature but of the realm, and of the king himself. However, even as the poem commemorates the occasion of Isabel's first child, the poem itself does not address the public or political sphere; it engages directly with the queen. More than mere laud, Cervantes' sonnet puts the poet (*ingenio*) into direct address with the divine lady. By way of apostrophe to a figure who is not absent in the traditional sense, but who is inaccessible by way of her loftiness, the speaker carves out a sphere of intimacy to create a private exchange within a public address. The queen's transformation from political body to ineffable divinity thus situated the poet in a curious form of ecstatic encomiastic experience, an encounter with ineffability. As the speaker advances through his verses, his form of address brings him into conversation with the *summum bonum*.

The 1567 sonnet makes clear that Cervantes' friendship with Gálvez de Montalvo, Francisco de Figueroa, and Pedro Laínez, among others, was not happenstance. The young poet was a precocious practitioner of their shared

[47] (Gálvez de Montalvo, *El pastor de Fílida*, 2006, 202, paranethetical mine). This tercet concludes the following sonnet by Siralvo:

"Divino rostro, en quien está sellado
el postrer punto del primor del suelo,
pues de aquél en quien tanto puso el cielo
tanto el pincel humano ha trasladado.
Rostro divino, ¿fuiste retratado
del que Natura fabricó de yelo,
o del que amor pasando el mortal velo
con vivo fuego, en mí dejó estampado?
Divino rostro, el alma que encendiste
y los ojos que helaste en tu figura
por ti responden, y por ellos creo . . .

poetic discourse. Cervantes was not the only poet to repurpose the pastoral for the political. In the tradition of the *contrafactum*, many poets transposed erotic poetry for devotional or encomiastic verse.[48] Pedro Laínez's three tropologically interchangeable sonnets to (1) his beloved Fili, (2) the Virgin Mary, and (3) the Princess Juana de Austria, in which the *contrafactum* of the love poem for Fili was employed not only for religious poetry (to the Virgin Mary) but also for encomiastic work (to the Princess), resituate Cervantes' sonnet within poetic practices of the literary culture shared by his contemporaries.[49] In fact, the inclusion of Cervantes' 1567 sonnet in ms. Espagnole 373 (BNF) – the only known record of it – attests to his position within this poetic milieu. A record of poetic production and collation, the compiler of the manuscript included Cervantes within this collection of poetry pertaining to the changing culture of Pastoral Petrarchism in the court. The sonnet shares a page with the start of Lope de Rueda's *entremés*, from a period during which the playwright was known to have performed for the queen and princess at court. Poetry by Diego Hurtado de Mendoza, Garcilaso de la Vega, Fernando de Herrera, and Pedro de Padilla, as well as a translation of Horace by Fray Luis de León and an anonymous translation of Petrarch's Sonnet 17, "Piovonmi amare lagrime,"

[48] The term *contrafactum* was examined by Bruce Wardropper (1958) in order to clarify the practice of rewriting certain erotic literary works in such a way that the profane sentiment was substituted by a religious one. "¿Qué es, pues, un *contrafactum*? Diremos que es una obra literaria (a veces una novela o un drama, pero generalmente un poema lírico de corta extensión) cuyo sentido profano ha sido sustituído por otro sagrado. Se trata, pues, de la refundación de un texto. A veces la refundación conserva del original el metro, las rimas, y aun–siempre que no contradiga al propósito divinizador–el pensamiento. El nombre de la dama amada se sustituye con el de la Santa Virgen; lo erótico se convierte en el amor cristiano" (B. Wardropper, *Historia de la Poesía lírica a lo divino en la Cristiandad Occidental*, Madrid: Revista de Occidente, 1958, 6–8).

[49] "Fili" // Hermosísima Fili, en quien florece / alto valor y rara hermosura, / y en cuyos claros ojos y figura / el bien del alto cielo resplandece; / por quien dulce y suave me parece / la pasada y presente desventura, / viendo en tan alta cumbre mi ventura, / que te acuerdas del mal que me adolece; / el cual, aunque me priva de la gloria / que el alma recibía sólo en verte, / no me podrá quitar el contemplarte. / Porque este bien, ni el tiempo ni la muerte / ni amor ni desamor pueden ser parte / para apartarme ya de mi memoria.

// "Virgen Mary" // O, so, de quien es rayo el sol del cielo, / con cuyo resplandor era alumbrada / mi alma, que en tinieblas sepultada / vivió sin ver tu lumbre en este suelo! / No sufras, claro sol, que escuro velo / de ausencia cubra esta alma desdichada, / que, aunque de donde estás está apartada, aspira siempre a ti con alto vuelo. / Temor de olvido, grave mal de ausencia, / del tiempo el vario curso y de Fortuna, / y el mal no te ver, estoy pasando; / mas por rodar del cielo, sol y luna, / no temas, claro sol, que tu presencia / olvide, pues por fe la estoy mirando.

// "Juana de Austria" // Altísima princesa, en quien el cielo / con abundante mano a derramado / la gloria y el valor tan extremado, / por quien se estima en alto precio el suelo; / cuyo saber, beldad y honesto celo, / digo de eternamente ser loado, / nos muestra claro ser claro traslado / de aquel que te levanta a tanto vuelo; / sin en los altos oídos se consiente / llegar alguna vez el bajo canto, / disculpa hallará mi atrevimiento, / pues ver los claros ojos y alta frente / bañados con tan largo y tierno llanto, / subió tan alto mi atrevido intento" (Laínez, *Obras*, 1951, vol. II, 214 [Fili], 196–197 [Virgin Mary], 226 [Juana de Austria]).

among many other works, were included. But most of the poetry was recorded anonymously. Taken as a whole, the manuscript reveals the ways in which this particular moment in literary history celebrated the legacies of Petrarch and Garcilaso whilst cultivating the poetry of Hurtado de Mendoza, Figueroa, Laínez, Padilla, Herrera, and others. The inclusion of the Marquis de Montesclaros and the Duke of Lerma indicates that the manuscript was also a record of the way in which early seventeenth-century court culture looked back on the previous decades of the sixteenth century.[50] As if opening onto an inverted world, the collection reverses the cultural values of hegemonic, masculine, Counter-Reformation Spain. Substituting religiosity with eroticism, and the Judeo-Christian god with the Platonically ideal beloved lady as *summa belleza*, or the fickle deity Love, this was an erotic theology fashioned out of philosophical and literary readings of the Classical world, entangled with the folkloric and Islamic inheritance of Iberia.[51] This was the Arcadian discourse in which Cervantes, Lope de Vega, and Góngora – innovators of the novel, *comedia*, and lyric, respectively – cut their first lines and phrases.

One of several compilations of sixteenth-century poetry preserved in the BNF, ms. Espagnole 373 consists of 164 folio pages of lyric verse, much of which is anonymous and almost all of which takes place within a pastoral landscape. The opening "Romance" invokes the idyllic setting in which most of the subsequent poetry is keyed:

> Junto a una clara fuente
> en lo hondo de un collado
> lugar fresco y apacible
> para un hombre libertado
> estaba un triste pastor
> entre las flores sentado
> con la flecha de Cupido
> el corazón traspasado
> . . .

[50] Juan de Mendoza y Luna, III Marquis de Montesclaros (1571–1628).

[51] "In realità l'audace lezione dell'eroticismo allegorico di Ibn al Farid ha preceduto, se non ispirato, parte della poesia religiosa europea moderna. Ancor prima, sia pure per vie traverse, nemmeno è del tutto improbabile che essa abbia potuto influenzare la lirica d'amore profano di un dissimulante Francesco Petrarca . . . Nel poemi di Ibn al-Farid, intuibilmente l'amata assente della poesia preislamica diventa l'essenza divina di cui il *sufi* è in cerca, finché essa non si ricongiunga e quasi si confonda con la propria essenza" eds. A. Almarai, P. Blasone, P. Branca, and O. Capezio, *Poesia araba dalle origini al XIII secolo*, Libri Mediterranei, 2015, 9). See also: (Ponce-Hegenauer, "Lyric and Empire," 2021).

y para mostrar su pena
desta manera ha hablado . . .

(Beside a clear fountain
in the depths of a mountain pass
a cool and amenable place
for a free man,
there was a sad shepherd
seated among the flowers
with Cupid's arrow
pierced through his heart
. . .
and to show his pain
in this manner he has spoken . . .)[52]

The collection opens like a pastoral work of prosimetric fiction (such as the *Fílida*); it sets the scene in what would be a peaceful and idyllic natural world were it not for the weeping victim of love and his sorrowful verses. As was typically the case, the shepherd in this opening poem is stricken with Cupid's arrow with such force that he cares neither for himself nor for his flock. But the poem is not a lyric in the traditional sense of an isolated first-person speaker: the poem performs narrative work before giving voice to the main "character," whose discourse is lyrical. The verses with which the poem opens act as a poetic prelude of narrative exposition to the lyric speaker. Like the prosimetrum of the pastoral novel, both narrative and lyric content take shape within a single work, here entirely versified. Because the culture of Pastoral Petrarchism consistently understood lyric as a revelation of a private interior, the poetics practiced in it typically took an interest in recontextualizing lyric expression within narrative exposition. By way of the framing verse, the reader eavesdrops on the shepherd and watches him "raise his tearful eyes to the heavens and sound his rabel."[53] The reader witnesses the lyric as a textual artifact (a lyric poem) and the immediate expression of a literary character (akin to prose fiction). As the

[52] (BNF, ms. Espagnole 373, 1r–1v).

[53] "De recelo y ausencia combatido
me tiene ciego Amor en tal estado
que me fuera mejor no haber nacido
pues tengo de morir desesperado
de la mas Alta cumbre soy caído
en el profundo abismo descuidado
mis males sin Remedio pues no hay cura
que valga donde falta la ventura."

(BNF, mss. Espagnole 373, 1v-2r).

reader overhears the outpourings of the shepherd's interior, the poem shifts from classical amorous suffering – a blindness caused by love – to real desperation, caused by the shepherd's fall from what he calls the highest nest into a profound abyss (a Platonic descent away from the divine lady). In the position of eavesdropper, the reader is moved into a position akin to most pastoral characters (from the other side of the page into the narrative scene), who often behold their fellow characters in moments of private poetic rapture. That is, the structure of the lyric-narrative poem wraps the reader into the place of the text.

The opening poem of the manuscript invokes several of the central themes of Pastoral Petrarchism, and it may be that the compiler selected this poem in particular for exactly that reason. As a "canción desesperada," the poem anticipates the tragic "suicide-poem" of the shepherd-poet Grisóstomo in the famous pastoral episode of the first part of the *DQ*.[54] In this poem, the erotic experience resulted from a star-crossed or ill-fated lack of fortune, impersonal and cosmological. As the speaker of the "Jubileo y confusión de Amor" in the same collection declared, "Viendo me predestinado / con la ley de vuestro amor (Seeing myself predestined / with the law of your love)," which itself echoed Garcilaso's "os ha cortado a su medida" ("my soul has cut you to its measure," Sonnet 5).[55] Repeating the common complaint of the pastoral novel, the shepherd in the opening poem laments that his beloved lady has married another shepherd. A friend has sent a letter with the unhappy news. He goes on to engage in a long lyrical curse against the lost shepherdess (no doubt, a lady of the court). The *romance* (a medieval folk narrative-ballad or a "modernization" of the tradition by "los modernos" of the 1580s) with which the manuscript opens is one of many poetic forms of pastoral discourse encountered in the compilation which brings together lyric and narrative within a single versified poem (akin to the way in which the pastoral prosimetrum unifies verse and prose in a story of the lyric lives of its characters). Whilst not a unified narrative, the manuscript does invite the reader into a shared *logos amoenus* shaped by the poems as a collective.[56] It should be remembered that even Montemayor's *Diana*, Gálvez de Montalvo's *Fílida*, and Cervantes' *Galatea* retained the threads of lyric incompleteness within the 'totality' of the narrative.

[54] The "Canción desesperada" itself "es anterior al *Quijote*, y su versión original es la que se guarda en los plúteos de la Biblioteca Colombina" (J.B. Avalle-Arce, 'Grisóstomo y Marcela: Cervantes y la verdad problemática', *Nuevos deslindes cervantinos*, Barcelona: Ariel, 1975, 96).

[55] (BNF, mss. Espagnole 373, 91v).

[56] There is also a "Vida de Aldea" (BNF, mss. Espagnole 373, 18v–22r).

Like the prosimetrum, the manuscript collected various verse forms, such as the *canción*, the *soneto*, and *coplas* (sometimes taking the form of a gloss). The *soneto* and *canción* had precedents in the work of Petrarch, Sannazaro, and Garcilaso. Several of Garcilaso's sonnets were copied into the manuscript. Though these were widely available in numerous printings, such as the copy that Tomás Rodaja carries to Italy in the *Licenciado vidriera*. Their inclusion evidences the living influence of Garcilaso and Boscán within the culture of Pastoral Petrarchism.[57] This is true for the anonymous translation of Petrarch's "Llueven amargas lágrimas a mis ojos (Bitter tears rain from my eyes)."[58] The *glosa*, in which a small verse (*letra*), usually two to four lines, is glossed by a lengthier poem intended to elucidate and play upon the full meaning of the *letra*, also appears frequently throughout the manuscript and underscores the intertextuality of Pastoral Petrarchism. These glosses take the form of games in pastoral fiction, as in Book VI of Cervantes' *Galatea* (1585). In the second part of the *DQ* (1615), they are a favorite pastime of the son of the Caballero del Verde Gabán. Like the *motes* of the *terrero*, *letras y glosas* were a form of flirtation and entertainment in the court, not always without consequence for the participants. Providing in addition a record of reception, the compiler comments on several poems, indicating how subsequent readers might understand his curation of the text. For example, next to the *coplas* that begin "Ojos que tal muerte dais (Eyes that give such a death)," the compiler writes, "buenas me parecen (they seem good to me)."[59]

Not all of the work is anonymous, as in the "Coplas en vituperio de la vida de Palacio y alabanza de aldea. Hechas por Gallegos secretario del Duque de Feria (Couplets in vituperation of Palace life and praise of the village. Made by Gallegos secretary of the Duke of Feria" (10 r–18 v). "Vituperation" had been a common theme of the pastoral since Guevara's *Menosprecio de corte* (1548), which Cervantes reinvented with the "Canción de Lauso" in the *Galatea*, which itself rewrote Cervantes' own "Epístola a Mateo Vázquez" composed in Algiers.[60] Another set of poems includes a "Carta. Del Marques de Montesclaros a Lerma (Letter from the Marquis of Montesclaros to Lerma)" (23 r–25 v), a "Redondilla del mismo [El

[57] These are followed by another sonnet, "Pues tuve corazón para partirme" (128v). On this sonnet: (A. Alatorre, "Sobre la 'gran fortuna' de un soneto de Garcilaso," *Nueva Revista de Filología Hispánica*, 24.1, 1975). Alatorre connects it to glosses given by Antonio Pérez in his continuation of *La Diana*.

[58] (BNF, mss. Espagnole 373, 281v). [59] (BNF, mss. Espagnole 373, 8v).

[60] See: (Morel-Fatio, "Les 'Coplas' de Gallegos," *Bulletin Hispanique*, 1901). There is also a "Vida de Aldea" (BNF, mss. Espagnole 373, 18v–22r).

Marques de Montesclaros]" (25 v), a "Respuesta [presumably by Lerma]" (25 v–31 v), and an "Otra de Francisco Nuñez de Velasco a Gaspar Yañez de Lerma en favor de la primera que le sirvió el de Montesclaros" (31 v).[61] All of these underscored the rich intertextuality of this literature as a form of discourse and exchange that directly involved life at court. The same is observable in the versified epistles included in López Maldonado's *Cancionero* of 1586. The collection was not lacking in the pastoral elegy – *Et in arcadia ego.* Two sonnets can be found for the death of Doña Isabel de Borja, whom the text identifies as the Countess of Lerma (she was the mother of the first Duke of Lerma). The first of the two sonnets is an allegory in the form of a dialogue between Life and Death (47 v). The mysterious figure of Gila Giraldo (*La serrana de la vera* of *romances* and Vélez de Guevara's tragedy) also appeared in the "Coplas de Gila Giralda hechas por R. L. M. d. S. M." (112 r–113 r). Read within the lexicon of Pastoral Petrarchism, as evidenced in mss. Espagnole 373, Cervantes' 1567 sonnet for Isabel is more than a panegyric meant to attain protection or a livelihood; it keys the most important tropes of court and poetic practice in order to posit the figure of the speechless poet (*ingenio*) before the ineffable lady. This genuflection was one that would recur in much of Cervantes' work. It appears with particular force at the close of his 1579 *octavas* for Antonio Veneziano's *Celia*, and remains present in the figures of Persiles and Sigismunda in his final narrative work.[62]

The "birth" of the poet was also the beginning of the end of Isabel's court. In 1567 Figueroa departed for the thriving literary court of the Count of Benavente, Viceroy of Valencia, where he would remain until his return to Alcalá in 1571.[63] The year 1568 was one of scandal and grief following the death of the prince and heir in July, after he had been confined to his room on 17 January for his alleged conspiracy with the Dutch against his father. These machinations could not have been far from the ears of Cervantes, whose close friend and lyric mentor, Pedro Laínez, was *camarero* to Prince Carlos, and likely authored the anonymous eyewitness *relación* of these events.[64] Laínez then passed into the service of Archduke Ernesto of Austria, and from Ernesto to Don Juan

[61] Likely the Francisco Nuñez de Velasco who authored the *Diálogos de contención entre la milicia y la ciencia/ en los cuales se discurre sobre el valor destas dos insignes facultades* (Valladolid: Juan Godinez de Millis, 1614).

[62] See also Chapter 4.

[63] (Figueroa, 1989, 39–43); (N.F. Marino, "The Literary Court in Valencia, 1526-36," *Hispanófila*, 104, 1992, 1–15).

[64] "Nos imaginamos a Cervantes enterándose del fin trágico del príncipe: sin duda, de la boca misma de su amigo Pedro Laínez, el poeta camarero al que se atribuye una relación manuscrita del arresto"

de Austria, whom he accompanied at the Battle of Lepanto in 1571, where he coincided with Cervantes (a meeting recalled later between Damón and Lauso in the *Galatea*).[65] An illegal duel in June 1568 resulted in the exile of Hurtado de Mendoza to Granada.[66] The uprising of the *moriscos* in the Alpujarras (1568–1571), which Hurtado de Mendoza, critical of Philip's II violent oppression, recorded in his *Guerra de Granada*, drew those Castilian soldier-poets who were not destined for Italy or the Low Countries to the south of Spain.[67] On October 3, 1568, following complications with her pregnancy, the young queen died.

Before leaving Madrid for Rome, Cervantes contributed several elegiac poems on the death of Isabel, published by López de Hoyos in the

(J. Canavaggio, *Cervantes. En busca del perfil pérfido*, Madrid: Espasa-Calpe, 1992, 2nd ed., 49). Astrana Marín narrates the same incident to which Laínez was a witness: "Sobre el acontecimiento hay la versión anónima de un testigo presencial, ayuda de cámara del Príncipe, obra, en nuestra opinión, del gran amigo de Cervantes, Pedro Laínez, que era el único escritor y poeta entre los ayudas de cámara de don Carlos" (*Vida ejemplar*, vol. II, 168). For the complete version of the anonymous testimony: (L.-P. Gachard, *Don Carlos et Philippe II*, Brussels: E. Devroye, 1863, Appendix B). An extensive narration of the incident can also be found in: (R. Menéndez Pidal, ed. *Historia de España, España en tiempo de Felipe II, 1556–1598*, Madrid: Espasa-Calpe, 1958, vol. I, 752–777).

65 (Astrana Marín, 1949, vol. II, 296–300).

66 "Nada, empero, podría dar tan clara muestra de lo que en realidad era en aquel tiempo la vida de Palacio, en cuanto a las damas y galanes, como las sabrosamente chismosas cartas que por los años de 1562 se cruzaron entre doña Magdalena de Bobadilla, poetisa y gran latina, dama de la Princesa de Portugal doña Juana, y don Juan de Silva, después conde de Portalegre, que tuvo la alegría en el alma aún más que en el título. En tales donosas epístolas, bajo el pintoresco disfraz de todo un onomasticón tomado de los libros de caballerías (más leídos entonces por las damas que los de horas de la Santísima Virgen), se cuentan mil donaires palaciegos del orden amatorio, y hasta algún lance aldeano en que lo picante pesa un si es, no es, de la raya. Esta ingeniosa Bobadilla se llama en su escrito, "la saudosa Corisandra", y Silva, "el caballero don Florestán". Y si, leídas tales cartas, se quiere ampliar, examinando otros documentos, la noticia de las invenciones, intrigüelas y dimes y diretes con que procuraban no aburrirse las guardadísimas damas de la cámara de la Reina, bien colmarán las medidas de nuestra curiosidad las redondillas en que don Diego de Leyva, hermano del Príncipe de Áscoli, se despidió festivamente de Casa de la Princesa y la respuesta que en otros versos le dió don Diego Hurtado de Mendoza, tan destemplada y satírica que, motivando entre los dos en los corredores de Palacio un lance en que Mendoza, para defenderse, echó mano a un puñal, trajo por consecuencia la prisión y el subsiguiente destierro de ambos"(Rodríguez Marín, "La Fílida de Gálvez de Montalvo," 22).

For the pseudonymic epistles of Bobadilla and Silva: (BNE, mss. 1439); (Rodríguez Marín, "La Fílida de Gálvez de Montalvo," 22, n.1). For a selection of Leyva's verses which mention Bobadilla: (Astrana Marín, *Vida ejemplar*, 1949, vol. II, 201–204).

67 (D. Hurtado de Mendoza, *Guerra de Granada*, ed. B. Blanco-González, Madrid: Castalia, 1970); (C. Johnson, *Transliterating a Culture: Cervantes and the Moriscos*, Newark: Juan de la Cuesta, 2010). For poetry on the Battle of Lepanto: (López de Toro, *Los poetas de Lepanto*, Madrid: Instituto Histórico de Marina, 1950); (E.R. Wright, S. Spence, and A. Lemons eds. *The Battle of Lepanto*, Cambridge: The I Tatti Renaissance Library, 2014). Also: (M. Gaylord, "Arms, Men and the Risks of Synecdoche," *Renaissance Society of America*, New York, 2004).

commemorative volume *Hystoria verdadera*, which was printed the following year (1569). In his *epitafio*, Cervantes focused on the figuration of Isabel as a peacemaker, a French flower who became the symbol of temperate valor and unification on Spanish soil.[68] Reconciler of difference, the symbol of the olive branch as crown was a fitting pastoral image for Isabel as peacekeeper. As the light of the west ("lucero de occidente") and *summum bonum* ("nuestro bien"), her olive branch was reminiscent of Petrarch's laurel, she of Petrarch's Laura. A curious transposition from the pastoral court to the idyllic Elysian fields, the epitaph figured Isabel as *la mejor flor de la tierra* which had been transplanted to a *locus amoenus*. In the *cuatro redondillas castellanas*, which López de Hoyos introduced as the work of "nuestro caro y amado discípulo," Cervantes began by voicing the collectively dashed hopes of the Spanish people (*nuestra suerte* and *nuestro reposo*).[69] He introduced the figure of *invencible muerte* as a famous thief and a fierce tyrant who had made off with *el valor del ser humano*. Reviving techniques from his 1567 sonnet, in the *redondillas* the collective voice gave way to a direct apostrophe to the deceased queen, whom the speaker addressed with the informal and intimate "tu." This staging of private

[68] "Epitafio //. Aquí el valor de la española tierra, / aquí la flor de la francesa gente, / aquí quien concordó lo diferente, / de oliva coronando aquella guerra; / aquí en pequeño espacio veis se encierra / nuestro claro lucero de occidente; / aquí yace enterrada la excelente / causa que nuestro bien todo destierra. / Mirad quién es el mundo y su pujanza / y cómo, de la más alegre vida, / la muerte lleva siempre la victoria; / también mirad la bienaventuranza / que goza nuestra reina esclarecida / en el eterno reino de la gloria" (Cervantes, *Poesías*, 2016, 136).

[69] Typically associated with the *estudio de la villa*, López de Hoyos attribution of "our dear and loved disciple" is typically assumed to be a reference to the early grammar school. As López de Hoyos was the official court chronicler, however, it could just as easily refer to Cervantes' role as a young poet active in court culture. Pages and other minor members of the court were likely educated in small private or informal schools like the *estudio*.

"Redondilla // ... Cuando dejaba la guerra / libre nuestro hispano suelo, / con un repentino vuelo / la mejor flor de la tierra / fue transplantada en el cielo; / y, al cortarla de su rama, / el mortífero accidente / fue tan oculto a la gente / como el que no ve la llama / hasta que quemar se siente."

Cuatro redondillas castellanas a la muerte de Su Majestad // Cuando un estado dichoso / esperaba nuestra suerte, / bien como ladrón famoso / vino la invencible muerte / a robar nuestro reposo; /y metió tanto la mano / aqueste fiero tirano, / por orden del alto cielo, / que nos llevó deste suelo / el valor del ser humano. // ¡Cuán amarga es tu memoria, / oh, dura y terrible faz! / Pero en aquesta victoria / si llevaste nuestra Paz, / fue para dalle más gloria; / y aunque el dolor nos desvela, / una cosa nos consuela: / ver que al reino soberano / ha dado un vuelo temprano / nuestra muy cara Isabela. // Una alma tan limpia y bella, / tan enemiga de engaños, / ¿qué pudo merecer ella / para que en tan tiernos años / dejase el mundo de vella? / Dirás, Muerte, en quien se encierra / la causa de nuestra guerra, / para nuestro desconsuelo, / que cosas que son del cielo / no las merece la tierra. // Tanto de punto subiste / en el amor que mostraste / que, ya que al cielo te fuiste, / en la tierra nos dejaste / las prendas que más quesiste. / ¡Oh, Isabel Eugenia Clara, / Catalina, a todos cara, / claros luceros las dos, / no quiera y permita Dios / se os muestre Fortuna avara!" (Cervantes, *Poesías*, 2016, 137–140).

exchange complicated the public function of the poem and thrust the lyric "I" of the poet into relation with his subject, Isabel. The poet volleyed between the public "we" and the private "I," a fierce negotiation between interior and exterior also at work in the pastoral prosimetrum and which perhaps was most famously codified in Petrarch's prologue sonnet "Voi ch'ascoltate." The oratorical and public voicing of collective grief gave way to the poet's lyric intimacy with the queen for whom the living poet's direct address stretched beyond the grave. In the final four lines, the figure of the prophet-poet emerges to address Isabel's two daughters. From the collective to the individual, the public to the private, the past to the future, the dead to the living, the poet navigates the spheres of grief as an intermediary, a speaker whose own lyric voice and personal anguish consistently stakes itself as lyric interiority within the public sphere.

In his lengthy *elegía* the apostrophic dynamism of Cervantes' early poetry increases. The speaker moves from addressing first the public, then Cardinal Espinosa (protector of López de Hoyos and possibly also of Cervantes), then Isabel's daughters, and then Isabel herself.[70] The poem opens with a publicly directed rhetorical question which echoes the conclusion of the 1567 sonnet: Will the effect of the poet's song be powerful enough to do justice to his subject? Perhaps in an allusion to Book X of Ovid's *Metamorphoses*, the speaker invokes the orphic power of pastoral elegy to recall the deceased Eurydice.[71] This question gives way to a familiar address ("tu") to Cardinal Espinosa which posits the departure of the queen as an insurmountable disaster. Public grief gives way to pastoral figurations reminiscent of the court culture that Isabel had cultivated. Where Gómez de Tapia sang of an eternal spring in his *Égloga*, Cervantes sings of a saddened summer and a scorched paradise.[72] Spring has turned to winter, an inverted sovereignty which again invokes the figuration of Isabel as a lost peacemaker. The untimeliness of the queen's death appears as the awaited fruit withered by an early frost. The poet returns to Ovidian imagery, employing the figure of impassioned Mars against the peace of the Elysian fields freed from the dangers of Charon's boat. The poet then returns to the direct address of the Cardinal, weaving him into the landscape of the poem as the loyal shepherd and imploring

[70] For the complete elegy: (Cervantes, *Poesías*, 2016, 141–148).

[71] (Cascardi, "Orphic Fictions") and (F. de Armas, ed., *Ovid in the Age of Cervantes*, University of Toronto Press, 2010).

[72] I have retained Cervantes proper as the poet rather than the disembodied "speaker" common to twentieth-century criticism.

him to lift the burden of grief from his flock. As if taking the cardinal by the hand, the poet directs his attention to the suffering of Philip in the sixteenth stanza, imploring the cardinal as a *divino ingenio* to opine on the uncertainty of human life and the necessity of hope. A new rhetorical question reintroduces the uncertainty of the poet, who recalls the inconsolable nature of the loss, and the two young daughters whom Isabel has left behind.

Then, suddenly, in the twenty-first stanza, the poem turns into an apostrophe to the deceased queen. Breaking entirely from the dedication to the Cardinal, the speaker invokes the dead queen and directs her attention to the state of things on earth. As if for her instruction, the orphic poet summons the grief of the natural world, a pastoral *locus amoenus* where *et in arcadia ego*. The happiest bird does not fly but pours forth its sad and dolorous song. But the divine lady is worthier of the heavens. In the twenty-fifth stanza the poet assures Isabel that collectively those on earth will console themselves with the legacy of her daughters. Then as the speaker turns toward the future, his address to the deceased queen begins to fade back to earthly concerns. The poet grows increasingly philosophical, again employing the device of a rhetorical question in order to develop the form of the elegy as a meditation on mortality. He returns to his original address to the cardinal. He reminisces on the figure of the young queen whose majesty is augmented by her disembodiment. Then the poem becomes an apostrophe to Death. The public address gives way to the intimacy of the poet's own feeling as he takes Death's action as a personal affront resulting in his own grief. In this confrontation with Death, which folds the speaker into the poem as one of its actors, Cervantes first employs one of his favorite metaphors for storytelling, a "roto hilo (broken thread)," at once the thread of a tale and a thread cut by the fates. In this direct confrontation with Death, the twenty-one-year-old poet posits his own lyric voice (a contender for immortality in letters).

Shortly after his poetic contributions for the death of Isabel, either in the fall of 1568 or the winter of 1569, Cervantes left for Italy.[73] He was in Rome between 1569 and 1571 prior to his time as a soldier-poet in the Mediterranean campaigns in service to Don Juan de Austria, the third Duke of Sessa (Gonzalo Fernández de Córdoba), and Marco Antonio Colonna. The nature of Cervantes' departure for Rome and his subsequent

[73] Both Rufo and Laínez benefited from the patronage of Don Juan de Austria while traveling in his immediate entourage to Lepanto. Rufo served as the prince's chronicler (Astrana Marin, *Vida ejemplar*, vol. II, 296–298). Following the arranged marriage of Magdalena Girón, Luis Gálvez de Montalvo also left Madrid to enlist as a soldier in the Alpujarras.

service with Cardinal Giulio Acquaviva has been clouded in ambiguity. According to a document discovered in the Archives of Simancas, royal provision was issued on September 15, 1569 for the arrest of a student by the name of Miguel de Cervantes, who was charged with injuring Antonio de Sigura in a duel. Miguel de Cervantes had apparently fled to Seville and as consequence of the royal provision it was decreed that he should publicly lose his right hand and be exiled for ten years.[74] While palace duels and their subsequent exiles were common during this period (as with Hurtado de Mendoza), and Cervantes' pertinence to the court of Isabel would no doubt have provided the occasion, the incident is chronologically problematic. The date, September 15, 1569, is nearly a year after the departure of Cervantes to Italy, which likely occurred between the funeral exequies for Isabel in mid-October 1568, when Giulio Acquaviva's arrived in Madrid, and his return to Rome in December 1568. Cervantes' status as a young poet was at a peak when the young Acquaviva arrived at the Madrileño court, just days after the passing of Isabel. Near contemporaries in age and both *aficionados* of poetry, their meeting may have been arranged by López de Hoyos or the Cardinal Espinosa; it provides the most reasonable explanation for Cervantes' sojourn in Italy. Given Cervantes' mention of his service with Giulio Acquaviva (d. 1574) in the dedication of the *Galatea* (1585) to Ascanio Colonna, Acquaviva's presence in the Madrileño court during Isabel's funeral exequies, and his subsequent return to Rome that winter, it is reasonable to believe that Cervantes came into his service and accompanied him at that time.[75] It is likely that the culprit of the 1569 Sigura affair pertains to a homonym.[76] Moreover, Cervantes' request for a *limpieza de sangre* (a certificate of "purity of blood" which was frequently requested as a way of discriminating against *marranos* and *moriscos*) from Rome, obtained on his behalf by his father the following year, was likely necessitated by Cervantes' service as *camarero* to Giulio Acquaviva. Acquaviva himself became *camarero* to Pius V.[77] The acquisition of this

[74] (Canavaggio, *Cervantes, En busca*, 52); (Astrana Marín, *Vida ejemplar*, 1949, vol. II, 185).

[75] Billi di Sandorno has argued that Cervantes' Italian sojourn was motivated by a distant relation, the archbishop of Salerno, Gaspar de Cervantes (A. Billi di Sandorno, "¿Por qué fué a Italia Cervantes?," *Revista Bibliográfica y Documental*, 1950, vol. IV, 109–129). There is a coincidence of distant lineage and the clerical ties to Espinosa, but the possibility is less likely than Acquaviva's return to Rome. Morel-Fatio's argument against Cervantes' association with both Acquaviva and, later, Colonna, is predicated on a scholarly trend of taking the author to be an *ingenio lego* isolated from the spheres of literary and political power in which he clearly participated: (Morel-Fatio, "Cervantes et les cardinaux," 1906).

[76] ". . . del mismo modo que ya se sabe que hubo dos Juan y dos Rodrigo, tal vez llegue un día en que se descubra que hubo dos Miguel de Cervantes" (Canavaggio, *Cervantes, En busca*, 53).

[77] (Astrana Marín, *Vida ejemplar*, vol. II, 186–187).

document would have proved difficult if the Sigura affair had taken place in September 1569. While the Acquaviva and Sigura remain matters of speculation, by the time of the acquisition of the *limpieza de sangre* in 1569, Cervantes was in Rome and, by his own account, in the service of Acquaviva.

Cervantes' early poetry for Isabel and his sojourn in Rome left an indelible mark on his poetic imagination. Late in the fourth book of his Heliodoran Byzantine Romance, *Los trabajos de Persiles y Sigismunda* (post. pub. 1617), the aging poet interpolated a final sonnet into his literary corpus which reconfigured the 1567 sonnet to Isabel as an apostrophe to the *caput mundi* itself. In this last known work of lyric verse, given in the Petrarchan style to the figure of the pilgrim, and at a distance of nearly five decades, Cervantes reconfigured the conceptual structure with which he had begun his poetic career. Before the immanent ineffability the mortal *ingenio* was once again suspended and speechless.

> ¡Oh grande, oh poderosa, oh sacrosanta,
> alma ciudad de Roma! A ti me inclino,
> devoto, humilde y nuevo peregrino,
> a quien admira ver belleza tanta.
> Tu vista, que a tu fama se adelanta,
> al ingenio suspende, aunque divino,
> de aquel que a verte y adorarte vino
> con tierno afecto y con desnuda planta.
> La tierra de tu suelo, que contemplo
> con la sangre de mártires mezclada,
> es la reliquia universal del suelo.
> No hay parte en ti que no sirva de ejemplo
> de santidad, así como trazada
> de la ciudad de Dios al gran modelo.
>
> (Oh great, oh powerful, oh sacrosanct,
> beneficent[78] city of Rome! I, a devote, humble,
> and new pilgrim who is struck by admiration
> to see such beauty, genuflect before you.
> The sight of you, which exceeds your fame,
> suspends the *ingenio*, although divine,
> of he that came to see you and adore you
> barefoot and with a tender affect.[79]
> The earth your land, mixed with the blood

[78] "En sentido latino, proicia, benéfica," (J.B. Avalle-Arce in Cervantes, *Los trabajos de Persiles y Sigismunda*, Madrid: Castalia, 1969, 426, n.490).

[79] (Covarrubias, *Tesoro*, 1995, 22).

of martyrs, that I contemplate
is the universal relic of the earth.
There is not a single part of you that does not serve as an example
of sanctity, as if traced
from the great model, the city of God.[80]

[80] (Cervantes, *Poesías completas*, 1974, 321).

CHAPTER 3

Figura of the Poet: *Pastoral Petrarchism as the Practice of Ingenious Gentlemen*

The poetry of the 1560s, 1570s, and 1580s participated in the widespread practice of Petrarchism which developed over the course of the sixteenth century in Europe by way of translations, imitations, invocations, and mythologizations of the *figura of the poet*, Francesco Petrarca.[1] This chapter focuses on the Pastoral Petrarchism of the middle and late sixteenth century, from Montemayor to (early) Lope de Vega. Studies of Spanish Petrarchism have typically skirted this middle period between Garcilaso and Góngora (with isolated treatments of Herrera).[2] But the period from the 1550s to the 1590s was crucial to Cervantes' own formation as a poet.[3]

[1] This chapter should not be confused with Robert Durling's monograph *The Figure of the Poet in Renaissance Epic* (Harvard University Press, 1965), which focuses on the narrator-poet and author in epic. The term *figura of the poet* may engage twentieth-century discourse on the "authorial figure," informed by Roland Barthes ("The Death of the Author") and Michel Foucault ("What Is an Author?"). There is no space to elaborate on this here. The interest of the present chapter is to recover and explore the *figura of the poet* particular to the practices of sixteenth-century Pastoral Petrarchism.

[2] Navarette (*Orphans of Petrarch*) traces Spanish Petrarchism from its "canonization" by Pietro Bembo back its earliest Iberian practitioners, the Marquis de Santillana and the treatises of the Salamanca school (*translatio studii*) in the 1490s. He recovers the early translation and imitation of Garcilaso and Boscán but skips the entire middle of the century to arrive at Fernando de Herrera's 1580 *Anotaciones* of Garcilaso, which Navarette promptly calls "the end of Petrarchism in Spain." This ignores Montemayor, Figueroa, Laínez, Gálvez de Montalvo, Miguel de Cervantes, Pedro de Padilla, López Maldonado, and the young Lope de Vega, to name only a few Pastoral Petrarchan poets writing in Castilian. The oversight is not unique to Navarette – it is indicative of widespread scholarly practices and the literary history of the Spanish Golden Age. For Herrera: (Navarrete, *Orphans of Petrarch*, 126–189); (Torres, *Love Poetry*, 60–94); (L. Middlebrook, "Fernando de Herrera Invented the Internet: Technologies of Self-containment in the Early Modern Sonnet," in D.R. Castillo and M. Lollini, *Reason and Its Others*, Nashville: Vanderbilt University Press, Hispanic Issues, 2006, 61–78); (J. Montero, *Fernando de Herrera y el humanism sevillano en tiempos de Felipe II*, Seville: Colección Giralda, 1998); (F. Rodríguez Marín, *El divino Herrera y la Condesa de Gelves, Conferencia leída en el Ateneo*, Madrid: Bernardo Rodríguez, 1911).

[3] Both Torres (*Love Poetry*) and Navarrete (*Orphans of Petrarch*) follow the Garcilaso, Herrera, Góngora grouping. For Petrarchism at large: (Lefèvre, *Una poesia per l'Imperio*); (Kennedy, *Petrarchism at Work*). For Cervantes and poetry: (A.L. Galanes, "Cervantes: el poeta en su tiempo," in *Cervantes, Su obra y su mundo*, Madrid: Edi-6, 1981, 159–178); (M. Menéndez Pelayo, "Cervantes considerado como poeta," 257–268).

While Petrarch's *Secretum* did not, as far as is known, circulate widely during the sixteenth century, *I trionfi* and the *Canzoniere* singularly determined lyric discourse for European poets.[4] The translations of Petrarch into Castilian by Fernando de Hoces (1554), Salmon Usque (1567), and Francisco Trenado de Ayllón (ca. 1595) evidence the *figura* of Petrarch at play in the pastoral poetry of Montemayor, Figueroa, Laínez, Gálvez de Montalvo, Cervantes, Padilla, López Maldonado, and others.[5] In like manner, sixteenth-century Roman lyrical works and the culture of the Renaissance garden, as exemplified by Munzio Manfredi and Vicenzo Orsini, respectively, attest to the practice of pastoral poetics within the larger Mediterranean sphere that Cervantes encountered during his time in Rome (1569–1571).[6] While the present chapter cannot include an

[4] The earliest translation of Petrarch into Castilian that is available in the National Library of Madrid (BNE, mss. 9223) is *Flores e sentençia del libro de maestre Francisco Petrarcha poeta, en el qual loa la vida apartada llamada solitaria* . . . The translation is attributed to Pedro Díaz de Toledo. See: (M. Villar Rubio, *Códices petrarquescos en España*, Padua: Antenore, 1995, 218–220); (Deyermond, *The Petrarchan Sources*, 141–142); and (G. Grespi, *Traducciones castellanas de obras latinas e italianas contenidas en manuscritos del siglo XV en las bibliotecas de Madrid y El Escorial*, Madrid: Biblioteca Nacional, 2004, 192). Early translations of Petrarch's poetry housed in the BNE such as mss. 17969 (*Canciones y poemas varios*) evidence the central role that the Italian poet played for Garcilaso, Boscán, and Hurtado de Mendoza. See: (M. de Riquer, *Juan Boscán y su cancionero barcelonés*, Barcelona: Archivo Histórico, casa del Arcediano, 1945, 44–45). The manuscript also records works by "El Príor de San Juan," Don Hernando de Toledo, "El Clavero" de Alcantara, Don Luis Osorio, Don Garcia de Toledo, Gutierelo Pez de Padilla, the Marques de Villafranca, and Don Juan de Mendoza. "El Príor de San Juan" probably refers to Antonio de Zúñiga y Guzmán (1480–1533), who fought for the emperor in the rebellion of the Comuneros in 1521 and who was named Viceroy of Cataluña the following year. He had been named as a "Continuo de la Casa Real" in 1506 by Ferdinand II of Aragon and had been a member of the court since the reign of the "Catholic Kings." Don Hernando de Toledo probably refers to "The Iron Duke," Don Fernando Álvarez de Toledo, third Duke of Alba (1507–1582), who had cultivated a long friendship with Diego Hurtado de Mendoza. He was a known patron and writer of poetry at court. Don Luis de Osorio is probably the uncle of Isabel de Osorio, lady of the Empress Isabel of Portugal and her daughters Juana and María of Austria. The group may be regarded as belonging to the court of Charles V in the 1520s and 1530s.

[5] (F. Petrarch, *Los triunfos de Francesco Petrarca, ahora nuevamente traducidos en lengua Castellana, en la medida, y número de versos, que tienen en el Toscano, y con nueva glosa*, ed. and trans. H. De Hoces, Medina del Campo: Guillermo de Millis, 1554, unpaginated [iir]); (F. Petrarch, *De los sonetos, canciones, mandriales y sextinas*, ed. and trans. S. Lusitano, Venice: Nicolao Beuilaqua, 1567); (F. Petrarch, *Translation of the sonnets of Petrarch, with a commentary by Francisco de Ayllon* . . ., ed. and trans. F. Trenado de Ayllón, British Library (BL), Egerton Collection, ms. 2062, ca. 1595, unpaginated [A5r], translation mine).

[6] (M. Calvesi, *Gli Incantesimi di Bomarzo, Il Sacro Bosco tra arte e letteratura*, Milan: Bompiani, 2000); (M. Fagiolo, "Bomarzo e le idee di Vignola e di Ligorio," in eds. S. Frommel and A. Alessi, *Bomarzo: il Sacro Bosco*, Milan: Electa architettura, 2009, 66–75); (G. Polizzi, "Il Sacro Bosco e la questione dei generi letterari: allegoria, epopea, arcadia," in eds. S. Frommel and A. Alessi, *Bomarzo: il Sacro Bosco*, Milan: Electa architettura, 2009, 104–113); (J. Theurillat, *Les Mystères de Bomarzo et des jardins symboliques de la Renaissance*, Geneva: Les Trois Anneaux Geneve 1973); (L. Morgan, *The Monster in the Garden: The Grotesque and the Gigantic in Renaissance Landscape Design*, University of Pennsylvania Press, 2016); (B. Croce, "La lirica cinquecentesca," in *Poesía popolare e poesía d'arte*, Bari: Laterza, 1946); (R. Lapesa, "Los géneros líricos del Renacimiento: La herencia cancioneresca," in

examination of pastoral poetics in northern Italy, it should not be forgotten that Hurtado de Mendoza, Figueroa, Don Juan de Austria, Gonzalo Fernández de Córdoba, third Duke of Sessa, Francisco Aldana, and others spent time immersed in literary academies active in these areas.[7] Montemayor himself died in Piedmont.

For sixteenth-century pastoralists, the Petrarch of the *Laura* was always also the Petrarch of the *laurel*. Beginning with the alleged rediscovery of the grave of Petrarch's beloved Laura in 1533, the mythologization of Petrarch as a divine lyric lover held the force and sway of historical fact throughout the century. The *tenzone* that circulated among Eufrasia Placidi de' Venturi, Laudomia Forteguerri, Virginia Martini Casolani Salvi, Virginia Luti di Salvi, Eufrasia Marzi Borghesi, Camilla Piccolomini de' Petroni, and Girolama Biringucci de' Piccolomini of Siena following Alessandro Piccolomini's pilgrimage to Petrarch's grave in 1540 was indicative of Petrarch's historical status among mid-century humanists, literati, and poets.[8] As the model of the *divino ingenio*, the poet's lyric love for Laura showed all aspiring *ingenios* the path to an immortal afterlife in letters.[9] While Petrarch's theme of Daphne (with its connections to the laurel tree/ Laura) and Apollo harkened back to an Ovidian pastoral, for the duration of this chapter the pastoral will be understood within the context of sixteenth-century Castilian poetics and cultural practices (as discussed in the previous chapters).[10] This form of Petrarchism, written within literary conceptions of classical Arcadia in which poets assigned pastoral

Homenaje a Eugenio Asensio, Madrid: Gredos, 1988, 259–275); (I. López Alemany, "El sonsoneto y la práctica poética cortesana del siglo XVI," *Revista de Estudios Hispánicos*, 50.3, 2016, 583–603). See Chapter 4 for Antonio Veneziano.

7 (Navarrete, *Orphans of Petrarch*). For the unique literary career of Aldana (P.J. Lennon, *Love in the Poetry of Francisco Aldana, Beyond Neoplatonism*, London: Tamesis, 2019); (F. de Aldana, *Poesías*, ed. E. Rivers, Madrid: Espasa-Calpe, 1966). For the Italian academies: (C. Celenza, "Academy," in eds. A. Grafton, G.W. Most, and S. Settis, *The Classical Tradition*, Harvard Univesity Press, 2013, 1–3); (R. Ciardi "'A Knot of Words and Things': Some Clues for Interpreting the *Imprese* of Academies and Academicians," in eds. D. Chambers and F. Quiviger, *Italian Academies of the Sixteenth Century*, London: Warburg Institute, 1995, 37–60); (J. Montegu, *An Index of Emblems of the Italian Academies*, London: Warburg Institute, 1998).

8 For participants in the *tenzone*: (K. Eisenbichler, *The Sword and the Pen: Women, Politics, and Poetry in Sixteenth-Century Siena*, Notre Dame University Press, 2012, 15–57).

9 Albert Ascoli's *Dante and the Making of Modern Author* (Cambridge University Press, 2008) also looks at the poet through a variety of figurations and the tension between the time of the author and the author's own individuation. However, my use of the *figura of the poet* in this chapter will speak specifically to Petrarch as poetic icon of the sixteenth century, particularly for poets writing in Castilian.

10 For Ovid in sixteenth-century literature: (A. Keith and S. Rupp, eds., *Metamorphosis: The Changing Face of Ovid in Medieval and Early Modern Europe*, Toronto: Centre for Reformation and Renaissance Studies, 2007); (F. de Armas, ed., *Ovid in the Age of Cervantes*, University of Toronto Press, 2010); (Cascardi, "Orphic Fictions").

pseudonyms to themselves and to their beloveds, produced new poetic figurations of the Petrarchan lover and beloved as shepherd-poets. The temporality of this *locus amoenus* situated lover, beloved, and landscape beyond the scope of biological and geological time, in what Cervantes in the *Galatea* refers to as a *tercia naturaleza*, and Harry Sieber, drawing on Frank Kermode's discussion of the *aevum* in the *Cueva de Montesinos* episode of the *DQ*, calls "literary time."[11] In this other Arcadian nature, the conventional practices of Petrarchism were a precondition for the imitative and innovative features of poetics in Spain, in which shepherd-poets lyrically lamented their erotic woes within a narrativized landscape. While Petrarchism has received a wide array of treatments in English, the Romance languages, and comparativist studies, the *figura of the poet* understood within these poetics, particularly Spanish Petrarchism in the pastoral mode, requires further elaboration.[12]

This chapter argues that Pastoral Petrarchism in Spain should be understood as a set of cultural and poetic practices that were distinguished by their own historical particularity even as they cultivated a conception of lyric temporality in the erotic authorial mode. This lyric temporality was a weaving of historical and literary time into a sempiternal temporality, a being almost always eternal. Unlike timelessness (a favorite erotic conceit), sempiternal or lyric temporality overflows the bounds of historical time whilst retaining the traces of historical particularity. Rather than the erasure of time, it is a type of "longue durée" which exceeds the biological and geological limits of "man and nature." It is both the product of and suited to the paradoxical understanding of language, particularly poetic language, as at once historical and transhistorical.[13] While Covarrubias did

[11] "Aquí se ve en cualquiera sazón del año andar la risueña primavera con la hermosa Venus en hábito subcinto y amoroso, y Céfiro que la acompaña, con la madre Flora delante, esparciendo a manos llenas varias y odoríferas flores. Y la industria de sus moradores ha hecho tanto, que la naturaleza, encorporada con el arte, es hecha artífice y connatural del arte, y de entrambas a dos se ha hecho una tercia naturaleza, a la cual no sabré dar nombre" (Cervantes, *Galatea*, 1961, vol. II, 170). (Sieber, "Literary Time," 268). See also the discussion of literary time in the palace *invenciones* of Isabel de Valois and Juana de Austria in Chapter 1; (E. Rhodes, "*La Galatea* and Cervantes' 'Tercia Realidad'," *Cervantes*, 8, 1988, 17); (Ponce-Hegenauer, "Lyric and Empire"). On imitation and genre: (Cruz, *Imitación y Transformación*); (C. Guillén, *Literature as System: Essays Toward the Theory of Literary History*, Princeton University Press, 1971).

[12] (Kennedy, *Petrarchism at Work*); (Ramachandran, "Tasso's Petrarch"); (Lefèvre, *Una poesia per l'Imperio*); (Braden, *Petrarchan Love and the Continental Renaissance*); (Dubrow, *Echoes of Desire*); (Navarrete, *Orphans of Petrarch*); (Greene, *Post-Petrarchism*); (Cruz, *Imitación y transformación*); (Waller, *Petrarch's Poetics*); (Deyermond, *The Petrarchan Sources*); (Vento, *Petrarchismo y concettismo*).

[13] "If, by virtue of its own subjectivity, the substance of the lyric can in fact be addressed as an objective substance – and otherwise – one could not explain the very simple fact that grounds the possibility of the lyric as an artistic genre, its effect on people other than the poet speaking his monologue – then it

not include the Dantean term "sempiterno" in his *Tesoro* of the Castilian language, it was a word that Cervantes employed early in his career as a poet in his 1579 Petrarchan *octavas* for Antonio Veneziano ("llanto sempiterno").[14] Pedro Laínez, Cervantes' lyric mentor in the court of Isabel de Valois, also used the term in his sonnet to Montemayor to describe the Portuguese poet's immortal fame ("renombre sempiterno").[15]

The Tuscan gloss on "sempiterno," given by Francesco Alunno in his *Fabrica del mondo*, was "quasi sempre eterno, & sempre durante (almost always eternal, and everlasting)."[16] "Sempiterno" aptly described the particularization of infinity in erotic affect, acts of poiesis, and literary immortality as understood in the culture of Pastoral Petrarchism. From the mythologization of Petrarch as an immortal lyric-lover, there emerged the *figura of the poet* as a *divino ingenio* whose *rime sparse* won for himself and his beloved lady a timeless afterlife of literary accomplishment: a becoming "almost always eternal" in the world of letters.[17] While it could be argued that Petrarch already conceived of lyric poiesis as such via his inheritance from Dante and the Ancients, the invention of moveable type in the middle of the fifteenth century popularized the *figura of the*

is only because the lyric work of art's withdrawal into itself, its self-absorption, its detachment from the social surface, is socially motivated behind the author's back. But the medium is language. The paradox specific to the lyric work, a subjectivity that turns into objectivity, is tied to the priority of linguistic form in the lyric; it is that priority from which the primacy of language in literature in general (even in prose forms) is derived. For language is itself something double. Through its configurations it assimilates itself completely into subjective impulses; one would almost think it had produced them. But at the same time language remains the medium of concepts, remains that which establishes an inescapable relationship to the universal and to society. Hence the highest lyric works are those in which the subject, with no remaining trace of mere matter, sounds forth in language until language itself acquires a voice" (T.W. Adorno, "On Lyric Poetry and Society," in ed. Rolf Tiedemann, *Notes to Literature*, Columbia University Press, 1991, 43).

14 "Solo me admira el ver que aquel divino / cielo de Celia encierre un vivo infierno / y que la fuerza de su fuerza y sino / os tenga en pena y llanto sempiterno" (Cervantes, *Poesías completas*, 1974, 347–350; verse 4, lines 1–4). See Chapter 4 for discussion.

Cervantes uses it again to create a euphemism for death, "sempiternal noche" in his last work: (Cervantes, *Persiles*, 1:4, 68).

15 (Laínez, "A [Jorge de] Montemayor," in *Obras*, 1951; vol. II, 233–234). See Chapter 1 for discussion.

16 "Sempiterno. Lat. quasi sempre eterno, & sempre durante. PET[RARCA] Renda a quest'occhi le sue luci prime, O li condanni a Sempiterno pianto. Quanto più vale Sempiterna bellezza, che mortale . . .. Sempiternare val. fare sempiterno. Lat. perpetuare. DAN[TE]. Quando la rota, che tu Sempiterni Desiderato a se mi fece atteso" (Alunno, *Fabrica*, 3v).

17 "Petrarca ofrece una nueva manera de imitar, tanto en su teoría poética como en la práctica, así como brinda una nueva manera de interpretar la historia" (Cruz, *Imitación y transformación*, 2). Also, as cited in Cruz: (Waller, *Petrarch's Poetics*).

In 1512, the *Triunfos*, translated by Antonio de Obregon, and with a commentary by Bernardo Illicinio, were printed at Logroño by Arnao Guillen de Brocar (BNE, R/2540). In 1513 *De los remedios contra prospera et aduersa fortuna* was translated by Francisco de Madrid and printed in Seville by Iacobo Cronberger (BNE, R/3407).

poet throughout the sixteenth century, in which the Tuscan poet's sempiternal afterlife was fully realized. In addition to the poet's literary afterlife, sempiternal temporality also figured as a poetic conceit informed by sixteenth-century philosophical discourse on love in which the infinity of love was an immanent experience. The sempiternal-erotic instant thrust the poet into the temporality of a "timeless" Arcadia, or in the cases of Dante and Petrarch, beyond the mortal coil. This ecstatic feature of erotic experience as an opening into sempiternal temporality was popularized in the erotic mysticism that came out of mid-sixteenth-century Iberian readings of Judah Abravanel's *Dialoghi d'amore*. But it was also a primary feature of the lyrical temporality articulated by Petrarch in the *rime sparse*. From the 1508 manuscript copy of Petrarch's *Canzoniere* which pertained to the Spanish governor of Milan, Juan Fernández de Velasco, fifth Duke of Frías, Petrarch's own "Tacer non posso" gave voice to this sempiternal affect:

Ma si, com huom talhor; che piange, et parte
Vede cosa, che gliocchi e'l cor alletta;
Cosi colei, perch'io son in prigione,
Standosi ad un balcone;
Che su sola a suoi di cosa perfetta;
Cominciai a mirar con tal desio;
Che me stesso, e'l mio mal posi in oblio.
I era in terra, e'l cor in paradiso
Dolcemente obliando ognialtra cura;
Et mia uiua figura
Far sentia un marmo, e'mpeir di merauiglia ...

(But as a man who sometimes weeps, departs,
then sees something that draws his eyes and his heart;
I am this way with her because I am in prison,
she standing at a balcony;
she who alone was a perfect thing;
I began to look with such desire
that I myself and my ill were placed in oblivion.

I was on earth and my heart in Paradise,
sweetly placing in oblivion every other care;
and my living figura
was made to feel a marble and to fill with wonder ...)[18]

[18] (Petrarch, *Obra poética*, ms. Vitr/22/3 [BNE], 122r, emphasis mine, transcription in accordance with manuscript). This citation is taken from the poem "Tacer non poffo; et temo, non adopre," which is

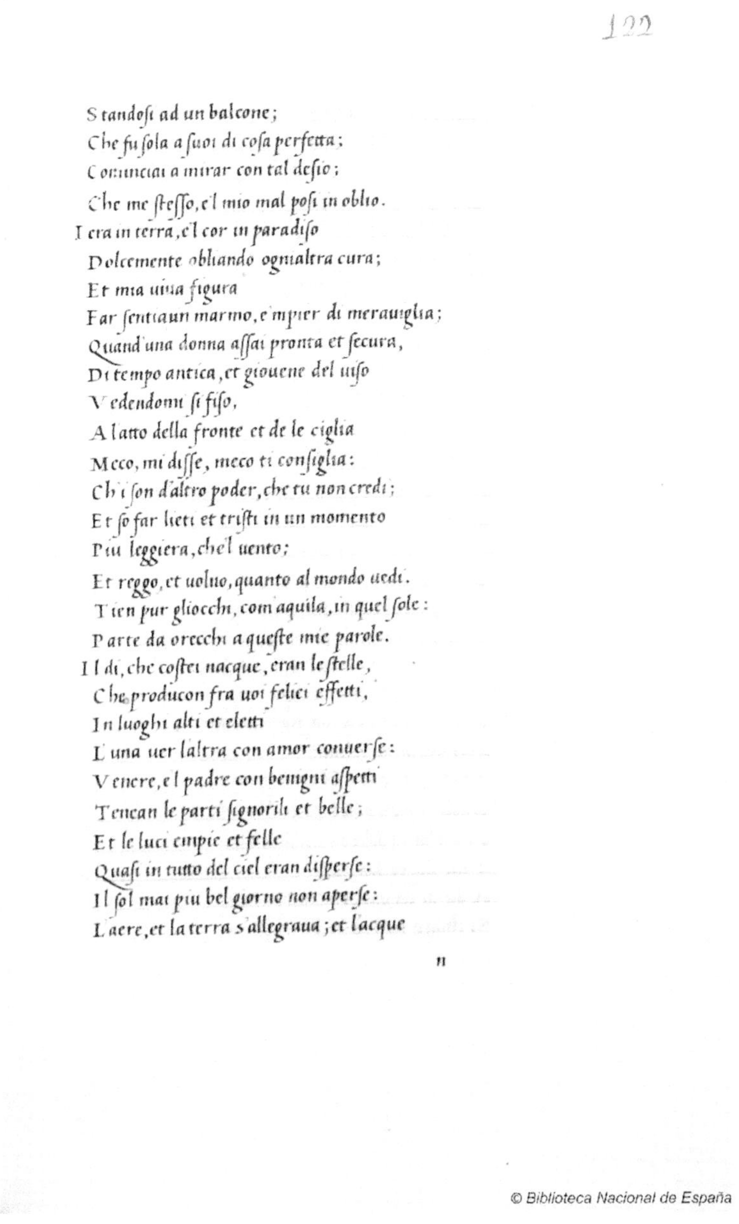

122

Standosi ad un balcone;
Che fu sola a suoi di cosa perfetta;
Cominciai a mirar con tal desio;
Che me stesso, e'l mio mal posi in oblio.
I era in terra, e'l cor in paradiso
Dolcemente obliando ogni altra cura;
Et mia uiua figura
Far sentiua un marmo, e'mpier di merauiglia;
Quand'una donna assai pronta et secura,
Di tempo antica, et giouene del uiso
Vedendomi si fiso,
A l'atto della fronte et de le ciglia
Meco, mi disse, meco ti consiglia:
Ch'i son d'altro poder, che tu non credi;
Et so far lieti et tristi in un momento
Piu leggiera, che'l uento;
Et reggo, et uoluo, quanto al mondo uedi.
Tien pur gliocchi, com'aquila, in quel sole:
Parte da orecchi a queste mie parole.
Il di, che costei nacque, eran le stelle,
Che producon fra uoi felici effetti,
In luoghi alti et eletti
L'una uer l'altra con amor conuerse:
Venere, e'l padre con benigni aspetti
Tenean le parti signorili et belle;
Et le luci empie et felle
Quasi in tutto del ciel eran disperse:
Il sol mai piu bel giorno non aperse:
L'aere, et la terra s'allegraua; et l'acque

n

Fig. 3.1 Petrarch, "Tacer non posso, et temo non adopre," *Obra poética*, ms. Vitr/22/3, BNE, 1508, 122r. Imágenes procedentes de los fondos de la Biblioteca Nacional de España

While influenced by Dante, the Petrarch of the *Canzoniere* moved through the allegory and epic of the *Paradiso* into the immediacy of lyric experience. In the wake of Petrarchan discourse, the biographically inflected poetry of Pastoral Petrarchism redounded upon a dual experience of sempiternity: *eros* and *poiesis*.[19] The concept of erotic contemplation as an ecstatic experience, described by Judah Abravanel in the *Dialoghi d'amore*, and the act of poiesis as a shaping of literary time disrupted the "I" of linear chronological (or biographical) time and gave rise to a lyric temporality within a *tercia naturaleza*: a lyric "I" as a being "almost always eternal" (*sempiterno*). Sempiternal temporality was at work in the erotic affect as an experience of temporal limit (i.e. the infinity of love), poetic authorship in pastoral prosimetric lyrics (poiesis and the *ingenio* as a "timeless" faculty), and the becoming immortal of the *figura of the poet* through centuries of readership (the *divino ingenio* as a transhistorical construction). In the case of erotic affect and poiesis, lyric could be understood to accord with an entirely different temporality (a sempiternity or a *tercia realidad*) than that of narrative meaning-making. In the case of '"posthumous immortality," the narrative arc of a lyric life exceeded the biographical markers of birth and death. Because the Arcadian landscape accommodated lyric time, the *figura of the poet* thrived in the mid-late sixteenth-century Spanish pastoral.

contained in this manuscript. For the modern Italian, see the critical edition (F. Petrarch, *Canzoniere*, eds. S. Stroppa and P. Cherchi, Torino: Einaudi, 2011, 502-507). (All modern citations of Petrarch are from this edition unless otherwise noted.) The manuscript is dated to 1508 and, according to Milagros Villar Rubio, belonged to the library of the Condestable de Castilla, Juan Fernández de Velasco, fifth Duke of Frías (ca. 1550–1613): (Villar Rubio, *Códices petrarquescos*, 208–210). Juan Fernández de Velasco served as the governor of the Duchy of Milan from 1592 to 1600. He was married to María Girón de Guzmán, daughter of the first Duke of Osuna, Pedro Girón de la Cueva. It should be remembered that Pedro was the elder brother of Magdalena, the Fílida of Gálvez de Montalvo's *El pastor de Fílida*, discussed in Chapter 2. Juan Fernández de Velasco and María Girón had two children. Their daughter Ana de Velasco y Girón was later married to Teodósio II, Duke of Braganza (their child became King Juan IV of Portugal in 1640). With his second wife, Joana de Córdoba y Aragón, Juan Fernández subsequently had three children; the youngest, Mariana Fernández de Velasco, later married the seventh Duke of Alba, António Alvarez de Toledo. The inclusion of this manuscript in the library of a major Castilian grandee in the closing decades of the sixteenth century reiterates the power of Petrarchism at that time. The manuscript itself is distinguished for the beauty of its illuminations (P. Durrieu, *Manuscrits d'Espagne remarquables* ..., s.n., 1893). Page 184v contains the note "Ludovicus Vicentinus Scribebat. MDVIII." Ludovico Vicentino degli Arrighi (1475–1527) was a papal scribe and author of *La Operina* (1522). He was later involved in printing and the design of typeface. Given his biographical dates, it is likely that Juan Fernández was not the first owner of the manuscript, but either received it as a gift or purchased it in Milan or elsewhere.

[19] I employ the term *erotic* instead of *amorous* because the *erotic* includes corporeal affect which involves the whole of the lyric "I" as subjectivity. For temporal play in sixteenth-century Petrarchism: (Braden, *Petrarchan Love*).

Prior to the publication of the *DQ*, this was Cervantes' primary literary milieu in Spain.

In addition to sempiternal temporality, this chapter makes use of the term *figura* as informed by Arezu and Marno, who distinguish the "phenomenal, perceptible form (*schema* or *typos*)" of *figura* from the "*morphe* or *eidos*" of *forma*: "Accordingly, the word [*figura*] soon acquired additional meanings of perceptible, external, superimposed, and potentially transient form, incl. the imprint of a seal, shadow, ghost, and deceptive semblance."[20] Arezu and Marno trace the history of *figura* from its initial use in Terence's *Eunuchus* to its use by Erich Auerbach and interlocutors in postwar American and European literary criticism. While the term today is heavily indebted to the history of biblical exegesis and derivative reading practices, in this chapter the term indicates the distinction between *eidos* as transcendental and unchanging essence, and *figura* as the morphological and transient apparition of perceptible *schemata* or *topoi* becoming. In this way, *forma* may be considered deductive and hierarchical (from a pre-given form), whereas *figura* is inductive and relational (arising out of particulars). The *figura of the poet* took shape out of particular figurations of the poet – Petrarch's "et mia viva figura" – through the reception, imitation, and reinvention (refiguration) of the poetic body of work (as authorial corpus and as a collective body of poetry over time). In this space, allegory and history were intertwined in the restaging of lyric interiority as literary text. In allegory, historical meaning as linear gave way to metaphorical meaning as multidirectional. In history, the metaphorical meaning of the interior was particularized to the language and experience of the poet. The sempiternal temporality of literary Arcadia

[20] (F.M. Arezu and D. Marno, "Figura," in ed. Roland Greene, *The Princeton Encyclopedia of Poetry and Poetics*, R. Princeton University Press, 2012, 485–486). I will return to the work of the term "imprint of a seal" in my discussion of Judah Abravanel's *Dialoghi d'Amore* in Chapter 4. The term *figura of the poet* shares some features but should not be confused with Robert Durling's influential study *The Figure of the Poet in Renaissance Epic* (Harvard University Press, 1965), in which Durling is attentive to the relationship between biographical identity and poetic individuality, as well as inherited convention and poetic individuality. This dynamic between the received and the invented is ultimately put to use in Durling's conception of the poet-narrator as a creator-god and the work as a type of cosmos. For Durling, Petrarch as the lyric lover is secondary to his interest in the epic achievements of Chaucer, Dante, and Ariosto. However, this chapter argues that the *figura of the poet* cut by Petrarch in sixteenth-century Petrarchism became the less obvious generative force of the novel and the subject throughout modernity. In this chapter, the *figura of the poet* takes an immanent rather than a transcendental stance, which does not figure in Durling's dichotomy between the transcendental and the natural world. For figurations of the poet as author: (Ascoli, Albert Russell, *Dante and the Making of a Modern Author*, Cambridge University Press, 2008).

became the *logos amoenus* in which lived experience underwent a *poetic figuration* and opened a doorway for the entry of the lyric "I" into the place of mythic time. The confluence of lyric and narrative in the literature of Pastoral Petrarchism, such as Cervantes' *Galatea*, played a significant role in the conception of the modern novel.

In the language of sixteenth-century poetry, the lyric "I" active in the *figura of the poet* would have been referred to as the poet's eroticized soul or *alma*, at times spirit or *anima*, as the feminine Psyche (regardless of the sex or gender of the speaker), and as the poet's creative faculty or *ingenio*. Garcilaso de la Vega's "Soneto V" is a ripe example of this use of *alma* in an erotic rather than a religious context:

> Escrito está en mi alma vuestro gesto
> y cuanto yo escribir de vos deseo:
> vos sola lo escribisteis; yo lo leo,
> tan solo que aun de vos me guardo en esto.
> En esto estoy y estaré siempre puesto,
> que aunque no cabe en mí cuanto en vos veo,
> de tanto bien lo que no entiendo creo,
> tomando ya la fe por presupuesto.
> Yo no nascí sino para quereros;
> mi *alma* os ha cortado a su medida;
> por hábito del *alma* misma os quiero;
> cuanto tengo confieso yo deberos;
> por vos nací, por vos tengo la vida,
> por vos he de morir y por vos muero.
>
> (Your visage is written in my soul,
> and everything that I would want to write of you,
> you yourself wrote it; I just read it,
> and in such solitude that I keep myself even from you.
> I am in this and will always be here,
> even though all that I see in you overflows my limits,
> of so much good I believe that which I don't comprehend,
> taking my faith as a presupposition.
> I wasn't born but for to love you;
> my soul has cut you to its measure;
> by habit of the same soul I love you;
> I confess that everything I have I owe you;
> I was born by you, by you I have life,
> by you I must die and I die for you.)[21]

[21] (G. de la Vega, *Poesía castellana*, eds. J. Jiménez Heffernan, I. García Aguilar, and P. Ruiz Pérez, Madrid: Akal, 2017, 109).

Within the sempiternal space of erotic experience, the poetry of what Menéndez Pelayo called in his *Historia de las ideas estéticas* an "erotic mysticism" everywhere liberated the *figura of the poet* from various forms of discourse (scriptural, inquisitorial, historical, imperial, etc.) by repurposing them in the language of the beloved. This novelizing of discourse through lyrical poiesis complicates Bakhtin's notion of poetic discourse as monoglot. In these cultural and poetic practices, the discourse of the poet was an active and unstable linguistic field.[22] In Garcilaso's ecstatic erotic encounter, it is the beloved who gives him a new language ("vos sola lo escribisteis; yo lo leo / . . . de tanto bien lo que no entiendo creo"). He is born of her. Or, in Dante's figuration, she writes his *vita nuova*. It is because the beloved exceeds the limits of comprehension and the capacity for linguistic expression that the poet's heuristic use of language subverts and revises all other forms of discourse in the approximation of the beloved's ineffability. She authors him. He authors discourse.

Garcilaso's sonnet is paradigmatic of the way in which Pastoral Petrarchism resituated Platonic transcendence – a stairway of ascent to the *summum bonum* – as an embodied erotic affect which engages the being of the beloved lady as an immanent *summa belleza*. As affective experience, the traditional Platonic ascent is reconfigured as a coming through language to an ineffable presence, the beloved as immanence before the *figura of the poet* as *alma* or *ingenio*. This is the exact motif that Cervantes' 1567 sonnet takes up and reformulates for his encomiastic purpose.[23] Because this *figura of the poet* silently existed within and repurposed various forms of discourse (through their appropriation and reformation, rather than evacuation and negation), the logic of sempiternity also became the logic of ineffability. Lyric poetry developed at and developed the limits of

[22] "In poetic genres, artistic consciousness – understood as a unity of all the author's semantic and expressive intentions – fully realizes itself within its own language; in them alone is such consciousness fully immanent, expressing itself in it directly and without mediation, without conditions and without distance. The language of the poet is *his* language, he is utterly immersed in it, inseparable from it . . . The language of the poetic genre is a unitary and singular Ptolemaic world outside of which nothing else exists and nothing else is needed. The concept of many worlds of language, all equal in their ability to conceptualize and to be expressive, is organically denied to poetic style . . . In poetry, even discourse about doubts must be cast in a discourse that cannot be doubted . . . The unity and singularity of language are the indispensable prerequisites for a realization of the direct (but not objectively typifying) intentional individuality of poetic style and of its monologic steadfastness" (Bakhtin, *Dialogic Imagination*, 285–286, emphasis in original). Heavily inflected by the nineteenth-century (Hegelian) notion of lyric poetry, this description of poetic discourse as monoglot is less efficacious within the contours of convention, imitation, invention, and pseudonymic layers of sixteenth-century Pastoral Petrarchism.

[23] See Chapter 2 for a discussion of this sonnet.

language. Writing on these poetics in Cervantes' *Galatea*, Mary Gaylord has observed,

> Even before it begins, Cervantes seems to invite us to reject it as a form of discourse inadequate to the tasks of evoking the intricacies of sentimental life . . .. [he] makes the central issue of pastoral art not sentiment but the way that sentiment can be expressed. Orompo's words call into question the power of language to communicate truth about the self.[24]

In so doing, the *figura of the poet* rendered the many discourses which it drew upon and reassembled inadequate, both as they were given and even once they had been remade as poetry. These frequent appeals to the conceit of ineffability subverted the power of language to the power of the beloved's embodied presence. From *eros* to *poiesis, amans* to *auctor,* after over a century of readership (1374–1508), Petrarch as the ecstatic lyric-lover had achieved another poetic figuration as a *divino ingenio* in Spain.[25] By 1550, Garcilaso had also been dubbed within this order of the immortals. By 1560, Montemayor's *Cancioneros* won him "renombre sempiterno" and the *Diana* brought the Castilianized practice of Pastoral Petrarchism into vogue in Habsburg Spain.[26]

~

On July 27, 1625, in the censure for Lope de Vega's *Triunfos Divinos con otras rimas sacras* (Madrid: viuda de Alonso Martín, 1625), Juan de Jáuregui hailed Lope's *contrafacta* of Petrarch's *Trionfi* as "más divinos que los del Petrarca (more divine than those of Petrarch)."[27] How did Petrarch attain such a status in Spain that this *figura of the poet* would continue to capture the imagination of Spain's most renowned poets and define the measure of poetic divinity well into the seventeenth century? While the Tuscan poet's influence can be felt in the works of the Marquis de Santillana and Ausias March, Petrarchism (and, it could be argued, works of lyric poetry as printed corpus) did not take off in Spain until after the rise of early lyric printings following the posthumous publication of Garcilaso and Boscán in 1543. Additionally, early translations of Petrarch influenced poetic lexicons in Spain, a facet of sixteenth-century language development evident in Covarrubias' *Tesoro de la lengua* of 1611. It was to Petrarch's

[24] (Gaylord Randel, "The Language of Limits," 257–258).

[25] The *figura of the poet* is never singular, but is always engaged with other *figuras*, never fully grasped, contained, or possessed. "Aspro core et feluaggio et cruda voglia / In dolce humile angelica figura" (Petrarch, *Obra poética*, 1508, 102r).

[26] (Laínez, "A [Jorge de] Montemayor," in *Obras*, 1951, vol. II, 233–234).

[27] (Lope de Vega, *Triunfos Divinos*, Madrid: viuda de Alonso Martín, 1625, unpaginated [3v]).

Tuscan verses that the lexicographer frequently appealed in the elaboration of his own language, as in the striking case of "fábula."[28] The 1562 translation of Ausias March's fifteenth-century Petrarchan poetry from Valencian to Castilian by the Portuguese courtier-poet and pastoral novelist Montemayor gave breadth and depth to the tradition of Petrarchan poetry in Spain as it simultaneously reinvigorated the Castilian tongue with authors of local and foreign dialect. Petrarchism in Spain was not simply a matter of repeated tropes and forms; from the outset, Castilian itself, as a "vulgar tongue," was resonant with discursive meaning that extended well beyond the confines of a single "national" language.[29]

The ways in which Boscán and Garcilaso realized their own lyric projects affected the way in which Petrarch was translated later in the century and foregrounded the reimagining of Petrarch's lyric project for the major Spanish poets of the sixteenth century. This reimagined project included Petrarch's sempiternal sense of the erotic event and the authorial act, but it also rendered the ambition to secure a posthumous literary life an historical fact. Their lyric project dubbed Petrarch a *divino ingenio* and reinforced this aspect of the Petrarchan project amongst poets writing in Castilian. Following the renown won by Boscán and Garcilaso, the most significant period of Petrarchan poetry in Spain unfolded in the wake of Jorge de Montemayor's verse *Cancioneros* of 1554 and 1558, and the prosimetric *Diana* (1559).[30] In his 1554 collection of poetry, Montemayor opened the Italianate section of his *Obras de Amores* (*Sonetos Canciones y Epístolas*) with a prologue sonnet.[31] The sonnet was a rewriting of Petrarch's "Voi ch'ascoltate" which developed the relationship between love and lyric production practiced by Boscán and Garcilaso.[32]

28 Covarrubias cites from the "Voi ch'ascoltate" in the Italian: (Covarrubias, *Tesoro*, 1995, 531–532).

29 This was in addition to Spain's medieval linguistic growth in which the development of Castilian was influenced by both Arabic and Hebew, not to mention the numerous dialects.

30 The first of these (*Las obras de George de Montemayor: repartidas en dos libros*, Anvers: Iuan Steelsio, Juan Lacio, 1554) was dedicated to the Princess Juana and her husband, Don Juan, Prince of Portugal, in whose service Montemayor was then employed ("criado de sus Altezas"). The second (*Segundo Cancionero de George de Montemayor*, Anvers: Juan Latio, 1558) was dedicated to Gonzalo Fernández de Córdoba, third Duke of Sessa, patron of the Cervantes family.

31 According to the edition of Rhodes and Montero, the second sonnet in the Italianate section served a similar function: (Montemayor, *Poesía selecta*, 2012, 133).

32 From the prologue: "Quien vio tan gran dessero en Castilla de las obras de Boscán, cuyo ingenio y alto estilo está manifiesto a los que desapasionadamente le miren, y después las sentencias que sobre él han dado. Y cuando les pide razón, no saben dar otra sino que es mejor lo que escribió Garci Lasso de la Vega; como si lo que es bueno dejase de serlo porque haya otra cosa mejor. Yo osaría jurar que darían los que han de ver este libro cuanto les pidiesen, por otro Garci Lasso encuadernado con él ..." (Montemayor, *Poesía completa*, 6).

Los que de amor estáis tan lastimados
que el remedio buscáis en causa ajena,
y con ver mayor mal curáis la pena
a que os da causa amor y sus cuidados;
  venid a ver mis versos, do pintados
veréis graves tormentos, grave pena,
que están vivos en mí, do amor ordena
que estén para este efecto diputados.
  Y aunque sufrido hayáis pena y tormento
y nunca ver podáis lo que esperastes,
o con ausencia estéis siempre lidiando;
  en viendo la pasión que amando siento,
luego confesaréis que nunca amastes,
o si algún tiempo amastes fue burlando.

(Those that are all so hurt by love
that you seek a remedy in other people's thoughts,
and in seeing a greater ill you cure the pain
that love and its thoughts cause you,
  come to see my verses, where painted
you will find grave torments, grave pain
that are alive in me, where love ordains
that they are representatives of this effect.
  And even though you all have suffered pain and torment,
and never can see what you hoped for,
or in absence are always embattled;
  in seeing the passion that I feel in loving
you will confess that you never loved,
or if at some time you loved it was but a joke.)[33]

In his prologue sonnet, Montemayor addressed a particular type of reader (a reader of Petrarchism, a "popol tutto"), someone who had been unfortunate in love and who, as consequence of their misfortune, sought a remedy in like misfortunes. He thus invited Petrarch's amorous reader of the "Voi ch'ascoltate" into the space of his own erotic suffering.[34] Conscious also of his Iberian models, in the first two lines of the first quatrain Montemayor repeated the medical ("remedio") and legal

[33] (Montemayor, *Poesía completa*, 592).

[34] "Voi ch'ascoltate in rime sparse il suono / di quei sospiri ond'io nudriva 'l core / in sul mio primo giovenile errore / quand'era in parte altr'uom da quel ch'i' sono, / del vario stile in ch'io piango et ragiono, / fra le vane speranze e 'l van dolore, / ove sia chi per prova intenda amore, / spero trovar pietà, nonché perdono. // Ma ben veggio or sí come al popol tutto / favola fui gran tempo, onde sovente / di me medesmo meco mi vergogno; / et del mio vaneggiar vergogna è 'l frutto, / e 'l pentérsi, e 'l conoscer chiaramente / che quanto piace al mondo è breve sogno" (Petrarch, *Canzoniere*, 1).

("causa") metaphors for amorous struggle that Boscán had employed in his own version of a prologue sonnet in the Italianate section of his poetry, with which Montemayor was doubtless familiar.[35] The second quatrain engaged the Horatian conceit of verbal art as painting ("ut pictura poesis") such that lyric verse was conceptualized as the space in which the internal torments of the poet's lived experience were made visible ("pintados") for the reader, just as the sound of Petrarch's sighs were rendered as *rime* in the "Voi ch'ascoltate."[36] In the tercet Montemayor went on to address three types of readers suffering amorous distress: those who suffered pain and torment, those whose hopes were never satisfied, and those who waited in indefinite uncertainty for the absent beloved. These typologies of amorous suffering were later recalled by Cervantes in the four-part eclogue found in Book III of the *Galatea*, in which the shepherd-poets known as the *triste* Orompo, *celoso* Orfenio, *ausente* Crisio, and *desamado* Marsilio compete for the prize of greatest amorous suffering. Notably, Cervantes added jealousy to Montemayor's list.[37] Montemayor's characterization of various forms of amorous distress was a significant change from Petrarch's general "popol": it populated the audience with types of lyric lovers. This anticipated his creation of the characters of the pastoral novel by a few years. In the turn of the final tercet Montemayor claimed a pyrrhic victory by saying that he had suffered most. The magnitude of his suffering would make a joke ("burla") of the love his readers claimed to have suffered. This shift from Petrarch's lamented *breve sogno* to Montemayor's "burla" at the close of the sonnet directly informed the lyric trajectory of the poets writing in subsequent decades during the blossoming of pastoral fiction in Spain.

Montemayor's *songbooks* were not his only contribution to the rise of Pastoral Petrarchism. The *Diana*, as a lyric in prose, also assumed the Petrarchan project of immortalizing the beloved lady. The *Diana* combined the influences of Petrarch's *Canzoniere* and Sannazaro's *Arcadia* to

[35] "Nunca d'amor estuve tan contento / que'n su loor mis versos ocupasse, / ni a nadie consejé que s'engañasse / buscando en el amor contentamiento. /Esto siempre juzgó mi entendimiento: / que d'este mal tod'hombre se guardasse, / y assí, porqu'esta ley se conservasse, / holgué de ser a todos escarmiento. / ¡O! vosotros que andáys tras mis escritos / gustando de leer tormentos tristes, / según que por amar son infinitos, / mis versos son deziros. «¡O benditos / los que de Dios tan gran merced huvistes / que, del poder d'amor, fuéssedes quitos!»" (J. Boscán, *Obras Poéticas*, eds. M. de Riquer et. al., Barclona: Universidad de Barcelona, 1957, 92). See also: (J. Boscán, *Obra completa*, ed. Carlos Clavería, Madrid: Cátedra, 1999, 121)

[36] This conceit became increasingly popular over the course of the sixteenth century, such that Covarrubias cited directly from Horace's text in his definition of the word "poeta": (Covarrubias, *Tesoro*, 1995, 827).

[37] This is reprised in the "Curioso Impertinente" of the *DQ I*, the *Celoso extremeño* of the *Novelas ejemplares*, and Book IV of the *Persiles y Sigismunda*.

give a new literary genre to the European scene. (Sannazaro himself was a Petrarchan poet.)[38] From Montemayor onward the Spanish pastoral novel was a prosimetric genre born of the Petrarchan project in which lyric and narrative were formally (verse and prose) and thematically (erotic and pastoral) interwoven in the poetic work of immortalizing the beloved lady and garnering sempiternal fame.[39] That Petrarch's achievement in verse ultimately was in service of his beloved Laura was widely recognized in Montemayor's *Diana*, as is evident in one of the three laudatory poems included in the front matter of the 1559 printing. Don Gaspar de Romani's sonnet underscored Petrarch's lyric project as primarily concerned with the immortalization of Laura and hailed the *Diana* in this light.[40] He situated Montemayor's *Diana* within a long poetic tradition that included Homer, but which privileged Petrarch. Like Petrarch's Laura, Diana was famed for her beauty ("por hermosura celebrada / que quantas en el mundo hermosas fueron," lines 10–11) and Montemayor for his lyric triumph ("de quién así el laurel tan justamente / merezca más, que cuantos escribieron," lines 13–14). This metamorphosis of the lyric project into the prosimetrum highlighted one of the most dynamic aspects of the Spanish pastoral novel: its status as a *roman à clef.* Diana was understood to be both a fictional character and an historical personage in Montemayor's intimate autobiography, just as "Laura" was understood to have been both the exalted beloved of Petrarch's lyric and a lady of Montserrat loved by Francesco Petracco. Fifty years after the *Diana*, in that first of modern European novels, Dulcinea would serve the same purpose in the pseudonymic immortalization of AQ's *giovanile errore* for Aldonza Lorenzo.[41] Thus the

38 (Kennedy, *Uses of Pastoral*, 37–57).

39 Verse was typically set to music: (M. Fuellana, *Libro de música para vihuela, intitulado Orphenica Lyra*, Seville: Martín de Montesdoca, 1554). The lyric shepherds of the *Diana* are also musicians. As a young courtier, Montemayor had served as a *cantor* in the court of Juana and her sister.

40 "Si de Madama Laura la memoria / Petrarca para siempre a levantado / y Homero assí de lauro a coronado / escrevir de los griegos la victoria. / Si los Reyes también para más gloria / vemos que de contino an procurado / que aquello que en la vida an conquistado / en muerte se renueve con su historia. // Con más razón serás ¡ o excelente / Diana!, por hermosura celebrada, / que quantas en el mundo hermosas fueron. / Pues nadie mereció ser alabada / de quien assí el laurel tan justamente / merezca más, que quantos escrivieron" (Montemayor, *Diana*, 1970, 4).

41 AQ's transformation of Aldonza Lorenzo into Dulcinea: "¡Oh, cómo se holgó nuestro buen caballero cuando hubo hecho este discurso, y más cuando halló a quien dar nombre de su dama! Y fue, a lo que se cree, que en un lugar cerca del suyo había una moza labradora de muy buen parecer, de quien él un tiempo anduvo enamorado, según se entiende, ella jamás lo supo ni le dio cata dello. Llamábase Aldonza Lorenzo, y a esta le pareció ser bien darle título de señora de sus pensamientos; y, buscándole nombre que no desdijese mucho del suyo y que tirase y se encaminase al de princesa y gran señora, vino a llamarla «Dulcinea del Toboso»" (Cervantes, *DQ*, 1999, I: 1, 44).

pastoral novel came to serve the same function as Petrarch's *Canzoniere*: the immortalization of the beloved for posterity and the crowning of the poet whose work it was to do so. Gálvez de Montalvo's *pastor de Fílida* likewise took its pseudonymous title from the lady it was intended to commend to posterity.[42] In the *Galatea* (1585) and the *Viaje del Parnaso* (1614), Cervantes also cast Galatea and Silena as sempiternal figures.[43]

It is significant that Montemayor's Petrarchan prosimetrum, as a precursor to Cervantes' novelistic fiction, did not take the epic or the tragic as its primary model. Its generic origin was the lyric, the Petrarchan lyric.[44] Montemayor's conception of narrative as arising out of the lyric interior was fitting given his spiritual disposition. The emphasis on interiority was in keeping with his personal branch of religious faith, the Portuguese practice of *iluminismo*, which he explored in his *Diáologo spiritual* (unedited manuscript, 1540s) and for which his *Obras de devoción* (of the 1554 *Cancionero*) and the *Cancionero espiritual* (1558) were censored.[45] Only his erotic verse went unimpeded by the Valdés *Index*. In Montemayor's *Obras de Amores*, verse acted as a means of turning the poet inside out or of making the individual interior visible to the exterior linguistically. This register was made legible by the legacy of Petrarch. Within a rigidly hegemonic socio-cultural world that did not otherwise value subjective intimacy, Montemayor's pastoral fiction resituated lyric interiority at the center of the narrative drive within literary prose.[46] Replacing the geographical contours of the Byzantine Romance

[42] See Chapter 2. [43] (Cervantes, *Poesías*, 320–323).

[44] Both in English literary studies and Spanish Golden Age scholarship, lyric has come in for some controversy. The lyric project articulated by sixteenth-century Castilian poets responds both to the diachronic need for historical reconstruction and to the synchronic coincidence of preoccupation with the human interior in verse poetry. See: (Middlebrook, *Imperial Lyric*); (eds. Jackson and Prins, *The Lyric Theory Reader*); (Culler, *Theory of the Lyric*); (Burt, "What Is This Thing Called Lyric?"). In Golden Age studies, the language of empire has played a central role in critical assessments of literary form and style (Middlebrook, *Imperial Lyric*). That poets were economically, and occasionally (all puns intended), tied to patrons who also occupied positions of military and political prowess is absolutely certain (Harry Sieber, "The Magnificent Fountain: Literary Patronage in the Court of Philip III," *Cervantes*, n.2 1998, vol. XVIII, 85–116). But a recent critical tendency to assume that such politically strategic positions always embodied an approach to literature representative of Nebrija's famous dictum is to obscure any other aesthetic orientation to the production of lyric verse, an oversight which inevitably privileges a political, economic, and imperial hegemony over diverse aesthetic and literary histories.

[45] For more on this aspect of Montemayor's body of work: (E. Rhodes, *The Unrecognized Precursors of Montemayor's Diana*, Columbia: University of Missouri Press, 1992). For reformation thought in Spain: (M. Bataillon, *Erasme et l'Espagne recherches sur l'histoire spirituelle du XVIe siècle*, Geneva: Droz, 1998).

[46] On the time and place of the *DQ* and Cervantes: (J.A. Maravall, *Utopia y Contrautopia en el 'Quijote'*, Santiago de Compostela: Pico Sacro, 1976).

with the amenable landscape of an Iberian Arcadia, Montemayor's *Diana* put lyric subjectivity into action by recontextualizing lyric verse within narrative plots. Within the pages of pastoral fiction, the distinction between interior lyric space and exterior narrative space, as seen in the prologue sonnet above, exaggerated the role of the lyric in the rise of novelistic plots through its linguistic externalization by shepherd-poets in his pastoral fiction. In the *Diana*, lyric verse was the way in which shepherd-poets and poetesses made their private lives visible or intelligible to their peers (and to the reader). As such, the community of lyric speakers created new forms of collective utterance. Once given voice in lyric verse, Pastoral Petrarchism situated the invisible, ineffable, and sempiternal aspects of human experience at the genesis of novelistic plot in *novedades* of prose fiction.[47] This organic and unpredictable generation of narrative plot out of the contingent confluences of several lyric drives brought history and allegory together within the space of a new form of literary fiction: the novel. It also transformed the singular *figura* of Petrarch into the communal practice of Pastoral Petrarchism by a multitude of shepherd-poets in the Habsburg court. In the decade that followed Montemayor's death in 1561, Figueroa, Laínez, Gálvez de Montalvo, and Cervantes populated this community of shepherd-poets in Madrid, of which ms. Espagnole 373 was a key example.[48]

Working within these complex multilingual sites of enunciation, translators often justified their work as pedagogical contributions intended to assist the poor talented *ingenio lego* who by whatever misfortune lacked the direct knowledge of the Tuscan language necessary for access to Petrarch's works.[49] But in practice the work of translation was often viewed as lyric authorship in its own right and intended to showcase the divinity of the translator's own *ingenio* in the view of his poetic peers. Most of the Pastoral Petrarchan poets writing after the middle of the sixteenth century (Montemayor, Hurtado de Mendoza, Figueroa, Laínez, Gálvez de Montalvo, Cervantes, and Aldana) read Tuscan and many had traveled throughout Italy for extended periods of time. In the cases of Figueroa and Aldana, the poets composed original poetry in both Castilian and Tuscan.

47 For this interior/exterior feature of Lukács' thought in *Theory of the Novel*, see the Coda.

48 See Chapter 2.

49 "El tercero fruto es haber sacado a luz en España en esta obra el arte de la poesía vulgar en rimas; pues con mucha razón se puede decir que este autor es el maestro a quien deben imitar y seguir para no errar todos los que tratan de la poesía, por lo qual no me deberán poco los altos ingenios de España" Petrarch, *Translation of the Sonnets*, ca. 1595, unpaginated [4r], translation mine).

The same was true of Iñigo Herrera y Velasco, who contributed one laudatory sonnet in Castilian and another in Tuscan to Francisco Trenado de Ayllón's 1595 translation and "Comento" of Petrarch. While these poets took pride in ennobling the Castilian language by way of unprecedented lyric feats, they took nearly equal pride in the broad transnational, transhistorical, and multilingual erudition that was the science of poetry. As such, poetic practice in sixteenth-century Spain everywhere dismantled imperial hegemony from within: by inverting the force of Antonio de Nebrija's dictum, the Castilian language was transformed from a tool of national purity for imperial expansion into a bastion of heterogeneous polyglossia, as understood within imperium studies.[50] As linguistic agents, poems themselves were understood to exercise pedagogical work on the translator during the writing process, on the reader, and on the common tongue. As a divine master of the science of poetry, Petrarch's lyric corpus was not just a holding place for cliched forms, tropes, and styles; it was a repository of epistemologically efficacious secrets and linguistic resources. As Boscán wrote in the prologue to his Italianate poetry:

> Petrarca fue el primero que en aquella provincia le acabó de poner en su punto, y en éste se ha quedado y quedará, creo yo, para siempre. Dante fue más atrás, el cual usó muy bien dél, pero diferentemente de Petrarca.
>
> (Petrarch was the first that in that province [Italy] put his stamp, and in this he has remained and will remain, I believe, forever. Dante was further back, who also put this to good use, but differently than Petrarch.)[51]

As science, poetry appealed to truth, a truth perhaps available to an author in the sustained engagement of translation. Thus, translation of the Tuscan poet, in practice, was often understood as a literary feat in its own right.

By the time of Fernando de Hoces' 1554 translation of *I trionfi*, dedicated to Don Juan de la Cerda, Duke of Medinaceli, the self-consciousness of the translator was pronounced.[52] In the dedication, the translator situated himself as a successor of the *Toscano* poets Garcilaso and Boscán in his attention to the transposition of verse metrics from Tuscan to Castilian ("la medida del verso [the measure of the verse]"). De Hoces claimed that by the middle of the sixteenth century, the Petrarchan metrics of Garcilaso and Boscán had been so successful that other translations of Petrarch into

[50] "Imperium studies challenges the self-sufficient histories of nation and empire by arguing for their imbrication and competition: only a plural history of the intersections among them can provide the full picture" (Fuchs, "Another Turn for Transnationalism," 412).

[51] (Boscán, *Obra completa*, 119, brackets mine).

[52] (Petrarch, *Los triunfos*, 1554, unpaginated [iir]).

traditional Castilian metrics had caused the poet's work to be ignored. The Petrarchan metrics of Garcilaso and Boscán had outshone lesser translations of the Tuscan model, which had failed as lyric feats of metered verse poetry.[53] De Hoces explained that he had used some leisure time the previous summer to undertake a new translation "en la misma medida y numero de versos, que el Toscano tiene (in the same measure and number of verses that the Tuscan has)," thus improving his translation through fidelity to the verse metrics of the original, and extending Petrarch's influence from the level of word to the measure of cadence. For his commentary, de Hoces declared himself to have chosen the middle path: neither as brief nor as lengthy as the two previous commentaries by Alexandro Vellutello and Bernardo Illucinio (Obregón's translation), respectively.[54] By situating himself within the practice of his predecessors, de Hoces made a symbolic claim to surpass them. Practicing a formulaic humility, without which no author of any kind could publish, he pointed out that he had undertaken the translation only for the contentment of his friends, and that he had pursued publication only upon their request. This was a gentleman's leisurely enterprise only on the surface; the front matter of his text revealed De Hoces' earnest preoccupation with his work as lyric art. In addition to the dedication, De Hoces also gave extensive commentary on the act of translation in the prologue "Al Lector," wherein he excused the elimination of several words from the original in order to perfect the metrics of his text. Taking the translation as more than transposition, or even imitation, he then situated his own sonic fidelity as lyric art in relation to a literary culture populated by Don Diego Hurtado de Mendoza, the secretary Gonzalo Perez, Don Juan de Coloma, Garcilaso de la Vega, and Juan Boscán.[55]

[53] Among these translations was Antonio de Obregon's (*Francisco Petrarca con los seis triunfos de toscano, Sacados en castellano con el comento que sobrellos se hizo*, ed. B. Illicinio, trans. Obregon, Logroño: Arnao Guillen de Brocar, 1512).

[54] Alexandro Vellutello had been one of the earliest authors of a *vita* of Petrarch; he was also mentioned by Trenado de Ayllón in his 1595 translation.

[55] "También quiero prevenir al lector, que hallara en esta traducción, algunas cosas quitadas, y muchas de otra manera puestas de como están en lo Toscano .... Pero en fin me pareció que era mejor aventurarme a este inconveniente, que no a contradecir la opinión de tantos, como los que el día de hoy son de voto, que al pie de la letra, se imite también en esto la manera del verso Italiano, como en todas las otras cosas: puesto caso que no es justo que ninguno condene por malo aquello que don Diego de Mendoza, y el secretario Gonzalo Pérez, y don Juan de Coloma, y Garcilaso de la Vega, y Juan Boscán, y otras muchas personas doctas tienen probado por bueno. Y en fin concluyo con suplicar al lector perdone entrambos estos dos defectos juntamente con todos los otros, que no hallara muchas cofas quitadas, o trocadas, por donde se estrague el sentido del lugar adonde estaban puestas: y las que hallare que lo dañan, podrá las enmendar, para que la traducción sea menos a mal, de lo que al presente va" (Petrarch, *Los triumphos*, 1554, viiir–viiiv).

Printed in 1554, De Hoces' translation set the stage for the subsequent Castilianization of Petrarch's lyric poetry undertaken by Salomon Usque Hebreo, whose translation was printed in 1567 in Venice, the same year that Cervantes composed his own ecstatic encomium (in the style of the Petrarchan sonnet) for Isabel de Valois.[56] This translation was dedicated to Alexandre Farnese, Principe de Parma y Placencia; in the dedication, Usque assured the dedicatee that the challenge of translating Petrarch, "ha sido mayor de lo que à mi profesión y débil ingenio convenía (is greater than that which is in keeping with my profession and weak *ingenio*)."[57] Not to be confused with his uncle (the cardinal), Alessandro (1545–1592) was a contemporary in age to Don Juan de Austria, Isabel, and Cervantes. An international man of letters, Farnese appeared in the anonymous *Memoire pour la reine* as a key visitor to Isabel's court in 1560.[58] Usque signed the dedication "Salusque Lusitano". His name, in fact, was Solomon ben Abraham Usque (ca. 1530–ca. 1596). He was a Portuguese *marrano* whose father, Abraham ben Solomon Usque, had moved his family to Ferrara in the 1540s. His father (also known as Duarte Pinhel) ran a printing press in Ferrara from 1552 to 1558. The family moved to Venice in 1558 and from there Salusque Lusitano traveled to the capital of the Ottoman Empire (modern-day Istanbul), where he ran a printing press from 1560 to 1561. He wrote in Spanish, Portuguese, Italian, and Hebrew, and he is known to have authored a Purim play about Queen Esther in the spring of 1558 (printed in 1559).[59] Not only did the Petrarchan lexicon that he translated everywhere disrupt the linguistic hegemony of imperial Castilian, but Usque himself, as an exiled Sephardic Jew working in the intellectual and textual interstices between the Ottoman and Habsburg empire, upset imperial hegemony with translation as poiesis. When Usque cited Cicero on translation, that words should be weighed rather than counted, he implicitly adjusted both Petrarch's Tuscan and the Castilian translation to the legibility of his own particular logos as a cosmopolitan exile at the crossroads of empire.

[56] (Petrarch, *De los sonetos*, 1567).
The author was also known as Duarte Gómez de Castelo Branco, Solomon Usque, and Solomon of Huesca. He was born around 1530 at Castelo Branco, Portugal. He is thought to have died around 1596.

[57] (Petrarch, *De los sonetos*, 1567, iir). The work had three privileges: one from the king of Spain, one from the regent of Flanders, and one from the city of Venice.

[58] (Anonymous, *Memoire*, 68r).

[59] (C. Roth, "'Salusque Lusitano' (An Essay in Disentanglement)," *The Jewish Quarterly Review*, 34.1, 1943, 65–85); (G. Zavan, *Gli ebrei, i marrani e la figura di Salomón Usque*, Treviso: Editrice Santi Quaranta, 2004); (A. Galanté, *Hommes et choses juifs portugais en Orient*, Constantinople: Société Anonyme de Papeterie et d'Imprimerie, 1927).

In addition to Usque's dedication, Alonso Ulloa, a Spanish translator active in Venice, contributed a prologue to the reader in which he wrote:

> Porque ansí como el que quiere hacer una Canción o un Mandrial [sic] en Toscano, abre el Petrarca, y escoge aquella, o aquel mas le agrada, y a su semejanza, en cuanto a los versos, y a la orden, compone la suya, lo puedan los nuestros Españoles hacer, aunque tengan las obras de Boscán, de Garcilaso de la Vega, de Don Diego de Mendoza, de Jorge de Montemayor, y de otros Autores, que con mucha gravedad y saber, han escrito en esta suerte de verso, a imitación del Petrarca.

> (Because in the same way that one who wants to make a *Canción* or a *Mandrial* in Tuscan opens Petrarch, and choses this or that [poem] that most pleases him and in its likeness, in keeping with the verses and the [metrics], composes his own, our Spaniards can do the same, even though they have the works of Boscán, of Garcilaso de la Vega, of Don Diego [Hurtado] de Mendoza, of Jorge de Montemayor, and of other Authors who with much seriousness and expertise have written in this type of verse in imitation of Petrarch.)[60]

Ulloa thus reviewed the major Spanish precedents of the culture of Pastoral Petrarchism (Boscán, Garcilaso, Hurtado de Mendoza, and Montemayor) as of 1567, and testified to the role of convention and imitation in poetic practices at the time. His prologue made a case for the efficacy of Usque's metric fidelity in Castilian to the original Tuscan as vital to the continued development of Iberian poetry for the next generation of poets writing in Castilian: Figueroa, Laínez, Cervantes, Gálvez de Montalvo, López Maldonado, Padilla, Góngora, Liñán de Riaza, Lope de Vega, and others, most of whom appeared as shepherds in Cervantes' *Galatea*.

The myth of Petrarch in translation during what Fernando Marías has called the "long sixteenth century" in Spain came to a close with an unedited manuscript now housed in the British Library.[61] Ms. Egerton 2062 contains large fragments of a translation into Castilian with commentary of Petrarch's *Canzoniere*, the "Comento del Petrarca," by Francisco Trenado de Ayllón, author of the early modern Italian language textbook *Arte muy curiosa por la cual se enseña muy de raíz el entender y hablar la lengua italiana* (Medina del Campo, 1596).[62] Intended as a companion piece to his textbook, Trenado de Ayllón's

[60] (Petrarch, *De los sonetos*, 1567, unpaginated vr). Alonso de Ulloa (15?–1580), sometimes referred to as Alfonso de Ulloa, was involved in a number of Italian–Spanish translations (mostly histories) in Venice during the sixteenth century.

[61] (F. Marías, *El largo siglo xvi. Los usos artísticos del renacimiento español*, Madrid: Taurus, 1989).

[62] (J. Canals, "Francisco Trenado de Ayllón y el léxico petrarquista," *AISPI. Actas XXIII*, 2005, 62–76).

translation of Petrarch, for reasons unknown, never went to print, and the extant 1595 manuscript copy in the British Library is incomplete. Nonetheless, this manuscript contains valuable indications as to the way in which Petrarchism developed over the course of the sixteenth century in Spain and in direct conversation with Cervantes' own literary milieu. In the prologue to his *Arte*, Trenado de Ayllón himself situated his work as such:

> . . . pareciéndome, que con esta Arte y con aquellas Rimas, habré hecho dos cofas de grande aprovechamiento, para dar entera noticia en España, de aquella lengua: Siendo este el mas derecho camino y mas claro modo de cuantos es posible darse, para inteligencia de una lengua extranjera: pues sirviendo esta Arte de la verdadera Teórica, y viniendo luego el Lector a la practica, leyendo aquellas rimas, se hallará con estas dos cosas tan señor de aquella lengua, como de la propia que tenemos por uso
>
> (. . . seeming to me, that with this Art [textbook] and those Rhymes [translation and commentary], I will have done two things of great benefit, in order to give complete notice of that [Tuscan] language in Spain: this being the most direct path and the clearest manner of the many that could be given, for the intelligibility of a foreign language, since this Art being served of the true Theory, and the Reader coming then to the practice, reading these rhymes will find themself with both of these things as much a master of that language as the one that we have for our use.)[63]

Trenado's translation demonstrated that at the close of the sixteenth century Pastoral Petrarchism maintained a decisive influence on the formation of Castilian poets and of the language itself through their practice, "a quien a su patria hace tal beneficio como este (to they who to their country make such a great benefit as this)."[64] This was a destabilizing conception of national language, one which inverted imperial linguistic expansion by resituating foreign and lyrical tongues at the foundation of linguistic development.

Both Trenado de Ayllón's published *Arte muy curiosa* and his unpublished "Comento del Petrarca" were accompanied by encomiastic sonnets from his contemporaries which further situated the texts within the literary moment for which they were composed. Alonso de Ledesma Butrago's laudatory sonnet for the "Comento" indicated, in unambiguous terms,

[63] (F. Trenado de Ayllón, *Arte muy curiosa por la cual se enseña muy de raíz, el entender y hablar la Lengua Italiana, con todas las reglas de la pronunciación y acento, y declaración de las partes indeclinables, que a esta Lengua nos oscurecen*, Medina del Campo: Santiago del Canto, 1596, unpaginated [A6v], brackets mine).

[64] (Trenado de Ayllón, *Arte muy curiosa*, unpaginated [A7r]).

both the way in which Petrarch continued to be held up as the figure of the divine poet in translation, and the way in which translation itself came to be understood as a poetic achievement.

> El tesoro de Italia tan copioso
> sacado de la rica y fértil vena
> del divino Petrarca, toda llena
> del oro de las ciencias más precioso.
>   Su dueño, a su nación le da gracioso,
> Abierto, fácil, claro; más ordena
> Que esté con llave a la nación ajena
> Por que lo Bueno siempre fue costoso.
>   Otro Pizarro el gran Trenado ha sido
> que a pura fuerza de su ingenio raro
> descubre tales indias con su nave:
>   Y el tesoro cerrado y ascondido
> nos deja el español abierto y claro
> que tal ingenio, nos sirvió de llave.
>
> (The copious treasure of Italy
> extracted from the rich and fertile vein
> of the divine Petrarch, all full
> of the gold of the most precious sciences.
>   Its owner makes his nation grateful,
> open, easy, clear; but he ordains
> that this is [locked] with a key to the nearby nation
> because the Good was always costly.
>   Another Pizzaro has been the great Trenado
> who by the pure force of his rare *ingenio*
> discovers such *Indias* with his ship:
>   such an *ingenio* served us as the key
> that the closed and hidden treasure
> discloses to us the Spanish, open and clear.[65]

In this sonnet, the poet exchanged the "glory" of the imperial colonizer for the triumph of the translingual poet-translator. To the discourse of political and economic power, Ledesma brought the gold of that most precious of sciences, poetry. In a curious play on *translatio studii* and *translatio imperii*, which resulted in the retention of neither practice, the *Indias* became a metonym for Petrarch's body of work. Trenado de Ayllón's act of translation became both navigation and discovery, a flourish which reworked the Petrarchan trope of the shipwrecked lover lost at sea into

[65] (Petrarch, *Comento del Petrarca*, ca. 1595, unpaginated [iiv]). The poetic conceit coincidentally reappears in John Keats' "On First Looking into Chapmen's Homer."

the successful voyager whose destination was the source itself: Petrarch. In a marvelously destabilized conception of imperial expansion, the *llave* that sealed the treasure from comprehension was transformed into the *llave* which opened it for new lyric revelation in that high science of poetry. In this way, both original poet (Petrarch) and translator (Trenado de Ayllón), as *llaves*, were engaged in the "mining" of poetic gold.

To a critical eye, the terrestrial violence of the mining of precious metals, reminiscent of Potosí, and the linguistic domination associated with imperial expansion and conquest, doubtless may situate Ledesma's metaphors within the purview of empire.[66] Upon closer investigation, however, poetry and, in particular, poetic translation continuously destabilized the very hegemonies whose modes of power the poem appropriates and upends by way of metaphor.[67] Ledesma's sonnet did more than highlight the "mimetic rivalries occurring among emergent empires at the very time they solidify power"; it subverted the mimetic rivalries themselves to the logic of a poetry without a single imperium.[68] Understood as an *imperial contrafactum*, the sonnet reshaped political ideology into poetic ingenuity by employing the same conceits for different ends, such that Castilian was rewritten by Tuscan from within.[69] This should not be misunderstood as a likening of poetry to empire, which would amount to a rather flat pasting-over of Nebrija's dictum on top of the poetic work. Ledesma did not write in simile. Through the work of metaphor, by repurposing the language of empire as the *vehicle* for the *tenor* of the poem, Ledesma unraveled the logic of empire with the logic of poetry which everywhere disrupted and transformed the cultural hegemony, linguistic purity, and orders of sameness on which empire (and later nation state) relied.[70] Like the model of Petrarch himself, the translator's work underscored the heteroglossia of poetic discourse and the ultimate ineffability of its secrets,

66 On metallurgy as post-colonial elision of metaphor and actuality: (A.M. Bigelow, *Mining Language: Racial Thinking, Indigenous Knowledge, and Colonial Metallurgy in the Early Modern Iberian World*, University of North Carolina Press, 2020).

67 On lyric as disruptive of imperial hegemony: (Ponce-Hegenauer, "Lyric and Empire").

68 (Fuchs, "Another Turn for Transnationalism," 412).

69 The term *contrafactum* was examined by Bruce Wardropper (1958) in order to clarify the literary practice of substituting a profane sentiment with a religious one. "¿Qué es, pues, un *contrafactum*? Diremos que es una obra literaria (a veces una novela o un drama, pero generalmente un poema lírico de corta extensión) cuyo sentido profano ha sido sustituído por otro sagrado. Se trata, pues, de la refundación de un texto. A veces la refundación conserva del original el metro, las rimas, y aun–siempre que no contradiga al propósito divinizador–el pensamiento. El nombre de la dama amada se sustituye con el de la Santa Virgen; lo erótico se convierte en el amor cristiano" (B. Wardropper, *Historia de la Poesía lírica a lo divino en la Cristiandad Occidental*, 1958, 6–8).

70 For the structure of metaphor: (ed. R. Greene, "Tenor and Vehicle," *Princeton Encyclopedia of Poetry and Poetics*, 1421–1422).

which belonged to no single language at all.[71] Ledesma's sonnet, and implicitly Trenado's project, undermined imperial logic with poetry's openness to the complicated multilingual space, the *location of culture*, that translation invoked and animated.[72]

The sphere of influence to which Trenado de Ayllón's "Comento" was tied was not limited to the poets who sang his praises in the front matter. The inclusion of the printing approbation authored by Juan Rufo Gutiérrez linked the sites of poetic production associated with Trenado's work to the very literary milieu in which Miguel de Cervantes circulated during the final decades of the sixteenth century.[73] In addition to authoring the *Seiscientas apotegmas* (1596), Rufo was also an epic poet whose own *Austriada* of 1584 (an encomiastic epic for the late Don Juan de Austria) had been printed with laudatory poems from several of his contemporaries, including Luis de Góngora and Miguel de Cervantes.[74] Don Juan (1545–1578), the ill-fated hero of Lepanto, had also been a major patron and practitioner of poetry, a near contemporary in age to Rufo and Cervantes, who were both born in 1547.[75] While much good work has been done on epic poetry and the Battle of Lepanto, the laudatory poems included in the front matter of Rufo's *Austriada*, like Ledesma's sonnet for Trenado, underscore the way in which the logic of empire was subverted by the logic of poetry, a lyric take on the contest of *armas y letras*.[76] Thus, Ledesma's sonnet and Trenado de Ayllón's "Comento" must be read within a larger literary sphere that everywhere

[71] (J. Abravanel, [Leone Ebreo], *Dialogues of Love*, ed. Rossella Pescatori, trans. D. Bacich, University of Toronto Press, 2009, 279).

[72] "Being in the 'beyond', then, is to inhabit an intervening space, as any dictionary will tell you. But to dwell 'in the beyond' is also, as I have shown, to be part of a revisionary time, a return to the present to redescribe our cultural contemporaneity; to reinscribe our human, historic commonality; *to touch the future on its hither side* . . .the intervening space 'beyond', becomes a space of intervention in the here and now . . .. The borderline work of culture demands an encounter with 'newness' that is not part of the continuum of past and present. It creates a sense of the new as an insurgent act of cultural translation. Such art does not merely recall the past, refiguring it as a contingent 'in-between' space that innovates and interrupts the performance of the present" (H.K. Bhabha, *The Location of Culture*, London: Routledge, 1994, 7, emphasis in original).

[73] (R. Ramírez de Arellano, *Juan Rufo: Jurado de Córdoba: estudio biográfico y crítico*, Madrid: Hijos de Reus, 1912). For Rufo and the Academia Imitatoria: (G. Ponce-Hegenauer, "A Novel Community: Pastoral Pseudonyms, *La Galatea*, and the *Academia Imitatoria* in Madrid, 1585," *Romance Studies*, n.3–4, vol. XXXI); (P. Marín Cepeda, *Cervantes y la corte de Felipe II: Escritores en el entorno de Ascanio Colonna (1560–1608)*, Madrid: Polifemo, 2015).

[74] No stranger to the art of translation, Góngora had also contributed a laudatory poem to the 1580 translation of Camoes epic poem *La Lusiada*, by Gómez de Tapia (whose commemorative eclogue on pastoral festivities at Aranjuez set the stage for Cervantes' first sonnet in Chapter 2): (Gómez de Tapia, *La Lusiada*, 1580, 2r–2v).

[75] For Cervantes' sonnet for Rufo's *Austriada*: (Cervantes, *Poesías*, 159–160).

[76] For the *Austriada*, poetry, and the Battle of Lepanto: (P. Marín Cepeda, "Entre pliegos anda el juego: Juan Rufo y las cortes literarias en el tiempo de *La Austriada*," *Calíope*, 2017, vol. XXII,

privileged the way in which lyric discourse rewrote empire from within: at the level of language. Fifteen years after the *Austriada*, when he authored the approbation for Trenado's translation, even an epic poet such as Rufo Gutiérrez considered Petrarch the quintessential poetic exemplar for *ingenios* writing in Castilian. Rufo wrote:

> Por comisión de los señores del Real consejo he visto la declaración y traducción del Petrarca, en tres volúmenes hecha por Fran[cisco] Trenado de Ayllón vecino de Villalpando. Y ha sido trabajo muy agradable y muy loable y que merece muy gran premio, y en beneficio no solo de la lengua española, más en favor de la curiosidad y doctrina de que algunos buenos ingenios carecen por no entender lengua tan rica y hermana de la nuestra como es la italiana. Y así por esto como por el Petrarca (a quien debidamente se dio el título de Divino) conviene que por todo se alabe y engrandezca, y que dignísimamente merece el que tan fielmente y a tan buen autor declaro y tradujo la licencia de imprimirla que pide ... en Madrid. 20. de septiembre de 1595. años.
>
> (By the commission of the gentlemen of the *Real consejo* I have seen the commentary and translation of Petrarch, in three volumes made by Francisco Trenado de Ayllón, neighbor of Villalpando. And it has been a very agreeable and laudable work and [one] that deserves a very great prize, and is to the benefit of not only the Spanish language, but also in favor of the curiosity and doctrine which some good *ingenios* lack for not understanding such a rich language, and sister of ours, as is Italian. So for this as for Petrarch (to whom it rightly was given the title of *Divino*) it is advisable that it is praised and aggrandized for all, and that it dignifiedly deserves – it that so faithfully and by such a good author is declared and translated – the license to print that is requested ... in Madrid. 20 of September of 1595. years.)[77]

Rufo's approbation rendered Petrarch's divinity one of transnational recognition, a sempiternal figure of the poet in Spain.[78]

But Trenado's translation was not simply a matter of linguistic pedagogy; his text configured the conceptual building blocks of this Petrarchan lexicon in the "Advertencias al lector para que mejor pueda entender todas las cosas contenidas en esta obra (Advertisements for the reader in order that they may better understand all the things contained in this work)"

165–188); (M. Blanco, "La batalla de Lepanto y la cuestión del poema heroico," *Calíope*, 19.1, 2014, 25–53); and (Wright, Spence, Lemons, *The Battle of Lepanto*).

77 (Petrarch, *Translation of the Sonnets of Petrarch*, ca. 1595, unpaginated, [vir]).

78 (Lefèvre, *Una poesia per l'Impero*). Instances in which imperial Spain was modified by its conquered territories have been thoughtfully studied in the case of Colonial Peru: (G. Lamana, *Domination Without Dominance: Inca-Spanish Encounters in Early Colonial Peru*, Duke University Press, 2008).

located in the frontmatter of his "Comento."[79] These included glosses of abbreviations such as M.L. for "Madama Laura," discursive definitions for words with a rich conceptual architecture, such as *Anima*, *Destino*, *Concepto*, *Objeto*, *Subjeto*, and *Afecto* (Spirit, Destiny, Concept, Object, Subject, and Affect), and formal and metrical features such as *Estilo*, *Rimas*, *Poema*, and *Madrigal* (Style, Rhymes, Poem, and Madrigal). Following this critical apparatus, Trenado's translation opened with a *vita* of the poet. Drawing on previous works of this kind, Trenado's "Vida del Petrarca" intertwined story and history in a version of biographical prose fiction in the style of the Byzantine Romance. His narrative surged *in medias res* into the drama of the Guelphs and Ghibellines in thirteenth-century Florence: "Ardía en su mayor furor dentro en Florencia, el inhumano fuego de los dos bandos Guelfos y Gebellinos (It burned in its greatest furor within Florence, the inhuman fire of the two bands Guelph and Ghibelline)."[80] The story has begun with the exile of Petrarch's parents, Ser Petracco and Eletta Cnigiani, from Florence to Arezzo. Foreshadowing the fire (and ice) of Petrarch's own erotic life, the opening sentence elides *ardía/furor/fuego* in a form of simile that figures both erotic and poetic *furore* as fire in the *vita*. Trenado mythologizes the poet over the course of eighteen narratively dynamic pages, including the tale of Petrarch saving a copy of Vergil from the towering flames of a burning building.

But the "Vida" is only one part of the myth of Petrarch in translation to which Trenado paid homage. The narrative preliminaries move on to Petrarch's lady, Laura, at Cabrières. Over the course of sixteen more pages, the "Origen de Madama Laura, con la descripción del Valle de Valclusa (Origin of Madame Laura, with the description of the Valley of Valclusa)" reprises Velutello's early sixteenth-century investigation into the identity of Laura.

In the retelling Trenado leads the reader to the 1533 "re-discovery" of the "Sepulchro de Madama Laura," at which point Trenado relates the following:

> Demás de lo dicho, hay un autor moderno; que en lo que toca al Sepulcro de Madama Laura dice, que en el Año 1533 por industria del curioso Mauricio Sceba fue hallada en una sepultura antigua de una capilla del monasterio de san Francisco de Avigñon una caja de plomo atada con un hilo de alambre

79 (J. Huang and C. Yan, "The Cultural Turn in Translation Studies," *Open Journal of Modern Linguistics*, n.4, 2014, vol. IV, 487–494); (Bhabha, *The Location of Culture*); (S. Bassnett and A. Lefevre, eds. *Translation – History – Culture*, Continuum, 1998).

80 (Petrarch, *Translation of the Sonnets of Petrarch*, ca. 1595, unpaginated, [9r]).

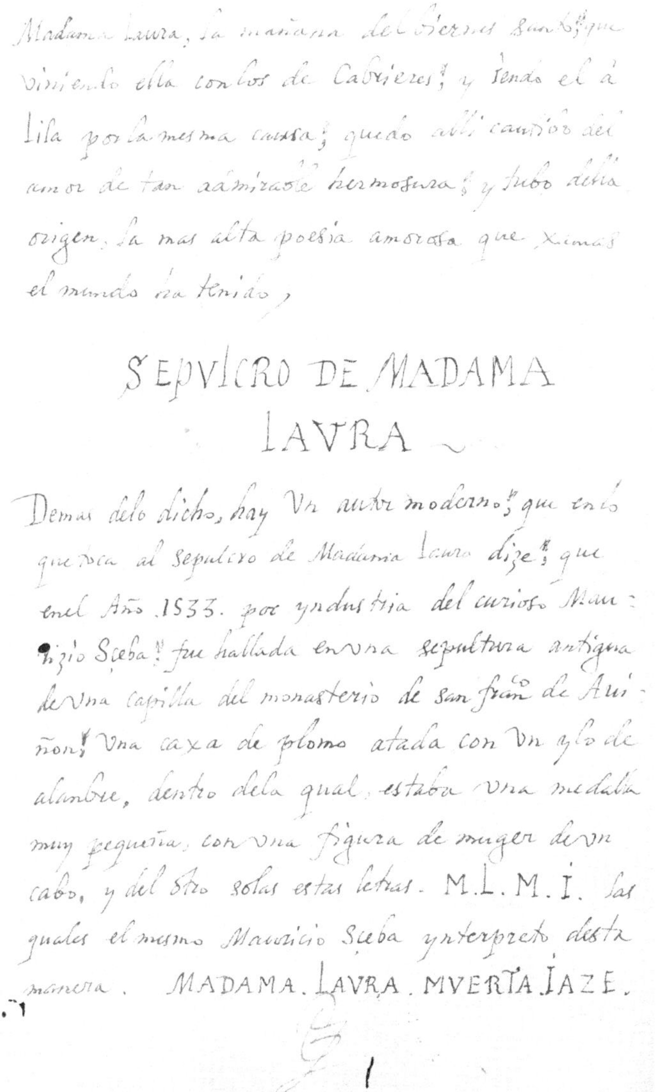

Madama Laura, la mañana del Viernes Santo; que viviendo ella con los de Cabrieres; y siendo él à Lila por la mesma caussa; quedo alli cautivo del amor de tan admirable hermosura; y tubo della origen, la mas alta poesia amorosa que xamas el mundo ha tenido,

SEPVLCRO DE MADAMA LAVRA

Demas delo dicho, hay Vn autor moderno; que en lo que toca al sepulcro de Madama Laura dize; que enel Año 1533. por yndustria del curioso Mauricio Sceba; fue hallada en vna sepultura antigua de vna capilla del monasterio de san franco de Aviñon; Vna caxa de plomo atada con Vn hilo de alanbre, dentro dela qual, estaba vna medalla muy pequeña, con vna figura de muger de vn cabo, y del otro solas estas letras. M.L.M.I. las quales el mesmo Mauricio Sceba ynterpreto desta manera. MADAMA. LAVRA. MVERTA. IAZE.

Fig. 3.2 Trenado de Ayllón, *Comento del Petrarca*, modern pagination, 26v, ms. Egerton 2062, British Library

> dentro de la cual estaba una medalla muy pequeña con una figura de mujer de un cabo y del otro solas estas letras. M. L. M. I. las cuales el mismo Mauricio Sceba interpreta desta manera. MADAME. LAURA. MUERTE. ÍAZE. Y así mismo estaba en la dicha caja un pergamino y en el escrito el siguiente soneto . . .
>
> (In addition to the stated, there is a modern author who, touching upon the sepulcher of Madame Laura, says that in the year 1533 by the diligence of the curious Mauricio Sceba in an ancient sepulcher of a chapel of the monastery of San Francisco of Avigñon was found a lead box tied with a thread of wire within which there was a very tiny medal with the *figura* of a woman on one side and on the other only these letters. M. L. M. I. the which the same Mauricio Sceba interpreted in this manner. MADAME. LAURA. MUERTE. ÍAZE. And even then, in the same stated box a parchment and on it was written the following sonnet . . .)[81]

While it is unlikely that the sonnet was written by Petrarch, what is of interest here is that it received sufficient circulation over the course of the sixteenth century to make its way into Trenado's translation as an authentic historical document, such that he included both the original Italian and the Castilian translation in his manuscript.[82] Situating both Petrarch and Laura as highly influential figures for the sixteenth century, Trenado recounted how King Francis I of France (d. 1547) built a marble edifice to Petrarch's beloved Laura and had this adorned with epitaphs in various languages, again underscoring the transnational, multilingual, and sempiternal nature of the *figura of the poet.*[83] So impassioned was the king that he himself wrote a small poem of eight lines for Madame Laura in French, which Trenado also includes in the original, followed by a translation "a la letra (to the letter)".

The body of the "Comento" opened with Petrarch's prologue-sonnet "Voi ch'ascoltate," accompanied by two and half pages of exegesis, which Trenado de Ayllón called an *exposición.* Throughout his exposition,

81 (Petrarch, *Translation of the Sonnets of Petrarch*, ca. 1595, unpaginated, [26v–27r]). The legend of the 1533 rediscovery of Laura's tomb was treated as an historical event well into the early part of the twentieth century. See comments in: (W. Dudley Foulke, *Some Love Songs of Petrarch, Translated and Annotated and with a Biographical Introduction*, Oxford University Press, 1915, 211–213).

82 (Petrarch, *Translation of the Sonnets of Petrarch*, ca. 1595, unpaginated, [27r–27v]). Trenado then goes on to an extended exegesis of the sonnet attributed to Petrarch which he has just translated. In the context of his *Arte muy curiosa*, this was part of his pedagogy of delight. Trenado also included a formal prologue, "El autor al lector. Respondiendo a las objeciones quele podrían ser puestas" (Petrarch, *Translation of the Sonnets of Petrarch*, ca. 1595, unpaginated, [30r–32r]).

83 For an extended discussion of Petrarch as transnational poet of the sixteenth century and Petrarchism as a translingual European phenomenon: (Lefèvre, *Una poesia per l'Imperio*).

Trenado gave glosses of the poems in Castilian into which he inserted the original Tuscan, one line at a time. The translator-as-pedagogue repeated this process for each of the ninety-two sonnets, eleven songs, three madrigals, and three sestinas contained in this large fragment of the "Comento." In Trenado's translation and exposition of Petrarch's "Canción 8" ("Per che la vita è breve"), the reader discovers the Castilian version of Petrarch as an immortal or *divino ingenio*:

> El amoroso pensamiento
> que mora dentro en vos, me se descubre
> de tal manera; que me saca del corazón toda otra alegría
> por lo cual palabras y obras
> salen de mi tan cumplidas entonces, que yo espero
> hacer me inmortal, aunque la carne muera.
>
> (The amorous thought
> that dwells within you, is revealed to me
> in such way that it takes every other joy out of my heart
> for the which words and works
> then come out of me so complete that I hope
> to make myself immortal, even though the flesh dies.)[84]

Following nearly two hundred years of translation into Castilian, this then was the state of Petrarch as the *figura of the poet* at the close of the sixteenth century. As a model chiseled by two hundred years of readership, and modernized by the work of the *divino* Garcilaso, the *figura of the poet* became both literary and biographical exemplar for poets writing throughout the century and for the shepherds who spoke in their texts. By combining the lyric legacy of the poet-lover with the narrative context of the *vita*, the prosimetric form of pastoral fiction soon gave way to Cervantes' first modern novel: a *vita* of the ingenious AQ which bookends the lyric apostrophes of dQ.

84 "*l'amoroso pensiero* dice el poeta, que aquel amoroso pensamiento que esta en su corazón, che el cual pensamiento, *aluerga dentro in voi* mora dentro ojos hermosos ojos (estando siempre imaginando en su alta hermosura) *mi si discopre tal* dice que seledescubre en el entendimiento en tanta manera hermoso, *che mi trahe del cor ogni altra gioia* que le saca del corazón cualquier otra alegría, siendo aquella tal, que ella sola no cabe en el: *onde parole & opre escondime si fatte allhor* por lo cual, salen del poeta entonces palabras y obras escritas en rimas de sus alabanzas, tan altas, *ch'i spero farmi imortal perche la carne muoia* que el espera hacer de inmortal fama de poeta, aun que muere el cuerpo desasiéndose en tierra" (Petrarch, *Translation of the Sonnets of Petrarch*, ca. 1595, unpaginated [227v–228r]).

CHAPTER 4

The Form of Beauty: Lyric Lovers in the Mediterranean World

On April 19, 1584, Antonio de Eraso signed the *privilegio* for the *Cancionero* of Gabriel López Maldonado, a lengthy collection of verse poetry consisting of some 64 folios (Madrid: Guillermo Droy, February 5, 1586). Just a few months earlier, on February 22 of that same year, he also signed the *privilegio* for Cervantes' own pastoral prosimetrum, the *Galatea* (Alcalá: Juan Gracián, 1585),[1] to which López Maldonado contributed an encomiastic sonnet (reprinted at the close of the 1586 *Cancionero*). Cervantes, in turn, contributed an encomiastic sonnet to López Maldonado's *Cancionero.*[2]

In the years following his ransom from Algiers, Cervantes successfully rejoined the circle of urban shepherd-poets in Madrid, many of whom he encoded under pastoral pseudonyms in the *Galatea*. As a testimony to the triumph of this literary *locus amoenus*, López Maldonado's *Cancionero* is a significant source on the confluence of lyric practice and erotic philosophy during this period. His *Cancionero* contained an extensive paratextual apparatus which included López Maldonado's own *prólogo* on the art of poetry and a dedication to Doña Thomisa de Borja y Enriquez, whom the poet

[1] "'De López Maldonado, Soneto': Salen del mar, y vuelven a sus senos / después de una veloz larga carrera, / como a su madre universal primera, / los hijos della largo tiempo ajenos. / Con su partida no la hacen menos, / ni con su vuelta más soberbia y fiera, / porque tiene, quedándose ella entera, / de su humor siempre sus estanques llenos. / La mar sois vos, ¡oh *Galatea* estremada!, / los ríos, los loores, premio y fruto / con que ensalzáis la más ilustre vida. / Por más que deis, jamás seréis menguada, / y menos cuando os den todos tributo, / con él vendréis a veros más crecida" (Cervantes, *Galatea*, 1961, vol. I, 13).

[2] "*De Miguel de Ceruantes en loor del Autor y de la obra.* / SONETO. // El cafto ardor de vna amorofa llama, / vn fabio pecho a fu rigor fujeto, / vn defden facudido y vn affecto / blando, que al Alma en dulce fuego inflama. / El bien y el mal a que combida y llama / de Amor la fuerça y poderofo effecto / eternamente en fon claro y perfecto / con eftas rimas cantara la fama / Lleuando el nombre vnico y famofo / vueftro, felice Lopez Maldonado / del moreno Etyope al Cyta blanco / Y hara que en valde del Laurel honrofo / efpere alguno verfe coronado / fI no os imita y tiene por fu blanco" (G. López Maldonado, *Cancionero de López Maldonado, Dirigido al ilustrísima Señora, Doña Tomasa de Borja y Enríquez mi señora, y de las villas de Grajar y Valverde y su tierra*, Madrid: Guillermo Droy, 1586, unpaginated, [iv recto–iv verso]).

CANCIONERO DE

La otra es, que aunque con dulce canto
ayan ſido por el tan leuantadas
que paſſan el lugar de las eſtrellas
Es ſu ingenio diuino tal, y tanto
que del mundo ſeran mas eſtimadas
ellas por el, que lo ſera el por ellas.

SONETO. 57.

En loor del Cancionero de Pedro de Padilla.

vean tesoro de varias poesias de Padilla

Eſta reſplandeciente y viua llama
que alumbra al mundo y regozija el Cielo.
eſta que illuſtra el gran ſeñor de Delo
y deſde el Taxo al Ganges ſe derrama
Eſta cuya virtud incita y llama
con nueuo exemplo a todos los del ſuelo
y preſta porque de, mas alto el buelo
mil ojos y mil alas a la Fama.
No la encendio el varon que con ſu pluma
canto del gran Troyano el claro nombre.
ni el otro por dos lauras celebrado.
Que dèſtos y de todo mortal hombre
eres, ò gran Padilla tu la ſuma
y tal llama en tal pecho ſe ha criado.

SONETO. 58.

Al miſmo en loor de ſu Romancero

Auien

LOPEZ MALDONADO 188

Auiendo de cantar del duro Marte
la ſangre en tantas partes derramada,
por la Eſpañola victorioſa eſpada
que en mil regiones ſu furor repartê
Con diuina inuencion, ingenio, y arte
primero en vueſtra Cythara catada
fue la Dioſa de Cypro, y la dorada
penetrante ſaeta, en toda parte.
Hiziſtes lo que ſuele vn gran maeſtro
que en la acordada lyra va templando
la aguda conſonancia con la graue
Mas que no templarà el ingenio vueſtro?
y diuina inuencion conque acordando
furor de guerra vays, y amor ſuaue.

SONETO. 59.

A la Galatcha de Miguel de Ceruantes.

Salen del Mar y bueluen a ſus ſenos
deſpues de vna veloz, larga carrera
como a ſu madre vniuerſal primera
los hijos de ella largo tiempo agenos
Con ſu partida no la hazen menos
ni con ſu buelta mas, ſoberuia y fiera
porque tiene quedandoſe ella entera
de ſu humor, ſiempre, ſus eſtanques llenos
La mar ſoys vos, ó Galathea eſtremada
los rios, los loores premio y fruto

Z 2 con

Fig. 4.1 López Maldonado, *Cancionero* (1586), Imágenes procedentes de los fondos de la Biblioteca Nacional de España

Dianaen exceder a los mortales
en caſtidad de eſtilo con pureza.
Mercurio las hiſtorias marañadas, (ue
Marte el fuerte vigor q̃ el braço os mue-
Cupido, y Venus, todos ſus amores,
Apolo las canciones concertadas
ſu ſciencia las hermanas todas nueue
y al fin el dios ſilueſtre ſus paſtores.

DE LOPEZ MALDONADO.

Soneto.

Salen del mar, y bueluen a ſus ſenos
deſpues de vna veloz larga carrera
como a ſu madre vniuerſal primera
los hijos della largo tiempo agenos.
Con ſu partida no la hazen menos
ni con ſu buelta mas ſoberuia y fiera
porque tiene quedandoſe ella entera
de ſu humor ſiempre ſus eſtãques llenos.
La mar ſoys vos o Galatea eſtremada
los rios, los loores, premio y fruto
conque enſalçays la mas illuſtre vida:
Por mas que deys, jamas ſereys menguada
y menos quando os den todos tributo
con el vendreys a veros mas creſcida.

PRIMERO LIBRO
de Galatea.

Mientras q̃ al triſte lamentable accento
del mal acorde ſon del canto mio,
en Eco amarga de canſado aliento
Responde, el monte, el prado, el llano, el rio
demos al ſordo y preſſuroſo viento
las quexas que del pecho ardiente y frio
ſalen a mi peſar, pidiendo en vano
ayuda al rio, al monte, al prado, al llano.

Crece el humor de mis canſados ojos
las aguas deſte rio, y deſte prado
las variadas flores ſon abrojos
y eſpinas que en el alma ſ'han entrado.
No eſcucha el alto monte mis enojos
y el llano de eſcucharlos ſe hã canſado,
y aſsi vn pequeño aliuio al dolor mio
no hallo en mõte, en llano, en prado en rio.

Crey que el fuego que en el alma enciende
el niño Alado, el lazo, con que aprieta

A la red

Fig. 4.2 Cervantes, *La Galatea* (1585), Imágenes procedentes de los fondos de la Biblioteca Nacional de España

served at that time. The front matter included laudatory verses from those in the poet's milieu. Luis de Vargas, Cervantes, Vicente Espinel, Juan de Vergara, Lope de Vega, Gonzalo Gómez de Luque, Diego Durán, Pedro de Padilla, Liñán [de Riaza], Diego de Aguiar, and Lazaro Luis Liranzo all contributed poems for this paramount publication of their lyric compatriot.[3]

The body of the *Cancionero* opened with López Maldonado's "Definición de Amor," a versified capstone and introduction to the lyric project these poets shared which gave shape to their philosophical outlook, which was informed by Judah Abravanel's (Leone Ebreo, León Hebreo) *Dialoghi d'amore* (Rome, 1535). Taking an approach that was more explicit than the use of intertextuality or borrowed lyric conceits, López Maldonado identified Judah Abravanel by his Hispanized penname, León Hebreo, in this opening poem.

Difinicion de Amor.

La Difinicion de Amor
fegun el Ouidio aduierte
es fer vna dulce muerte
y vna vida con dolor.
Vn acuerdo y vn oluido
dize, y vn mundo al reues,
que haze no fer lo que es:
y fer lo que nunca ha fido.
Y aquel famoso Leon,
por fobre nombre el Hebreo,
dize, que Amor es deffeo
de fegura poffefsion.
Vna lenta calentura
que quema hafta el poftrer hueffo,
y que al mas maduro fefo
condena a mayor locura.

(*Definition of Love*
The definition of love
according to what Ovid warns
is to be a sweet death
and a painful life,
a reminiscence and thing forgotten,

[3] (López Maldonado, *Cancionero*, unpaginated, [iv recto–xi verso]). Many of these poets appear in the "Canto de Calíope" of the *Galatea*. The shared poetic discourse was also evident in the inclusion of verse epistle exchanges with Doctor Campuzano, Gálvez de Montalvo, Vincente Espinel, and an anonymous interlocutor.

LOPEZ MALDONADO. 1

Difinicion de Amor.

LA Difinicion de Amor
ſegun el Ouidio aduierte
es ſer vna dulce muerte
y vna vida con dolor.
Vn acuerdo y vn oluido
dize, y vn mundo al reues,
que haze no ſer lo que es:
y ſer lo que nunca ha ſido.

Y aquel famoſo Leon,
por ſobrenombre el Hebreo,
dize, que Amor es deſſeo
de ſigura poſſeſsion.
Vna lenta calentura
que quema haſta el poſtrer hueſſo,
y que al mas maduro ſeſo
condena a mayor locura.

Mario Equicola tambien
con ſu ingenio celeſtial,
dize que Amor es vn mal
agradecido por bien.
Vna ſabroſa dolencia
que aſsi agraua los ſentidos
que quando mas adormidos
entienden mejor ſu ſciencia.

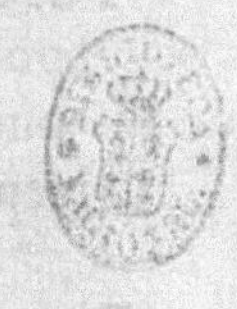

A Otras

Fig. 4.3 “Definición de Amor,” López Maldonado, *Cancionero* (1586), 1r, Imágenes procedentes de los fondos de la Biblioteca Nacional de España

he says, and an inverted world,
which renders without being what is,
and gives being to that which never has been.
  And that famous León,
for pseudonym, the *Hebreo*,
says that Love is desire
for a secured possession.
  A slow fever
that burns even the last bone,
and even the most mature brain
it condemns to the greatest madness.)[4]

Moving from Ovid's inverted world to Abravanel's desire for a thing possessed, López Maldonado keyed poetic forays in erotic philosophy, not only for the contents of his own *Cancionero*, but also for the network of poets that radiated outward from the many laudatory poems and versified epistles contained in his work. This same milieu, which nurtured the genesis of Cervantes' own pastoral novel (1585) and his subsequent poetic fictions, shared an intellectual sphere with Italian poets that had developed in the middle decades of the sixteenth century through the reception of Abravanel's *Dialoghi d'amore* (Rome, 1535), following the posthumous printing by humanists and literati active in Siena. As Cervantes stated in the prologue to the *DQ I* (1605), "Si tratáredes de amores, con dos onzas que sepáis de la lengua Toscana, toparéis con León Hebreo que os hecha las medidas. (If you want to treat amorous matters, with the two ounces that you know of the Tuscan language, you'll bump into León Hebreo who cut your measurements)."[5] That Cervantes was a deep reader of Abravanel was not only evident from this mention in the prologue to the *DQ I*. Less remarked upon, but far more foundational, was the debate on love between the shepherd-poets Tirsi and Lenio in Book IV of the *Galatea*, a debate which dramatized key arguments in Abravanel's philosophy within the circle of poets shared by Cervantes and Maldonado at that time.[6] In conjunction with poetic trends in Rome, Naples, Sicily, and Algiers, this milieu of the 1580s situates Cervantes' 1579 epistle in *octavas* to Antonio Veneziano and his early versified drama, the *Trato de*

[4] The poem also names Mario Equicola. For complete text, see: (López Maldonado, *Cancionero*, unpaginated, 1r–4v).

[5] (Cervantes, *DQ*, 1999, prologue, 16).

[6] (López Estrada, "La influencia italiana"). See Chapter 5 for the possible identification of Lenio with López Maldonado. For complete debate on love between Lenio and Tirsi: (Cervantes, *Galatea*, 1961, vol. II, 43–71).

Argel, as part of a multilingual poetic practice in the early modern Mediterranean informed by readings of Abravanel's *Dialoghi*.[7]

By his own account, by 1569 Cervantes was serving in the court of a young Neapolitan nobleman, Giulio Acquaviva, in Rome, where Vicenzo Orsini's *boschetto* at Bomarzo was one of many private pastoral gardens cultivated by various Italian nobleman throughout the region.[8] Within these botanical and textual landscapes, the beloved lady was frequently figured as the *summa belleza* or *summum bonum*, an apparition of the form of beauty in the sensory world.[9] As such, pastoral poetry set the poet's erotic soul (the *figura of the poet*) into motion within the immanent framework of a sempiternal Arcadia. Because Neoplatonism in the Renaissance, and particularly in Renaissance Spain, has been consistently generalized to a Christian framework, this chapter necessarily recuperates the philosophy of Judah Abravanel through the reception of the *Dialoghi d'amore* in the poetries and cultural practices of Pastoral Petrarchism. Abravanel's text accomplishes the convergence of Ficino's Neoplatonism, Jewish mysticism and Kabbalistic thought, Hermeticism, medieval Islamic philosophy, and a proto-pantheism, written from the vantage point of a Sephardic Iberian exile in Italy. Through an examination of Abravanel's third dialogue, on the "Origin of Love," this chapter reconsiders the ways in which poets conceptualized their own erotic experiences.

This chapter situates Cervantes' poetic interpolations on erotic experience within this transnational milieu informed by Abravanel's *Dialoghi*, and offers a first literary reading of the *octavas* that Cervantes composed from solitary confinement in Algiers and sent to Veneziano in Palermo in

[7] For the *Trato de Argel*: (M. de Cervantes, "Comedia Llamada Trato De Argel Hecha Por Miguel de Cervantes, Que Estuvo Cautivo En Él Siete Años," ed. M. del Valle Ojeda Calvo, in ed. L. Gómez Canseco, *Comedias y Tragedias*, Real Academia Española, 2015, 2v.; v.2, 909–1004).

[8] "Cardinal Gianfrancesco Gambara at Bagnaia created an extensive garden which included a wood as well as a formal water-centred garden. At Caprarola Cardinal Alessandro Farnese had a series of formal gardens round his palace, but in his inner, secret garden the intruding natural rocks and cliffs were used as elements of fountains and stone tableaux. Cardinal Madruzzo at Soriano nel Cimino also created a garden endowed with fountains and often grotesque statuary. And members of the Orsini clan, lords of their respective domains, each devised gardens exploiting the natural and historical qualities of the land. Maerbale Orsini made a garden, now vanished, at Penna, and at Pitigliano Niccolo IV Orsini created a park on the high plateau of tufa rock that juts out opposite his town .... Natural caves almost indistinguishable from Etruscan cave-tombs abounded and Niccolo enhanced them with carved decorations, keeping alive memories of the long-gone Etruscans .... Not far away and at about the same time another of the Orsini lords was creating an equally impressive but much more enigmatic park, the Sacro Bosco or Sacred Wood of Bomarzo" (J. Sheeler, *The Garden at Bomarzo, A Renaissance Riddle*, London: Frances Lincoln Limited, 2007, 7–8).

[9] For the apparition of the form of beauty in the beloved: (Plato, "Phaedrus," in eds. J.M. Cooper and D.S. Hutchinson, *Complete Works*, Indianapolis: Hackett, 1997, 506–556; esp. 250d–255e, 528–532).

1579. Veneziano's own place as a poet writing within the Habsburg territories of the "Two Sicilies" and in a language other than Tuscan is recovered in relation to Cervantes' poetic work. This chapter concludes with Cervantes' earliest dramaturgical work, the *Trato de Argel* (Algiers or Madrid, ca. 1575–1582), in which he continued to develop the concept of love as faith within the confluence of Islamic and Christian paradigms in which erotic concepts typically appropriated religious discourse, a reverse of the classic poetic *contrafactum*.[10] Finally, this chapter gestures toward Cervantes' heroines, the female lyric lovers Zara and Silvia of the *Trato de Argel* and the many women found throughout his fiction, who should be situated within the lyric discourse of several Italian poetesses writing at that time (such as Virginia Salvi, Gaspara Stampa, and the philosopher-poet Tullia d'Aragona). Often ignored in contemporary critiques of Petrarch and Petrarchism, the activities of poetesses throughout the sixteenth century prepared the way for the woman as protagonist in early novelistic fiction. Through attention to this voicing of the lyric "I" by the "*summa belleza*," this chapter suggests *en passant* the Italian sources for Cervantes' "discovery" of poetic intersubjectivity, and the articulation of female desire that he would soon develop in the characters of Teolinda, Leonarda, and Rosaura in the *Galatea* following his return to Madrid in the autumn of 1580.[11]

~

[10] (Canavaggio, *Cervantès dramaturge*, 19).

[11] (eds. E. Fernández and M. Alcalá Galán, *Sex and Gender in Cervantes: Essays in Honor of Adrienne Laskier Martín*, Frankfurt: Reichenberger, 2019). It has often been suggested that Galatea the character is an underdeveloped blank slate, but the marriage plot of the later books, and in particular her lyric of Book V, suggest that her discretion does not amount to the erasure of her interiority: "¿A quién volveré los ojos / en el mal que se apareja, / si, cuanto mi bien se aleja, / se acercan más mis enojos? // A duro mal me condemna / el dolor que me destierra, / que si me acaba en mi tierra, / ¿qué bien me hará en el ajena? // ¡Oh justa amarga obediencia, / que por cumplirte he de dar / el sí que ha de confirmar / de mi muerte la sentencia! // Puesta estoy en tanta mengua, / que por gran bien estimara / que la vida me faltara, / o, por lo menos, la lengua. // Breves horas y cansadas fueron las de mi contento; / eternas las del tormento, / mas confusas y pesadas. // Gocé de mi libertad / en mi temprana sazón; / pero ya la subjeción / anda tras mi voluntad. / Ved si es el combate fiero / que dan a mi fantasía, / si al cabo de su porfía / he de querer, y no quiero. / ¡Oh fastidioso gobierno, / que a los respectos humanos / tengo de cruzar las manos / y abajar el cuello tierno! // ¿Que tengo de despedirme / de ver el Tajo dorado? / ¿Que ha de quedar mi ganado, / y yo triste he de partirme? / ¿Que estos árboles sombríos / y estos anchos verdes prados / no serán ya más mirados / de los tristes ojos míos? // Severo padre, ¿qué haces? / Mira que es cosa sabida / que a mí me quitas la vida / con lo que a ti satisfaces. // Si mis sospiros no valen / a descubrirte mi mengua, / lo que no puede mi lengua / mis ojos te lo señalen. / Ya triste se me figura / el punto de mi partida, / la dulce gloria perdida / y la amarga sepultura. / El rostro que no se alegra / del no conocido esposo, / el camino trabajoso, / la antigua enfadosa suegra, // y otros mil inconvenientes, / todos para mí contrarios, / los gustos extraordinarios / del esposo y sus parientes. // Más todos estos temores / que me figura mi suerte, / se acabarán con la muerte, / que es el fin de los dolores" (Cervantes, *Galatea*, 1961, vol. II, 133–134).

The type of erotic spirituality explored in Judah Abravanel's *Dialoghi d'amore* (Rome, 1535) was a topic of philosophical investigation throughout the sixteenth century, following Marsilio Ficino's late fifteenth-century Platonic academy in Florence and his translation of the Platonic corpus, particularly the *Symposium* and the *Phaedrus*. In Spain, philosophical forays into the mystery of love date to texts produced during medieval Islamic rule, such as Ibn Hazm's *The Ring of the Dove (Tawq al-Hamamah).*[12] By the turn of the sixteenth century, a renewed interest in the confluence of natural philosophy and erotic philosophy, which would culminate in Giordano Bruno's *Heroic Frenzies* (1585), underwent a revival in circles of humanists, nobility, poets, and artists across Europe.[13] Judah Abravanel (ca. 1460–ca. 1521), an exiled Sephardic Jew who had settled in Naples and Genoa at the end of the fifteenth century, became a key interlocutor in poetic and cultural understandings of erotic love and philosophy during this period.[14] As a child, his family passed from service to the Portuguese crown to the court of Ferdinand and Isabel, where his father, Isaac, prospered until the expulsion of Jewish peoples in 1492, a moment which resulted in the loss and forced baptism of Judah's youngest son, Isaac. Also a poet, Judah later lamented this loss in his own lyric poetry. He had served as court physician in Spain and continued his practice in Naples, where he likely coincided with the *Accademia Pontiniana* and the 1504 printing of Jacopo Sannazaro's *Arcadia*, just a couple of decades prior to Garcilaso and Boscán. His *Dialoghi* were set between two intimate interlocutors, Philo and Sophia, in the privacy of an idyllic landscape which recalled Sannazaro's pastoral and Plato's *Phaedrus*. Plagued by various manifestations of antisemitism, Abravanel worked in Genoa before returning to Naples, where little historical record of him remains for the period after 1521. While the learned explorations of Jewish mysticism by his father, Isaac, appealed to creation *ex nihilo* (against the Aristotelian tradition of Maimonides) and often rejected both Platonic and Aristotelian traditions, Judah's syncretic approach to Platonic (particularly the *Timaeus*, the *Symposium*, and the *Phaedrus*) and Neoplatonic texts came to fruition in his complex work of Renaissance Platonism. Less studied today, Abravanel's *Dialoghi* became a bestseller throughout the sixteenth century (it had been reprinted at least sixteen times by 1607). In addition to the Italian

12 (Ibn-Hazm, *The Ring of the Dove: A Treatise on the Art and Practice of Arab Love*, trans. Anthony Arberry, London: Luzac Oriental, 1994).

13 On the sonnet sequence: (G. Bruno, *Giordano Bruno's The Heroic Frenzies*, ed. and trans. P. E. Memmo, Jr., Chapel Hill: University of North Carolina Press, 1966, 32–46).

14 (Abravanel, *Dialogues*, 2009, 4). All citations in English translation are from this edition, unless otherwise noted. He should not be confused with his father, Isaac, also a philosopher and commentator, Isaac.

reprintings, during the sixteenth century there were as many as four French and five Spanish translations, as well as one into Latin.[15] Spinoza is thought to have had his own annotated copy nearly a century later (a probable source for the fifth book of the *Ethics*). This link in intellectual history may, in fact, point to the pantheistic tendencies in Abravanel's work which are still debated by scholars today. There is no place to treat the full scope of the work here, but several features of the *Dialoghi* were absorbed into the poetic practices of the literary pastoral. This resulted in an erotic cosmology in which the divine, beloved lady frequently figured as a natural form of Beauty.[16] The erotic allegory was an embodied metaphor for the Renaissance commonplace of art versus nature.

Abravanel's *Dialoghi* was first printed posthumously in Italian in Rome in 1535, nearly fifteen years after its author disappeared from the historical record.[17] It is unknown whether the first printing was the original version of Abravanel's text, which could have been written in Hebrew, Latin, or a number of vernacular languages prior to its appearance in Italian. The humanist who saw to the printing of the work, Mariano Lenzi, a nephew of Claudio Tolomei, made no mention of a translation from a manuscript original.[18] It remains a matter of speculation as to why Abravanel's text remained unpublished until nearly fifteen years after his disappearance from the historical record, and why it was that Mariano Lenzi had the work printed and dedicated to Madonna Aurelia Petrucci in 1535. Mariano Lenzi was likely a practicing humanist; thirty years later, Mutio Manfredi's *Donne Romane* included a poem by Lorenzo Lenzi, presumably a relation likewise involved in poetic circles in Rome.[19] While little is known of

[15] "Between 1535 and 1607 it had gone through sixteen separate editions in Italy alone and was translated into Latin once, French twice and Spanish at least five times. In addition to the testimony of the printing press we have the words of the literati of the sixteenth century itself. Lauded by authors as far afield as Benedetto Varchi (1503–1565), Tullia d'Aragona (1510–1556), Alessandro Piccolomini (1508–1579), Pontus de Tyard (1521–1605), Michel de Montaigne (1533–1592) and Miguel de Cervantes (1547–1616), and translated into Spanish by Garcilaso de la Vega the Inca (1539–1616), it is obvious that the work was a critical success among readers throughout the Christian world. The Jewish reaction would seem to have been more restrained in that century. It was only in the seventeenth century that Baruch of Urbino undertook a Hebrew translation, though this was only published (in Lyck, Poland) in the second half of the nineteenth century. The question of the original language ... of course remains a *vexata quaestio* among scholars" (Novoa, "Leone Ebreo's Dialoghi d'amore," 62–63).

Also: (Eisenbichler, *The Sword and the Pen*); (Abravanel, *Diálogos*, 2009, 47–55).

[16] (Abravanel, *Dialogues*, 2009, X-XI). [17] (Abravanel, *Dialogues*, 2009, XI).

[18] (J.N. Novoa, "New Documents Regarding the Publication of Leone Ebreo's *Dialoghi d'amore*," *Hispanica Judaica*, 5, 2007, 271–282).

[19] Lenzi's poem was dedicated to Madonna Settima Mazzei Maddaleni (M. Manfredi, *Donne Romane, Rime d'diversi. Raccolte, & Dedicate al Signor Giacomo Buencompagni. Da Mutio Manfredi*, Bologna: Alessandro Benacci, 1565, 753–758).

Mariano Lenzi, Aurelia Petrucci, a Sienese patrician, was a practicing poet and known lady of letters amongst humanist circles in Siena, which then included a number of female interlocutors.[20] Her mother's family, the Piccolomini of Siena, may have been in possession of the original manuscript.[21] She was the dedicatee of a translation of Book IV of Vergil's *Aeneid* by Bartolomeo Carli Piccolomini (1503–ca. 1538), and of another dialogue concerning amorous philosophy, the *Dulpisto* (1540), by the founder of the Sienese *Accademia degli Intronati*, Antonio Vignali (1500–1559).[22] Aurelia's cousin, Alessandro Piccolomini, had been the initiator of a *tenzone* (epistolary exchange in verse) amongst several ladies of Siena concerning his pilgrimage to Petrarch's birthplace just a few years prior to the printing of the *Dialoghi*.[23]

[20] "Petrucci, Aurelia (1511–1542) Born in Siena. Daughter of Borghese Petrucci (1490–1526), ruler of Siena from 1512, and Vittoria Todeschini Piccolomini, great-niece of the humanist pope Pius II. Borghese Petrucci was overthrown in a coup in 1516 and exiled. Aurelia was raised under the protection of her uncles Giovanni and Alessandro Todeschini Piccolomini. Married (1) Giovanfrancesco di Iacopo Petrucci, a second cousin, exiled after the expulsion of Aurelia's uncle and his cousin, Fabio Petrucci, in 1523; (2) Camillo Venturi (probably c. 1531). Two children from each marriage. Aurelia was the dedicatee of various literary works, including the first edition of Leone Ebreo's *Dialoghi d'amore* (1535). The writer Alessandro Piccolomini commemorated her death with a funeral oration that constructs her as a heroic feminine ideal" (V. Cox, ed. and trans., *Lyric Poetry by Women of the Italian Renaissance*, Baltimore: Johns Hopkins University Press, 2013, 397).

(Eisenbichler, *The Sword and the Pen*, 59–99); (L.A. Stortoni, ed., *Women Poets of the Italian Renaissance: Courtly Ladies & Courtesans*, trans. M. Prentice Lillie, New York: Italica Press, 1997, 41–43).

[21] (J. Abravanel, *Diálogos de amor. Vol. 1: Texto Italiano, Notas e Documentos*, vol. II: *Versão Portuguesa & Bibliografia*, ed. and trans. G. Manuppella, Lisbon: Instituto Nacional de Investigação Científica, 1983).

[22] "This translation was part of a group effort by six contemporary men at rendering into Italian the first six books of Virgil's *Aeneid*. Each man translated one book and dedicated it to a woman .... The long-absent Sienese intellectual and diplomat Claudio Tolomei (1492–1556), who for many years represented the Sienese Republic at the French court, apparently never met Aurelia but was inspired by her reputation for beauty and intellect to write to her and send her a complimentary copy of one of his works on the Tuscan language" (Eisenbichler, *The Sword and the Pen*). For poetics in this milieu: (C. Tolomei, *Versi e regole della nuova poesia toscana*, Rome: Antonio Blado d'Asola, 1539).

"About fifteen years earlier, in 1525–1527, he had composed and published, under his academic name of 'Arsiccio Intronato,' the absolutely scurrilous dialogue *La Cazzaria*, a vulgar but riotously funny conversation between Arsiccio (Vignali himself) and his friend Sodo Intronato (Marc'Antonio Piccolomini) .... Not surprisingly, when he sent his *Dulpisto* to press in 1540 Vignali found it advisable to publish it anonymously, though he felt no need to safeguard the identity of the dedicatee of the work. In the brief, one page dedicatory letter addressed to Aurelia Petrucci and dated 20 May 1540, Vignali indicates that his dialogue is part of a series of works currently being composed by various members of the Sienese Academy of the Intronati in honor of Aurelia Petrucci .... The *Dulpisto* is very much in line with the standard discussions of love penned in the sixteenth century and presents the usual Renaissance ideas about love in a socially much more acceptable and literarily much more elegant manner than the earlier *Cazzaria*" (Eisenbichler, *The Sword and the Pen*, 66–68).

[23] For the *tenzone*: (Eisenbichler, *The Sword and the Pen*, 15–57).

In the dedication of Abravanel's *Dialoghi* to Petrucci, Lenzi compared the relationship held by Pythagoras, Plato, and other ancient philosophers to Mercury with the relationship that Lenzi held to the "goddess" Petrucci. He suggested that her influence, as divine intellect and exemplary lady, would have far exceeded that which Mercury had been thought to exercise on ancient authors.[24] Lenzi made Petrucci the *specchio* (or ideal exemplar) for prospective readers of Abravanel's philosophy.[25] For Lenzi, Petrucci became the figure of Sophia (wisdom), the beloved lady of Philo and co-participant in their dialogues.[26] When Lenzi wrote that, "in my desire to repay this great debt I owe you, but recognizing the limits of my own talents and not having produced anything worthy of myself, I send you the fruits of another's labour,"[27] he invoked the Platonic idea of intellectual conception and procreation in literary works, and the pastoral ideal of the intellectual garden, what Richard Cody has called "the landscape of the mind."[28] While Abravanel's relation to this first publication remains a mystery, it is clear that the work appeared within and was directed to an influential circle of humanists and literati active in northern Italy, most of whom were poets versed in the practices of Pastoral Petrarchism.

Of her two surviving poems, one attests to Aurelia Petrucci's lyrical engagement with Abravanel's erotic cosmology.[29] Both sonnets originally appeared in print in an early collection of women's poetry, the *Rime diverse d'alcune nobilissime, et virtuosissime donne*, collected by M. Lodovico

[24] "Fu antichissima usanza degli scrittori di Egitto i santissimi libri da loro scritti indirizzare Mercurio . . . ." For full text: ([Judah Abravanel] Leone Ebreo, *Dialoghi d'amore*, Rome, 1535, unpaginated).

[25] "vedesi certo dalli ingegni purgati altro non esser in vita nostra se non uno specchio, & una Idea del mondo come si convenga vivere agli altri: & quelli, che insanguati nelle cose terrene non possono alzarsi in un subito a questo celeste pensiero, pur che voltino gli occhi in voi, illustrati dal vostro reggio, a poco a poco si purgane, & dell'alta contemplazione della vostra divinità si fanno degni" (Abravanel, *Dialoghi*, 1535, unpaginated).

[26] "The repetition and parallel structure . . . elevate the discussion of love to a higher sphere, something reminiscent of the medieval Italian tradition of the *donna angelicata* . . . a concept best illustrated by Dante in his *Divine Comedy*" (Eisenbichler, *The Sword and the Pen*, 65).

[27] ([Abravanel], *Dialoghi*, 1535, unpaginated [2*verso*]); all Italian citations from this edition unless otherwise noted. English translation: (Abravanel, *Dialogues of Love*, 2009, 23–24); all English translations from this edition unless otherwise noted. For the court of Isabel, the most likely version is the French of Parc Champenois (Lyon, 1551), dedicated to Isabel's mother, Catherine de' Medici. For the Castilian translation in circulation during the 1570s and 1580s, the 1568 translation printed in Venice is a good source. As Cervantes attests in the prologue to the *DQ I*, most poets likely read the text in the original Italian (Tuscan).

[28] (Cody, *Landscape of the Mind*).

[29] Only Petrucci's sonnet to Siena appears in (ed. Cox, *Lyric Poetry*, 311) and (ed. Stortoni, *Women Poets*, 42–43).

Domenichi (Lucca: Vincenzo Busdraghe, 1559).[30] Virginia Cox has pointed to the mid-sixteenth century as the apogee of women's lyric poetry in the "High Renaissance," and it is fitting, given the wide influence of the *Dialoghi* on Petrarchism, that Petrucci's sonnet on Abravanel's text appeared at the forefront of Domenichi's 1559 *Rime diversi*.[31] In her sonnet, Aurelia politely defers from the role of divine exemplar which Lenzi had attributed to her in his dedication with the formulaically humble gesture that her *ingegno* ("torbido e tosco [turbid and course]") is not up to the task of adjudicating the argument of Abravanel's text. With a quick allusion to Petrarch's "Voi ch'ascoltate," her sonnet suggests that Lenzi's admiration was of an amorous (if not youthful) error. In the sextet she interrupts her status as a divine and exemplary lady by invoking her own amorous and political suffering and exile. Her discretion, paradoxically, renders Petrucci a figure of wisdom, the Sophia of the *Dialoghi* to whom Lenzi had likened her. In writing the sonnet, she performs the role of "*specchio & una Idea*." Her inclusion as the opening poet in the *Rime diverse* in 1559 and her status as dedicatee of the original printing of the *Dialoghi* mark her as likely to have been among the many female Italian *ingegni* of whom the young poet Cervantes may have become aware upon his arrival in Rome in 1569, ripe inspiration for the heroines of his later fiction.[32]

30 The volume included the poetesses: Anna Golfarina, Athalanta Savese, Alda Torella Lunata, Berenice G. Cassandra Petrucci, Clarice de Medici, & de gli Strozzi, Claudia dall Rovere, Candida Gattesca de gli Alluminati, Cornelai Brunozzi de Villani, Catherina Pellegrina, Diamante Dolsi, Ermellina Arringhierei de Cerretani, Egeria da Canossa, Florenza G. Piemontese, Fausta Tacita, Francesca B. Sanese, Giulia Braccali de Ricciardi, Gentile Dotta, Gaspara Stampa, Suor Girolama Castellana, Gostanza Davala, Duchessa d'Amalfi, Honorata Pecci, Hortensia Scarpi, Hippolita Mirtilla, Isabella Riaria de Pepoli, Isabella di Morra, Lluia Torniella Bonromea, Laudomia da Sangallo, Lucretia Figliucci, Leonora Falletta da San Giorgio, Lucretia di Raimondo, Laudomia Forteguerri, Lisabetta da Cepperello, Livia Poeta, Lucia Bertana, Maddalena Pallavicina de Marchesi di Ceva, Maria Lagnosca Solera, Maria Martelli de Panciatichi, Maria da Sangallo, Maria Spinola, Narda N. Fiorentina, Olimpia Malipiera, P.S.M., Pia Bichi, Reina di Navarra, Silvia di Somma, Contessa di Bagno, Selvaggia Braccali de Bracciolini, Silvia Marchesa de Piccolomini, Virgina Gemma de Zuccheri, Veronica Gambara di Correggio, Virginia Martini de Salvi, and Vittoria Colonna Marchesa di Pescara.

31 *"Di Mad. Aurelia Petrucci"*: "Di quel, ch'il buon Filon disse a Sofia, / Mal posso giudicar, ch'Io ben conosco / Esser l'ingegno mio torbido, & tosco, / Ne tanto in sè capir la mente mia. / Però l'error' in vostro biasmo sia, / Ché mal prato esser può d'orrido bosco; / E Amor spesso veder fa torto, e losco, / Anchor che buon giudicio in altri stia. / Più ricche donne il bel paese nostro / Di Me ritien, ricche, dic'Io del bello, / Ch'attribuite a Me co'l chiaro inchiostro. / Io provo il Ciel troppo contrario, & fello; / Et de' suoi doni in Me sì pochi ha mostro, / ch'Io son d'ogni dolor continuo ostello" (A. Petrucci, "Di quel, ch'il buon Filon disse a Sofia," in ed. M. Lodovico Domenichi, *Rime diverse d'alcune nobilissime, et virtuosissime donne*, Lucca: Vincenzo Busdraghe, 1559, 9). (Eisenbichler, *The Sword and the Pen*, 63–66, 71–72); (ed. Cox, *Lyric Poetry*, 23–34).

32 For women writers at the time: (Cox, *Lyric Poetry*); (V. Cox, *The Prodigious Muse: Women's Writing in Counter-Reformation Italy*, Baltimore: Johns Hopkins University Press, 2011).

While the first translation of the *Dialoghi* into Castilian was not printed until 1568, the work had already appeared in a French translation dedicated to Isabel's mother, Catherine, as early as 1551, while Isabel was still a princess in her mother's court. Copies of the French translation may have arrived in Spain with Isabel's entourage in 1560, but this would not have been the first appearance of the work in Spain, where the Tuscan original was already in circulation. Abravanel's text was also the key philosophical treatise behind Montemayor's *Diana* (1559).[33] Several editions of Abravanel's *Diálogos* appeared in Castilian translation over the course of the sixteenth century. Abravanel was not a fleeting presence of the 1560s.[34] The most famous of these translations was accomplished by the Inca Garcilaso de la Vega in 1590. In addition to Montemayor, Cervantes, and López Maldonado, Abravanel's influence has been noted in the work of the Argensola brothers, Villamediana, and Figueroa.[35] To this we may add Gálvez de Montalvo, Padilla, Laínez, and Aldana. These authors were likely also familiar with the work of Marsilio Ficino and perhaps those of Tullia D'Aragona and Mario Equicola.[36] If the *figura of the poet* was the model for the life and legacy of the lyric lover, Abravanel provided the conceptual framework for an erotic spirituality by which Petrarch's exemplary *Canzoniere* and *Trionfi* were read, understood, and imitated. Abravanel gave shape to the way in which the beloved was conceptualized by the lyric lover as the *lady of his thoughts* and keeper, not only of the poet's heart, but also of his soul.

The *Dialoghi d'amore* consist in three dialogues undertaken between Philo, and his beloved, Sophia. Philo-Sophia, or "lover of wisdom," together made philosophy.[37] The first dialogue treats the difference

[33] "para darnos cuenta del impacto que una obra de este tipo (que venía, por otra parte, a ahondar en la brecha abierta por *El Cortesano*) causó en la literatura de la época, tanto en poesía como en prosa, . . . de los Argensola, Villamediana, Figueroa o, finalmente, Jorge de Montemayor y Cervantes, autores estos últimos que en la *Diana* y en el libro IV de *La Galatea*, respectivamente, no sólo continúan y siguen una vía amorosa neoplatónica, sino que llegan a reproducir pasajes completos de los *Diálogos de amor* de Hebreo" (J-M. Reyes Cano in J. Abravanel, *Diálogos de amor*, ed. J-M. Reyes Cano, Barcelona: PPU, 1993, 59).

[34] Spanish printings: *Los Diálogos de amor* . . . (Venice: con licenza delli Superiori, 1568); *Philographia universal* . . . (Zaragoza: Lorenço y Diego de Robles Hermanos, 1584); *La truduzion del Indio* . . . (Madrid: Pedro Madrigal, 1590); *Los diálogos de Léon Hebreo* . . . (Zaragoza: Lorenço de Robles, 1593); *Dialogos de Amor* . . . (Venice: 1598).

[35] (Reyes Cano in Abravanel, *Diálogos*, 1993, 59).

[36] (Byrne, *Ficino in Spain*) Menéndez Pelayo writes: "La oscuridad que envuelve la persona de Judas Abarbanel no se extiende a su libro . . . influyendo portentosamente en los místicos y en los poetas eróticos del siglo XVI" (M. Menéndez Pelayo, *Historia de las ideas estéticas en España, Siglos xvi y xvii*, ed. D. Enrique Sánchez Reyes, 3rd ed., Madrid: Consejo Superior de Investigaciones Científicas [1888], 1962, vol. II, 11).

[37] (Abravanel, *Dialogues*, 2009, 25–27, 73–75, 165–169).

between love and desire, the union of the active and contemplative life via moderation, love of god as efficient and formal cause, and the connection between carnal and spiritual love through the three facets of reason. (In López Maldonado's "Definición de amor," love as the desire for a thing already possessed was taken from the first dialogue.) The second dialogue develops a microcosmic/macrocosmic cosmology around the human as a simulacrum of the tripartite universe: earthly, heavenly, and divine. This coincides with the medieval tradition of the *pequeño mundo del hombre*, and gives voice to the role of allegory as both concealment and preservation of mystical truths.[38] Mythopoeia is understood to "preserve truth from temporal change through fixed versification."[39] Love is a unifying agent between the intellect, the world-soul, and the terrestrial world (sun, moon, earth), which is figured through the human as intellect-soul-body.[40] The lengthy third dialogue treats erotic ecstasy or alienation, debates on the soul and intellect, the interplay of imagination and intellect in philosophical understanding, cognition of the form of Beauty, the cosmic androgyny of god (origin of Intellect and Wisdom), the production of love by Beauty and Knowledge, the particular aim of love as the enjoyment of the Beautiful, and the universal end of love to make the beloved more perfect.[41] All three of the dialogues drew upon Empedocles, Anaxagoras, Pythagoras, Plato, Plotinus, Aristotle, Porphyry, Spanish and Italian Kabbalah (ex. *The Zohar*), Averroes, Avicenna, Al-Farabi, Ibn-Gabirol, Maimonides, Boethius, Ficino, Pico della Mirandola, Francesco Cattani da Diacceto, and Yohanan Alemanno.[42] This vast syncretic approach, evident also in Pico della Mirandola's unfinished fragment *On Being and the One*, was key to Abravanel's text.

The third dialogue stages the love of Philo for Sophia in such a way that their discourse is enacted within the idyllic quasi-pastoral setting of the text. In this dialogue, Philo introduces Sophia to the concept of erotic ecstasy or alienation, which became crucial for the poets of pastoral literature – enamored shepherds frequently were thrown "fuera de si (outside of oneself)," an affect of which Lenio emphatically complains in his argument against love in Book IV of the *Galatea* (taken explicitly from Abravanel's *Dialoghi*).[43] This erotic ecstasy, which may be understood as a form of meditation, is the intense retreat of the intellect into a concentrated unity

[38] (Francisco Rico, *El pequeño mundo del hombre: varia fortuna de una idea en la cultura española*, Barcelona: Ediciones Destino, 2005, 22); (Cacho-Casal, *La esfera del ingenio*).

[39] (Abravanel, *Dialogues*, 2009, 74). [40] (Abravanel, *Dialogues*, 2009, 73–75).

[41] (Abravanel, *Dialogues*, 2009, 168). [42] (Abravanel, *Dialogues*, 2009, 25).

[43] "Y es tan mala el alegría de los amantes, que los saca fuera de sí mesmos, tornándolos descuidados y locos" (Cervantes, *Galatea*, 1961, vol. II, 49).

in the contemplation of the beloved such that the bodily senses go dormant. Philo first experiences and then elucidates this for Sophia. At the opening of the third dialogue, the intellectually eager and erotically aloof Sophia repeatedly calls to Philo, who is caught up in the very erotic ecstasy or alienation that he will soon explain to her. Once she jolts him back into his senses, he elucidates this experience:

> Since you would like me to tell you what you already know, I say that my mind, as it often is, was withdrawn in contemplation of the beauty formed in you, whose image is impressed upon it, and which is always desired. This caused me to take leave of my perception of what is outside me . . . Because if your radiant beauty had not entered through my eyes, it could not have perforated my perception and imagination as deeply as it did. It could not have penetrated my heart, or have thus chosen my mind for its eternal habitation, forming your image like a sculpture upon every part of it. The rays of the sun do not pass through the heavenly bodies and the elements beneath them to the earth more quickly than the effigy of your beauty passed into the centre of my heart and into the core of my mind . . . "Ecstasy," or we can name it "alienation," caused by loving meditation, which is more than half-death.[44]

Philo's reference not only to the two-dimensional image, but to the three-dimensional sculpture underscores Sophia's active position at the core of Philo's intellect. This ecstatic alienation of the senses into the intellectual realms was made possible only by way of contemplation of the beloved (*in te belleza*).[45] In pastoral literature, this made way for the lyrical formulation of the beloved as the *summa belleza* wherein the Platonic form of beauty was conflated with the *summum bonum*, the Good, and life-giving force.[46] This was at least partly owed to the fact that from Plato onward, the Good shared an eidetic relationship with Beauty.[47] In Diotima's ladder, as discussed by Socrates in the *Symposium*, the physical figure of the beloved as beautiful was only the first step in an ascent through all bodies and ideas to an ineffable form of absolute or pure beauty.[48] But for the poets of Pastoral Petrarchism, this ineffable form of absolute or pure beauty was an immanent and active force within the image of the beloved, specifically

[44] (Abravanel, *Dialogues*, 2009, 171). For Spanish: (Abravanel, *Diálogos*, 1993, 326–327). For the Italian: (Abravanel, *Dialoghi*, 1535, 98v).

[45] The differences with Descartes' "alienation" will have to be undertaken in another place.

[46] (Plotinus, *The Enneads*, ed. L.P. Gerson, trans. G. Boys-Stones et al., Cambridge University Press, 2018, 1.6 and 1.7, 92–107).

[47] (Plato, "Phaedrus," 254b, 531).

[48] (Plato, "Symposium," *Complete Works*, 457–505; 210a-212b, 492–494).

within the figuration of the beloved's gaze. The *summa belleza* of the beloved was not only a question of the beautiful face or figure (as found, for example, in the *blazon*), but also consistently referred to the gaze of the beloved; the "window to the soul" was a crossroads between the corporeal and incorporeal, between the natural world and *summum bonum*.[49] This rendering of love "at first sight," understood as the meeting of two gazes, was informed by Abravanel's discussion of the eyes as a diaphanous liminal organ at the crossroads of the metaphysical and the physical.[50] Philo continues:

> It can be seen that the organ of vision is more clear, spiritual and of greater artifice than those of the other organs. The eyes are unlike the other parts of the body; they are not flesh, rather [they are] brilliant, diaphanous and spiritual; they seem like stars and overtake in beauty the other parts of the body.[51]

While Abravanel's concept of erotic ecstasy or alienation renders the bodily senses dormant, it retains within pure intellection the sensory ground of the erotic event and the Otherness of the beloved within the concentrated unity of the intellect.[52] The experience is at once sensual, emotional, and intellectual. The eyes are the organ or sense that facilitate this process because, as Philo explains, they are a gateway that connects the corporeal and incorporeal worlds. In the erotic experience, the lovers' gazes become the nexus of two Heraclitan rivers. Sophia's beauty shines through her eyes and it is via the eyes that she pierces and penetrates Philo's core. This emphasis on the sight of the beloved's gaze also appeared in Gálvez de Montalvo's unedited sonnet of July 22, 1583, which the poet included in a letter to Ascanio Colonna.[53] The sextet glossed this penetration by way of the eyes:

49 "Natura naturata" and "natura naturans" *avant la lettre*.

50 "Il viso e solo il conoscimento di tutti i corpi, l'audito aiuta alla cognizione delle cose, non pigliandola da le medesime cose, come l'occhio, ma pigliandola d altro conoscente, mediate la lingua: la quale o l'ha conosciuta per il viso, overo inteso da quel che ha veduto: in modo che l'antecessore dell'audito, e il uso. & conmunemente l'orecchia suppone l'occhio, come origine principale a l'intellettuale cognitione, gli altri tre sensi sono tutti corporali, fatti piu presto per conoscimento, & uso delle cose necessarie alla sostentatione dell'animale, che per la cognitione intellettuale . . .. peroche per le cose corporee si conoscono l'incorporee: le quali l'anima piglia dall'audito, per informatione d'altrui: & dal viso, per propria cognitione de corpi . . .. Nissuno di questi dui visi, corporeale, & intellettuale, puo vedere senza luce che l'illumini: et il viso corporale, & oculare, non puo vedere senza la luce del sole, che illumina l'occhio, e l'oggetto sia d'aere, o d'acqua, o d'altro corpo trasparente, o diaphano . . .. // Il strumento, tu il vedi quanto e chiaro, piu spirituale, & artificiato che l'istrumenti delli altri sensi: che gli occhi non simigliano all'altre parti del corpo; non sono carnali, ma lucidi, diaphani, e spirituali: paiono stelle, & in bellezza tutte l'altre parti del corpo eccedono (Abravanel, *Dialoghi*, 1535, 103r and 105r); (Abravanel, *Dialogues*, 2009, 178–181).

51 (Abravanel, *Dialogues*, 2009, 181). For Spanish: (Abravanel, *Diálogos*, 1993, 343).

52 (Abravanel, *Dialogues*, 2009, 179).

53 (Ponce-Hegenauer, "A Novel Community"); (Marín Cepeda, *Cervantes y la corte*).

No son guiadas tus saetas de arte
que hieran menos al que mas se avise;
el que una vez entre tus hierros pise
no querra libertad en otra parte.
  No tendra envidia el que supiere amarte
al que en favor con las estrellas frise
ni son tus lazos soberana Nise
de los que el tiempo a desatares parte
  Llega a la vista de la vista al pecho
del pecho al corazón y dél al alma
pasa la fuerza de tus ojos tiernos
  Por quien las flechas hacen bien su hecho
de los hierros amor lleva la palma
y son los lazos justamente eternos.

Your arrows are not guided by art,
that hurt least the one who is most informed;
he who once stepped behind your bars
will not want liberty anywhere else.
  He who knows how to love you won't be envious of
he who, when favored, has grazed the stars,
nor are your ties, sovereign Nise,
of a kind that time unravels, parts.
  It arrives to the sight from the sight to the breast,
from the breast to the heart and from there to the soul,
the force of your tender eyes [gaze] passes;
  For whom the arrows do well their deed,
from the irons love raises the palm,
and the ties are justly/just now eternal.[54]

The movement of the beloved's gaze ("la *fuerza* de tus ojos tiernos") from the lover's eyes to his breast, from the breast to the heart, and from the heart to the soul lyricized the way in which the gaze (as inner form of beauty or *summa belleza*) took hold of the lover's interior as the "eternal abode" in Abravanel's philosophy: the active *force* at the unity of the intellect in erotic alienation. It is no accident that the poet rhymes "tiernos" (line 11), her *tender* eyes, with "eternos" (line 14), his *eternal* entanglement: "tiernos" become "eternos". If the 1981 untitled work of the American feminist and artist Barbara Kruger, declared, "[His] gaze hits the side of [her] face" (brackets mine), within Pastoral Petrarchism, Abravanel's philosophy determined that

[54] In the translation I have retained the double meaning for "justo" both for its temporal placement as "just now" (the poem as speech act) and for the quality of being "fair" or "just". (BSS, "Gálvez de Montalvo to Ascanio Colonna," 22 July. II.C.F.1583); (Ponce-Hegenauer, "A Novel Community"); (Marín Cepeda, *Cervantes y la corte*).

her gaze hit the center of *his* soul. Beauty was in the eyes of the beholder, but it was also in the eyes of the beheld. As the form that, according to Plato's *Phaedrus*, "shines through" to the sensible world, the supersensible beauty contained in the beloved's gaze penetrated the lovers' intellect in the ecstatic erotic event of bodily alienation. It was within this conception of "love at first sight" that AQ was able to retain his *giovanile errore* for Aldonza Lorenzo well into his geriatric vision of them as dQ and Dulcinea.[55]

In the poetry of Pastoral Petrarchism, from Garcilaso's *mi alma os a cortado a su medida* onward, poets versed in Abravanel's philosophy typically used the word *alma* (soul) to describe the nature and stakes of this erotic experience. *Alma* involved the *ingenio* and *entendimiento* of the lover in Abravanel's process of erotic intellection as a spiritual event. Because the *entendimiento*, the *memoria*, and the *voluntad* together formed the tripartite structure of the soul, the affect of the beloved's gaze engaged the intellectual as the spiritual. When Philo referred to the interior effigy of the beloved as a penetration of the sight *nel centro del cuore, e nel cuor della menta*, he made Sophia not only the heart of his world but also the world of his intellect. While this erotic alienation of the bodily senses in the intellection of the beauty of the beloved could be confused with the Cartesian evacuation of the experiential world, Abravanel's erotic philosophy retained the physical otherness of the beloved as a sensory ground at the core of intellectual unity, and thus prohibited a divorce between the intellectual and the perceptual, the soul and the body, the transcendent and the immanent. In Descartes, the spiritual facet of the mind was reserved for a single monotheistic god and divorced from sensory experience. Like Sophia, dQ's transformation of Aldonza Lorenzo into Dulcinea del Toboso was figured as the *lady of his thoughts*.[56] It merits clarification that this imprint of the beloved in the lover was not a biographical identity but a formal unity in the shape of beauty.

The result of this divinization of the beloved Other, at the core of the lover's intellect, became the ground for the production of a heterodox poetry of *erotic mysticism* (Menéndez Pelayo) which reimagined Abravanel's erotic cosmology within lyric formulations of a literary Arcadia.[57] The heterodox passions explored by Garcilaso de la Vega and Jorge de Montemayor produced a radical poetic conceit in the shepherd-poets of the 1560s, 1570s, and 1580s in which the beauty of the mortal beloved lady became the divine *summa*

[55] (Ponce-Hegenauer, "La muerte de Aldonza Lorenzo").
[56] (A. Baras Escolá, "Una lectura erótica del *Quijote*," *Cervantes*, 12.2, 1992, 79–89).
[57] (Menéndez Pelayo, *Historia de las ideas estéticas*, II).

belleza and sovereign of the poet's soul. The shepherd-poets of Spain took seriously the myth of the pastoral and the formal reality invoked in Abravanel's erotic cosmology, such that the Arcadian "communion of the pure" opened directly onto the revelation of love as the eternal knot of the universe.[58] This poetry replaced the traditional monotheistic godhead with the allegorical figure of Love and, at times, with the divinized figure of the beloved lady herself. Where the *poesía a lo divino* or *contrafactum* had "translated" secular language into religious expression, the poetry of Pastoral Petrarchism transposed, reworked, and reinvented mystical discourse as an erotic theology. Cervantes himself depicted this thematic with the lyric verses of the many shepherd-poet lovers of the *Galatea*, as in the case of Lauso.[59] Through the appropriation of political and religious discourse for erotic poetry, the *figura of the poet* and the beloved encoded the divine or sempiternal aspects of human experience within the idyllic *locus amoenus.* While these linguistic structures were already evident in the Spanish Petrarchism of the Habsburg court in the 1560s, and in Cervantes' earliest poetry for Isabel de Valois, Cervantes explicitly engaged these conceptual and linguistic registers in his 1579 octaves for Antonio Veneziano's "*canzoniere*," the *Celia.*

When Cervantes, "the poet," departed Madrid for the *caput mundi*, he joined a tradition of journeys to Rome common to European writers of his day, and for several centuries thereafter.[60] According to Frederick de Armas' account, it was during this Roman period that Cervantes first encountered the Vatican frescos of Giulio Romano (*Sala di Constantino*) and Raphael (*Stanze della Segnatura*), which later inspired the ekphrastic content of Cervantes' early play, the *Numancia*, composed either in Algiers (1575–1580) or shortly after his return to Madrid.[61] Cervantes' own Roman

58 "... la lírica amorosa fue adquiriendo un cierto tono y significado spiritual y trascendente que en un principio le era ajeno, lo que desembocó en los *contrafacta*, las versiones *a lo divino* de la literatura profana" (Reyes Cano in Abravanel, *Diálogos*, 1993, 57). In Sánchez de Lima's *Arte poética* of 1585, the dialogue on poetic practice takes place between shepherds. Wind's *Pagan Mysteries* is still the source on erotic love and cultural practice.

59 See Chapter 6.

60 "Italian sojourns were almost *de rigueur* for Spanish poets ... Cervantes' voyage, then, resembled the ones of Acuña, Aldana, the brothers Argensola, Cetina, Figueroa, Garcilaso, Hurtado de Mendoza, Medrano, Santillana, and Villamediana. Such voyages were facilitated by the fact that the kingdom of Naples was part of the Spanish empire, while other regions of the peninsula were under Habsburg influence" (F. de Armas, "Cervantes and the Italian Renaissance," in ed. A.J. Cascardi, *Cambridge Companion to Cervantes*, Cambridge University Press, 2002, 32-57; 32). See also: (F. de Armas, *Cervantes, Raphael, and the Classics*, Cambridge University Press, 1998) and (F. de Armas, *Quixotic Frescos: Cervantes and Italian Renaissance Art*, University of Toronto Press, 2006).

61 For the Italian source of the *Numancia*, Trissino's *Sofonisba*: (G. Ponce-Hegenaur, "'Trissinian Tragedy', Cervantes and *La Numancia*: Anonymous Traditions and Canonized Authors," *MLN*, 2011, 126.4, 709–737).

reminiscences in the prologue to the *Galatea*, particularly his service to Giulio Acquaviva, who was himself a chamberman of Pius V, place him squarely within this Vatican milieu.[62] While no writing by Cervantes from the Roman period has survived, much of the cultural and literary practices that he found there reinforced his early experience as a poet in the Madrileño court. For most of the sixteenth century, literary culture in Rome had been determined by the tastes and preferences of the many Medici, Carafa, and Farnese popes, cardinals, lesser clergy, and visiting noblemen.[63] Despite the reforms of Pius V (Antonio Ghislieri 1504–1572, pope 1566–1572), who sacked the Vatican court jester and outlawed prostitution, the tradition of Renaissance gardens and villas as the *locus amoenus* of pastoral culture became increasingly popular among the Roman elite, who wielded significant power within the walls of the Vatican but also sought relief from the strict environs of Pius V. Two paradigmatic indications of the state of Pastoral Petrarchism in mid-sixteenth-century Rome were Mutio Manfredi's collection of various poets and their ladies, *Alle Donne Romane* (1565), and Vicenzo Orsini's *Boschetto* at Bomarzo. Manfredi's *Alle Donne Romane* brought together the work of contemporary poets within the virtual *locus amoenus* of a printed collection of poetry. Orsini's "little wood" reimagined erotic Renaissance texts (Ovid, Petrarch, Ariosto) through statuary and tablature within the wooded countryside below the Orsini palace at Bomarzo (about 100 kilometers, or two days' travel, from Rome). This is not to mention the hundreds, if not thousands, of local and foreign poets, musicians, artists, intellectuals, and minor nobles who made possible the cultivation of aristocratic life at the Palazzo Colonna, the Villa Farnese, and several other palaces and gardens.[64] Cervantes' own position as *camarero* to Giuilio Acquaviva,

62 (De Armas, Frederick, *Cervantes, Raphael, and the Classics*, Cambridge University Press, 1998, esp. Chapters 2–4).

63 (L. Pastor, *History of the Popes: From the Close of the Middle Ages: Drawn From the Secret Archives of the Vatican and Other Original Sources*, London: K. Paul, Trench, Trübner & Co., 1899, vol. XVII, 70–71, 86); (F. de Cervantes, "Cervantes in Italy: Christian Humanism and the Visual Impact of Renaissance Rome," *Journal of the History of Ideas*, 66.3, 2005, 325–350; 327 and 330).

64 Cardinal Alessandro Farnese, brother-in-law to Vicino Orsini, was one of the most powerful figures in Counter-Reformation Papal Politics. His patronage of the arts was evident in his gardens at Caprarola (Villa Farnese) and on the Palatine Hill: "Il recinto degli Orti va ricollegato insieme a tipologie antiche e alla nuova concezione dell'*hortus conclusus* come giardino pensile, quale viene attuata dal Vignola nei due «giardini segreti» di Caprarola. I due più modelli di recinto antico appaiono il *Castrum Praetorium* (che verrà nel '600 adattato a Vigna) e le Terme di Diocleziano che proprio intorno al 1560 erano state riconsacrate nello spazio interno (S. Maria degli Angeli) e ri-usate nel perimetro esterno (*Horti Bellaiani*). Bisogna poi ricordare gli altri recinti delle Terme di Constantino sul Quirinale (dove sorgerà il palazzo-giardino dei Borghese, poi Pallavicini-Rospigliosi), delle terme di Tito sull'Esquilino (rappresentate nella pianta del Bufalini in forme in qualche modo analoghe ai progetti per Villa

a well-known young man of letters and a patron of literary culture, placed the young poet squarely within the political, literary, and pastoral settings of Rome.[65] He would have been immersed in the world of sixteenth-century Petrarchism that flourished throughout the Italian peninsula in the years leading up to Aristotelian controversies over Ariosto's *Orlando Furioso* (ca. 1516) and Tasso's *Gerusalemme liberata* (1581).[66]

Within these circles of influence, the unification of the Vatican, Venice, and Spain in the "Holy League" likely inspired Cervantes' decision to become a solider-poet in the style of Garcilaso. In 1571 he traveled south in order to take up arms, and fought under Don Juan de Austria, Marco Antonio Colonna, and Andrea Doria at the Battle of Lepanto.[67] His close friend and fellow author, Juan Rufo Gutiérrez, to whom Cervantes would devote a laudatory sonnet for Rufo's *Seiscientos apotegmas* (1594), traveled as the *cronista* of Don Juan de Austria during the Battle at Lepanto.[68] Cervantes' lyric mentor, Pedro Laínez, was also under Don Juan's protection.[69] The

Madama) e delle Terme di Caracalla (da cui provenivano alcuni capolavori della collezione farnesiana; queste terme costituirono inoltre un modello spaziale per Villa d'Este a Tivoli" (M. Fagiolo, 'Arche-Tipologia Degli Orti Farnesiani' in ed. G. Morganti, *Gli Orti Farnesiani Sul Palatino*, Rome: École Française de Rome, Sopraintendenza Archeologica di Roma, 1990, 246).

"Cardinal Alessandro regarded Caprarola as his own and the dynasty's shop window ... the most important figure in the Counter Reformation, Carlo Borromeo, who during his visit ironically asked whether paradise could be fitted out as splendidly as Caprarola's villa and park" (H. Gamrath, *Farnese Pomp, Power and Politics in Renaissance Italy*, Rome: 'L'Erma' di Bretschneider, 2007, 175). Also: (Clare Robertson, *Il Gran Cardinale: Alessandro Farnese, Patron of the Arts*, Yale University Press, 1992).

65 Since the sack of Rome by the troops of Charles V on May, 1527, the *caput mundi* was fully threaded with Spanish power. "Together with these functionaries in the papal bureaucracy, were the numerous Spanish *camereros*, or stewards, who served in the papal palace in the 1560s and 1570s. Francisco de Reynoso, Diego Jorge, a cleric from Seville, Sylvestro de Guzman, and Don Gaspar de la Concha all appear in the records in this capacity. Another Spaniard, Francisco de Soto, held the positions of cantor and chaplain for the papal chapel in the 1560s" (T.J. Dandelet, *Spanish Rome, 1500-1700*, Yale University Press, 2001, 145). Habsburg possessions in Milan, Naples, and Sicily brought a large portion of Italy under Spanish control. For Spain and Italy: (M.J. Levin, *Agents of Empire: Spanish Ambassadors in Sixteenth-century Italy*, Cornell University Press, 2005); (J.L. Colomer, *España y Nápoles: Coleccionismo y Mezenazgo Virreinalles en el siglo XVII*, Madrid: Centro de Estudios Europa Hispánica, 2009); (J. Martínez-Millán, M. Rivero Rodríguez, C. Alvarez Nogal, eds., *Centros de poder italianos en la monarquía hispánica (siglos XV-XVIII)*, Madrid: Polifemo Ediciones, 2010); (B. Croce, *La Spagna Nella Vita Italiana Durante La Rinascenza*, 2nd ed., Bari: Laterza, 1922).

66 Contact with the Aristotelian translations, commentaries, and debates over Epic and Romance in the *Orlando Furioso* and *Gerusalmme liberata* in Rome is indubitable. (E.C. Riley, *Cervantes's Theory of the Novel*, [1st ed. Oxford University Press, 1962], Newark: Juan de la Cuesta, 1992, 57–67); (Forcione, *Cervantes, Aristotle and the Persiles*); (S. Zatti, A.R. Ascoli, S. Hill, *The Quest for Epic: From Ariosto to Tasso*, ed. D. Looney, University of Toronto Press, 2006); (B. Weinberg, *A History of Literary Criticism in the Italian Renaissance*, University of Chicago Press, 1963, vol. II).

67 (Wright, Spense, Lemons, eds., *The Battle of Lepanto*).

68 (Astrana Marín, *Vida ejemplar*, vol. II, 296). Rufo returned to Spain following the victory in October 1571. Rufo was also the author of the *aprobación* for Trenado de Ayllón's translation and commentary of Petrarch (ca. 1595), discussed in Chapter 3.

69 (Astrana Marín, *Vida ejemplar*, vol. II, 299).

poets Gabriel López Maldonado, Andrés Rey de Artieda, and Cristóbal Virués were among the numerous soldier-poets present at the Habsburg victory.[70] This entourage of Castilian poets circumscribed around the young and illegitimate Habsburg prince, Don Juan de Austria, would come together again in Madrid for the cultivation of the "urban-pastoral" during the 1580s. Many appeared as shepherd-poets under pastoral pseudonyms in Cervantes' *Galatea* (1585). Wounded during the Battle of Lepanto, Cervantes convalesced at the hospital in Messina, where festivities commemorating the battle were celebrated on October 31, 1571, and where he remained until at least March 9, 1572, according to payment records for the injured soldiers.[71]

For the next four years he served as a solider-poet in campaigns throughout the Mediterranean, passing through Navarino, Tunis, la Goleta, and Corfu. He spent time in military ports in Messina, Palermo, Naples, and Sardinia before his attempted return to Spain from Naples in September 1575.[72] The poets Luis Barahona de Soto and Andrés Rey de Artieda were with him at la Goleta. He was favored by two significant literary patrons during his military campaigns: Don Juan de Austria and the third Duke of Sessa, Gonzalo Fernández de Córdoba (a longtime patron of the Cervantes family and of Juan Latino, a poet and active participant in the literary salons of Italy).[73] Both men provided the young soldier-poet and hero of Lope de Figueroa's *tercio de la sacra lega* with numerous special payments and letters of commendation.[74] In the *Capítulo VIII* of the *Viaje del Parnaso* (1614), Cervantes recalled his early time in Naples, but none of his lyric verse survives from this time.[75] He definitively returned to Naples on February 14, 1574, where he remained, with the exception of a stay in Genoa, until his departure for the Madrileño court on *El Sol* on September 20, 1575 as a decorated soldier-poet.[76] On September 26, 1575, he was captured, along

[70] (Astrana Marín, *Vida ejemplar*, vol. II, 297–299).

[71] (Astrana Marín, *Vida ejemplar*, vol. II, 396).

[72] (Astrana Marín, *Vida ejemplar*, vol. II, 383). He wintered in Sardinia, and then served the Duke of Sessa at la Goleta and Marco Antonio Colonna in subsequent campaigns.

[73] (S. Bargali, ed., *Delle lodi dell'Academie, orazione di Scipione Bargagli da lui recitata nell'Accademia degli Accesi in Siena, All'Illustrissimo Signore Scipione Gonzaga principe*, Florence, 1569).

[74] (Astrana Marín, *Vida ejemplar*, vol. II, ch. 23).

[75] (Cervantes, *Poesías*, 2016, 387–392); (Astrana Marín, *Vida ejemplar*, vol. II, 409–429). We may speculate that some of his Neapolitan poetry found its way into the interpolated tale of the *dos amigos*, Timbrio and Silerio, in the *Galatea*. On the "dos amigos": (J.B. Avalle-Arce, "El cuento de los dos amigos. Cervantes y la tradición literaria," *Nueva Revista de Filología Hispánica*, 11, 1957, 1–35). A large portion of books, manuscripts, and archives in Naples were incinerated or destroyed during the heavy bombing of the city from 1940 to 1943; much of the sixteenth-century historical and cultural record was lost at this time. Not only early works by Cervantes but perhaps also documents related to Maria de Zayas may have disappeared as a result of this destruction.

[76] (Astrana Marín, *Vida ejemplar*, vol. II, 409).

with his brother, by Arnaut Mamí (who appeared in his later fiction), and sold into captivity in Algiers.[77]

The *Topografía de Argel*, written by Antonio de Sosa and posthumously published as a text by Diego de Haedo (Valladolid: 1612), reconstructed life in Algiers in the 1570s from the perspective of a European captive.[78] Sosa recalled Cervantes by name and described his repeated escape attempts, highlighting his noble valor before the Algerian king, who bestowed unusual favor on the young soldier-poet and stayed his execution even after his fourth escape attempt. Along with Ruffino di Chiambery and Antonio Veneziano, Antonio de Sosa formed part of a multilingual, intercultural, and transnational sphere of *ingenios* with whom Cervantes wrote whilst captive in Algiers. The Algerian *lingua franca*, for example, appears in the *Trato de Argel*.[79] In contrast to the absence of any surviving literary compositions dating to the author's Italian period, several works survive from his time in captivity. As Carroll B. Johnson has observed, "the five-year Algerian experience was arguably the most important in the writer's life."[80] Two laudatory sonnets for Ruffino di Chiambery, a letter and poem in *octavas* for Antonio Veneziano, and the *Epístola a Mateo Vázquez* were all written in Algiers.[81] Cervantes' earliest drama, the *Trato de Argel*, was composed either while in captivity or soon after his return to Madrid, when

77 See: the tale of Timbrio and Salerio in the *Galatea*, the *Amante liberal*, the "Captive's Tale" and the story of Ana Félix in the *DQ* for Cervantes' fictional reworkings. (Astrana Marín, *Vida ejemplar*, vol. II, 453–454).

78 (A. de Sosa, *An Early Modern Dialogue with Islam: Antonio de Sosa's Topography of Algiers*, ed. M. A. Garcés, trans. D. de Armas Wilson, University Notre Dame Press, 2011).

79 (M.A. Garcés, *Cervantes in Algiers: A Captive's Tale*, Vanderbilt University Press, 2002, 105), and (M.A. Garcés, *Cervantes en Argel, Historia de un cautivo*, Madrid: Gredos, 2005); (N. Martínez de Castilla and R.G. Benumeya Brimau, *De Cervantes y el Islam*, Madrid: Ministerio de Cultura, 2006), in particular Ahmed Abi-Ayad's article in the same volume, "Argel: la otra cara de Miguel de Cervantes" (59–69).

80 (Johnson, *Transliterating a Culture*, 2010, 287). Johnson does not discuss Cervantes' lyric work. He focuses on the *Información de Argel*, Antonio de Sosa's section on *Diálogo de los mártires de Argel*, and the "Captive's Tale" of the *DQ*. In *Cervantes in Algiers*, María Antonia Garcés briefly comments on the friendship which Cervantes cultivated with Antonio Veneziano whilst in Algiers. The Sicilian poet appears in her study three times: (1) a brief mention of Cervantes' octaves; (2) discussion of the various circles Cervantes encountered in Algiers; and (3) a second cursory mention of Cervantes' composition of poetry whilst in Algiers (2002, 67, 105, and 127). On Cervantes' octaves for Veneziano, Garcés writes: "Accordingly, in spite of his heavy chains and of 'the many fancies wearying' him, Cervantes contrived to write two [sic] glum *octavas* in response to Veneziano's long poem singing his love for "Celia" (2002, 67).

81 (Gonzálo, *La epístola a Mateo Vázquez*, 2010); (R. Pina Piras, *La Información en Argel de Miguel de Cervantes: Entre Ficción y Documento*, Universidad de Alcalá, 2014): (Johnson, *Transliterating a Culture*, 285–307). (E. Mele, "Miguel de Cervantes y Antonio Veneziano," *Revista de archivos, bibliotecas y museos*, n.29, 1913, 82–90); (A. Veneziano, *Libro delle rime siciliane*, ed. G.M. Rinaldi, Palermo: Centro di studi filologici e linguistici siciliani, 2012).

he began writing for the *corrales* around 1582. The *Información de Argel* is also an important legal document dating to this phase of the author's life.[82]

Cervantes' poetry from his Algerian captivity reveals a young poet engaged with the complex lyric discourse of his literary moment. His two 1577 sonnets for Bartolomeo Ruffino di Chiambery appeared in a manuscript intended for another noblewoman and patron associated with Cervantes' early poetry, Marguerite de Valois, Duchess of Savoy (1523–1574), aunt of Isabel de Valois, dedicatee of the *Rime degli Academici Eterei* (Venezia: da Comin da Trino, 1567), and the original intended of Philip II. Ruffino di Chiambery's manuscript, *Sopra la desolazione della Goleta e Forte de Tunisi*, was dedicated to Emmanuel Philibert, Duke of Savoy, her husband. Cervantes' two laudatory sonnets can be dated to between his capture on September 26, 1575 and the dedication of the work on February 3, 1577.[83] Within the trans-imperial literary culture in Algiers, they demonstrate Cervantes' understanding of the *ingenio* as a divine creative and sempiternal poetic faculty, and his use of the word as a synonym for the author:

> pues, libre de cadenas vuestra mano,
> reposando el ingenio, a la alta cumbre
> os podéis levantar seguramente
>
> (well, your hand free of chains,
> [your] *ingenio* in repose, to the high peak
> you can raise yourself, without a doubt)[84]

and

> ¡Felice ingenio, venturosa mano,
> que, entre pesados yerros apretado,
> tal arte y tal virtud en sí contiene!
>
> (Happy *ingenio*, fortunate hand,
> that, clenched among heavy irons,[85]
> such art and such virtue are contained within![86]

[82] (M. de Cervantes, *Información de Argel*, ed. A.J. Sáez, Madrid: Cátedra, 2019).

[83] (Astrana Marín, *Vida ejemplar*, vol. II, 453, 528). [84] (Cervantes, *Poesías*, 2016, 149).

[85] I have taken "yerro" to be a homonym for "hierro". The line refers to the author's captivity.

[86] (Cervantes, *Poesías*, 2016, 151). Cervantes' use of "mano" with "ingenio" in both sonnets underscores the correlation between the creative faculty and the physicality of the authorial act. As El Saffar observes of the narrators of the *DQ*, "The problem is that Cide Hamete represents a preoccupation on Cervantes' part not so much with the limitations of narrative perspectives as with the problem of an author who must exist on two different temporal planes: that of his actual physical existence, and that of his projected, imagined story" (El Saffar, *Distance and Control*, 19).

The same correlation is evident in the work of Focillon: "Watch your hands as they live their own free life. Forget for a moment their function, forget their mystery. Watch them in repose; the fingers

The speaker likens Bartolomeo's authorial toils to a shackled hand, a fitting metaphor considering that both were captive at that time, and assures Bartolomeo that with his hand freed, his *ingenio* will soon enjoy a state of repose, presumably on the heights of Parnassus. The House of Savoy was not the only source of patronage invoked during Cervantes' time in Algiers. His *Epístola a Mateo Vázquez* solicited the protection of one of Philip's most powerful ministers, Secretary of State Mateo Vázquez de Leca, whom Cervantes may have known since his time at grammar school.[87] While this verse epistle did not secure for Cervantes the royal ransom and protection for which he hoped, the poet did rewrite the *Epístola* and insert it as the *Canción de Lauso* in the *Galatea* (1585) upon his return to Spain.[88]

Aside from any number of lost works, the most significant literary work to have survived the Algerian captivity was Cervantes' poem in *octavas* for the Sicilian poet Antonio Veneziano.[89] A near contemporary in age to Cervantes, Veneziano was born in Monreale on January 7, 1543. He spent most of his adult life as the poet laureate of the city of Palermo, until his untimely death in 1593 in a fire in the fortress of Castellammare, where he was being held prisoner as the alleged author of a poster pasted in the Piaza degli Bologni that denounced the Spanish viceroy, Don Diego Enrique de Guzmán, Count of Alba de Liste.[90] As a boy he had been educated by Jesuits in Palermo and then sent to Rome to study in the *Collegio Romano* under Francisco de Toledo. He abandoned religious pursuits and returned to Palermo, where his literary talents were recognized while he was working

are lightly drawn in, as if the hands were absorbed in a reverie. Watch them in the sprightly elegance of pure and useless gestures, when it seems that they are describing numberless possibilities gratuitously in the air, and, playing with one another, preparing for some happy event to come. Although they can imitate the silhouettes and the behavior of animals by casting their shadow on a wall by candlelight, they are much more beautiful when they imitate nothing at all. Sometimes, left to themselves when the mind is active, they move ever so faintly. On an impulse they stir the air, or they stretch their tendons and crack their knuckles, or else they close tightly to form a compact mass which is truly a rock of bone. Sometimes it happens that, first raised, then lowered, one after the other in invented rhythms, the fingers trace, nimble as dancers, choreographic bouquets" (H. Focillon, *The Life of Forms in Art*, trans. C. Beecher Hogan and G. Kubler, 2nd ed., New York: George Wittenborn, 1963, 66).

87 (Astrana Marín, Vida ejemplar, vol. II, 532) (Gonzalo, *La epístola a Mateo Vázquez*, 2010, esp. 188–201).

88 Lauso was Cervantes' own pastoral pseudonym. The author seems to have acknowledged this explicit surfacing of autobiography beneath the pastoral veil by having Lauso's friend, Damón (a pseudonym for Pedro Laínez), deliver the *Canción de Lauso* in the shepherd's absence. See Chapters 5 and 6.

89 (A. Veneziano, *Ottave*, ed. A. Rigoli, Turin: Einaudi, 1967); (G. Pitré, "Antonio Veneziano nella leggenda populare siciliano," *Archivo Storico Siciliano*, XIX, 1894, 3–11); (M.C. Ruta, "Le ottave di Cervantes per Antonio Veneziano e Celia," *Bolletino del Centro di Studi filologici e linguistici siciliani*, 1979, vol. XVI, 171–185); (G. Millunzi, "Antonio Veneziano," XIX, 1894, 18–198); (ed. Marco, *Antonio Veneziano*, 2000).

90 (Mele, "Miguel de Cervantes," 83); (Veneziano, *Ottave*, 1967, 25–27).

as an *escribano*. He was commissioned for various municipal celebrations which would have had similar stylistic qualities to those that took place at the court of Isabel de Valois.[91] He designed and authored triumphal arches with epitaphs, *motes*, verses, and paintings, frequently allegorical and highly symbolic; much of this ephemera has been lost.[92]

As poet laureate of Palermo, Veneziano wrote in the Sicilian language at a time when Italian authors still vied for primacy of dialect as part of the *questione della lengua*. Bembo's project for the Toscano of the *tre corone* (Dante, Petrarch, and Boccaccio) would not fully come to fruition until the late nineteenth-century unification of Italy.[93] Along with the Provençal of the troubadour poets, Sicilian was regarded as a sophisticated and ancient poetic language, one which staked a claim to the invention of the sonnet. In combination with the fifteenth-century court of Alfonso in Naples, the twelfth-century *scuola siciliana* held primacy of place in the lyric traditions of the Habsburg territories.[94] In 1543 the Syracusan historian and poet employed by Charles V from 1525 to 1532, Claudio Mario Arezzo, in his *Osservanti di la lingua siciliana et canzoni in lo proprio idioma* (Messina: Pietruccio Spira, 1543), drew attention to the fact that Dante, and to a larger extent Petrarch, had credited the *scuola siciliana* as foundational to Tuscan poetic practices.[95] Thus, the curious case of Petrarchism in early modern Sicily constituted a double *imitatio* that returned the lyrics of the Tuscan poet to their Sicilian predecessors, and reinvented the sixteenth-century continental phenomenon of Petrarchism through Sicilian popular, folk, and oral traditions.[96] This was not unlike the revival

91 (A. Veneziano, *Pantheon Ambiguo: La Fontana Pretoria Di Palermo Nell'analisi Formale e Nel Commento di Antonio Veneziano e Francesco Baronio Manfredi*, eds. G. La Monica and S. Iannone, Palermo: Flaccovio, 1987).

92 "El recibió el encargo de escribir epígrafes para los hombres ilustres y los hechos memorables de la ciudad, y el de erigir los arcos triunfales que, ornados de festones, pinturas, versos y motes, se levantaban para honrar la entrada de algún personaje de gran importancia. Poco de esto imprimió y mucho permanece inédito: entre lo más interesante figura el arco descrito en 1588 a favor de Ludovico de Torres, Segundo Arzobispo de Monreal de este nombre; notable el que se levantó á la entrada de Mons. D. Diego Haedo, Arzobispo de Palermo, escrito en lengua española y versos latinos, por él mismo traducidos en versos españoles" (Mele, "Miguel de Cervantes," 84). It is possible that Veneziano carried Antonio de Sosa's manuscript of the *Topografía de Argel* to Sicily, where it would later be discovered and published under the name of Diego de Haedo: (Sosa, *An Early Modern Dialogue*).

93 Well into the twentieth century, poets such as Ignazio Buttitta (1899–1997) continue to write in Sicilian.

94 (G. Sajeva, *La Lingua Siciliana Nella Poesia*, Palermo: Boccone del povero, 1924, vol. II).

95 See Chapter 3; "Dila inuention di Rimi," in (C.M. di Arezzo, *Osservantii dila lingua siciliana, et canzoni in lo proprio idioma*, Messina: Ad Instantia di Paulo Siminara, 1543, 5r–5v).

96 (Vento, *Petrarchismo y concettismo*). For the Arabic tradition in the Sicilian lyric: (Ponce-Hegenaur, "Lyric and Empire"); (K. Mallette, *European Modernity and the Arab Mediterranean: Toward a New Philology and a Counter-Orientalism*, University of Pennsylvania Press, 2010); (K. Mallette, *The Kingdom of Sicily, 1100-1250: A Literary History*, University of Pennsylvania Press, 2005); (Almarai, Blasone, Branca, and Capezio, eds., *Poesia araba*, 2015, 7–12).

of the popular romance tradition within the erudite poetics of Pastoral Petrarchism in 1580s Madrid.[97]

The primacy of Sicilian poetics in Renaissance Petrarchism was a tradition to which Veneziano laid claim in the 1581 dedication to Marco Antonio Colonna.[98] Voicing his argument in Sicilian, Veneziano wrote:

> Starria friscu Homeru chi fu grecu e scrissi grecu, Horaziu chi fu d'undi si parlava latinu e scrissi latinu, lu Petrarca chi fu tuscanu e scrissi tuscanu, s'a mia, chi su sicilianu, non mi convenissi componiri sicilianu.
>
> (Would I be a new Homer, who was Greek and wrote Greek; Horace, who was from where Latin was spoken and wrote Latin; Petrarch, who was Tuscan and wrote Tuscan, if it did not suit me – who am Sicilian – to compose in Sicilian.)[99]

Placing himself within this venerable tradition, Veneziano put particular emphasis on being the first to accomplish or perfect certain poetic feats in Sicilian. In a dedicatory letter to Francisco Lo Campo, Baron of Campofranco, Veneziano boasted, "iu sù lu primi chi nesciu a stu ringu di mandarin in luci canzuni siciliani (I was the first to give birth to Sicilian *canzuni*)."[100] This desire for primacy in one's own language was interwoven with the project that any *divino ingenio* undertook to immortalize his beloved lady, a primacy of literary invention that Cervantes explicitly claimed in the prologue to his *Novelas ejemplares* (1613).[101] Veneziano also opened up a cultural world of magic and mysteries, a Hermeticism commonly associated with Ficino's Platonic academy. While the necromancy practiced by the Numantinos in Cervantes' other early drama (the *Numancia*) has been a source of critical confusion and discomfort, Veneziano was known as a wizard, in the tradition of Vergil, Ovid, and Boccaccio.[102]

[97] For *romancero* culture in Madrid: (Carreño, *Romancero*, 28).

[98] Marco Antonio Colonna (1535–1584): Roman nobleman, general at Lepanto, Habsburg Viceroy of Sicily from 1577 to 1584, and father of Ascanio, to whom Cervantes dedicated the *Galatea*, just months after Marco Antonio's death (which Cervantes laments in the dedication).

[99] For modern edition: (Veneziano, *Rime*, 2012, 4) (Ponce-Hegenauer, "Trissinian Tragedy") on the problems of Renaissance canon formation. My sincere thanks to Professor Karla Mallette for her assistance with this translation.

[100] (Mele, "Miguel de Cervantes").

[101] Harry Sieber has observed this concept of the primacy of poiesis in the *Novelas ejemplares*: "Ejemplar en este sentido es lección literaria (o «estética», si se quiere) más bien que lección moral" (in M. de Cervantes, *Las novelas ejemplares*, ed. H. Sieber, Madrid: Cátedra, 2001, vol. I, 15).
Cervantes in his *prólogo* writes: "que yo soy el primero que he novelado en lengua castellana, que las muchas novelas que en ella andan impresas, todas son traducidas de lenguas estranjeras, y éstas son mías propias, no imitadas ni hurtadas; mi ingenio las engendró, y las parió mi pluma, y van creciendo en los brazos de la estampa" (*Las novelas ejemplares*, 2001, vol. I, 52).

[102] "como acontece con Virgilio en Nápoles, Ovidio en los Abruzos y Boccaccio en Certaldo, alcanzó la reputación de mago" (Mele, "Miguel de Cervantes," 82).

On 25 of April, 1579, Veneziano embarked from Palermo with Don Carlos de Aragón, Duke of Terranova, for the court in Madrid.[103] The sailing party was overtaken by eight Algerian corsair galleys. Don Carlos escaped, but Veneziano, who was traveling in the second galley, was taken prisoner and transported to Algiers.[104] It is curious to consider that both poets would have met amongst the literary environs of the court in Madrid had they both avoided capture during their passage from Italy to Spain. Veneziano's captivity, from late spring to early fall 1579, constituted a period of intense literary production. It was during his captivity that he composed the *Celia*, a *cancionero* of 289 *estrambote* (lyrics in "the old style"). The *estrambote* were octaves consisting of two hendecasyllabic quartets rhymed ABAB: ABAB. In his poetry, the confluence of Pastoral Petrarchism and Abravanel's erotic philosophy took the form of the divine beloved lady to metaphorical heights. Literally the "heaven," his *Celia* became the source of the poet's own spiritual captivity.[105] Cervantes' *octavas*, composed in the autumn of 1579 in response to and in the style of the *estrambote* of Veneziano's songbook, the *Celia*, proved him to be an insightful reader of Veneziano's corpus as well as a virtuoso of the lyric apostrophe. They survive by way of Veneziano's transcription of Cervantes' letter and verses, along with Veneziano's sonnet response, in his own autograph manuscript (ms. P10, Biblioteca centrale della Regione Siciliana, Palermo), which he began in Algiers and was still augmenting at the time of his incarceration and death in Palermo. Veneziano's creative power was sufficient to inspire the city of Palermo to use municipal funds to pay his ransom from Algiers.[106]

103 Veneziano was on his way to the Habsburg court and the very circles of poets Cervantes had left and to whom he would return, and with whom he would compose the *Galatea* in the first years of the 1580s. The Italian painter of the Habsburg court, the teacher and confidant of Isabel de Valois Sofonisba Anguissola, lost her husband to the same journey (M.W. Cole, *Sofonisba's Lesson: A Renaissance Artist and Her Work*, Princeton University Press, 2019, 134 and 146). Don Carlos escaped, Veneziano was captured, and her husband, Fabrizio Moncada, was drowned.

104 (Mele, "Miguel de Cervantes," 1913, 84–85) and (Veneziano, *Ottave*, 1967, 18–19).

105 "canzuni antichi [sic], como aún hoy llaman los sicilianos, según consta Pietré, sus octavas de dos cuartetos endecasílabos, de rimas alternas [ABAB: ABAB], en las que aparece el desarrollo psicológico de su amor, mostrando las angustias y tormentos de su ánimo y su agitada pasión con viveza expresiva y representación interna desusada y nueva" (Mele, "Miguel de Cervantes," 85).

106 "Verdadero poeta, Veneziano triunfó, y mostró tales facultades de fantasía y arte, que le levantaron sobre sus compañeros, hasta colocarlo junto a los más inspirados poetas italianos del siglo XVI; resulta original hasta cuando imitó al Petrarca, y le conocemos aun cuando se vale de imágenes petrarquescas, porque expresó afectos verdaderos y propios de su alma; rica efusión y sentimientos sinceros, su poesía derive con larga vena de motivos é inspiraciones de cantos populares, en los cuales, en compensación aún sobrevive un eco de sus cantos" (Mele, "Miguel de Cervantes," 85). Also: (Vento, *Petrarchismo y concettismo*).

Fig. 4.4 Antonio Veneziano, *Canzuni amurusi siciliani* (In Algeri, 1579), frontispiece. ms. XI.B.6, *Biblioteca centrale della Regione Siciliana "Alberto Bombace," Palermo Su concessione dell'Assessorato regionale dei Beni Culturali e dell'Identità Siciliana, Dipartimento Beni Culturali e dell'Identità Siciliana*

Veneziano's inclusion of Cervantes' *octavas* is evidence of Cervantes' status as a poet in the Habsburg territories prior to the publication of any of the prose works that have made him famous in modernity. Veneziano's preservation, curation, and engagement with the words of his lyric interlocutor and fellow captive calls into question several later judgments against Cervantes as a poet, including the poet's own self-deprecating remarks. Antecedent even to the dedication to Marco Antonio Colonna (Habsburg viceroy of Sicily 1577–1584), written in December 1581, the self-contained unit of the *Celia* formed by the title page, "libro primu," and correspondence with Cervantes can likely be dated to the Algerian captivity and ransom. The correspondence with Cervantes appears at the conclusion of this section. As Gaetana Maria Rinaldi has observed, the title page of the autograph manuscript and the "libro primu" (the *Celia*) were both almost certainly completed in Algiers.[107] Like Petrarch, Veneziano returned to, revised, altered, and augmented his body of vernacular poetry throughout the final decades of his life. The autograph manuscript and its copies were a lifetime achievement, abruptly concluded with Veneziano's untimely death. That Veneziano included Cervantes' octaves as a compendium to his explicitly autobiographical *Celia* indicates that Cervantes knew the work in Algiers and was esteemed a worthy interlocutor. When he composed the octaves of 1579, his lyric epistle was already bound up in the poetics that both authors shared. This is not only a powerful indication of the way poetic practice broke down boundaries (linguistic, geographical, imperial) throughout the sixteenth century, but also a powerful signal to contemporary scholars of the status of Cervantes as an internationally recognized poet more than two decades prior to the publication of the first part of the *DQ*.

Cervantes' *octavas* and accompanying letter to Veneziano were written following his fourth escape attempt from solitary confinement in the prison of Hasan Pachá.[108] Less than ten years after the court chronicler, López de Hoyos, had published Cervantes' early court poetry as the featured poet in the 1569 printing of the funeral exequies for Isabel de Valois, Cervantes must have been disappointed to see the city of Palermo ransom Veneziano while he received no aid from the court in Madrid. In the *Trato de Argel*, the character Saavedra voices complaints over the

[107] (Veneziano, *Libro delle rime*).

[108] (Garcés, *Cervantes en Argel*, 414); (Veneziano, *Ottave*, 1967, 19).

See: Antonio de Sosa's *Topografía de Argel* (published as authored by Diego de Haedo), printed in Valladolid in 1612, for contemporary accounts of Cervantes' escape attempts, and (Garcés, *Cervantes en Argel*, 413–414).

Habsburg failure to address the plight of Spanish captives in Algiers.[109] By 1579 Don Juan de Austria and Gonzalo Fernández de Córdoba, third Duke of Sessa, whose letters of commendation Cervantes had carried on *El Sol*, had died. His versified plea to the court, the *Epístola a Mateo Vázquez*, went unanswered. He gave up his first opportunity to return home so that his younger brother could go, and was not ransomed until 1580, a year after his octaves for Veneziano, and then by way of the intervention of his mother, Leonora, and the aid of Trinitarian friars. The rescue came just days before he was to be sent to the Ottoman capital, Constantinople, as a gift. He returned to Madrid undecorated and in debt for the heavy ransom, owing largely to the letters of commendation that he had carried from his two deceased patrons.

Veneziano's ransom, one year earlier than that of Cervantes, did not impede the lyric exchange that the two poets had begun in captivity. On the contrary, it provided the young Castilian poet with the opportunity to opine on the erotic poetics then practiced within Habsburg Sicily, a viceregal territory of the Spanish empire. While the two poets were close friends, Cervantes' letter that accompanied the octaves gestured toward a subservience or genuflection, which may in part have been formulaic, but which may also have been indicative of the hope for literary patronage in the form of a ransom from Veneziano's peers and patrons in Palermo.[110]

"Al señor Antonio Veneziani.
[octavas]
Señor mío:

Prometo a Vuestra Merced como cristiano, que son tantas las imaginaciones que me fatigan, que no me han dejado cumplir como quería, estos versos que Vuestra Merced envío, en señal del buen ánimo que tengo de servirle, pues él me ha movido a mostrar tan presto las faltas de mi ingenio, confiado que el subido de Vuestra Merced recibirá la disculpa que doy y me animará a que, en tiempo de más sosiego, no me olvide de celebrar, como pudiere, el *cielo* que a Vuestra Merced tiene tan sin contento en esta tierra, de la cual Dios nos saque y a Vuestra Merced llegue a aquella donde su *Celia* vive.

En Argel, los seis de noviembre 1579.
De Vuestra Merced verdadero amigo y servidor,
Miguel de Cervantes."

109 (M. de Cervantes, "Trato de Argel," in eds. L. Gómez Canseco, *Comedias y Tragedias*, vol. I, 909–1004).
110 (J. Trueba Lawand, *El arte epistolar en el renacimiento español*, Madrid: Tamesis, 1996).

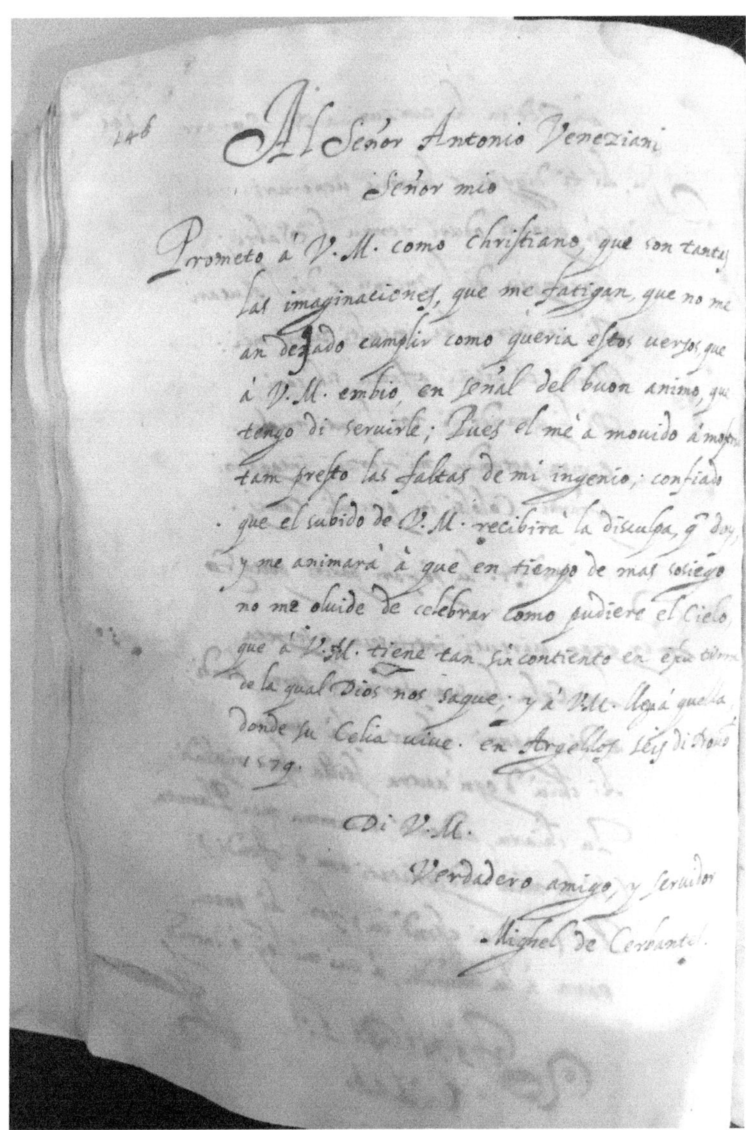

146 Al Señor Antonio Veneziani

Señor mio

Prometo à V.M. como christiano, que son tantas las imaginaciones, que me fatigan, que no me an dexado cumplir como queria estos versos, que à V.M. embio, en señal del buen animo, que tengo di seruirle; Pues el me à mouido à mostrar tam presto las faltas de mi ingenio; confiado que el subido de V.M. recibirà la disculpa, q̃ doy, y me animarà à que en tiempo de mas sosiego no me oluide de celebrar como pudiere el Cielo que à V.M. tiene tan sin contiento en esta tierra de la qual Dios nos saque; y à V.M. lleuà aquella donde su Celia viue. en Argel à seis di Nouie. 1579.

Di V.M.

Verdadero amigo, y seruidor

Miguel de Ceruantes.

Fig. 4.5 Antonio Veneziano, *Canzuni amurusi siciliani* (In Algeri, 1579), 146, ms. XI. B.6, *Biblioteca centrale della Regione Siciliana "Alberto Bombace," Palermo Su concessione dell'Assessorato regionale dei Beni Culturali e dell'Identità Siciliana, Dipartimento Beni Culturali e dell'Identità Siciliana*

("To the Sir Antonio Veneziani.
My sir:

I promise Your Grace as a Christian that I am fatigued by so many imagined things, that they have not permitted me to complete as I wanted the verses that I send to Your Grace, as a sign of the good intention that I have to serve you, well, it has moved me to show so soon the faults of my *ingenio*, confident that the heightened [*ingenio*] of Your Grace will accept the excuse that I give, and it will give me spirit in a time of greater peace when I will not forget to celebrate as I can the *cielo* that has Your Grace so discontented on this earth, and that God free us of that [captivity], and [make] Your Grace to arrive where your *Celia* lives.

In Algiers, the 6th of November 1579.
From Your Grace's true friend and servant,
Miguel de Cervantes.")[III]

The humility that Cervantes demonstrated by asserting the "faltas de mi ingenio" was formulaic by that time, and the use of "V.M.," or "Vuestra Merced," was in keeping with the usage between poets and patrons. Cervantes' promise of future compositions, "en tiempo de más sosiego," echoed the closing lines of his first laudatory sonnet for Bartolomeo Ruffino di Chiambery, also composed in Algiers in 1577 (cited above). While no ransom came of these octaves, Veneziano did transcribe both the poem and the accompanying letter for posterity in his own autograph manuscript, followed by his own original sonnet response, thus creating a critical dialogue at the conclusion of the *Celia*.

In his twelve-stanza poem, composed in *octavas* (*ottava rima*) and modeled on Veneziano's own Sicilian version of the octave (the *estrambote*), Cervantes drew upon the Petrarchan exaltations of the divine beloved and the power of the lyric apostrophe that he had developed in his earlier encomiastic poetry for Isabel de Valois. Veneziano's own *rime* had hyperbolized the trope of the divine beloved lady with the eponymous pseudonym of *Celia* for the object of his thoughts. In this eleven-octave response to Veneziano's *canzuni amurusi* for *Celia*, Cervantes played with the significance of *cielo*, not only in reference to the lady, but also through various religious and scientific valences. At times, *cielo* was a nirvana or paradise; at others, the physical heavens; at

[III] (Cervantes, *Poesías*, 2016, 152, italics mine).

others, the Aristotelian conception of *forma e materia* (evident in the work of Pomponazzi, Tasso, Bruno, etc.).[112] Because this conceptual play relied upon the understanding that *cielo* always meant more than one thing, whilst also always indicating Veneziano's beloved, *Celia*, in the translation that follows I have left both *cielo* and *Celia* untranslated so as to make their use easily identifiable to the reader in English. Abravanel's discussion of an erotic ecstasy or alienation in which the mind was concentrated on the sculpture of the beloved provided ample ground for Cervantes' description of Veneziano's poetic process.[113] Cervantes' use of *sempiterno* was also indicative of his knowledge of Italianate poetic vocabulary and corresponding conceits for the *figura of the poet* and the erotic event.[114]

But the *octavas* for Veneziano also represented a marked departure from the young soldier-poet's earlier work through a deliberate reformulation of the tropes and conceits of Pastoral Petrarchism into a controlled, decisive, and sage position of poetic authority on erotic comportment. In place of the tortured Petrarchan lover, Cervantes substituted the naked vulnerability of the vanquished genuflection. This move anticipated the hyperbolic spiritual love of dQ roughly twenty-five years later.[115] By ventriloquizing a direct address to *Celia* in the closing three octaves of his poem – what Veneziano *should* say – Cervantes rewrote the convention of amorous Petrarchan tropes which he had deployed throughout the poem in keeping with Veneziano's own erotic discourse. In place, Cervantes interposed the genuflection before the divine exalted lady of *their* thoughts. The resonance with Dante's *Divina Commedia* was evident, particularly in the use of Empyrean Heaven in the second stanza. Thus, Cervantes' interjection on Veneziano's behalf was not only an exchange between friends, but also an interjection into the most established conventions of erotic verse, a discourse which the two poets shared. By way of this lyrical intervention, Cervantes made a decided and unambiguous choice to favor genuflection and submission over struggle and complaint. Together, Cervantes' *octavas* and Veneziano's sonnet reply serve as interpretive devices for the 289 *estrambote* of the *Celia*, and the general topography of their shared poetic discourse. Because these verses are seldom read, are not widely available,

112 For example, "Burno afferma con Aristotele che «duplex enim est natura: forma et materia»," (V. Zaffino, "Giordano Bruno Lettore Della 'Fisica' di Aristotele," *Revista di Filosofia Neo-Scolastica*, 107.4, 2015, 853–866; 863 and esp. 856–858).

113 Note also the correlation between *mano* and *ingenio* in his sonnets for Chiambery.

114 See Chapter 3 for sempiternal temporality and the *figura of the poet*.

115 "Está ahí la sin par Dulcinea del Toboso, gloria de estas riberas, adorno de estos prados, sustento de la hermosura, nata de los donaires y, finalmente, sujeto sobre quien puede asentar bien toda alabanza, *por hipérbole que sea*," (Cervantes, DQ, 1991, II:73, 1213–1214, italics mine).

and to my knowledge, remain untranslated, I have included them here in their entirety for ease of access for Spanish and English speakers.

1
Si el lazo, el fuego, el dardo, el puro yelo
que os tiene, abrasa, hiere y pone fría
vuestra alma, trae su origen desde el cielo,
ya que os aprieta, enciende, mata, enfría,
¿qué nudo, llama, llaga, nieve o celo
ciñe, arde, traspasa o yela hoy día,
con tan alta ocasión como aquí muestro,
un tierno pecho, Antonio, como el vuestro?

2
El cielo, que el ingenio vuestro mira,
en cosas que son dél quiso emplearos
y, según lo que hacéis, vemos que aspira
por Celia al cielo empíreo levantaros;
ponéis en tal objeto vuestra mira
que dais materia al mundo de envidiaros:
¡dichoso el desdichado a quien se tiene
envidia de las ansias que sostiene!

3
En los conceptos que la pluma vuestra
de la alma en el papel ha trasladado
nos dais no solo indicio pero muestra
de que estáis en el cielo sepultado,
y allí os tiene de amor la fuerte diestra
vivo en la muerte, a vida reservado,
que no puede morir quien no es del suelo,
teniendo el alma en Celia, que es un cielo.

4
Solo me admira el ver que aquel divino
cielo de Celia encierre un vivo infierno
y que la fuerza de su fuerza y sino
os tenga en pena y llanto sempiterno;
al cielo encamináis vuestro camino,
mas, según vuestra suerte, yo dicierno
que al cielo sube el alma y se apresura,
y en el suelo se queda la ventura.

5
Si con benino y favorable aspecto
a alguno mira el cielo acá en la tierra,

obra ascondidamente un bien perfeto
en el que cualquier mal de sí destierra;
mas si los ojos pone en el objeto
airados, le consume en llanto y guerra
ansí como a vos hace vuestro cielo:
ya os da guerra, ya paz, y fuego y yelo.

6
No se ve el cielo en claridad serena
de tantas luces claro y alumbrado
cuantas con rica habéis y fértil vena
el vuestro de virtudes adornado;
ni hay tantos granos de menuda arena
en el desierto líbico apartado
cuantos loores creo que merece
el cielo que os abaja y engrandece.

7
En Scitia ardéis, sentís en Libia frío,
contraria operación y nunca vista;
flaqueza al bien mostráis, al daño brío;
más que un lince miráis, sin tener vista;
mostráis con discreción un desvarío,
que el alma prende, a la razón conquista,
y esta contrariedad nace de aquella
que es vuestro cielo, vuestro sol y estrella.

8
Si fuera un caos, una materia unida
sin forma vuestro cielo, no espantara
de que del alma vuestra entristecida
las continuas querellas no escuchara;
pero, estando ya en partes esparcida
que un fondo forman de virtud tan rara,
es maravilla tenga los oídos
sordos a vuestros tristes alaridos.

9
Si es lícito rogar por el amigo
que en estado se halla peligroso,
yo, como vuestro, desde aquí me obligo
de no mostrarme en esto perezoso;
mas si me he de oponer a lo que digo
y conducirlo a término dichoso,
no me deis la ventura, que es muy poca,
mas las palabras sí de vuestra boca.

10
Diré: «Celia gentil, en cuya mano
está la muerte y vida y pena y gloria
de un mísero captivo que, temprano
ni aun tarde, no saldrás de su memoria:
vuelve el hermoso rostro, blando, humano,
a mirar de quien llevas la victoria:
verás el cuerpo en dura cárcel triste
del alma que primero tú rendiste.

11
Y, pues un pecho en la virtud constante
se mueve en casos de honra y muestra airado,
muévale al tuyo el ver que de delante
te ha un firme amador arrebatado;
y si quiere pasar más adelante
y hacer un hecho heroico y estremado,
rescata allá su alma con querella,
que el cuerpo, que está acá, se irá tras ella.

12
El cuerpo acá y el alma allá captiva
tiene el mísero amante que padece
por ti, Celia hermosa, en quien se aviva
la luz que al cielo alumbra y esclarece;
mira que el ser ingrata, cruda, esquiva
mal con tanta beldad se compadece:
muéstrate agradecida y amorosa
al que te tiene por su cielo y diosa».

1
(If the rope, the fire, the dart and the pure ice
that binds, burns, wounds, and chills
your soul, originates in the *cielo*,
since it ties, ignites, kills, and freezes you,
what is this knot, flame, injury, snow or ice
that lately squeezes, burns, pierces, and freezes–
as I show here in this lofty opportunity–
a tender breast, Antonio, such as yours?

2
The *cielo* that your *ingenio* regards[116]
has kept you employed in its matters,
and, according to what you do, we see that *Celia*

[116] *Ingenio* for poet-lover.

aspires to the Empyrean *cielo* to lift you up;[117]
you put your gaze on such a sight
that you give the world reason[118] to envy you.
Happy the unhappy one who is
envied for the anguish he sustains!

3[119]
In the concepts that your quill
transposed[120] from your soul onto the page[121]
you not only give signs, but prove[122]
that you are entombed in the *cielo*.
Up there, the strong fortune[123] has you
in love, alive in death, in life put out;
since he who is not of the earth cannot die,
having the soul in *Celia*, who is a *cielo*.

4
It just astonishes me to see that divine
cielo of *Celia* encloses a living hell,

117 "Nel ciel che più de la sua luce prende," (Dante, *Paradiso*, ed. and trans. R.M. Durling, Oxford University Press, 2011, 1:4, 22). In the same volume, Durling notes, "Named only once in the poem (*Inf.* 2.21 and note), and here by circumlocution, this is the Empyrean, the last, or tenth, heaven, also the 'first heaven' (*Purg.* 30.1) and 'the supreme edifice of the world . . . in which the whole world is enclosed.' (*Conv.* 2.3.11). *Ep.* 13.67–72 defines it as the sphere containing all the others, contained by none, remaining still while the others, moving within it, receive its formative power (see *Par.* 1.122, 2.111–14 and notes; also *Conv.* 2.3.9–11); this embracing stillness, which means it lacks nothing, justifies that it receives 'most' of God's light. The Empyrean is emphasized in the *Epistle* and in *Paradiso* (see 2.112, 4.31–32, 22.61–66, 23.108, 27.110, 30.39, etc.) because it is the pilgrim's goal (lines 121–26), and the final casue of the poet's life and his poem" (*Ibid.*, 32). See also: (R. Kay, "Dante's Empyrean and the Eye of God," *Speculum*, 78.1, 2003, 37–65); however, in the practices of Pastoral Petrarchism, the "Eye of the Beloved" becomes the Empyrean.

118 The use of "materia," translated as "reason," introduces the play on *forma y materia* into the poem. For "materia" as reason or argument: (Covarrubias, *Tesoro*, 1995, 741).

119 The reader may quickly hear John Donne's (1572–1631) "Batter my heart, three-person'd God" echo the first stanza. It is not unreasonable to imagine that Donne was familiar with works of this kind, though Cervantes' verses to Veneziano are not known to have circulated. The list was also employed widely by Italian poets such as Bembo and Stampa. For example: "Arsi, piansi, cantai, piango, ardo, e canto" (G. Stampa, *The Complete Poems*, eds. and trans. J. Tylus and T. Tower, University of Chicago Press, 2010, 80) and "Altri mai foco, stral, prigione o nodo," and corresponding notes: (ed. Cox, *Lyric Poetry*, 95).

120 "2. Trasladar. Vale algunas veces interpretar alguna escritura de una lengua en otra," (Covarrubias, *Tesoro*, 1995, 933).

121 Note that the soul requires translation into language in this view, a sharp juxtaposition with the modern view, which has moved from a conflation of soul and mind to a subjugation of the same in language. Cervantes uses the verb "trasladar," which includes the notion of translation but which is founded in the notion of movement. "Trasladar" does not require that the movement or transposition be from one language to another.

122 The skepticism regarding language throughout this stanza is pronounced, a juxtaposition between soul and quill (spiritual and textual) which is lost if "soul" is conflated with "mind" as a linguistically bound thinking thing of reason.

123 For "diestra" as fortune: (Covarrubias, *Tesoro*, 1995, 427).

and that the force of its force and fate,
have you in a state of sorrow and sempiternal weeping.[124]
You walk your path to the *cielo*,
but, in accordance with your luck, I discern
that your soul ascends and hastens to the *cielo*,
and fortune remains on the earth.

5
If with a kind and a propitious appearance
the *cielo* looks to someone here on earth,
it works a perfect good
that exiles every bad.
But if angered eyes are set upon the object,
he is consumed with sorrow and war
as happens to you with your *cielo*:
now it gives you war, now peace, and fire and ice.

6
The *cielo* is not seen in serene clarity
with clear illuminated lights as numerous
as the rich and fertile virtues
with which you have adorned your [*cielo*];
nor are there as many fine grains of sand
in the remote Libyan desert as numerous
as there are lauds, I believe, deserved
by the *cielo* that topples and aggrandizes you.

7
In Scythia you burn. In Libya you feel cold –
contrary operation, never before seen;
you greet good with weakness, injury with enthusiasm;
more than a lynx you are watching, though you be blind;
you show with discretion a delirium
that takes the soul, conquers the reason,
and this conflict is born from her
who is your *cielo*, your sun, and star.

8
If it were a chaos, a unified *materia*
without *forma*, this *cielo* of yours,[125]
it would not surprise me that the continuous complaints
of your sorrowful soul went unheard.
But, being already dispersed in parts
that form a foundation of such rare virtue,
it is a marvel that [she] has deaf

[124] See Chapter 3 for a discussion of the sempiternal.

[125] See: n.112 and n.117 in this chapter.

ears to your sad howls.[126]

9
If it is licit to plead on a friend's behalf
when he finds himself in a dangerous state,
I, as yours, am obliged from now on
not to be lazy in the task;
but if I must oppose what I am saying
and conduct this to a happy end,
we shan't trade lots (mine is very little)
but trade the words, yes, from your mouth.

10
I will say: "Gentle *Celia*, in whose hand
lies the death and life and sorrow and glory
of a miserable captive who, neither sooner
nor later, will let you from his memory:
turn your soft pretty face, human,
to look on one over whom you are victorious;
you will see the body in the hard, sad prison
of the soul that you first conquered.

11
And since a breast of constant virtue
is moved and angered in cases of honor,
move yours to see that before you,
you have a steadfast lover ravished,
and, if you wish to go further
and do a final heroic deed,
rescue [to where you are] his soul by loving it;
the body, which is here, will follow after it.

12
The miserable lover who suffers for you
has the body here and the soul captive there,
beautiful *Celia*, in whom the light that illuminates
and gives clarity to the *cielo* is revived;
see that being crude, aloof, ungrateful, bad,
he is pitied with so much beauty:
show yourself grateful and loving
to him who has you for a heaven and a goddess.")[127]

In the first three octaves, Cervantes' reading of Veneziano's *Celia* and Abravanel's erotic intellection comes to fruition in the trope of the captive

[126] For *alaridos* (howls): (Covarrubias, *Tesoro*, 1995, 39–40).
[127] (Cervantes, *Poesías*, 2016, 153–156).

lover before the sovereign divine lady, or *Celia* (sky or heaven). Cervantes depicts Veneziano as looking to the sovereign, the "cielo empíreo" of the *summa belleza*, in the hope of an ascent at once intellectual and sensual. As such Veneziano's suffering is enviable.[128] *Celia* serves as a protector of the lover even as she subjugates him, much like the *serenísima reina* of Cervantes' first sonnet for Isabel de Valois. In the fourth octave Cervantes treats Veneziano's Petrarchan suffering, and warns that while *Celia* inspires ascent, Veneziano's corporeal suffering remains. The poet lover should purify his gaze and look to *Celia* with love rather than desire, a distinction again drawn from Abravanel. The virtuous path of the lover was to adorn *Celia* with laudatory verses as countless as the stars and grains of sand (sixth stanza), an explicit reference both to Petrarch's *rime sparse* and to the nearly 300 *estrambote* of the *Celia* that Veneziano composed while in Algiers. At mid-length, the poem returns to the language of the first octave, recalling the burning, freezing, fainting, and fighting, and resituates these Petrarchan commonplaces within an exotic landscape ("Scitia" and "Libia"). *Celia* becomes a lynx who drives Veneziano discreetly mad. As in erotic intellection, she has penetrated his soul and conquered his mind (as her eternal abode). *Celia* is the "cielo," "sol," and "estrella" of Veneziano's world.

In the ninth octave, the poem begins to turn on a *volta* which plays upon the speaker's demonstrated mastery of their shared poetics. As if donning a pastoral pseudonym and shepherd's garb, in the three closing octaves, Cervantes becomes the exemplary lover in a direct address to *Celia*. When the final octave concludes by reaffirming the address through the repetition of *Celia's* name, it highlights the special case of apostrophe in the poem, which is already an epistle to Veneziano. Within that initial address to Veneziano, the reader discovers a ventriloquized apostrophe to *Celia*. On this rhetorical device (which touches on the sempiternal temporality of the lyric), Jonathan Culler has observed:

> Apostrophe resists narrative because its *now* is not a moment in a temporal sequence but a *now* of discourse, of writing. This temporality of writing is scarcely understood, difficult to think, but it seems to be that toward which the lyric strives. Proverbial definition calls the lyric a monument to immediacy, which presumably means a detemporalized immediacy, an immediacy of fiction .... However, the very brazenness with which apostrophe declares its strangeness is crucial, an indication that what is at issue is not a predictable relation between a signifier and a signified, a form and its meaning, but the

[128] In the *Viaje del Parnaso* (1614), he is again envious of lyric inspiration: "Jamás me pude ver sólo un momento, / Pues cuando subir quiero, se está queda" (M. de Cervantes, *Viaje del Parnaso*, ed. F. Rodríguez Marín, Madrid: C. Bermejo, 1935, 16).

> incalculable force of an event. Apostrophe is not the representation of an event; if it works, it produces a fictive, discursive event.[129]

As apostrophe, Cervantes' *octaves* to Veneziano produce "a fictive, discursive event," which is the development of the poetic and conceptual lexicon of Pastoral Petrarchism through the poet's revision of the very commonplaces and figures that the poem engages. This creates a sempiternal moment in literary time. As a ventriloquized apostrophe, Cervantes' declaration *as* Veneziano *to Celia* produces a second event (within the primary apostrophe of the epistle to Veneziano). This second event gives fictional (but not narrative) realization to the poet's own authorial position on erotic comportment: a new formulation birthed within conventional erotic discourse. Like the literary time of the palace *invenciones* of Isabel de Valois and Juana of Austria, the sempiternity of the poets of Pastoral Petrarchism, and the chronotopic dynamism of lyric subjectivity in the *Galatea*, the "immediacy of fiction" undertaken in the closing apostrophe thrusts the lyric "I" (Cervantes as speaker to Veneziano) into the literary time of the "fictive, discursive event" (Cervantes' voice as the perfected lover of *Celia*).[130] By ventriloquizing Veneziano in the apostrophic event, Cervantes takes up the role of the "good lover," the exemplar of right erotic comportment. In doing so, Cervantes the poet took a full step of authorial distance back from the amorous topoi of the poem, even as he engaged them.[131] He took an "authorial role" over Veneziano's lyric circumstances and the general topoi of his "songbook," the *Celia*. On these terms, the captivity of the body by the conquered soul recalled the erotic ecstasy or alienation described by Abravanel. The beloved *summa belleza* was *aliquid quo maius nihil cogitari potest*, spiritual sovereign of the lyric lover through erotic intellection. The question was not whether this process was in force, but how best to experience it. If this step outside of amorous expression gave Cervantes distance on the erotic event, it also established his lyric voice as a poetic authority on erotic ethics. Like Silerio in the *Galatea*, he woos on his friend's behalf. As the voice of erotic insight, Cervantes is 'dressed up' (*disfrazado*) as Veneziano in order to perform for Veneziano (and *Celia*) what the lover could and should be.[132] His

[129] (Culler, *The Pursuit of Signs*, 1981, 152–153, emphasis in original); (Culler, *Theory of the Lyric*).

[130] For sempiternity and the *figura of the poet*, see Chapter 3. For chronotopic dynamism in the *Galatea*, see Chapter 6.

[131] "This process of simultaneously renouncing and admitting involvement in a story is the same as that which will be experienced by every fictional narrator and dramatist throughout the [*DQ*]" (El Saffar, *Distance and Control*, 33).

[132] This was not Cervantes' only reimagining of Veneziano in his own works. Veneziano is also thought to have served as the inspiration for the character Riccardo in Cervantes' novela *El amante liberal*. As Leonardo Sciascia has observed: "Dove il Cervantes, senza ricordarlo direttamente, si è ricordato del

follow-through is long-reaching; over the course of the *DQ*, AQ as dQ will take the lover's genuflection to the grave. In the Stoic sense, he "holds the pose" indefinitely, or at least for sempiternity.

Of all the imaginative texts of Cervantes' oeuvre, the octaves to Veneziano offer the reader the most explicit expression of Cervantes' own authorial position on lyric love, the recurring theme of the *Galatea*, the *DQ*, the *Novelas*, and the *Persiles y Sigismunda*.[133] The *octavas* ventriloquized the author's own vision of erotic truth in 1579, in which Cervantes subverted all prior models, including Veneziano's *Celia*, to his own philo-poetic position.[134] It is little wonder that the poet later underscored the philosophical stakes of his eclogue-in-prose in the prologue to the *Galatea*.[135] In the octaves he revised Pastoral Petrarchism toward the genuflection of the lyric lover before the divine beloved (at once Dantean and Quixotic). The whole of the poet's experience in the court of Isabel, in Rome, as a soldier-poet in the Mediterranean, and as a captive in Algiers comes into focus in this explicit depiction of the Petrarchan lover in courtly genuflection. As Richard Cody has observed, the chivalric and the pastoral share a communion of the pure.[136] This lyric outlook was recapitulated and voiced by the character Antonio at the close of the *Persiles y Sigismunda*, who says of the pilgrim-lovers Persiles and Sigismunda (Periandro and Auristela): "No todos los amores son precipitados ni atrevidos, ni todos los amantes han puesto la mira de su gusto en gozar a sus amadas, sino con las potencias de su alma. (Not all loves are hasty or insolent, nor have all lovers put the aim of their pleasure in enjoying their lovers, but in the powers of their soul.)"[137] While Petrarch, Sannazaro, Castiglioni, Garcilaso, and Montemayor influenced the poetic lexicon in which Cervantes wrote, it was Veneziano (like Laínez

Veneziano, e più della sua Celia, a noi pare sia nella novella *El amante liberal*, quando l'infelice Riccardo, siciliano prigioniero dei turchi, descrive la bellezze di Leonisa: 'Y te pregunto primero si conoces en nuestro lugar de Trápana una doncella a quien la fama daba nombre de la más Hermosa mujer que habia en toda Sicilia . . . una di cui i poeti cantavano'. . . che pare la trascrizione di una ottava del Veneziano, e lealmente il Cervantes averte che così 'los poetas cantaban': i poeti siciliani, di una fanciulla siciliana" (Veneziano, *Ottave*, 1967, 20–21).

133 Even *Rinconete y Cortadillo* breaks the mode of the picaresque through the introduction of the *dos amigos*.

134 (Riley, *Cervantes's Theory*, 26–34).

135 ". . . así no temeré mucho que alguno condemne haber mezclado razones de filosofía entre algunas amorosas de pastores, que pocas veces se levantan a más que a tratar cosas del campo, y esto con su acostumbrada llaneza. Mas advirtiendo–como en el discurso de la obra alguna vez se hace–que muchos de los disfrazados pastores della lo eran sólo en el hábito, queda llana esta objeción" (Cervantes, *Galatea*, 1961, vol. I, 8).

136 (Cody, *Landscape of the Mind*, 60-61).

137 (M. de Cervantes, *Los Trabajos de Persiles y Sigismunda*, ed. J.B. Avalle-Arce, 1969, 462).

and Gálvez de Montalvo) who served as a contemporary interlocutor in his lyric imagination.[138]

~

At the time that Cervantes perfected the fictive lyric event of the apostrophe (or shortly thereafter), he also staged a dramatic space in which women became active lovers within the tropes and conceits of Pastoral Petrarchism in the *Trato de Argel.* The lyric love explored by many of Cervantes' heroines was likely rooted in the erotic philo-poetics voiced by several Italian poetesses whose works were printed during Cervantes' time in the Italian territories. Like Aurelia Petrucci of the dedication of Abravanel's *Dialoghi*, poetesses such as Veronica Gambara, Vittoria Colonna, Barbara Salutati, Virginia Salvi, Chiara Matraini, Gaspara Stampa, Veronica Franco, Livia Spinola, Dianora Sanseverino, Vicenza Armani, Fiammetta Soderini, Orsini Cavaletti, Moderata Fonte, and the philosopher-poet Tullia d'Aragona lent immediate experiential ground to the *figura* of female Petrarchan lovers in Cervantes' many fictive works.[139] The publication of the *Rime diversi* (1559), in which Petrucci's sonnet appeared, was one of many collections of poetry by women in circulation when Cervantes arrived in Rome. These poetesses created a precedent for the lyric drives of Cervantes' fictional heroines, such as Teolinda and Rosaura of the *Galatea*, Dorotea and Zoraida/Maria of the *DQ I*, Preciosa of *La gitanilla*, Altisidora and Ana Félix of the *DQ II*, and Sigismuda of the *Persiles y Sigismunda*. In addition to better known poetesses recuperated in the work of Cox, Tyllus, and others, the publications of literary academies in the "Two Sicilies" evidence the active participation of poetesses throughout Habsburg Italy.

[138] Cervantes' *octavas* anticipate those of Elicio at the opening of the *Galatea*. As Vicente Gaos notes, "Los mismos elementos, *fuego, lazo, flecha y hielo* figuran también en dos composiciones del libro I de *La Galatea*, las que empiezan: 'Mientras que al triste lamentable acento' y 'Afuera el fuego, el lazo, el hielo y flecha'," (in Cervantes, *Poesías completas*, 1974, 347). Compare the first stanza of the *octavas* to stanzas 1 and 4 in Elicio's first song: "Mientras que al triste lamentable accento /del mal acorde son del canto mío, / en Eco amarga de cansado aliento / responde el monte, el prado, el llano, el río, / demos al sordo y presuroso viento / las quejas que del pecho ardiente y frío / salen a mi pesar, pidiendo en vano / ayuda al río, al monte, al prado, al llano. // . . . // Yo sí que al fuego me consumo y quemo, / y al lazo pongo humilde la garganta, / y la red invisible poco temo, / y el rigor de la flecha no me espanta; / por esto soy llegado a tal estremo, / a tanto daño, a desventura tanta, / que tengo por mi gloria y mi sosiego, / la saeta, la red, el lazo, el fuego, // . . .," (Cervantes, *Galatea* 1961, vol. I, 15–16).

Both *octavas* drew upon Veneziano's *estrambote* for *Celia*: "Celi, planeti e vui, causi secundi, / chi distinguiti motu, tempu et huri, / chianti, arburi, frutti, xhiuri e frundi, / chiani allegri, auti munti e valli oscuri, / ripi, xhiumi, vui sausi e vui, duci undi, / feri salvaggi e vui, mansi e sicuri: / si di vui comu di mia non s'ascundi, / cuntati a la mia donna lu miu arduri" (Veneziano, *Libro delle rime*, 33.)

[139] While the *figura of the poet* may appear at odds with the psychoanalytic view, the interest here is in how the modern psyche itself developed in the novelistic contours of Cervantes' prose fiction and versified dramaturgy from these lyric beginnings. For poetesses: (ed. Cox, *Lyric Poetry*).

A prime example are the sonnet replies of Laura and Marta Bonanno in the *Rime della Accademia degli Accesi di Palermo* (Palermo: Giouan Mattheo Mayda, 1571), which were contemporary with Cervantes' time as a soldier-poet in Sicily. Throughout his fiction, Cervantes' heroines become more than the poetic vision of his male protagonists. Even Dulcinea courts a life independent of AQ as the aging, "off-stage," and forever-enchanted Aldonza Lorenzo, whilst many of the characters of the novel voice objections to dQ's version of her existence. Both *figura of the poet* and *summa belleza*, the beautiful lady as the lyric lover inverted Veneziano's world, placing the *Celia* on earth and her beloved in the heavens. In the *Trato de Argel*, the confluence of Islamic and Christian faith gives way to an erotic theology in which characters of any religion or gender participate.[140]

While the *Trato de Argel* respects a unity of action consisting of the liberation of the Christian captive-lovers, the nature of the plot involves a number of erotic entanglements, which allowed Cervantes to deploy several lyric conceits within the versified drama. A proto-historical realism concerning the depiction of the suffering of Christian captives in Algiers and a critique of Philip II's impotency in their rescue occupies the central portion (over half) of the versified drama. But the amorous unity of action which bookends and is interwoven throughout the *comedia* concerns the happy fortune of two unfortunate captive-lovers (a dramatic conceit that actualized the metaphor of erotic love as spiritual captivity). It is precisely the disproportionately lengthy depiction of captive life in Algiers and the cruelty of some slave-owners which contrasts with and highlights the benevolence of the Algerian king and the power of love displayed by the amorous pair to soften the hearts of their captors.[141] While the pastoral typically provided a *locus amoenus* in which to incubate the lyric interiority of its protagonists, Cervantes' drama allegorized the landscape to reflect the inner captivity of amorous subjugation. In the *Trato de Argel*, Cervantes was not ambiguous about the sovereignty of love. Zahara, the Muslim Algerian owner of the Christian slaves Aurelio and Silvia abandons her religious faith to her passion for the "divine" Aurelio for whom she burns:

[140] The motifs of captivity and spirituality in this dramatic work are also evident in the attribution of the *Jerusalén* (a dramatization of Tasso's *Gerusalemme*) to Cervantes. See: (S. Arata, "La conquista de Jerusalén, Cervantes, y la generación teatral de 1580," *Criticón*, 54, 1992, 9–112).

[141] The captive lovers could be productively compared to Tasso's use of the same trope in the *Gerusalemme liberate*. See: (M. de Cervantes, *La conquista de Jerusalén por Godofre de Bullón*, ed. H. Brioso Santos, Madrid: Cátedra, 2009) for more on Arata's attribution of the *Jerusalén* to Cervantes.

¡Déjame a mí con Mahoma,
que agora no es mi señor,
porque soy sierva de Amor,
que el alma subjeta y doma!

(Leave Mahomed to me;
I'm not his servant anymore
because I'm a servant of Love
which subjugates and dominates my soul!)[142]

While this seeming disregard for the Islamic religion should be treated with a critical eye, it merits observation that the Abrahamic religions (Islam, Christianity, Judaism) are generally transformed into erotic faith in Cervantes' works. In the *Trato*, the Christian captive Aurelio makes full use of the divine beloved as keeper of his captive soul:

Pondérase mi dolor,
con decir, bañado en lloros,
que mi cuerpo está entre moros
y el alma en poder de Amor.
Del cuerpo y alma es mi pena;
el cuerpo ya veis cual va,
el alma rendida está
a la amorosa cadena.
Pensé yo que no tenía
Amor poder entre esclavos,
pero en mí sus recios clavos
muestran más su gallardía.

Ponder my pain,
in saying, bathed in cries,
that my body is among Moors,
and my soul in the power of Love.
My pain is of body and soul;
the body, already you see how it goes;
my soul is subjugated
to the amorous chain.
I thought that Love didn't have
any power among slaves;
but in me its hard nails
show best its gallantry.[143]

142 (Cervantes, "Trato de Argel," I: 229–232, 919). See also (*Ibid.*, II:1188–1190) for Silvia.
143 (Cervantes, "Trato de Argel," I: 25–36, 912).

It would be obtuse to ignore the fact that Cervantes' depiction of Muslim slaveholders in Algiers is critical, but in his critique his Muslim characters are neither reduced to an evil enemy nor flattened into the xenophobic reductions of his period, such as those particularly aggressive sentiments following the violent suppression of the uprising in the Alpujarras (1568–1571) which culminated with the expulsion of the moriscos in 1609. In Cervantes' poetry (writ large), Love as spiritual sovereign became the great equilizer which knew neither religious nor imperial boundaries.

CHAPTER 5

The Poet as Literary Character: Eclogues and Encomia in Madrid

In 1602, Philip III and Queen Marguerite of Spain traveled to Valencia de Don Juan to pay a visit to Jorge de Montemayor's aging shepherdess, Diana.[1] Then in her seventies, she was reputed to have retained the beauty which the Portuguese poet immortalized in the first Spanish pastoral novel, the *Diana* (Milan: Andrea de Ferrari, 1559).[2] The literary technique of the *roman à clef* (novel in key) was a key feature of pastoral poetics during the early modern period. The significance of this literary technique, which included not only the private histories of identifiable persons, but also the representations of their interiorities in lyric verse, has often been acknowledged, but its literary significance has been left largely unexamined.[3] As with Aristophanes' old comedies, this is due partly to the fact that many of the historical keys to the encoded references in the literature of Pastoral Petrarchism have been lost – the referents remain encrypted for later generations of readers. Nonetheless, within sixteenth-century literary production, the combination of personal history and poetic allegory in the *roman à clef* fostered a mimetic self-consciousness at the confluence of lyric interiority and narrative community which was directly involved in the genesis of modern novelistic fiction. It rendered the living *figura of the poet* the central protagonist of literary storytelling. As such, the technique of the *roman à clef* cannot be taken as separate from the poetics of these texts because it was not simply a pastoral habit in which to cloak one's own

[1] (H.A. Rennert, *The Spanish Pastoral Romances*, 35). [2] BNE R/41505.

[3] (Avalle-Arce, *La novela pastoril española*, 143); (Avalle-Arce, *La Galatea de Cervantes cuatrocientos años después: Cervantes y lo pastoril*, Newark: Juan de la Cuesta, 1985, 2); (Avalle-Arce, "*La Galatea:* The Novelistic Crucible," 8); (Collins, "Lauso, a Portrait"); (Gaylord, "The Language of Limits"); (J. Toribio Mendina, "El Lauso de la *Galatea* de Cervantes es Ercilla," *Romantic Review*, n.1, 1919, vol. X, 16–25); (Ponce-Hegenauer, "A Novel Community"); (E. Rhodes, "Sixteenth-Century Pastoral Books, Narrative Structure, and *La Galatea* of Cervantes," *Bulletin of Hispanic Studies*, 1989, 351–360); (Rhodes, "*La Galatea* and Cervantes' 'Tercia Realidad'"); (Stagg, "A Matter of Masks"); (Stagg, "The Composition and Revision"); (F. Valencia, "'El melancólico vacío': Poesía, poética y melancolía entre *La Galatea* de Cervantes y las *Soledades* de Góngora," doctoral thesis, Brown, 2010); (Valencia, "No se puede reducir a continuado término," vol. XXI, 81–106).

experiences. It took up the question of mimesis as a tension between art and nature, lyric utterance and shared storytelling, chronological time and the sempiternal temporality of the lyric at the heart of the poetic process, something that Alan Trueblood in his study of Lope de Vega's *Dorotea* called a tension between *erlebnis* and *poiesis*.[4]

Eight years prior to Cervantes' first sonnet for Isabel de Valois, when the *Diana* went to print in 1559, there was little doubt that the pastoral allegory was a thinly veiled mimetic reworking of the private life of the poet and his contemporaries within the sophisticated space of literary convention. The *Diana* was likely composed within the regency court of the Princess Juana of Austria in Valladolid (1554–1559), and much of the historical evidence that would facilitate a complete decoding of it has been lost. However, as Jorge de Montemayor explicitly acknowledged at the close of the Argument of the first book,

> Y de aquí comienza el primero libro y en los demás hallarán muy diversas hystorias, de casos que verdaderamente an sucedido, aunque van disfraçados debaxo de nombres y estilo pastoril.
>
> (And from here, where begins the first book, and in the others they will find different histories, of cases that truly have happened, although they go about disguised beneath the pastoral names and style.)[5]

Twenty-six years later, in the prologue to the *Galatea* Cervantes also highlighted the feature of the *roman à clef* within the tradition of Pastoral Petrarchism:

> Mas advirtiendo—como en el discurso de la obra alguna vez se hace—que muchos de los disfrazados pastores della lo eran sólo en el hábito . . .
>
> (But being advised (as in the discourse of the work it is sometimes done) that many of the disguised shepherds therein, were so only in "habit" . . .)[6]

Four years prior to the 1602 royal visit to Montemayor's aging shepherdess, Lope de Vega's *Arcadia* encoded the poet and his contemporaries at the court of Antonio Álvarez de Toledo, fifth Duke of Alba at Alba de Tormes.[7] While the publication of Lope de Vega's *Arcadia* (1598) is often considered to be the conclusion of the vogue of the pastoral novel (1559–1598), in his late work the

4 (Trueblood, *Experience and Artistic Expression*, 15). The tension implicitly invokes the phenomenological question of intentionality. However, there is no space to treat such wide historical and disciplinary implications here.

5 (Montemayor, *Diana*, 1970, 7).

6 (Cervantes, *Galatea*, 1961, vol. I, 8).

7 This feature of the *roman à clef* was widely recognized in the many laudatory poems contributed to the *Arcadia*. (Lope de Vega, *Arcadia, prosa y versos*, ed. A. Sánchez Jiménez, Madrid: Cátedra, 2012, 149–151 and 152–172).

Dorotea (1632) Lope recounted and reprised his early period of poetic growth in the culture of Pastoral Petrarchism in 1580s Madrid. Affirming what all of his contemporaries already knew, he wrote,

> La Diana de Montemayor fue una dama natural de Valencia de Don Juan, junto a León. Y Esla, su río, y ella serán eternos por su pluma. Así la Fílida de Montalvo, la Galatea de Cervantes, la Camila de Garcilaso, la Violante de Camões, la Silvia de Bernaldes, la Filis de Figueroa, la Leonor de Corte Real.
>
> (The Diana of Montemayor was a lady native to Valencia de Don Juan, next to León. And Ezla, its river, and she will be eternal by his plume. In the same way the Fílida of Montalvo, the Galatea of Cervantes, the Camila of Garcilaso, the Violante of Camões, the Silvia of Bernaldes, the Filis of Figueroa, the Leonor of Corte Real.)[8]

Just twelve years prior to Lope's *Dorotea*, the 1624 Lisbon reprinting of Montemayor's *Diana* included a dedication by Lourenzo Craesbeek in which he related an incident involving Montemayor in the garden of the Duchess of Sessa in which Diana's true identity was probed and discussed among the guests.[9] Well into the third decade of the seventeenth century, this pastoral blending of fact and artifice into literary artifact was still a topical point of interest and discussion. When Cervantes returned to Madrid in the 1580s this literary culture was at its height. As Gregorio de Godoy wrote in his laudatory sonnet for the 1582 printing of Gálvez de Montalvo's *El pastor de Fílida*:

> . . ., pues si queremos
> apartarle el reboço con cuidado,
> un Gálvez de Montalvo hallaremos,

[8] (Lope de Vega, *La Dorotea*, ed. E.S. Morby, University of California Press, 1958, Act II: Scene 2, 137–138).

[9] According to Rennert, "Some interesting gossip concerning Montemayor is given in the dedication written by Lourenço Craesbeek to the edition of the *Diana* which he printed at Lisbon in 1624. He tells us . . . 'So great was the fame of Montemayor that there was not a house in which the *Diana* was not read, nor a street in which its style was not extolled; everybody, however great, desired a personal acquaintance with its author, who was invited to that splendid entertainment which the Duchess of Sessa gave in her garden to the principal ladies of the Court. Montemayor, entering with some servants of the Duke, in whose house he was then lodged, the Duchess introduced him to her guests, who inquired about the beauty of *Diana*, about the grievous action of the shepherd in marrying her, and about other things about rustic shepherds, and about other things in his book, to which he replied with many gallantries, not a little proud of such good-fortune. The Marquise of Camarsa asked him: Sr. Montemayor, if you write such pleasing things about rustic shepherds, what would you do if you were asked to write about this garden, of these fountains and these Nymphs which you see here? To which Montemayor replied: All these things, my lady, are matter rather for wonderment than for the pen'" (Rennert, *The Spanish Pastoral Romances*, 31).

Montemayor's invocation of the trope of ineffability was native to the developing tradition of Pastoral Petrarchism to which he contributed in Spain.

tan hidalgo y galán como discreto
y tan discreto como enamorado.

(. . ., well, if we want
to carefully take from him the veil
a Gálvez de Montalvo we will find,
as gentleman and gallant as [he is] discreet,
and as discreet as he is enamored.)[10]

This chapter employs paratextual sources (front matter, dedications, prologues, and laudatory sonnets) to reconstruct the "urban-pastoral" milieu to which Cervantes returned in 1580, the site of production for his pastoral prosimetrum, the *Galatea* (1585). Drawing on the known manuscript annotation (ms. 2.856, BNE) that identifies Cervantes as the "Lauso" of the *Galatea*, in conjunction with a rich history of scholarship on the many pseudonyms of the text, this chapter updates understandings of the *Galatea* as a *roman à clef* through new attention to the biographical names encoded in pastoral pseudonyms for poets pertaining to the river Tajo in the "Canto de Calíope" (Book VI).[11] This decoding is crucial to an understanding of the *Galatea* within Cervantes' literary moment and authorial trajectory because it reveals a definitive change in the focus of the pastoral prosimetrum. Where this type of prosimetric fiction typically encoded the poet-shepherd amongst his patrons and other nobles of the court, the *Galatea* represented its author amidst his contemporary milieu of poets and thus rendered poetic practice (rather than aristocratic court culture) and its persons the characters of literary fiction. While comparative literary theory on the *roman à clef* has typically begun with the work of Madeleine de Scudery in seventeenth-century France, it is clear that in Spain the pastoral prosimetrum flourished as a *novela en clave* throughout the sixteenth century. Because the pastoral narrativized lyric interiority as a source of character drive and development from which plots arose organically, it introduced into the prose fiction of romances and chronicles a novel element of modern storytelling: immediacy and its contingencies.[12] In the *DQ* Cervantes extends the narrative force of lyric interiority begun in

[10] (Gálvez de Montalvo, *El pastor de Fílida*, 431).

[11] (Schevill and Bonilla in Cervantes, *Galatea* 1914); (Stagg, "A Matter of Masks"); (Stagg, "The Composition and Revision"); (Gaylord Randel, "The Limits of Language"); (Avalle-Arce, "Novelistic Crucible").

[12] For the *roman à clef* in French literature: (F. Drujon, *Les Livres à clefs. Étude de bibliographie critique et analytique pour servir à l'histoire littéraire*, Paris: Rouveyre, 1888, vol. II); (*Les Romans à clefs, Troisième colloque des Invalides, December 3, 1999*, Tusson, Charentes: Du Lérot, 2000); (A. Glinoer and M. Lacroix, eds., *Romans à clés: Les Ambivalences du réel*, Presses universitaires de Liège, 2014).

the *Galatea* beyond the characters to the narrator and historian, a development which facilitated the most modern and postmodern features of his text. The status of the *Galatea* as a *roman à clef* has been touched upon repeatedly since its publication in 1585.[13] Long acknowledged as

[13] This has been treated by Schevill and Bonilla, Juan Bautista Avalle-Arce, Francisco López Estrada and Maria Teresa López García-Berdoy, Geoffrey Stagg, and others. In their 1914 edition of the *Galatea*, Schevill and Bonilla write, "La circunstancia de que Cervantes . . . ha puesto a prueba el ingenio y la erudición de los cervantistas, para dar con los auténticos personajes a quienes el autor oculta bajo el rústico pellico del pastor . . .. Como quiera que sea, parece seguro que hay en su novela tres nombres, por lo menos, que encubren los de otros tres personajes perfectamente históricos: es uno de ellos *Tirsi*, que sin duda oculta al *divino* Francisco de Figueroa, de quien el mismo Cervantes cita los primeros versos de tres composiciones que en las colecciones de sus *Obras* figuran; el segundo es el *famoso pastor Meliso*, cuyas obsequias se celebran en el libro VI, y del cual constan pormenores en la *Galatea* que permiten identificarle con Diego Hurtado de Mendoza, de tan alta representación en la historia política y literaria del Renacimiento español; el tercero y último es el pastor *Astraliano*, de quien no debe dudarse que sea el propio D. Juan de Austria. Cualquiera otra identificación es problemática. Podría, sin embargo, juzgarse, con bastante verosimilitud, que *Larsileo*, el amigo de Lauso, es Mateo Vázquez; *Siralvo*, Gálvez de Montalvo (que se disfrazó con tal seudónimo en su *Pastor de Phílida*); *Crisio*, Cristóbal de Virués (que solía llevar ese nombre poético); *Artidoro*, Andrés Rey de Artieda; *Siluano* (también citado por Gálvez de Montalvo, y antes por Montemayor), Gregorio Silvestre; y que los *Matuntos*, padre e hijo, músico el uno y poeta el otro, tienen relación con el 'Matute', celebrado por López Maldonado en su elegía a D.a Agustina de Torres. *Damon*, para Fernández de Navarrete, es Pedro Laínez. En cuanto a *Lauso*, el mismo Navarrete opina que es Luis Barahona de Soto; aunque consideramos mucho más probable la conjetura de José María Asensio, para quien *Lauso*, 'verdadero amigo' de *Damon*, y amante de *Silena*, es el propio Cervantes. En cuanto a *Galatea*, según Lope de Vega (*Dorotea*, II, 2) no fué una 'dama imaginaria'; pero no hay fundamento sólido para identificarse con Catalina de Palacios Salazar y Vozmediano, con quien contrajo matrimonio Cervantes en Esquivias, el 12 de diciembre de 1584; como tampoco le hay para afirmar que *Elicio* sea el propio Cervantes. Otros nombres de la novela parecen recogidos por el autor en sus lecturas literarias: así, *Carino* (a quien vuelve a sacar Cervantes en el *Persiles*) constaba en la *Arcadia* de Sannazaro, y es además personaje de algunas comedias de Terencio; *Thelesio* es quizá reminiscencia del poeta y humanista italiano de ese nombre; *Belisa* aparece en Gálvez de Montalvo, y *Galatea* figuraba ya en Garcilaso. En otros casos, por último, los nombres parecen de pura invención. De todos modos, la identidad de seudónimos no autoriza para concluir nada seguro acerca de los personajes: así, *Galatea*, cantada por Garcilaso, lo fué también por Hernando de Acuña, Julián (o Julio) Íñiguez de Medrano, Fernando de Herrera, Argensola (Lupercio), Luis de Góngora y Damasio de Frías, y aparece como amada de *Damon* en el soneto de Figueroa que comienza: 'Vuelto Damon el rostro al occidente'; *Damon*, a su vez, fué nombre poético usado por Hernando de Acuña, Diego de Mendoza, Francisco de la Torre y Baltasar del Alcázar; *Amarili* o *Amarilis* fué celebrada por Gutierre de Cetina, por Cristóbal de Mendoza, por Manuel Bocano y por Jerónimo Fernández de Mata; *Artidoro* es el nombre del fingido autor griego de *Leandro el Bel*, novela caballeresca atribuida a Pedro de Luxán, e impresa en Toledo el año 1563; *Siluano* es nombre poético usado por Pedro de Padilla en algunos romances de su *Thesoro de varias poesías* (Madrid, 1580)" (Cervantes, *Galatea*, 1914, vol. I, XXIX–XXII).

Compare this assessment to the one given by Avalle-Arce nearly fifty years later in his 1961 edition of the *Galatea*, "Con toda intención he dejado para el final el problema de la realidad histórica encubierta en *La Galatea*. Lo he hecho así, porque entiendo que la cuestión está situada en la periferia de la literatura . . .. Sólo tres de las soluciones propuestas son seguras en mi opinión: Tirsi es Francisco de Figueroa; Meliso, don Diego Hurtado de Mendoza, y Astraliano es don Juan de Austria. Todas las demás son hipotéticas. Las que tienen mayores visos de probabilidad son las que identifican a Damón con Pedro Laínez y a Lauso con el propio Cervantes (entiéndase que un Cervantes poetizado, como en el caso de los demás personajes). Larsileo quizá sea el secretario Mateo Vázquez, no don Alonso de

a novel in key by Lope de Vega, early in the nineteenth century Fernández de Navarrete made several conjectures regarding the masked identity of the text's shepherd-poet lovers in his *Vida de Miguel de Cervantes.*[14] In 1902, José María Asensio identified Lauso with Cervantes, an identification later corroborated by Schevill and Bonilla in their 1914 edition of Cervantes' text, and by Avalle-Arce in 1961.[15] Late in the twentieth century, Juan Bautista Avalle-Arce, López-Estrada, Geoffrey Stag, and Mary Randel gestured toward the import of circles of poets writing contemporaneously to Cervantes' composition of the *Galatea.*[16] In one of the more explicit treatments of the matter, Geoffrey Stagg has written, "an even more venerable tradition, established by Virgil himself, authorized the introduction, suitably masked, of persons of influence with whom the author was anxious to ingratiate himself."[17] That in the *Galatea* Cervantes repurposed the encomiastic function of encoding noble personages for the priority of place given to the immortalization of a living community of poets is a possibility which has not fully been appreciated. But subsequent scholarship has yet to make sense of the *Galatea* amongst poets of the 1580s and has instead favored attention to the symbolic features of the text.[18] Recently, Marsha Collins has suggested a more allegorical reading of Lauso as symbolic of the poet in general, in Paul Alpers' terms a "representative

Ercilla, como creía Rodríguez Marín, pues el gran poeta épico no tenía gran influencia en la corte y Larsileo sí. Siralvo, con casi toda seguridad, es Gálvez de Montalvo. Y aquí dejo el problema, pues no veo que sus soluciones ayuden mucho a la comprensión de *La Galatea* como obra de arte" (Cervantes, *Galatea*, 1961, vol. I, XXX–XXI). Also: (*La Galatea*, eds. Francisco López Estrada and María Teresa López García-Berdoy, Madrid: Cátedra, 1995, 157–167).

"Cervantes puso nombre a sus personajes siguiendo un amplio criterio. Algunos de ellos son personas históricas disfrazadas con nombre y condición de pastor; unos pocos pueden llegar a identificarse, como Tirsi, Damón, Larsileo, Astraliano, Meliso y Lenio, que son los que escoge G. Stagg para su estudio (1972). Otro, como Arnaut Mami, aparece con su propio nombre y condición de corsario . . .," (Cervantes, *Galatea*, 1995, 60–61 and 113–119).

(Stagg, "A Matter of Masks," esp. 258–266).

[14] (M. Fernández de Navarrete, *Vida de Miguel de Cervantes Saavedra, escrita y ilustrada con varias noticias y documentos inéditos pertenecientes a la historia y literatura de su tiempo*, Madrid, 1819), as referenced by Schevill and Bonilla in (Cervantes, *Galatea*, 1914, vol. I, XXXI).

[15] Schevill and Bonilla give an obscure reference for José María Asensio as "Véase su artículo *Filena*, en el número 1. de la *Crónica de los Cervantistas*, fundada y dirigida por D. Ramón León Máinez" (Cervantes, *Galatea*, 1914, vol. I, XXXI). For the complete reference: (J.M. Asensio, "Filena, Novela Pastoril que se atribuye a Miguel de Cervantes por sus biógrafos," in *Cervantes y sus obras*, Barcelona: F. Seix, 1902).

[16] (Avalle-Arce, "*La Galatea:* The Novelistic Crucible"); (Stagg, "A Matter of Masks"); (Gaylord, "The Language of Limits"); and (Valencia, "'El melancólico vacío'").

[17] (Stagg, "A Matter of Masks," 256).

[18] Marín Cepeda's study of poets in correspondence with Ascanio Colonna (1583–1587) sheds light on literary patronage, but little advanced the inner workings of Pastoral Petrarchism and the development of novelistic fiction (Marín Cepeda, *Cervantes y la corte de Felipe II*).

shepherd."[19] Felipe Valencia has also tended toward a symbolic interpretation of the shepherd-poet Tirsi, long identified with Francisco de Figueroa: "Tirsi's identification with a historical poet as a nod within a supposed à clef game is less important than his function as what Antonio Prieto called a representative of great Italianate poetry and Neoplatonic wisdom who belongs to an era on the wane."[20] This turn toward the symbolic or allegorical features of Cervantes' pastoral prosimetrum singularly highlights one side of the tension that the pastoral, and Cervantes' pastoral in particular, takes up within its thematic content. This tension between history and allegory, lyric and narrative, story and trope, character and symbol cannot be severed without altering the shape of the work and the literary practices cultivated in it.

Throughout the *Galatea* Cervantes repeatedly called attention to this "matter of masks" as "the content of the poetry and what is said about it."[21] This was neither an accidental flourish nor a passing technique of an experimental work. The poet continued to exploit the formal features of the pastoral as a *roman à clef* in all of his subsequent prose fiction. Beginning in Book I of the *Galatea*, with the repeated change of names from the *pastor-homicidio* to the *pastor del bosque*, to the narratively situated *Lisandro*, Cervantes immediately called into question the permanence of the proper-signifier in the development of his characters, a gesture which explicitly pointed to the pseudonymic feature of pastoral practices as narrative transformation within his own community. Later in the same text, the shepherdesses Galatea, Florisa, and Teolinda are made to indicate the linguistic veil when they suppose that Lauso's amorous laments refer to a shepherdess whose true identity has been disguised beneath the pastoral pseudonym of Silena. This pseudonym within a text of pseudonyms itself was not static; as Marsha Collins has observed, "Lauso uses clever wordplay to equate his once beloved *Silena* with *Sirena* the devouring monster."[22] But the question of names, throughout Cervantes' fiction, is more than just wordplay. This polyonomasia became a key feature of Spitzer's

[19] "Yet Lauso, along with other characters and aspects of *La Galatea*, offers suggestive glimpses into Cervantes's views on the importance of the poet and poetry for the collective community of Spain and her empire, as well as all of humankind. In retrospect, Lauso constitutes an exemplar of Cervantes' personal rendering of what Paul Alpers has called the 'representative shepherd,' referring to the tendency of pastoral shepherds and shepherdesses to symbolize or signify–that is, 'represent' something or someone beyond themselves and the poetic and/or fictional anecdote in which they appear" (Collins, "Lauso, a Portrait of the Poet," 138–148, 144).

[20] (Valencia, "No se puede reducir," 89–106, 93).

[21] (Stagg, "A Matter of Masks") and (Valencia, "No se puede reducir").

[22] (Collins, "Lauso, a Portrait," 143).

understanding of linguistic perspectivism in the *DQ*.[23] Dating to at least Veneziano's use of the poetic *sobrenombre Celia*, Cervantes uses names, pseudonyms, and epithets to indicate a character's narrative coordinates. In his lyric-laden fiction, doubt about what *is* in a name surfaces as a narratively contingent process of naming which shatters notions of static identity by way of its appeal to immediacy.

In the 1580s, this nominal fluidity first appeared in the poetic practices of Cervantes and his milieu as a figural transformation of the biographical poet into his textual lyric voice. Lope de Vega's many pastoral pseudonyms are indicative of the way in which poets frequently changed their own "nome de vert," or that of their beloved, across the lyric stages of their lives.[24] From the outset, the pseudonym was not merely a one-to-one coded mask that could be put on and taken off; it marked the becoming of a persona, a *figura of the poet*, or a novelistic character out of the confluence of personal experience and the literary lexicon of its expression. Nor was this technique merely a play of metonymic similes. Cervantes consistently employed the nominal qualities of his characters to diverse effect. Situated so as to include both the pastoral techniques of poetic fiction and the community of poets from whose lives and works these practices arose, the *Galatea* brought about the poetic persona as novelistic character in the development of prosimetric fiction. Indeed, "poetry about poetry," as Mary Gaylord has observed, the *Galatea*, as sixteenth-century pastoral poetry about sixteenth-century pastoral poetry, raised the private lives and lyric interiors of "minor" poets to the order of literary (and novelistic) fiction. By way of poetic practice, a network of authors working in Madrid became the *ingenios* of the *Galatea*.[25]

By the time Cervantes returned to Madrid the foremost literary patrons of his youth were dead.[26] Francisco Figueroa's late sonnet "¿Hay quién quiera comprar nueve doncellas . . . (Is there anyone who wants to buy nine ladies?)" lamented the shift in the status of the eclogue from patronized

[23] (Spitzer, "Linguistic Perspectivism," esp. 49–50).

[24] (Lope de Vega, *Romances de juventud*, 15–23).

[25] (Collins, "Lauso, a Portrait"); (Valencia, "No se puede reducir"). This scholarly tendency to assume that the technique of the *roman à clef* may be divorced from the literary techniques and merits of the text dates, at least, to Schevill and Bonilla. The tendency appears consistently, and relatively unquestioned, throughout twentieth-century scholarship, as in the editions of Avalle-Arce and the articles cited above.

[26] Prince Carlos (d. 1568), Queen Isabel de Valois (d. 1568), Princess Juana de Austria (d. 1573), Don Diego Hurtado de Mendoza (d. 1575), Don Juan de Austria (d. 1578), Gonzalo Fernández de Córdoba, third Duke of Sessa (d. 1578), Queen Ann of Austria (d. 1580), Fernando Álvarez de Toledo, third Duke of Alba (d. 1582), Fadrique Álvarez de Toledo, fourth Duke of Alba (d. 1583).

court culture to the mercantile streets of Madrid through its ironic treatment of the nine muses.[27] Coincident with Philip II's increasing withdrawal within El Escorial (1584), the urbanite poets of the 1580s formed communities and academies of their own. This eventually led to the formation of the *Academia Imitatoria* with the Roman patron Ascanio Colonna, to whom the *Galatea* was dedicated, in the late 1580s.[28] During the 1580s, literary life migrated from the Alcázar to urban environs and what would soon and thereafter become the *barrio de las letras*. To a large degree the generation of poets whom Cervantes had left behind in Madrid in 1568 was still intact when he returned from Algiers. Following the death of Don Diego Hurtado de Mendoza on August 14, 1575, Francisco de Figueroa and Pedro Laínez (the Tirsi and Damón of the *Galatea*) became the two eldest and most respected poetic exemplars for the emerging generations of younger poets. Of those younger poets whose work had first begun to appear in the 1560s, Luis Gálvez de Montalvo and Gómez de Tapia both saw their pastoral poetry (which pertained to Isabel's reign) in print during the first years of the 1580s.[29] To this generation of the 1560s – Figueroa, Laínez, Gálvez de Montalvo, Cervantes, Gómez de Tapia, Juan Rufo Gutiérrez – a new generation, which included Pedro de Padilla, Gabriel López Maldonado, Luis Vargas Manrique, Doctor Campuzano, the *maestro* Garray, Diego Durán, Francisco Díaz, Liñán de Riaza, Luis de Góngora, and Lope de Vega, began to appear in the flowering of poetic publications that marked the years of the 1580s. In addition to these and other Madrileño poets, authors such as Gregorio Silvestre, Luis Barahona de Soto, and the Argensola brothers also passed through Madrid during this period.

The group which forged the core of Cervantes' literary milieu upon his return to Spain were the first of the decidedly urbanite poets, at times employed by individual nobleman and patrons, but no longer united under the cultural rubric of palace life. These urban poets of Madrid wrote

[27] "¿Hay quién quiera comprar nueve doncellas / esclavas a lo menos desterradas / de las tierras do fueron engendradas? / ¿Hay quién las compre? ¿Hay quien dé más por ellas? / Pues yo [os] prometo que solían ser ellas / hermosas, ricas, graves, y estimadas, / y aunque de muchos fueron recuestadas, / bien pocos alcanzaron favor dellas. / Ahora van las tristes mendigando / de puerta en puerta, rotas y baldías, / y por sólo el comer se venderían. / Pues no son muy golosas, que hallando / hierbas, flores u hojas, pasarían / con sombras frescas y con aguas frías" (Figueroa, *Poesía*, 1989, 246).

The nine ladies, of course, refer to the nine muses: Calíope, Clio, Euterpe, Erato, Melpomene, Polyhymia, Terpsichore, Thalia, and Urania.

[28] (Ponce-Hegenauer, "A Novel Community"); (Marín Cepeda, *Cervantes y la corte*).

[29] On the translations of Camoes: (D. Alonso, "La recepción de Os Lusiadas en España," in *Obras completes*, Madrid: Gredos, 1974).

with unprecedented autonomy and with an expressed interest – more with immortal fame than economic gain in mind – in the emerging book market.[30] It is important to remember that in Lope's *Proceso* for libel in 1587 and 1588, the author was still reluctant to say that he wrote *comedias* for money. While only six books were known to have been printed between 1561 and 1566 in Madrid, by 1579 as many as sixteen volumes appeared in a single year. Over the course of the decade of the 1580s as many as 168 volumes appeared in the city alone.[31] While several of these volumes included royal provisions, juridical and courtly decrees, and religious texts, the market was also flooded with volumes of poetry, annotations, translations, and new works of medicine and philosophy. For the first time in Spanish literary history, living authors writing in Castilian pursued the art of lyric verse and poetic practice in a public format. Sánchez de Lima's *El arte poética en romance castellano* (Alcalá: Juan Iñiguez de Lequerica, 1580), Pedro de Padilla's *Thesoro de varias poesías* (Madrid: 1580), Fernando de Herrera's *Anotaciones a la poesía de Garcilaso* (Seville: Alonso de la Barrera, 1580), Caldera's translation of *Os Lusiadas* (Alcalá: Juan Gracián,1580), and Gómez de Tapia's translation of *La Lusiada* (Salamanca: Joan Perier 1580) all appeared within the first year of the decade. The front matter to these publications alone included contributions from Pedro Laínez, Ruy López de Zúñiga, López Maldonado, Antonio Suarez, the *maestro* Garay, Luis Gálvez de Montalvo, the *maestro* Vergara, and Luis de Góngora, among others.

Following his ransom and return from Algiers in 1580, Cervantes briefly stopped in Madrid while in pursuit of the Habsburg court, which had been transferred temporarily to Lisbon for the annexation of Portugal.[32] On May 21, 1581, while the court was in Tomar, he undertook a secret royal mission to Oran. He returned to meet the court in Lisbon toward the end of July 1581.[33] The exact date of Cervantes' final return to Madrid from

30 For a clear index of the exponential increase in publications of imaginative literature between the founding of Madrid as a capital city in 1561 and the number of lyric publications by 1590, refer to: (C. Pérez Pastor, *Bibliografía madrileña, o, descripción de las obras impresas en Madrid*, [1891], fascim., Pamplona: Analecta, 2000, vol. III; vol. I). Also: (Y. Clemente San Román, *Tipobibliografía Madrileña: La imprenta en Madrid en el siglo xvi (1566–1600)*, Kassel: Edition Reichenberger, 1998, vol. I). For literacy in early-modern Spain: (T.J. Dadson, *Tolerance and Coexistence in Early Modern Spain, The Moriscos of the Campo de Calatrava*, London: Tamesis, 2014). For Lope de Vega's relationship to literary markets: (D. Gilbert-Santamaría, *Writers on the Market: Consuming Literature in Early Seventeenth-Century Spain*, Lewisburg: Bucknell University Press, 2005).

31 (Pérez Pastor, *Bibliografía madrileña*, vol. I, 1–165).

32 For the annexation of Portugal: (F. Bouza, *Imagen y propaganda: Capítulos de historia cultural del reinado de Felipe II*, Madrid: Akal Ediciones, 1998).

33 (Astrana Marín, *Vida ejemplar*, vol. III, 143–151).

Portugal is unknown. However, his contribution of an encomiastic sonnet to Pedro de Padilla's *Romancero* (Madrid: Francisco Sánchez, 1583) indicates that he had rejoined this circle of poets, whether in Madrid or in Lisbon, in time for the *licencia* and *privilegio* of this work, completed by Antonio de Eraso, on September 22, 1582 in Lisbon.[34] The *aprobación* for Padilla's text had been signed by Juan López de Hoyos, and it may be easily inferred that the court chronicler helped to welcome Cervantes back into the circles of poets writing in Madrid.[35] At home again within this urban pastoral, Cervantes wrote of Pedro de Padilla:

> Ya que del ciego dios habéis cantado
> el bien, y el mal, la dulce fuerza y arte,
> en la primera y la segunda parte,
> do está de amor el todo señalado,
> ahora, con aliento descansado
> y con nueva virtud que en vos reparte
> el cielo, nos cantáis del duro Marte
> las fieras armas y el valor sobrado.
> Nuevos ricos mineros se descubren
> de vuestro ingenio en la famosa mina,
> que al más alto deseo satisfacen;
> y, con dar menos de lo más que encubren,
> a este menos lo que es más se inclina
> del bien que Apolo y que Minerva hacen.

> Already of the blind god you have sung
> the good and the bad, the sweet force and art,
> in the first and second part,
> where love is signaled everywhere,
> now, with rested breath
> and with new virtue, that in you is distributed
> [by] the *cielo*, you sing to us of the hard Mars,
> the fierce arms, and the high valor.
> Newly mined riches are discovered

[34] Antonio de Eraso was Secretary of State to Philip II and Secretary of the Indies and of War. On Francisco de Eraso in a comparable post: (C.J. de Carlos Morales, "El poder de los secretarios reales: Francisco de Eraso," in ed. J. Martínez Millán, *La corte de Felipe II*, Madrid: Alianza, 1994, 107–148).

[35] According to his *aprobación*, the work was, "Principalmente, la historia de Flandes en Romances Castellanos, puesto con mucho artificio y decoro de la historia. También contiene Sonetos muy artificiosos de muy buenos conceptos, y agudas sentencias. Y ultra desto tiene una muy agradable variedad de Poesía, la cual hace, que la obra sea en si muy Ilustre y digna de que como Jardín de Floresta Española, para enriquecer nuestra lengua" (Laínez in P. de Padilla, *Romancero de Pedro de Padilla, En el cual se contienen algunos sucesos que en la jornada de Flandres los Españoles hicieron, Con otras historias y poesías diferentes, Dirigido al Ilustrísimo Señor Marques Mondejar*, Madrid: Francisco Sánchez, 1583, unpaginated, [iii]v).

of your *ingenio* in the famous mine
that satisfy even the loftiest desire;
   and, with giving the least of the much that they conceal,
even this little (which is still more) inclines
toward the good that Apollo and Minerva make/do.[36]

The full title of Padilla's work was the *Romancero de Pedro de Padilla en el cual se contienen algunos sucesos que en la jornada de Flandes los Españoles hicieron. Con otras historias y poesías diferentes* (Romancero of Pedro de Padilla in which are contained some of the events that happened in the *jornada* of Flanders.[37] With other different histories and poetries). The Renaissance motif of love and war, as reflected in the title and embodied in the soldier-poet, was repeated in Cervantes' sonnet.[38] The lyric lover, Padilla, was depicted as having sung of the "blind god," Love or Cupid, son of Venus, who is classically juxtaposed with Mars in the second stanza. This motif also appeared in Cervantes' early dramaturgy in which the

[36] (Cervantes, Poesías, 2016, 157–158). In 1582, the same year as the completion of the *Romancero*, Padilla's pastoral eclogues had appeared in print: (*Églogas pastoriles de Pedro de Padilla y juntamente con ellas algunos sonetos del mismo autor*, Seville: Andrea Pescioni, 1582). The volume was dedicated to Doña Anna de Mendoza, Duchess of Medina de Rioseco, not to be confused with the Princess of Eboli, Ana de Mendoza de la Cerda y de Silva Cifuentes, Duchess of Pastrana. In the prologue *Al lector*, Padilla wrote, "Son Églogas Pastoriles de differentes subjetos y composturas, donde con versos sueltos en lugar de prosa van ligados los demás que a diuersos propósitos se hizieron; solo pido que disculpe mi voluntad con los que saben alguna parte de las imperfectiones que lleuan" (Padilla, *Églogas pastoriles*, 2010, 50).

Laínez also contributed a laudatory sonnet to *Padilla's 1580 Thesoro de Varias Poesías*:

"*Soneto de Pedro Laynez al Avthor.* // De la varia, sotil, red amorosa / si ventura o razón no nos defiende / flaca es la mayor fuerça que pretende / rendir la que es y fue tan poderosa. / Seguir a Amor empresa es peligrosa, / huylle no aprouecha, antes ofende, / mas ya se puede amar, pues, ya se entiende / que ay passo cierto en senda tan dudosa. / Tú, famoso Padilla, hallaste, / pues con ventura y con razón pudiste / subir lo alto, asegurar lo incierto. / Los secretos de Amor que penetraste / tan viuamente aquí los descubriste, / que es ya lo obscuro y falso, claro y cierto" (Pedro de Padilla, *Thesoro de Varias Poesías*, eds. A. Valladares, J.J. Labrador Herraiz, R.A. DiFranco, México: Frente de Afirmación Hispanista, 2008, 36).

[37] On military history in Flanders as literary source: C. Hollingsworth, "The Source of Lope de Vega's Los Españoles en Flandes," *Hispanic Review*, 1974, 42.3, 279–292. Hollingsworth does not mention these seldom-studied pieces by Padilla.

[38] Edgar Wind, in his chapter "Virtue Reconciled with Pleasure" provides an altogether more appropriate depiction of the thought processes immediately relevant to these patrons and poets: "The ancient 'mystery' upon which they seized, was the unlawful union of Mars and Venus, from which issued a daughter named Harmony. Born from the god of strife and the goddess of love, she inherits the contrary characters of her parents: *Harmonia est discordia concors*. But her illegitimate birth, far from being a blemish, was taken for a sign of mystical glory, according to a rule set forth very clearly in Leone Ebreo's *Dialoghi d'amore*. In discussing the love and procreation of the gods as metaphors for universal forces in nature, he explained that 'when this union of the two parents occurs regularly in nature, it is called marriage by the poets, and the partners are called husband and wife; but when the union is an extraordinary one, it is styled amorous or adulterous, and the parents who bring forth are styled lovers'" (Wind, *Pagan Mysteries*, 81–82).

author wove military and political conflict into the amorous plots (the *Numancia*, the *Trato de Argel*, and the attributed *Jerusalén*). As with so much of the poetry of this period, Cervantes made the *ingenio* a central feature of the sonnet. The classical figuration of the poet as *vates* was rounded out by the positioning of Apollo and Minerva, in place of Mars and Venus, at the sonnet's close.[39] This modification after the *volta* shifted the dichotomy away from love and war toward the "divine science of poetry," as the summit of a contest between arms and letters, to which both love and war pertained. The 1583 printing included laudatory poems by Francisco de Montalvo and López Maldonado; the latter's *Cancionero* of 1586 again brought together Padilla and Cervantes amongst a growing textual community of living poets. In 1580 Padilla's *Thesoro de varias poesías*, the first of the two parts to which Cervantes referred (line 3 above), had included contributions from Pedro Laínez, Juan de Vergara, Ruy López de Zúñiga, Francesco Fortunato de Patti, Antonio Suárez, and again López Maldonado. The second of the two, *Églogas pastoriles* (1583), carried tercets by Gabriel de Arriaga and an approbation by Pedro Laínez.

Cervantes' metaphor of mining the *ingenio* was indicative of the accepted view of poiesis current amongst his contemporaries, as evidenced in the front matter of many of these works.[40] As the relatively small canon of amorous poets (Ovid, the *scuola siciliana*, the Provençal troubadours, the *dolce stil nuovo*, Dante, Petrarch, Boccaccio, Ausias March, and Sannazaro) grew to include Garcilaso, Boscán, Montemayor, Laínez, Figueroa, Herrera, Aldana, and others, the poets of the 1580s became increasingly aware of the stakes of their own *ingenios* as a literary legacy. As Pedro Laínez wrote in the *aprobación* to Pedro de Padilla's 1582 *Églogas pastoriles:*

> . . . todo me paresce digno de salir en público: el estilo es dulce, fácil, y propio, la inuención nueua, apazible y muy ingeniosa, y aunque en el discurso de la obra [h]ay algunos lugares ymitados y traduzidos, es con tanta

[39] For the poet as "Vates" and for "Furor Poeticus": (*Princeton Encyclopedia of Poetry and Poetics*, 1503–1504 and 531–533).

[40] On mining as metaphor and colonial practice: (Biegelow, *Mining Language*). For the work of the *ingenio*, for example, as depicted in Padilla's eclogues: "Pues que será escusado ingenio y arte / dezir la menor parte de las cossas / ricas, marauillosas no halladas / que en sí tiene çifradas mi pastora, / que el alma que le adora, solo entiende / y el bien que comprehende, como es tanto / ya del grosser canto, corta el hilo / porque tan baxo estilo es impossible / que diga lo possible, y a esta causa / hará la final pausa aquí la pluma, / y solo dirá, en suma, que no ay cosa / que se yguale a mi diosa en lo criado, / sino la fee y cuydado que yo tengo / con que viuo, descanso y me entretengo" (P. de Padilla, *Églogas pastoriles y juntamente con ellas algunos sonetos del mismo autor*, eds. A. Valladares, J.J. Labrador Herraiz, R.A. DiFranco, México: Frente de Afirmación Hispanista, 2010, égloga 4: ln. 452–465, 127-128).

facilidad y dulçura, que ygualan a sus primeros Auctores, y en muchas partes se les auentajan.

(... it all seems to me worthy of being brought out in public: the style is sweet, easy, and unique, the invention new, pleasant, and very ingenious, and although in the discourse of the work there are some places imitated and translated, it is with such facility and sweetness that they equal to their first Authors, and in many places excel them.)[41]

Doctor Juan Huarte de San Juan's *Examen de ingenios* of 1575 (augmented 1594) reinforced this understanding of the divine creative faculty of the *ingenio* (the act of poiesis) and the legacy which such a poet might garner for himself. While Huarte de San Juan's text has more frequently been discussed for its treatment of early modern humoral theory, as in the work of Otis Green, it was the doctor's conception of poiesis that is of interest here.[42] On this type of ingenious authorship, he wrote:

Como pareció en la invención de este nombre, *ingenio*, que para descubrirla fue menester una contemplación muy delicada y llena de filosofía natural. En la cual, discurriendo, hallaron que había en el hombre dos potencias generativas: una común con los brutos animales y plantas, y otra participante con las sustancias espirituales, Dios y los ángeles .... hablando con los filósofos naturales, ellos bien saben que el entendimiento es potencia generativa y que se empreña y pare, y que tiene hijos y nietos, y una partera (dice Platón) que le ayuda a parir. Porque de la manera que en la primera generación el animal o planta da ser real y sustantífico a su hijo, no lo teniendo antes de la generación, así el entendimiento tiene virtud y fuerzas naturales de producir y parir dentro de sí un hijo, al cual llaman los filósofos naturales *noticia* o *concepto*, que es *verbum mentis*.

(As it appeared in the invention of this word, *ingenio*, which in order to discover it a very delicate contemplation full of natural philosophy was required. In this discourse they found that there was in [the hu]man two generative potencies: one in common with the brute animals and plants, and the other a participant with the spiritual substances, God and the angels ... speaking with the natural philosophers, they well know that the *entendimiento* is a generative potency and it becomes pregnant and gives birth, and it has children and grandchildren, and a midwife (says Plato) which helps it give birth. Just as in the first animal or plant generation a real and substantial being is given to the child, not having one prior to the generation, in the same way, the *entendimiento* has the virtue and natural forces to produce and

41 (Padilla, *Églogas pastoriles y juntamente con ellas algunos sonetos del mismo autor*, 2010, 48).

42 (Green, "El ingenioso hidalgo," 176); (C. Orobitg, "Del *Examen de ingenios* de Huarte a la ficción cervantina, o cómo se forja una revolución literaria," *Criticón*, 2014, 23–39); (N. Ushijima, "Sobre los títulos del *Quijote*, La función del 'ingenio'," *Actas III-Actas Cervantinos*, 1990, 325–329).

give birth within itself to a child, which the natural philosophers call a *noticia* or *concepto*, which is *verbum mentis*.)[43]

Within this idea of authorial procreation (culled from Diotima in Plato's *Symposium*), intellectual gestation and birthing became metaphors for literary production (as an act of poiesis) employed by poetesses and poets throughout the sixteenth century.[44] For example, Maddalena Campiglia (1553–1595), author of the pastoral drama the *Flori*, who wrote for Felice Orisini Colonna (the mother of Ascanio), favored the birthing of the *ingenio* over that of children.[45] Cervantes exploits this understanding of poiesis in the narrator's references to the *DQ* as the "stepchild of his mind."[46] Indeed, this figuration of the author, as pregnant with thought, countered more militaristic and violent bids for immortality – the pen over the sword, as in the close of Cervantes' sonnet above. This deeply Platonic view of intellectual activity and reproduction was commonplace amidst the many prologues, dedications, and approbations authored by the poets of Pastoral Petrarchism. In a humility typical of dedicatory notes and prologues, Padilla took up Huarte de San Juan's language in his own genuflection before the reader in the prologue to his 1580 *Thesoro de varias poesías*:

> Aunque esta obra, por no tener determinado sujeto, no tenía necesidad de prólogo o prefación alguna, . . . sino la lástima de ver algunos hijos de mi pobre entendimiento tratados menos bien que merecen de muchos que no siendo sus padres los han hecho hijos adoptivos, para solo destruyrlos: y temeroso de que faltando yo se hiziese lo mismo con los que me quedauan, quise más subjetarlos a la piadosa censura de los buenos entendimientos, que dexarlos a elección de quien sabrá mejor acabarlos de hazer imperfectos, que corregirlos y perfectionarlos.
>
> (Although this work, for not having a determined subject, has no need of any prologue or prefatory remark, . . . the pity of seeing some children of my poor *entendimiento* treated less well than is deserved by many that, not being fathers, have taken adopted children only in order to destroy them, and fearful that being absent myself, they would do the same with those that I abandoned, I better wanted to subject them to the merciful censure of the

43 (J. Huarte de San Juan, *Examen de ingenios para las ciencias*, ed. G. Séres, Madrid: Cátedra, 1989; 186–188); (Plato, "Symposium," 206c-207c, 489–490).

44 The power of poiesis was ripe in the lyric topography well into the seventeenth century, as can be observed in the poetry of Juana Inés de la Cruz, such as "Détente, sombra de mi bien esquivo" in which the sonnet concludes, "poco importa burlar brazos y pecho / si te labra prisión mi fantasía" (J. I. de la Cruz, *Poesía lírica*, ed. J.C. González Boixo, Madrid: Cátedra, 14th ed., 2018, 124–125).

45 (L.J. Ultsch, "'Epithalamium Interruptum': Maddalena Campiglia's New Arcadia," *MLN*, 120.1, 2005, 70–92; 85–86).

46 (Cervantes, *DQ*, 1999, I: prologue, 9–10).

> good *entendimientos* than to leave them to the election of someone who will better know to finish them by making them imperfect, than correct them and perfect them.)[47]

In practice, Padilla's texts were more often lauded among a network of poets that shared this understanding of poiesis as procreation.

During this period, Cervantes contributed two laudatory poems and a sonnet on San Francisco to Pedro de Padilla's *Jardín espiritual* (1585), where Francisco de Montalvo and Luis Gálvez de Montalvo also appeared in the front matter.[48] He also contributed a laudatory sonnet in 1587 to Padilla's *Grandezas y excelencias de la Virgen*. Within the context of Pastoral Petrarchism, Padilla's turn away from the erotic poetry of his early volumes toward the religious devotion of his final works completed the Petrarchan trajectory devoted to the divine beloved, from Laura to the Virgin Mary. In the *Galatea*, the lengthy interpolated tale of Silerio similarly follows his transition from ill-fated lover to devout hermit, after losing both lady and friend in a byzantine turn of events. Perhaps most significant for the community of Pastoral Petrarchism, Cervantes contributed two laudatory poems to López Maldonado's *Cancionero* (1586), where he appeared alongside Don Luis de Vargas, Vicente Espinel, the licentiate Juan de Vergara, Gonzalo Gómez de Luque, Diego Durán, Pedro de Padilla, Diego de Aguiar, Lazaro Luis Liranzo, the licentiate Liñán [de Riaza], and the newly popular Lope de Vega. This collection brought together the entire milieu under the auspices of López Maldonado's "Definición de amor" and their ties to the philosophy of Judah Abravanel, as discussed in Chapter 4. During the second half of the decade, Cervantes wrote laudatory sonnets for Alonso de Barros' *Philosphia Cortesana moralizada* (Madrid: Alonso Gómez, 1587) and the doctor Francisco Díaz's *Tratado nuevamente impreso de todas las enfermedades de los riñones, vejiga y carnosidades de la verga y urina* (Madrid, 1588). In all of these works, he maintained the divine capacity of the *ingenio*, the excellence of sempiternal poetic feats, which competed with Greek and Tuscan posterity, the conceit of the river Tajo as a site of authorial production, and the figure of Apollo as presiding over compositions. While the last of these laudatory sonnets for Díaz's medical treatise may seem unlikely within the group of pastoral poets, the laudatory octave for Díaz in the "Canto de Calíope" of the

[47] (P. de Padilla, *Thesoro de Varias Poesías*, eds. A. Valladares, J.J. Labrador Herraiz, R.A. DiFranco, Moalde: Colección Cancioneros Castellanos, 2008, 35).

[48] (P. de Padilla, *Jardín espiritual, compuesto por F. Pedro de Padilla, de la orden de nuestra señora del Carmen*, Madrid: Guerino Gerardo Flamenco, a costa de Blas Robles, 1585, unpaginated).

Galatea suggests that he was also a poet within this network.[49] When Cervantes composed the laudatory sonnet for Díaz's text, he did so within the language of the pastoral:

Al Doctor Francisco Díaz, de Miguel de Cervantes, soneto.

Tú, que con nuevo y sin igual decoro
tantos remedios para un mal ordenas,
bien puedes esperar destas arenas,
del sacro Tajo, las que son de oro,
y el lauro que se debe al que un tesoro
halla de ciencia, con tan ricas venas
de raro advertimiento y salud llenas,
contento y risa del enfermo lloro;
que por tu industria una deshecha piedra
mil mármoles, mil bronces a tu fama
dará sin invidiosas competencias;
darate el cielo palma, el suelo yedra,
pues que el uno y el otro ya te llama
espíritu de Apolo en ambas ciencias.

You, that with new and unequaled decorum
order so many remedies for an ill,
you can very well expect from these sands,
of the sacred Tagus, those that are of gold,
and the laurel that is owed to that in which the treasure
of a science is found, with such rich veins
full of rare prescience and health,
contentment and levity for the sick grief;
that by your industry an uncut stone will give
a thousand marbles, a thousand bronzes
to your fame without envious competition;
the sky will give you peace, the earth herb,
well, the one and the other are already calling you
spirit of Apollo in both sciences.[50]

Apollo was both healer and poet. As with this laudatory sonnet for Díaz's *tratado*, in the "Canto de Calíope" of the *Galatea*, Cervantes also situated Díaz on the banks of the river Tajo, where the central action of the novel resides. It is within this context that we must come to understand the status

[49] "De ti, el doctor Francisco Diaz, puedo / assegurar a estos mis pastores / que, con seguro coraçon y ledo, / pueden auentajarse en tus loores. / Y si en ellos yo agora corta quedo, / deuiendose a tu ingenio los mayores, / es porque el tiempo es breue, y no me atreuo / a poderte pagar lo que te deuo" (Cervantes, *Galatea*, 1914, vol. II, 216, lines 5–12).

[50] (Cervantes, *Poesías*, 2016, 175–176).

of the *Galatea* as a *roman à clef*, not of court life but of ingenious writers and their lyric practices, gathering on the streets and in print during the early 1580s in Madrid.[51]

Housed in the Biblioteca Nacional of Madrid, ms. 2.856 provides one of the most curious early references to the pastoral encodings at work in pastoral poetics.[52] On the back of the final folio a number of stick-figure dueling *caballeros* have been set in action in the cartoon musings of the compiler. The entrenched relationship between pastoral practice and ingenious gentlemen is reinforced by the series of notes that the compiler has scrolled opposite these figures.

As an aid to the reader, or a note to self, the compiler offers the following cipher for pastoral pseudonyms in use amongst several poets of the period: Liñán [de Riaza] – Risselo; Lope de Vega – Belardo; Francisco de Figueroa – Tirsi; and Miguel de Cervantes – Lausso. While the accuracy of the manuscript has sometimes been called into question, its very existence reinforces the strength of place which the pastoral as *roman à clef* held in the imaginations of early readers. To the compiler of the manuscript whose doodles populate this spare page, there was little doubt that the pastoral elicited this type of decoding. When combined with textual clues contained within the novel and Cervantes' own return to the figure of Silena (Lauso's beloved) in the *Viaje del Parnaso*, it is reasonable to believe that the whimsical young scribe had some insight into these nominal *disfraces*.

Studies of the *Galatea* as a *roman à clef* have typically focused on select identifications based on scholarly knowledge of literary culture at the time. The first of these has long been the identification of Francisco de Figueroa with the elder shepherd-poet Tirsi. Within the *Galatea* Cervantes directly cited Figueroa's own poetry as that of Tirsi's. While Figueroa's works were published posthumously, they were recognizable to his contemporary

[51] "The printer of the Galatea, Juan Gracián, was not chosen by Cervantes .... Furthermore, Juan Gracián would die soon after: by 1588, the second edition of the Cancionero general de la doctrina cristiana of Juan López de Úbeda was published by the 'herederos de Juan Gracián.' But Gracián had been a distinguished printer, who in 1580 had brought out the first Spanish translation of Os Lusiadas of Camoens, done by his compatriot Benito Caldera. To be sure, the same four poets who praised Caldera's translation in Gracián's edition (el maestro Garay, Luis Gálvez de Montalvo, el maestro Vergara and Pedro Laínez) were allotted laudatory octaves in Cervantes' Canto de Calíope, and Pedro Laínez even appears as a character in La Galatea, under the poetic pseudonym of Damón. The same place, the same printer, and the same four poets appear in both works. I mention this en passant for I think that it would be worthwhile to reconstruct and study these provincial poetic cliques, because they might solve more than one small literary mystery of the times" (Avalle-Arce, "The Novelistic Crucible," 8).

[52] The manuscript is described by Astrana Marín (*Vida ejemplar*, vol. II, 429–431).

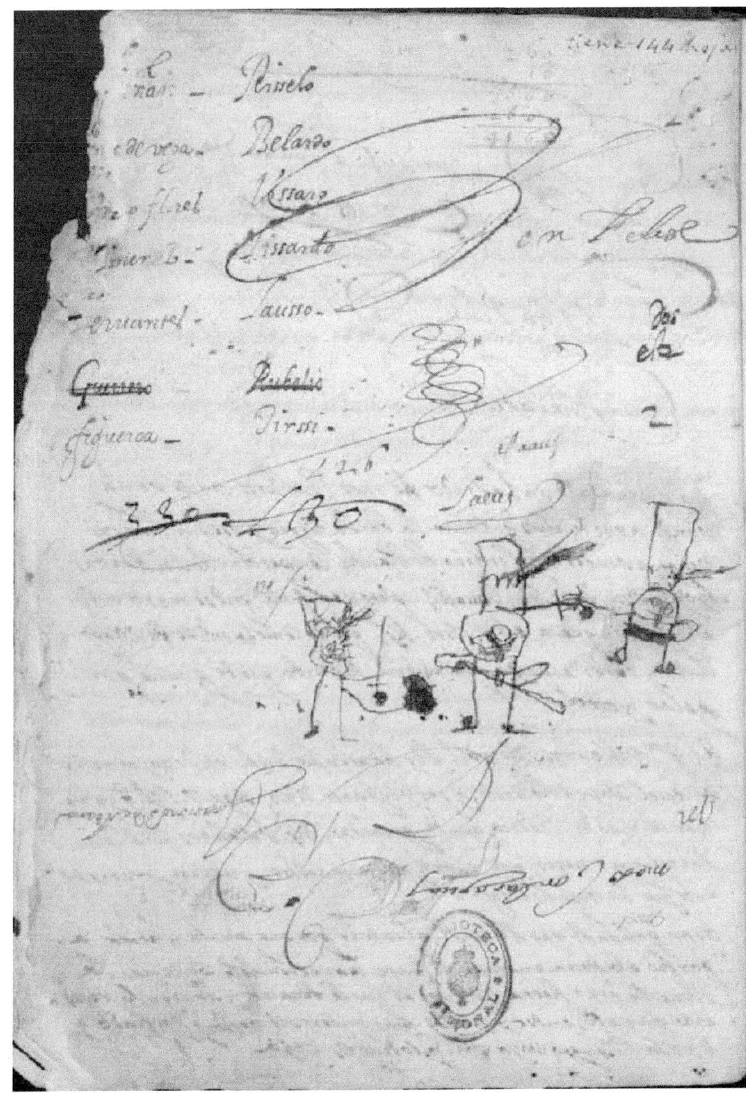

Fig. 5.1 Ms. 2.856, anonymous, unpaginated [last page with markings], Imágenes procedentes de los fondos de la Biblioteca Nacional de España

readers through manuscript circulation.[53] In Book II, the younger shepherd-poet Elicio declaims Tirsi's poetry while Tirsi is absent from the

[53] (F. Bouza, *Corre manuscrito, Una historia cultural del siglo de oro*, Madrid: Marcial Pons, 2001, 57).

scene. This inclusion of a younger poet declaiming the work of a senior poet was a narrative gesture mimetic of the very composition of the *Galatea.* Schevill and Bonilla identified these citations with Figueroa's Sonnet XXI, Sonnet XXVII, and Canción IV, printed in Pedro Craesback's 1625 edition of Figueroa's *Obras*, but already known in court and urban milieus in his lifetime.[54] In addition to these direct citations, Cervantes gave strong narrative indications that Tirsi was intended as a recognizable representation of the *divino* Figueroa, such as Elicio's praise

[54] Cervantes would have known Figueroa's poetry by way of friendship and manuscript circulation. The Canción figures in manuscript 2.864 of the Biblioteca Riccardiana (folios 7v–9r). This manuscript is cited by Schevill and Bonilla in their edition of the *Galatea* (1914). They also give the following reference: Eugenio Mele and Adolfo Bonilla, *Dos Cancioneros Españoles* (Madrid, 1904) 12. I have not yet had the opportunity to examine this manuscript.

"Soneto XXXI. . .¡Ah, de quan ricas esperanças vengo / al deseo más pobre i encogido / que jamás encerró pecho herido / de llaga tan mortal como yo tengo! / Ya de mi fee, ya de mi amor tan luengo, / que Phili sabe bien quan firme ha sido: / ya del fiero dolor con que he vivido, / i en quien la vida a mi pesar sostengo, / otro más dulce galardon no quiero, / sino que Phili un poco alce los ojos / a ver lo que mi rostro le figura: / que, si lo mira, i su color primero / no muda, y aun quiçá moja sus ojos, / bien será más que piedra helada i dura. . .Soneto XXVII. . . La amarillez i la flaqueza mia / el comer poco y el dormir perdido, / la falta quasi entera del sentido, / el debil passo, i la voz ronca i fria, / la vista incierta, i el más largo dia / en suspiros y quexas repartido, / alguno pensará que aya nacido / de la pasada trabajosa via. / I sabe bien Amor que otro tormento / me tiene tal, i otra razón mas grave / mi antigua gloria en tal dolor convierte. / Amor solo lo sabe, i yo lo siento. / ¡Si Phili lo supiesse! . . . ¡O mi suave / tormento! ¡O dolor dulce! ¡O dulce muerte!. . . Canción IV. . . Sale la Aurora, de su fertil manto / rosas suaves esparziendo i flores: / pintando el cielo va de mil colores, / i la tierra otro tanto, / quando la dulce pastorzilla mia, / lumbre i gloria del dia, / no sin astucia i arte, / de su dichoso alvergue alegre parte. // Pisada del gentil blanco pie, crece / la hierva, i nace en monte, en valle o llano: / qualquier planta que toca con la mano, / qualquier arbol florece. / Los vientos, si soberbios van soplando, / con su vista amansando, / en la fresca ribera / del rio Tybre sientase y m'espera. // Dexa por la garganta cristallina / suelto el oro que encoge el sutil velo; / arde de amor la tierra, el rio, el cielo, / i a sus ojos se inclina; / ella, de azules i purpureas rosas, / coge las más hermosas, / i, tendiendo su falda, / texe dellas despues bella guirnalda. // En esto vee que el sol, dando al Aurora / licencia, muestra en la vezina cumbre / del monte el rayo de su clara lumbre, / que el mundo orna i colora. / Turbase, i una vez arde i se aira, / otra teme y suspira / por mi luenga tardança, / i, en mitad del temor, cobra esperança. // Yo, que estava, encubierto, los más raros / milagros de [natura] i de amor viendo, / i su amoroso coraçón leyendo / poco a poco en sus claros / ojos, principio i fin de mi deseo, / como turbar los veo, / i, enojado conmigo, / temblando, ante ellos me presento, i digo: // "Rayos, oro, marfil, sol, laços, vida / de mi vida i mi alma i de mis ojos: / pura frente, que estás de mis despojos / más preciosos ceñida: / hevano, nieve, púrpura i jasmines, / ambar, perlas, rubines: / tanto vivo y respiro, / quanto sin miedo i sobresalto os miro." // Alça los ojos a mi voz, turbada, / [*i, mirando los mios, segura i leda, / sin moverlos, a mi se llega, i queda / de mi cuello colgada, / i assi está un poco embebecida; i luego, / con amoroso fuego, / blandamente me toca, / i bebe las palabras de mi boca*]. // Despues comiença, en son dulce i sabroso / (i, a su voz, cessa el viento i para el rio): / 'Dulce esperança mia, dulce bien mio: / fuente, sombra, reposo / de mi sedienta, ardiente i cansada alma: / vista serena i calma: / ¡muera aqui, si más chara / no me eres que los ojos de la cara!" // Assi dice ella, i nunca en tantos nudos / *[fue de yedra o de vid olmo enlazado, / quanto fui de sus brazos apretado, / hasta el codo desnudos; / i, entrando en el jardin de los amores, / cogi las tiernas flores / con el fruto dichoso: / ¿quien vio nunca pastor tan venturoso?]* (Cervantes, *Galatea*, 1914, vol. I, 246–249).

of Tirsi as exemplary among the shepherd-poets. By the early 1580s Figueroa, like Tirsi, had retired to the banks of the Henares, a renowned court poet who sought a reprieve in Alcalá toward the end of the 1570s. Tirsi's position as wizened mentor to the younger poets replicated the role that Figueroa played among Cervantes' milieu. In fact, it may have been Figueroa's status as a *divino ingenio* which led the author to include the poet's own work rather than attempt to invent verses characteristic of his style. He would have been seen as inimitable.

Tirsi's position at the head of a generation of poets served as a *clef* to several other figures dressed up in the pastoral garb. Tirsi and Damón, who reside on the banks of the Henares, are the venerated *dos amigos* of an elder generation which included the deceased shepherd-poet Meliso (long identified with Diego Hurtado de Mendoza). Damón has typically been identified with Pedro Laínez, the poetic companion of Figueroa; he was one of the only remaining poets of that generation by the opening of the 1580s, and Cervantes' lyric mentor since his days in the court of Isabel de Valois in the 1560s. This elder generation had its counterpart in the youngest and featured *dos amigos* of the text, Elicio and Erastro, whose mutual love for Galatea became the main plot on the banks of the Tajo. For reasons that I will expand upon below, I have speculatively identified Elicio and Erastro as Lope de Vega and Liñán de Riaza, respectively. In between the elders of the Henares (Tirsi and Damón) and the youths of the Tajo (Elicio and Erastro), Cervantes situated his own poetic persona, Lauso. In touch with both poetic epochs, and a longtime friend of Damón, Lauso, as newly returned to the banks of the Tajo after a period abroad, was made a sort of outlier in the generational divide.

Lauso's shepherdess, Silena, is the most mysterious of all; she does not explicitly appear within the action of the text, and has baffled scholarship for some time. She later appeared in Cervantes' *Viaje del Parnaso* (1614) shortly before the poet's death. Like the mysterious Aldonza Lorenzo behind the pseudonym of Dulcinea, the Silena of the *Galatea* remains hidden by the pastoral veil. She could not have been either Anna Francisca de Rojas or Catalina de Palacios Salazar because both women entered the author's life in 1584 after the *Galatea* had been completed (in late 1583 or January 1584) and submitted for the approbation and printing privilege (February 1584). The dedication to Ascanio Colonna was penned days after the death of his father, Marco Antonio, on April 1, 1584. However, neither Lauso nor Silena were unique to the *Galatea* within Cervantes' corpus. His *romance*, "La morada de los celos," did not appear in print during the 1580s but pertained to the same poetic community. The text was recorded in various forms subsequent to this period. It appeared as the "Romance a una cueva muy escura, por Miguel de

Çeruantes" in the *Cancionero* of the Duke of Estrada, now housed in the National Library of Naples.[55] In 1593, the work was printed in the *Flor de varios y nuevos romances.*[56] The poem also appeared in its most complete form in the 1600, the 1604, and various other printings of the *Romancero general.* The *romance* reiterated Cervantes' shared role in the group of poets known as *los modernos,* whose efforts to revitalize and reinvent the *romance* during the 1580s were championed by Lope de Vega and Liñán de Riaza.[57] Situated sometime in the 1580s, the *romance* recalled Isabel and Juana's palace *invenciones* and anticipated dQ's descent into the *Cueva de Montesinos.*

> . . . una entrada de un abismo,
> quiero decir una cueva
> profunda, lóbrega, oscura,
> aquí mojada, allí seca,
> propio albergue de la noche,
> del horror y las tinieblas.
>
> (. . . an entrance to an abyss,
> I want to say a cave
> profound, gloomy, dark,
> here damp, there dry,
> the very lodging of the night,
> of horror and of darkness.)[58]

[55] (ms. I-E, 49, fol. 94) See: (Cervantes, *Comedias y entremeses, Poesías sueltas*, eds. Roberto Schevill and Adolfo Bonilla, Madrid: Bernardo Rodríguez, 1922, vol. VI, 62–67); (Cervantes, *Poesías Completas*, 1974, 369–372). Sáez prints all three versions: the manuscript *Cancionero* of the Duke of Estrada, the 1593 printing, and the 1600 printing (Cervantes, *Poesías*, 2016, 189–194).

[56] According to Schevill and Bonilla, the 1593 text was largely inaccurate but contained interesting variants. See (Cervantes, *Poesías*, 2016, 189-191).

[57] "Yace donde el sol se pone / entre dos tajadas peñas / una entrada de un abismo, / quiero decir una cueva / profunda, lóbrega, escura, / aquí mojada, allí seca, / propio albergue de la noche, / del horror y las tinieblas. / Por la boca sale un aire / que al alma encendida yela, / y un fuego, de cuando en cuando, / que el pecho de yelo quema. / Óyese dentro un ruïdo / como crujir de cadenas / y unos ayes luengos, tristes, / envueltos en tristes quejas. / Por las funestas paredes, / por los resquicios y quiebras / mil víboras se descubren / y ponzoñosas culebras. / A la entrada tiene puesto[s], / en una amarilla piedra, / huesos de muerto encajados / de modo que forman letras, / las cuales, vistas del fuego / que arroja de sí la cueva, / dicen: «Esta es la morada / de los celos y sospechas». / Y un pastor cantaba a Lauso / esta maravilla cierta / de la cueva, fuego y yelo, / aullidos, sierpes y piedra, / el cual, oyendo, le dijo: / «Pastor, para que te crea, / no has menester juramentos / ni hacer la vista experiencia. / Un vivo traslado es ese / de lo que mi pecho encierra, / el cual, como en cueva escura, / no tiene luz, ni la espera. / Seco le tienen desdenes / bañado en lágrimas tiernas; / aire, fuego y los suspiros / le abrasan contino y yelan. / Los lamentables aullidos, / son mis continuas querellas, / víboras mis pensamientos / que en mis entrañas se ceban. / La piedra escrita, amarilla, / es mi sin igual firmeza, / que mis huesos en la muerte / mostrarán que son de piedra. / Los celos son los que habitan / en esta morada estrecha, / que engendraron los descuidos / de mi querida Silena». / En pronunciando este nombre, / cayó como muerto en tierra, / que de memorias de celos / aquestos fines se esperan" (Cervantes, *Poesías*, 2016, 191–193).

[58] (Cervantes, *Poesías*, 2016, 191).

The focus on jealously explicitly referred to the plot of Lauso and Silena in the *Galatea*, one that took up the problem of Lauso's jealousy as a story of the interior which thrust the unfolding of his plot into a type of chronotopic dynamism (discussed in Chapter 6). By exchanging the problem of an unwanted marriage (a classic of the pastoral prosimetrum, what is at issue for Galatea and Elicio) for the internal struggle of jealousy, Cervantes reoriented Lauso's narrative away from exterior obstacles toward the emplotment of the lyric interior.

If there were any doubt about the repeated presence of Silena in the author's poetic imagination, the fourth chapter of the *Viaje del Parnaso* (1614) placed the anonymous lady under her pastoral pseudonym within the author's literary legacy. To Delio, the author declares:

> Yo corté con mi ingenio aquel vestido
> con que al mundo la hermosa *Galatea*
> salió para librarse del olvido.
> . . .
> También, al par de Filis, mi Silena
> resonó por las selvas, que escucharon
> más de una y otra alegre cantilena,
> y en dulces varias rimas se llevaron
> mis esperanzas los ligeros vientos,
> que en ellos y en la arena se sembraron.
> Tuve, tengo y tendré los pensamientos,
> merced al cielo que a tal bien me inclina,
> de toda adulación libres y esentos.
>
> (I cut with my *ingenio* that dress
> with which for the world the beautiful Galatea
> went out in order to be liberated from forgetfulness.
> . . .
> Also, equal of Filis, my Silena
> resounded through the forests, that listened
> to more than one and another happy melody,
> and in sweet varied rhymes they were carried off,
> my hopes, by light winds,
> sewn in them and in the sands.
> I had, I have and I will have my thoughts,
> thanks to the *cielo* that to such a good inclines me,
> untethered and free of all adulation.)[59]

[59] (M. de Cervantes, "Capítulo Quarto," *Viaje del Parnaso*, ed. J.T. Medina, Santiago de Chile: Imprenta Universitaria, 1925, 132–141).

Thus, the quasi-autobiographical poet-speaker of the *Viaje* distinguished between "la hermosa Galatea," whose immortality the poet had tailored, and "mi Silena," who served both as the source of inspiration for his fleeting pastoral song, and ultimately the sempiternal ("tuve, tengo, y tendré") lady of his thoughts. If the Petrarchan project of poetic immortalization was reserved for the literary craft devoted to Galatea, the Petrarchan affect or *vita* of the poet was owed to the influence of Silena. The metaphor of the tailor recalled Garcilaso's "mi alma os ha cortado a su medida" of Sonnet 5 in order to render the poet the shaper of Galatea's literary afterlife. But the tribute to Silena reprised the most famous lines of Petrarch's "Voi ch'ascoltate," such that the Tuscan's "del vario stile in ch'io piango et ragiono / fra le vane speranze e 'l van dolore (the varied style in which I weep and reason / between vain hope and vain pain)," became "y en dulces varias rimas se llevaron / mis esperanzas los ligeros vientos (and in sweet varied rhymes they were carried away / my hopes by light winds)." Lauso's *rime* for Silena, ultimately sewn in the wind and sand, seemed to disentangle poetic immortality from erotic affect, the former a choice and the latter a fate. While Silena was still the poetic focal point of the aging speaker of the *Viaje*, her identity remains a mystery.

The other two identifications which consistently appear in scholarship are characters who do not feature within the action of the text, but who are mentioned due to their relevance to Lauso. They are Astraliano (Don Juan de Austria) and Larsileo (Mateo Vázquez). The "Canción de Lauso" in the *Galatea*, a revision of the *Epístola a Mateo Vázquez*, which Cervantes wrote and sent from Algiers, is said by Damón to have been sent by Lauso (Cervantes) to Larsileo (Mateo Vázquez). In the case of Astraliano, the reader is told that Damón and Lauso have not seen one another since before Astraliano headed north for military campaigns, that is, since the Battle of Lepanto and Don Juan's departure from Milan for the Low Countries. He died in Belgium of fever in 1578. In the case of Larsileo, Damón's recitation of the "Canción de Lauso," a versified epistle on the perennial theme of *menosprecio de corte y alabanza del aldea*, left little doubt about the true identities of these thinly veiled interlocutors.[60] In 2010, Sánchez Portero attempted to identify Liñán de Riaza with the *desamorado*

Unfortunately, in his 1925 edition, Medina gives the following note on the Castilianization of Cervantes' *latinismos*: "Notemos que en la edición príncipe está *pronto* escrito a la latina: *prompto*, como antes (911) *trasumpto:* formas que no es posible conservar por efecto de la rima" (Cervantes, *Viaje del Parnaso*, 1925; 131 n.1264). Cervantes' rhyming ear was not shared by Medina.

60 (A. de Guevara, *Menosprecio de corte y alabanza de aldea*, ed. A. Rallo Gruss, Madrid: Cátedra, 1984).

Lenio.[61] However, given Liñán's close friendship with Lope and the fact that both were conceived of as belonging to the youngest and most active generation within the group, particularly influential in the modernization of the *romance*, as well as Liñán's reputation as a rustic poet, the identification with Erastro is much more appropriate.[62] It is far more likely that Lenio served as a guise for López Maldonado of the 1586 *Cancionero*, whose reputation as a misogynist and enemy of love point toward his identification as the *hereje del amor* who contests with Tirsi in the famous debate on love drawn from Abravanel's *Dialoghi*.[63] Of the youngest generation of poets writing in Madrid during the first half of the 1580s, only Lope de Vega garnered the biographical and literary notoriety necessary for an identification with Elicio. It seems reasonable to conjecture that the *Galatea* depicts a crucial and overlooked moment in the early career of Lope de Vega (1580–1583) prior to the dissolution of his affair with Elena Osorio, her preference for Francisco Perrenot de Granvela, the suit for libel in 1587–1588, Lope's exile and abduction of Isabel de Urbina, and his own first literary reworking of the Osorio affair in his *Arcadia* (1598).[64] Speculatively, Elena Osorio is the Galatea of Cervantes' prosimetrum.

Something more must be said of the many shepherd-poets whom Cervantes gathers on the banks of the river Tajo throughout his text, and in particular of the geographical indications which the author is careful to provide for his readers. The central plot and narrative timeline of the *Galatea* takes place on the river Tajo (Madrid), and includes visits from several foreign shepherds. The community which most directly corresponds to and is enmeshed with the community of the Tajo is the community of the Henares (Alcalá). The shepherd-poets of both rivers pertain to the same milieu; they know one another through both personal friendship and literary fame. For example, Lauso (Tajo) is friends with Damón

61 (A. Sánchez Portero, "Correlación entre el Desamorado Lenio', Liñán de Riaza y el «Desamorado Don Quijote» de Avellaneda," *Lemir*, 2010, vol. XIV, 53–56).

62 "Al mismo grupo [generación de 1580] pertenece Pedro Liñán de Riaza, nacido en Toledo y de padres aragoneses, muerto en 1607. A él le dedica Lope varios sonetos (*Rimas*, núms. 54 y 92) y lo elogia en *La Filomena*. La atribuye el *Ramillete de flores* el romance «Pues ya desprecias el Tajo» (*Fuentes*, V, fol. 5), y es posible, como bien afirma José F. Montesinos, que su mismo nombre «atrajera romances espúrios». Lo considera este crítico como el iniciador («el cultor») más eficaz «de cierto realismo bucólico». La aldea arcádica, convencional, idealizada, es sustituida por la rústica, atenuada, según la convención, por las circunstancias de la vida pastoril cotidiana. Vista desde la corte adquiere una perspectiva irónica, incluso burlesca. Y de Liñán procede esta modalidad rústica, dentro de la temática pastoril" (Carreño, *El Romancero Lírico*, 28, square brackets mine).

63 (López Estrada, "La influencia italiana").

64 (Lope de Vega, *Dorotea*, ed. J.M. Blecua, Madrid: Universidad de Puerto Rico, Revista Occidente, [1955] 1996; 13–30).

(Henares). Tirsi (Henares) is famous throughout both communities. Tirsi and Damón (Henares) are privy to the courtship of Elicio and Galatea (Tajo). However, the Tajo needs not necessarily indicate poetic culture in Madrid. The vast river more readily referred to Toledo (as in the case of Gálvez de Montalvo's *El pastor de Fílida*) and may have been consistently employed in the pastoral fiction to indicate the location of the court in general, which in the early 1580s may have included itinerant stays in Portugal. Yet it is clear that Cervantes is using the Tajo as a metonym for his own circle of Pastoral Petrarchists who had settled in Madrid by the early 1580s. Madrid was also the only site of congregation for poets on the Tajo sufficiently close to the Henares to provide for easy visits from those of Alcalá (de Henares), as occurs in the text. This ambiguity regarding the community on the Tajo was clarified within the space of the *roman à clef.*

When Cervantes made poets, rather than ladies, the subject of the "Canto de Calíope" in Book VI of the *Galatea*, he unambiguously signaled to the reader that this was a work meant to commemorate poets and the practices of Pastoral Petrarchism then flourishing in Madrid's *barrio de las letras.*[65] In Book VI, the text supplied explicit clues for the identification of the shepherd-poets on the Tajo with their living counterparts in Madrid. The "Canto de Calíope" was divided into rivers in order to signal particular poetic communities throughout the Spanish-speaking world. Cervantes used the river Tajo in the "Canto de Calíope" to provide the biographical names of the many pseudonymic-shepherds whom he placed as characters on the banks of the Tajo within his poetic fiction. To my knowledge, no work of scholarship has been attentive to the list of poets whom Calíope places on the Tajo as a *clef* within the work. Twenty-eight poets appear on the river Tajo by way of Calíope's song. They are: Doctor Francisco de Campuzano,[66] Doctor Suarez de Sosa, Doctor Vaca, licenciate Dionisio Daza Chacón, *Maestro* Garay,[67]

[65] Both Montemayor and Gálvez de Montalvo included lengthy encomiastic poems which lauded a catalogue of noble ladies. Cervantes took the precedent of lauding poets from Gil Polo.

[66] Schevill and Bonilla give his name as Doctor Francisco de Campuçano, "fue médico del Rey. Hay versos suyos en el *Jardín espiritual* de Pedro de Padilla (Madrid, 1585); en el *Cancionero* de López Maldonado (Madrid, 1586) y en *El Pastor de Philida*, de Luis Gálvez de Montalvo (Madrid, 1582). Lope de Vega, en la *Dorotea* (acto IV, escena II) menciona al Dr. Campuzano entre los que llama 'grandes poetas de esta edad'" (Cervantes, *Galatea*, 1914, vol. II, 307–308).

[67] "Menciónale con elogio Lope de Vega en la *Arcadia* (libro V, *ad finem*), llamándole 'laureado y divino ingenio'; en la *Dorotea* (acto IV, scena II); en *El jardín de Lope* (*La Filomena;* Madrid, 1621; fol. 154v.), donde habla de 'Garay, en tantas letras eminente'; en la *Relacion de las fiestas que la insigne villa de Madrid hizo en la canonizacion de S. Isidro* (Madrid, 1622), y en el *Laurel de Apolo* (silva IV), donde se expresa así: 'En el doctor Garay hallarás luego / oposiciones al latino y griego, / felicísimo río, / cuando en aplauso de la docta Clío / le viste coronar méritamente, / y él dijo en sus canciones: / *Tengo una honrada frente, / de laurel coronada.* / Felice edad pasada, / que honrabas los científicos varones, / ¿cuándo será que premies y repares / la gloria de tus hijos, sacro Henares?'. También le loa Espinel en *La Casa de la Memoria* (folios 32 vuelto

Maestro Juan de Córdoba,[68] the Doctor Francisco Díaz,[69] Luján, Juan de Vergara,[70] licenciate Alonso de Morales Salado,[71] licenciate Hernando Maldonado, Marco Antonio de la Vega, Diego de Mendoza, Diego González Durán,[72] Gabriel López Maldonado,[73] Luis Gálvez de Montalvo,[74] Pedro Liñán de Riaza,[75] Alonso de

y siguientes), haciéndole natural de las riberas del Duero. Hay un soneto del Lic. Garay al frente de *Los Lusiadas*, de Camoens, traducidos por Benito Caldera (Alcalá, 1580). Otras poesías, sacadas de un códice que fué de D. José María de Alava, pueden verse en el tomo XLII de la *Biblioteca de Autores Españoles*. Finalmente, consérvanse composiciones de Garay, con otras de Juan de Salinas y de Baltasar del Alcázar, en un tomo en 4., manuscrito de fines del siglo XVII (70 hojas), que poseyó Aureliano Fernández-Guerra y hoy se halla en poder de D. Luis Valdés y Alberti; y en *El Cancionero de Mathias Duque de Estrada*" (Cervantes, *Galatea*, 1914, vol. II, 311–312).

68 Friend and perhaps the schoolmaster of Lope de Vega who lauds him in the *Laurel de Apolo* (silva IV) and in *El perergrino,* (libro IV, folio 179 vuelto, de la edición barcelonesa de 1605)". His Latin poems can be found in the *Tractatus Eleemosynae* ... of the licentiate Alfonso Iñigo de Valdés (Madrid, 1588) and in both editions of the *Diversas Rimas* of Vicente Espinel (Madrid, 1591)" (Cervantes, *Galatea*, 1914, vol. II, 311–312).

69 Doctor and surgeon of Philip II who dedicated his *Tratado nuevamente impresso de todas las enfermedades de los Riñones, Vexiga y carnosidades de la verga y urina* (Madrid, 1588) to Doctor Francisco Valles; Cervantes and Lope de Vega contributed laudatory sonnets. Díaz authored the *Compendio de Chirugia* (Madrid, 1575) and contributed a sonnet to Duarte Dias' *La Conquista que hicieron los poderosos y católicos reyes don Fernando y doña Isabel en el reino de Granada* (Madrid, 1590): (Cervantes, *Galatea*, 1914, vol. II, 314).

70 Doctor, surgeon, and poet whose poetry appeared in: Díaz's *Compendio de Chirugia* (Madrid, 1575), *Obras de Música para tecla, arpa y vihuela* (Madrid, 1578) by Antonio de Cabezón; Padilla's *Thesoro de varias poesías* (Madrid, 1580); *Método de la colección y reposición de las medicinas simples* (Madrid, 1581) by Luis de Oviedo; Lope's *Isidro* (Madrid, 1599); López Maldonado's *Cancionero* (Madrid, 1586); *Práctica y teórica de cirugía* by Daza Chacón (Valladolid, 1584); Lope's *La Hermosura de Angélica* (Madrid, 1602); the *Romancero historiado* of Lucas Rodríguez (Alcalá, 1585); the *Floresta de varia poesía* collected in México in 1577 (ms. 2.973 of the BNE); and Benito Caldera's translation of *Los Lusiadas* (Alcalá, 1580): (Cervantes, *Galatea*, 1914, vol. II, 314).

71 "[H]ay un soneto, con otros de Pedro Láinez y de Jun de Vergara, en las citadas *Obras de Musica* de Antonio de Cabezón (Madrid, 1578) y en el aludido *Methodo de la collection y reposicion de las medicinas simples*, de Luis de Oviedo (Madrid, 1581)" (Cervantes, *Galatea*, 1914, vol. II, 314).

72 "Hay un soneto suyo en las *Primeras tragedias españolas* de Antonio de Silva (Fr. Jerónimo Bermúdez), impresas en Madrid, el año 1577 .... Otra poesía del ... *Cancionero* de López Maldonado (Madrid, 1586)" (Cervantes, *Galatea*, 1914, vol. II, 316).

73 In addition to the *Cancionero* of 1586, his sonnet appeared in *Las obras de Boscan y Garcilaso trasladados en materias cristianas y religiosas* by Sebastián de Córdoba (Granada, 1575) and in *El Prado de Valencia* by Gaspar Mercader (Valencia, 1600). "Maldonado residió algún tiempo en Valencia, donde ingresó en la *Academia de los Nocturnos*, con el seudónimo de *Sincero*, en 1592. En el *Cancionero* de dicha Academia ... figuran composiciones de Maldonado. Hay además poesías suyas en el *Tesoro de varias poesías* (Madrid, 1580), en el Romancero (Madrid, 1583), y en el *Jardín espiritual* (Madrid, 1585) de Pedro de Padilla. Le alaban: Cervantes, en el *Quixote* (I, 6): Espinel, en *La Casa de la Memoria (Rimas, &)*; y Lope de Vega, en *La Dorotea* (VI, II)" (Cervantes, *Galatea*, 1914, vol. II, 316–317).

74 "El nombre poético de Gálvez de Montalvo era *Siralvo*, que aparece como autor de una epístola en verso (E: 'El pastor más humilde de la tierra') dirigida a *Clarinda*, en el manuscrito 3.358, folio 49 recto, de la Biblioteca Ricardiana" (Cervantes, *Galatea*, 1914, vol. II, 317–318). See the citation for Gálvez de Montalvo's July 13, 1587 letter to the Duke of Francavila from Rome, where Gálvez de Montalvo was in the service of Ascanio Colonna.

75 "Su nombre poético era *Riselo*. Coleccionáronse sus *Rimas* en la edición, bastante incompleta, de la *Biblioteca de Escritores Aragoneses* (Zaragoza, 1876). Cons. también: Pedro Espinosa, *Flores de poetas*

Valdés,[76] Pedro de Padilla, Gaspar Alfonso, Cristóbal de Mesa, Pedro de Ribera, Benito Caldera, Francisco de Guzmán, Capitán Juan de Salcedo Villandrando, Tomás Gracián Dantisco,[77] Baptista de Bivar, Balthasar de Toledo, and Lope de Vega. The division of poets into rivers did not accord to biographical place of origin, but to the regional divisions of poetic practice at the time that the novel was written. Among them, Doctor Campuzano, Juan de Vergara, Diego Durán, López Maldonado, Luis Gálvez de Montalvo, Liñán de Riaza, Pedro de Padilla, and Lope de Vega were not only poets of the Tajo according to Calíope, but also all appeared alongside Cervantes in the front matter to the 1586 printing of López Maldonado's *Cancionero*, a text which included the reprinting of López Maldonado's own laudatory sonnet for the *Galatea*. In addition to the front matter, the *Cancionero* included versified epistolary exchanges with Doctor Campuzano and Gálvez de Montalvo in the body of the text. Together, the *Cancionero* and the *Galatea* give a sempiternal afterlife to this active network within a shared poetic milieu.

In placing active poets, by name, on the banks of the Tajo, Calíope calls attention to the biographical counterparts to the shepherds of the fiction. She addresses the group of pseudonymically masked characters gathered on the Tajo to honor Meliso as being one and the same with the biographically identified poets that she names on the Tajo:

> Del claro Tajo la ribera hermosa
> adornan mil espíritus divinos,
> que hacen nuestra edad mas venturosa
> que aquella de los griegos y latinos.
> Dellos pienso decir sola una cosa:
> que son de vuestro valle y honra dignos

ilustres, segunda edición citada, núms. 110 y 124; E. Mele y A. Bonilla, *El Cancionero de Mathias Duque de Estrada (Revista de Archivos;* Madrid, 1902); idem id., *Dos Cancioneros españoles*, Madrid, 1904, páginas 8, 10 y 11; E. Mele, *Rimas inéditas* (de Aguilar, Espinel, Mercader, Tárrega, Liñán, Belvis y Guillén de Castro), Bordeaux, 1901 (tirada aparte del *Bulletin Hispanique*); A. Bonilla, *Anales de la Literatura Española;* Madrid, 1904; págs. 103–113; y el manuscrito 3.795–97 de la Biblioteca Nacional de Madrid. Lope de Vega, en muchos lugares de sus obras, cita con elogio a Liñán. La atribución a Liñán de *La Vida del Pícaro, compuesto por gallardo estilo en tercia rima* (cons. la edición A. Bonilla; Paris, 1902, pág.9) está reforzada por la circunstancia, que indica F. Holle en su reciente edición de *La hija de Celestina (Bibliotheca Romanica;* Strasburgo; pág.7) de Salas Barbadillo, de transcribir éste, en el *Caballero puntual* (1616; folio 45 vuelto), un terceto de dicha *Vida*, atribuyéndolo al 'lírico Liñán'. En el Archivo de la antigua casa ducal de Osuna hemos hallado, en copia manuscrita del siglo XVII, la siguiente glosa de Liñán, que aparece remitida por el conde de Cocentaina al de Salinas y Ribadeo . . ." (Cervantes, *Galatea*, 1914, vol. II, 320–321).

[76] There is an Alonso de Valdés in Espinel's *Diversas Rimas* (Madrid, 1591).

[77] Author of *Arte de escribir cartas familiares* (Madrid, 1589).

tanto cuanto sus obras nos lo muestran,
que al camino del cielo nos adiestran.

(A thousand divine spirits adorn
the beautiful bank of the clear Tajo,
who make our age more fortunate
than that of the Greeks and Latins.
Of them I think to say only one thing:
that they are of your valley and worth
as much honor as their works demonstrate,
which point us to the path of the *cielo*.)[78]

Calíope addresses Doctor Francisco Diaz in the familiar "tu" form and refers to his presence as a character among the other shepherds to whom she speaks. She again addresses the group directly in her octave for Juan de Vergara, whom she says is the friend of the shepherds.[79] Diego Durán is also named as a friend of the shepherds.[80] A similar familiarity is suggested in the octave for López Maldonado and made explicit in the octave for Gálvez de Montalvo that follows it.[81] Calíope's direct address to the shepherds of the Tajo recurs several times throughout her encomia of poets pertaining to the Tajo, including the octaves dedicated to Pedro Liñán de Riaza, Pedro de Padilla, and Benito Caldera. The section of her song dedicated to the poets on the Tajo concludes with their youngest member, a *verdadero amante*, Lope de Vega.

Muestra en un ingenio la experiencia
que en años verdes y en edad temprana
hace su habitación ansi la ciencia,
como en la edad madura, antigua y cana.
No entraré con alguno en competencia
que contradiga una verdad tan llana,
y más si a caso a sus oídos llega
que lo digo por vos, Lope de Vega.

78 (Cervantes, *Galatea*, 1961, vol. II, 193).

79 "El alto ingenio y su valor declara / un licenciado tan amigo vuestro / cuanto ya sabéis que es Juan de Vergara, / honra del siglo venturoso nuestro" (Cervantes, *Galatea*, 1961, vol. II, 196).

80 "Un conocido el alto Febo tiene, / ¿qué digo un conocido?, un verdadero / amigo, con quien sólo se entretiene / que es de toda ciencia tesorero. / Y es este que de industria se detiene / a no comunicar su bien entero, / Diego Durán, en quien contino dura/ y durará el valor, ser y cordura" (Cervantes, *Galatea*, 1961, vol. II, 198).

81 "¿Quien pensáis que es aquel que en voz sonora / sus ansias canta regaladamente, / aquel en cuyo pecho Febo mora, / el docto Orfeo y Arïón prudente? / Aquel que de los reinos del aurora / hasta los apartados de occidente, / es conocido, amado y estimado / por el famoso López Maldonado. // ¿Quien pudiera loaros, mis pastores, / un pastor vuestro amado y conocido, / pastor mejor de cuantos son mejores, / que de Fílida tiene el apellido? / La habilidad, la ciencia, los primores, / el raro ingenio y el valor subido / de Luis de Montalvo, le aseguran / gloria y honor mientras los cielos duran" (Cervantes, *Galatea*, 1961, vol. II, 198).

(Experience shows in an *ingenio*
who in green years and early age,
even then, makes his room this science,
as if of a mature, old, and grayed age.
I won't enter into competition with anyone
who contradicts a truth so plain,
and more, if by chance, this arrives to your ears,
I say it for you, Lope de Vega.)[82]

While it may risk imprudence to introduce speculation over the identities of other shepherds in the *Galatea*, it is curious that the central protagonists of the text, Elicio, Galatea, and Erastro, have never been given consideration in treatments of the novel as a *roman à clef*, particularly because Cervantes emphasizes the youthful expertise of Lope at the culmination of the list of poets whom Calíope places on the Tajo. This generational orientation also supports Cervantes' shift from the traditional focus of the pastoral novel on the author's beloved to Lauso's somewhat tangential plot with Silena. With the speculative nature of this treatment in mind, it is reasonable to consider the likelihood that the central plot of Cervantes' *Galatea* makes literary art of early content pertaining to the same subject matter that Lope de Vega treated in his early comedy *El verdadero amante*, his own pastoral novel, the *Arcadia* (1598), and his late "action in prose," the *Dorotea* (1632): the love affair between Lope and Elena Osorio.[83] Because the *Galatea* was completed by 1584, it must be understood that the ill-fated conclusion of that affair in no way figured in Cervantes' conception of the *Galatea*. On Edwin Morby's account, both the *Verdadero amante* and the *Dorotea* are needed to recover the full erotic history at work in these texts.

> *El verdadero amante* plainly treats a situation parallel to Marfisa's marriage and separation from Don Fernando, and the beginning of the latter's love for Dorotea. It ends before *La Dorotea* begins, portraying the inception of a passion whose dissolution is the theme of *La Dorotea*. The pastoral settings, the complications of plot, the interventions of such characters as the fathers of Jacinto and Amaranta, are distracting enough to obscure this essential fact, but not to conceal it entirely.[84]

82 (Cervantes, *Galatea*, 1961, vol. II, 203–204).

83 The theme of the "true lover," or *verdadero amante*, a Platonic question, appeared in the early comedy by that name – a comedy that Lope claimed was his first. For the speeches on the good lover: (Plato, "Phaedrus"). For various versions of the lover, including Diotima's discussion of the true lover: (Plato, "Symposium," 201d-212c, 484–494).

84 (E.S. Morby, "Reflections on *El verdadero amante*," *Hispanic Review*, 1959, vol. XXVII, 317–323; 321).

While Elicio's verses may have referred to (as in the case of Figueroa) or reinvented early verses of Lope's which had circulated amongst the members of this milieu between 1580 and 1583, precise identification of these verses in Lope's oeuvre has proved difficult. Antonio Sánchez Jiménez's recent edition of Lope's *Romances de juventud* squarely placed Lope within the renovation of the *romance* at this time, but even the *romancero pastoril*, which included works such as "El lastimado Belardo," has been dated to 1587–1608, that is, at least four to five years after the composition of the *Galatea*.[85] It is probable that Cervantes' use of the figure of the *verdadero amante* in the character of Elicio was inspired by a very young Lope, younger even than most of Lope's subsequent lyric self-portraits. The inclusion of Lope's laudatory *canción* in the front matter of López Maldonado's *Cancionero* (1586), the year following the publication of the *Galatea*, placed Lope squarely within this intimate circle of poets writing in Madrid and is the best indication of the type of poetry Lope may have been writing during the completion of the *Galatea*.[86] It is earlier even than the *romancero pastoril*, and showcases Lope as the youngest "star" member of

[85] (Lope, *Romances de juventud*).

[86] Rennert thought Lope's *canción* sufficiently different so as to require the author's name for it to be recognizable: (H. Rennert, *The Life of Lope de Vega*, Glasgow: Gowans and Gray, Ltd., 1904; n.1, 18). "*Canción del Autor de Lope de Vega* // Al facro afiento de la Cypria Diofa / que al mundo embia entre vna y otra nuue / aquel luzero y luminaria ardiente / vuestro diuino penfamiento fube / tocado dela llama licenciofa / donde las alas abrafar fe fiente /no menoles confiente / el fuego que le apura y acrifola / de vueftra Phili en la hermofura fola / pues conuertido en el al centro afpira / del tercero planeta / a quien efta fujeta / la inclinacion que a vuestra pluma infpira. // Diuinamente variays el canto / de vueftros penfamientos amorofos / y del Amor, la variedad de efetos / reduzidos a pechos generofos / donde fu honefto fer fe illuftra tanto / que el alma fola mueftra los fecretos / que en los pechos difcretos / la Venus celeftial engendra y cria, / gloria dela amorofa fantafia / tan diferente del valor que encierra / en fu difcurfo ciego, / en flechas, arco, y fuego / la humana Venus que nacio en la tierra. // Si de foberuios Principes y Reyes / tragedias graues con viftofo ornato / de quantas Perlas el Oriente encierra / armas, trompetas, bellico aparato / y en facrificios laureados bueyes / fangre, incendio, furor, enuidia y guerra, / de Egypto, o de otra tierra, / cantara vueftra Mufa? No le fuera / tan alta admiracion a quien la oyera, / pues el fujeto mifmo fe leuanta / pero fubir al cielo / con tan ligero buelo / vn folo penfamiento al mundo efpanta. // Para cantar feguros y encubiertos / muchos bufcaron choças y enrramadas, / filveftres flores chriftalinas fuentes / difponiendo en las lyras mal templadas / raros conceptos a la vifta inciertos, / pero al ingenio viuo tranfparentes / fus varios acidentes / pintaron mil, con aparato y pompa / porque la fequedad deshaga y rompa / pero vueftra diuina pluma y mano / fin ageno ornamento / leuanta vn penfamiento / que no le alcança penfamiento humano. // Como pintor difcreto aueys difpuesto / fobre la tabla de pafsiones propias / aqui el violado alli el azul y el verde / no mal formadas ni jamas inpropias / que con viuo pinzel las aueys puefto / donde ninguna fe efcurece o pierde / ya permitis recuerde / vna efperança muerta vn verde claro / ya del defden el vnico reparo / y en otra parte los rabiofos celos / de mas colores llena / que el Iris que ferena / las tempeftuofas nieblas delos cielos // Bien quifiera feñor qué aqui mis loores / vuestros meritos altos igualaran, / para llegar al cielo con mi pluma / pero ingenios mayores / fe puede colegir que atras quedaran / pues no los comprehende humana fuma / y todo fe refuma, / en que fe entienda, o Lopez Maldonado / que aquefte don de Apolo / en vueftro ingenio folo / no es Maldonado, fino Biendonado" (López Maldonado, *Cancionero*, 1586, vir–viiv).

the group of poets gathered in the *Cancionero*. While Lope's laudatory *canción* is not an example of his early love poetry, we may compare Lope's lyrics spoken by Don Fernando of the *Dorotea* with those of Elicio of the *Galatea*:

A mis soledades voy,
de mis soledades vengo,
porque para andar conmigo
me bastan mis pensamientos.
  No sé qué tiene el aldea
donde vivo y donde muero,
que con venir de mí mismo,
no puedo venir más lejos.
  Ni estoy bien ni mal conmigo;
mas dice mi entendimiento
que un hombre que todo es alma
está cautivo en su cuerpo.

(To my solitude I am going,
from my solitude I come,
because to go about with myself
my thoughts are enough.
  I don't know what's happening in the village
where I live and where I die,
that in coming from myself,
I can't come any further.
  I'm neither good nor bad with myself;
but my *entendimiento* says
that a man who is all soul,
is captive in his body.)[87]

Both Lope and Elicio feign simplicity whilst relying on Classical erudition and erotic mysticism for the development of their conceits.

¿Con qué milagro, amor, abres el pecho
del miserable amante que te sigue,
y de la llaga interna que le has hecho
crecida gloria muestra que consigue?
¿Cómo del daño que haces es provecho?
¿Cómo en tu muerte alegre vida vive?
La alma que prueba estos efectos todos

[87] (Lope de Vega, *Dorotea*, 1996, 120). For the erotic mysticism of the poem, see: (L. Spitzer, "A mis soledades," *Revista de Filología Española*, 1936, vol. XXIII, 397–400). See also: (W. Fichter and F. Sánchez y Escribano, "The Origin and Character of Lope de Vega's A mis soledades voy," *Hispanic Review*, n.4, 1943, vol. XI, 304–313).

la causa sabe, pero no los modos.

(With what miracle, Love, do you open the breast
of this miserable lover who follows you?
And of the internal wound that you have made
show increased glory, what do you achieve?
How is the damage you do profitable?
How does life live in your happy death?
The soul that tries out all these effects
knows the cause, but not the means.)[88]

In addition to the shared commonplaces of these two examples, Elicio's allusions to Classical mythology anticipate those which appear in Lope's poem for Maldonado's *Cancionero* and the early *romanceros*, and which were more fully developed in the *Arcadia*.[89] In spite of their subsequent rivalry, Lope retained a preference for Cervantes' *Galatea* well into the seventeenth century; he included it in his own playful revaluation of the amorous topoi of the 1580s in his 1613 *comedia*, *La dama boba*. As Nise's father complains of his erudite daughter:

Ayer sus librillos vi,
papeles y escritos varios;
pensé que devocionarios,
y de esta suerte leí:
Historia de dos amantes,
sacada de lengua griega;
Rimas, de Lope de Vega;
Galatea, de Cervantes;
. . .
Temo, y en razón lo fundo,
si en esto da, que ha de haber
un don Quijote mujer

(Yesterday I saw her books,
various papers and writings;
I thought they would be devotionals,

[88] (Cervantes, *Galatea*, 1961, vol. I, 25). Also: "Do mengua la esperanza y la fe crece / se descubre y parece el alto intento / del firme pensamiento enamorado, / que sólo confiado en amor puro / vive cierto y seguro de una paga / que al alma satisfaga limpiamente" (*Ibid*, vol. II, 88).

[89] For example, Sonnet 41: "Hermosos ojos, yo juré que había / de hacer en vos de mi rudeza empleo, / en tanto que faltaba a mi deseo / el oro puro que el Oriente cría. / Rústica mano desta fuente fría / ofrece el agua, mas mirad que a Orfeo / versos le dieron singular trofeo / de aquella noche que no ha visto el día. / Y pues por la crueldad que en toda parte / usáis conmigo, vuestro cuerpo tierno / puede temer la pena de Anaxarte; / no despreciéis el don, que al lago Averno / irá por vos mi amor venciendo al arte; / más tal hielo aun no teme el fuego eterno" (Lope de Vega, *Poesía selecta*, ed. Antonio Carreño, Madrid: Cátedra, 2013, 225–226).

and of this sort I read:
History of two lovers,
translated from the Greek;
Rhymes of Lope de Vega;
Galatea of Cervantes.
. . .
I fear, and in reason I found it,
if in this she gives herself, that there must be
a female don Quijote.)[90]

The relationship, personal and literary, between Lope de Vega and Cervantes has been explored by various scholars, but few have returned to the early years of the 1580s and the origins of this fraught friendship.[91] José Montero's 1999 article "Una amistad truncada: Sobre Lope de Vega y Cervantes" has done much to recover this crucial period in the formation of both major authors.[92] While the friendship between Cervantes and Lope de Vega would dissipate into spurious rivalry during the seventeenth century, during the first years of the 1580s Cervantes was a known and respected court poet and military hero, and Lope de Vega was a talented and highly regarded youth. With Tirsi and Damón (Figueroa and Laínez) as the two established senior poets, Lauso (Cervantes) as their respected junior newly returned from abroad, Lenio as an independent enemy of love (López Maldonado), and Elicio and Erastro (Lope de Vega and Liñán de

[90] Octavio's comment on his erudite daughter, Nise. See: (Lope de Vega, *La Dama Boba*, ed. D. Marín, Madrid: Cátedra, 2005; 146 and 148, verses 2113–2120 and 2145–2148). The history of two lovers is surely Helidorus' *Aethiopica*, which was anonymously translated into Spanish in 1554 as *Historia ethiopica de Heliodoro* (Anvers: Martin Nucio). In 1587, just two years after the *Galatea*, a new translation by Fernando de Mena was printed by Juan Gracián (printer of the *Galatea*) under the title *La historia de dos leales amantes Theagenes y Chariclea*.

[91] (J. Montero, "Una amistad truncada: Sobre Lope de Vega y Cervantes, (Esbozo de un compleja relación)," in *Memoria de Actividades del Instituto de Estudios Madrileños*, Madrid: Consejo Superior de Investigaciones Científicas, 1999, 313–336); (C.A. Barrera y Leirado, *Nueva biografía de Lope de Vega (1890)*, Madrid: Atlas, 1973), vols. I–II); (O. Green, "Lope and Cervantes: 'Peripateia' and Resolution," in eds. A.D. Kossoff and J. Amor y Vázquez, *Homenaje a W. Fichter*, 1971, 249–256); (J. Entrambasaguas, "Cervantes y Lope, el tiempo y el momento," *Anales de la Universidad de Chile*, 105, 1950, 235–244); (M.A. Buchanan, "Cervantes y Lope de Vega: their literary relations. A preliminary survey," *Philological Quarterly*, 1942, vol. XXI, 54–64); (A. González de Amezúa, *Lope de Vega en sus cartas, Introducción al epistolario de Lope de Vega Carpio*, Madrid: RAE, 1935–1943); (J.E. Hartzenbusch, "Cervantes y Lope en 1605," in *Las 1633 notas puestas por [. . .] a la primera edición del Quijote [. . .]*, Barcelona: Establecimiento Tipográfica, Narciso Ramírez y C., 1874, 193–202).

[92] "La primera etapa, de amistad, o al menos, cordialidad entre ambos escritores, se extendería desde el momento en que se conocieron, esto es, en torno a 1580 tras el regreso de Cervantes de su cautiverio argelino, hasta una fecha no concreta, pero que probablemente sería el año de 1587 o principios del siguiente, en todo caso el momento en que Lope ha de abandonar Madrid, desterrado tras los libelos contra Elena Osorio y su familia" (J. Montero Reguera, *Miguel de Cervantes: Una literatura para el entretenimiento*, Montesinos, 2007, 131).

Riaza) as two young talented shepherds of the Tajo, the reader garners an accurate depiction of the various generations of lyric poets who pertained to the practices of Pastoral Petrarchism at that time. In this way, the very community which the *Galatea* encodes and immortalizes comes clearly into focus.[93] While Elicio was not one of the many known pseudonyms of Lope de Vega, it is possible that Cervantes may have taken creative liberties with the pseudonyms for these two young poets by using names that were themselves inspired by the literary model of Sannazaro. It may also be that these correspond to earlier pseudonyms which had not been cemented into historical fact by the time the *Galatea* went to print. While Lope would appear, fifteen years later, in his own *Arcadia* (1598) as Belardo, the three works that most overtly pertain to the Elena Osorio affair, *El verdadero amante*, *Belardo el furioso*, and *La Dorotea* all cast him under different pseudonymic guises. In like manner, Lope used the name Filis to laud Elena, but he also used Dorotea and Belarda. There is nearly no way of knowing what pseudonym Lope used as early as 1581. Liñán de Riaza's close friendship with Lope de Vega, as exemplified in their epistolary correspondence and laudatory poems for one another, strongly suggests this pair of lyrical *dos amigos* as the protagonists of the central plot of the text.[94] Liñán's cultivation of the bucolic or rustic style of pastoral poetry was a pronounced feature of the work that he produced within this group.[95] Together they brought the folk genre of the *romance* to erudite fruition and reinvention during this crucial decade. It is reasonable to consider that the never completed second part of the *Galatea* (1585) was refigured in Lope's *Dorotea* (1632), an unmasked and urban denouement (1587–1588) of the courtship (1580–1583) that Cervantes had cast in pastoral fiction. Like the *Galatea*, Lope's late work explicitly referred to the same pastoral community, often by proper name, and to the pastoral genre as a *roman à clef*.[96]

[93] The generational gaps are as follows: Lope (b. 1562), Líñan de Riaza (b. ca. 1558), Cervantes (b. 1547), Laínez (b. ca. 1538) and Figueroa (b. ca. 1530).

[94] (J. de Entrambasaguas, "Cartas poéticas de Lope de Vega y Liñán de Riaza," in *Estudios sobre Lope de Vega*, Madrid: CSIC, 1958, vol. III, 225–261).

[95] See note 62.

[96] "Graves poetas son los desta edad, pero más querrán ellos imprimir sus obras que ilustrar las ajenas. Diego de Mendoza, Vicente Espinel, Marco Antonio de la Vega, Pedro Laínez, el doctor Garay, Fernando de Herrera, los dos Lupercios, don Luis de Góngora, Luis Gálvez de Montalvo, el marqués de Auñón, el de Montes Claros, el duque de Francavila, el canónigo Tárraga, el marqués de Peñafiel, que tanta gracia tuvo para los versos castellanos. . . Francisco de Figueroa y Fernando de Herrera, que entrambos han merecido nombres de divinos; Pedro de Padilla, el doctor Campuzano, López Maldonado, Miguel Cervantes, el jurado Rufos, el doctor Soto, don Alonso de Ercilla, Liñán de Riaza, don Luis de Vargas Manrique, don Francisco de la Cueva y el Licenciado Berrio, y este Lope de Vega" (Lope de Vega, *Dorotea*, 1958, 315–320).

In considering the possibility that the infamously discrete Galatea was intended to represent Elena Osorio (or an earlier beloved), the reader must consider the years 1580–1583. This makes the *Galatea* a particularly special version of the Osorio affair since even Lope's own pastoral novel, the *Arcadia*, was written with the concluding *desengaño* in mind. The *Galatea*, in contrast, remains arrested with its 1585 publication. The closing image of a troop of valiant shepherds following Elicio down the hill at sunrise as he makes his way to plead for Galatea's freedom is frozen in time. This may, in fact, be one reason why Cervantes never successfully found a way to bring forth the second part. In 1582–1583, Lope was around twenty to twenty-one years old. The events of the first part of the *Galatea* would have had to have concluded by January 1582. The timeline of the novel is just a week. By February 1582, Cervantes had already begun composition of the work. By July 1582, Lope had enlisted in the military campaigns in the Azores, seeing action at the Battle of Ponta Delgada. Of course, the *Galatea* could also refer to an earlier youthful love affair that the young Lope had experienced during the early 1580s, prior to that with Elena Osorio, and which coincided with Cervantes' return to Madrid. What is certain is that some poetic liberties would have to have been taken in the case of Elena, who was already married to Cristóbal Calderón when Lope fell in love with her. Such poetic alterations may seem out of place, but the problem of an unwanted arranged marriage had been one of the central conceits of pastoral fiction since Montemayor's *Diana*. Cervantes returned to the theme years later in the *Coloquio de los perros*, where we read,

> No se le quedaba entre renglones el pastor Elicio, más enamorada que atrevido, de quien decía que, sin atender a sus amores ní a su ganado, se entraba en los ciudados ajenos.
>
> (The shepherd Elicio did not write within the lines, more enamored than intrepid, of whom it is said that, without attending to his loves nor to his flock, he entered into distant concerns.)[97]

In this final comment, published nearly thirty years after the *Galatea*, the reader can detect the impossibility of the novel's second part following Lope's suit, abduction, exile, enlistment in the unfortunate Spanish Armada, and move to Alba de Tormes. Such unforeseen disillusionments may have seemed impossible when the first part of the *Galatea* went to print. Indeed, the novel concludes on the poetic optimism of action at dawn:

[97] (Cervantes, *Las novelas ejemplares*, 2001, vol. II, 307–308).

> Cuando Elicio acabó su canto, comenzaba a descubrirse por las orientales puertas la fresca aurora con sus hermosas y variadas mejillas, alegrando el suelo, aljofarando las yerbas y pintando los prados, cuya deseada venida comenzaron luego a saludar las parleras aves con mil suertes de concertadas cantilenas. Levantóse en esto Elicio, y tendió los ojos por la espaciosa campaña.
>
> (When Elicio finished his song, the fresh dawn with its beautiful colored cheeks began to show itself through the eastern doors, making happy the earth, pearling the herbs and painting the plains, whose desired arrival the chattering birds began to salute with a thousand types of arranged melodies. Elicio arose in this and spread his eyes over the spacious countryside.)[98]

There in the sunrise, Elicio sees two squadrons of shepherds coming toward him, led by his friends Arsindo and Lauso, and followed by Orompo, Marsilio, Crysio, and Orfenio. Tirsi and Damón have also come to aid in Elicio's plight. It is Lauso who announces the purpose of the group for his friend:

> En la compañía que traemos puedes ver, amigo Elicio, si comenzamos a dar muestras de querer cumplir la palabra que te dimos. Todos los que aquí ves vienen con deseo de servirte, aunque en ello aventuren las vidas.
>
> (In the company that we bring you can see, my friend Elicio, how we begin to give signs of our desire to keep the word that we gave you; everyone you see here comes with the desire to serve you, even if it means venturing their lives.)[99]

In the light of the dawn Elicio descends toward the home of Galatea to reason with her father, Aurelio, followed by a band of nearly twenty shepherds who are prepared to rescue Galatea by force if she is not to be rescued by reason. On the cusp of an amorous triumph, defended by a brotherhood of shepherd-poets, the plot of the first part of the *Galatea* concludes. What the narrator calls an "amoroso cuento y historia," and elsewhere an "égloga," is left in suspense.

To these identifications we may propose the additional identification of the widowed Orompo with the widowed Doctor Campuzano. Campuzano's poems, which appeared in López Maldonado's *Cancionero*, explicitly discussed his amorous grief as a widower. As is already known, Siralvo was the pseudonym of Gálvez de Montalvo in his own *El pastor de Fílida* of 1582. To review, the pseudonyms of the *Galatea* are as follows:

[98] (Cervantes, *Galatea*, 1961, vol. II, 265). [99] (Cervantes, *Galatea*, 1961, vol. II, 265).

Galatea – Elena Osorio (Madrid)
Elicio – Lope de Vega (Madrid)
Erastro – Liñán de Riaza (Madrid)
Lauso – Cervantes (Madrid)
Silena – unknown (also appears with Cervantes in *Viaje del Parnaso*)
Lenio – López Maldonado (Madrid)
Tirsi – Francisco de Figueroa (Alcalá)
Damón – Pedro Laínez (Alcalá)
Meliso – Diego Hurtado de Mendoza (deceased, celebrated in Madrid)
Siralvo – Gálvez de Montalvo (Madrid)
Astraliano – Don Juan de Austria (deceased, referenced)
Orompo – Doctor Campuzano (Madrid)
Larsileo – Mateo Vázquez (court, referenced)

I do not mean to suggest that these are the only historical personages in the novel which the author may have expected contemporary readers to recognize. He includes twenty-eight poets on the banks of the Tajo in the *Canto de Calíope* as explicitly sharing the same poetic space as the shepherds who listen to her song from the banks of the Tajo, where the story is set. This is not to mention the many shepherdesses (for whom there is little historical data) and foreign characters whose tales are interpolated into the work. While it is wise to proceed with caution when approaching this novel as a *roman à clef*, the relatively concise circle which characterized this literary milieu does make identification of poets with their corresponding pseudonyms easier than may previously have been assumed. The tradition of the *roman à clef* was a key literary technique of the pastoral prosimetrum. The *Galatea*'s focus on the "science of poetry" as a living practice, and the many narrative hints that Cervantes supplies throughout the text, make speculative identification part and parcel of interpretive work. It is actively a thematic that the text develops. As Lope de Vega wrote of López Maldonado's *Cancionero*, the matter of Pastoral Petrarchism was drawn from the *alma* and the *pensamiento* of the living poet.[100] This invited a novel immediacy into the fictions of a highly conventional form of writing which, in a gesture quintessential to the author's modernity, became a self-conscious feature of the work. While it is the case that Cervantes, Lope de Vega, and several other authors would gain considerable authorial and poetic distance from these immediate mimetic processes of the 1580s, this entanglement of the novel and the conventional in poetic practice left an indelible mark on prose fiction, dramaturgy, and the lyric.

[100] (López Maldonado, *Cancionero*, 1586, vir –viiv).

By transforming the *Galatea* into the prosimetric exploration of poetic practices as they were lived by the poet and his peers in Madrid in the 1580s, Cervantes placed the lyric life of the *figura of the poet* at the generative heart of novelistic fiction. In the *Galatea*, the *vita* of the poet is the source of the literary character.

CHAPTER 6

The Literary Character as Poet: Lyric Subjectivity, Chronotopic Dynamism, and Plot in the Galatea

Beginning in 1582 with the transition from verse to prose in Pedro de Padilla's *Églogas pastoriles* (Seville), a fluid movement which involved storytelling in verse and lyricizing in prose imbued the structure of pastoral poetics with unprecedented attention to the role of the human interior in the determination of novelistic emplotment.[1] This shift in the time/space (chronotopicity) of poiesis was also evident in the unfinished eclogue *Engaños y desengaños de amor*, by Cervantes' lyric mentor, Pedro Laínez (Damón of the *Galatea*). In these works, the technique of the *roman à clef* was more than cover and fodder for court gossip. It was explicitly involved in resituating the lyric life of the Petrarchan project at the generative heart of novelistic fiction. This constituted a narrativization of the *figura of the poet* in prose fiction.[2] Anthony Cascardi's study of the "self-legitimizing" fragmented subject in *The Subject of Modernity* easily finds a precedent in lyric subjectivity at the generative heart of the novelizing process which came about during the disintegration of social, religious, and political homogeneity at the turn of the seventeenth century. However, these nuances should not obscure the fact that the modern subject has been

[1] Because the pastoral prosimetrum was understood as a *roman à clef* which involved the biography of the poet and his peers, the term "emplotment" is suited to the narrative of *lyric subjectivity*: "**emplotment** … coined by Hayden White in his 1973 *Metahistory* to describe the way in which historians necessarily fashion their source material into narrative. Historiography (*q.v*), White argues, encodes historical data, which themselves do not constitute a story, into one of four possible intelligible plot types: tragic, comic, romantic or ironic …. Which type is deployed depends on the trope of figurative representation that dominates the historian's language and culture. These tropes, which correspond to the four emplotment types, include metaphor, metonymy, synecdoche and irony (*qq.v*) … the nature of historical events and the relationships between them are not inherent in the events themselves; rather, they are constituted through the very language used to describe them" (J.A. Cuddon and M.A.R. Habib, eds., *A Dictionary of Literary Terms and Literary Theory*, Wiley-Blackwell, 2013, 233). One need not adopt White's designations of plot types and tropes wholesale in order to comprehend the ordering of non-causally related material into a narrative arc.

[2] For Cascardi's take on Hegel's notion of modernity as the prosification of the world within the contours of the early modern, see the introduction to: (*Subject of Modernity*, esp. 64).

narrated both as a homogenized unity (a nearly absolute subject) and as a fragmented construction (inextricable from the networks of power in which it self-fashions).[3] This oscillation between the unitary and the fragmentary understanding of the subject is at the core of the lyric as a function of the self and, as this chapter will show, is natural to the chronotopic dynamism of the novel. Cascardi returned to the topic of prosification in "Orphic Fictions," where he observes:

> Recognizing that Garcilaso de la Vega stands at the headwaters of a living tradition of Spanish lyric poetry closely associated with the pastoral, but recognizing also the Orphic power of poetry as lost, if not *always*, then certainly *now*, might be reason enough to think that Cervantes's own success as a writer of prose fiction was predicated on the eclipse of the Orphic dream, that his success in prose was predicated on a 'prosification of the world' in which figures like Garcilaso could only be seen at a distance . . . And yet the world of prose continues to include poetry, both as *poesía* and more broadly as poiesis.[4]

The "how" of this latent inclusion of lyric poetry as the content and action at the foundation of modern fiction is the central interest of this chapter. During the final quarter of the sixteenth century, the transposition of the interior event into story led to the transformation of lyric sempiternity into narrative time.

This chapter makes use of the terms "lyric subjectivity," "chronotopic dynamism," and "plot" in order to treat the introduction of lyric temporality into narrative emplotment as the generative force for novelistic fiction. These terms are complex and fraught with debate. For the sake of simplicity, "lyric subjectivity" here refers to an interior temporality or sempiternal movement within the time and the space of narrative, that is, discursive and embodied action on the part of the poet, the literary character, and the poet as literary character.[5] "Chronotopic dynamism" here makes use of, but also takes issue with, Bakhtin's notion of the chronotope (as a unity of time/space in the human) in the novel; "chronotopic dynamism" is used to indicate that novelistic tendencies in pastoral fiction grew out of the fact that this unity was not solid but unstable, fragmentary, and contingent.[6] The character of

[3] For the autonomous subject: (J. Michelet, *La Renaissance*, 1855); (J. Burkhardt, *The Civilization of the Renaissance in Italy*, 1860); (W. Pater, *The Renaissance*, 1873), and its critique: (S. Greenblatt, *Renaissance Self-Fashioning*, University Chicago Press, 1980).

[4] (Cascardi, "Orphic Fictions," 25, emphasis in original).

[5] For *lyric subjectivity* and the *modern subject*, see the Coda.

[6] It is clear that Bakhtin did not have the pastoral prosimetrum in mind in his remarks on the idyllic chronotope: "This finds expression predominantly in the special relationship that time has to space in the idyll: an organic fastening-down, a grafting of life and its events to a place, to a familiar

the shepherd-poet is consistently rooted in the landscape of the text, but the lyric temporality of these characters uncouples space from time. The use of "plot" relies upon E.M. Forster's understanding of plot as a causal construction and Schlovsky's understanding of suyzet as the creatively sequenced presentation of events as a plot.[7] "Emplotment" is taken from Hayden White's usage to indicate the way in which disordered historical data are arranged into a narrative arc.[8]

As discussed in previous chapters, the poets of Pastoral Petrarchism understood Petrarch's *Canzoniere* as a series of repeatedly edited lyric utterances which amounted to an autobiographical totality or a *vita* of the poet in verse. From Montemayor's *Diana* (1559) onwards, this Petrarchan project of the *Canzoniere* was transformed into the pastoral prosimetrum.[9] Don Gaspar de Romani's 1559 laudatory sonnet for the *Diana* well illustrated a general understanding of the eponymous shepherdess not only as a real historical beloved, but also as a new Castilian Laura. Romani's sonnet recast Montemayor, Diana, and the novel itself within the tradition of the immortal lovers in letters. In the sonnet, addressed to Diana, Romani assured her that *so long lives this and this gives life to thee.* The narratological effect of this appeal to posterity was to introduce causal, and therefore chronological, validity to the sempiternal stasis of the lyric.[10] In layman's terms, this amounted to the historical effects of the infinity of love, the narrative practice of a sempiternal concept.[11] Where erotic poetry treated the sempiternal experience as unbounded, the narrative emphasis on an afterlife in letters linked lyric production to the emplotment of a poetic life. It gave to the lyric an endgame, a nearly eschatological one, and it was this "sense of an ending" that allowed for novelistic fiction to emerge from the space of the lyric.[12]

territory with all its nooks and crannies, its familiar mountains, valleys, fields, rivers and forests, and one's own home. Idyllic life and its events are inseparable from this concrete, spatial corner of the world" (Bakhtin, *Dialogic Imagination*, 225).

7 For sake of simplicity, I will not here engage Brooks understanding of plot and its many critiques. See: (Peter Brooks, *Reading for the Plot*, New York: Knopf, 1984, pp.12).

8 (Cuddon and Habib, eds., *A Dictionary of Literary Terms*, 233).

9 López Maldonado's later time in the *Academia de los Nocturnos* in Valencia was indicative of these types of inter-urban and international experiences. (A.M. Maldonado Cuns, "La definición de Amor según López Maldonado," in *Líneas actuales de investigación literaria: estudios de literatura hispánica*, Madrid: ISBN, 2004, 271–280); (J. Weiner, *Cuatro ensayos sobre Gabriel Lobo Lasso de Vega (1555–1615)*, Valencia: Universitat de Valencia, 2011).

10 For the role of causality in the transformation of story into plot: (E.M. Forster, *Aspects of the Novel*, New York: Harcourt, 1955, 83–104).

11 The conceit of the infinity of love finds its narrative realization in the "sempiternal" afterlife of the poet and lady in letters. The poetry itself is the unity of the conceit and the fulfillment.

12 (F. Kermode, *The Sense of an Ending*, New York: Oxford University Press, 1968).

Si de Madama Laura la memoria
Petrarca para siempre ha levantado,
y a Homero así de lauro ha coronado
escribir de los griegos la victoria,
Si los reyes también, para más gloria,
vemos que de contino han procurado
que aquello que en la vida han conquistado
en muerte se renueve con su historia;
Con más razón serás, ¡oh excelente
Diana!, por hermosura celebrada,
que cuantas en el mundo hermosas fueron;
Pues nadie mereció ser alabada,
de quien así el laurel tan justamente
merezca más que cuantos escribieron.

(If Petrarch has raised the memory
of Madame Laura for all time,
and Homer, in like manner, has been crowned
for writing about the Greek victory,
if kings also, for greater glory,
we see, have continually procured that
the thing which in life they have conquered
in death is renewed in history;
with greater reason you will be, oh excellent
Diana, celebrated for your beauty,
than however many in the world were beautiful;
well, nobody deserved to be praised
more than the one who justly the laurel
deserves, more than the many who wrote.)[13]

While Romani also mentioned Homer's epic achievement and the legacy of politico-military history, invoking the Renaissance debate of *armas y letras*, the language of the sextet set Diana and Montemayor within the figuration of Laura and Petrarch (Laura and laurel wreath) with which the sonnet began. The use of inherited Petrarchan topoi in the representation of contemporary experience underscored that the nearer to life the pastoral drew, the greater the degree of artifice it employed. Literary immortality was not a regional question contingent on dialect, but one that expanded geographically, linguistically, and temporally from contemporary Madrid to Ancient Greece by way of poetic convention. Gabriel de Arriaga's tercets for the front matter of Pedro de Padilla's *Églogas pastoriles* (1582) well illustrated this emphasis on the divine beloved and *divino ingenio* in the

[13] (J. de Montemayor, *Los siete libros de La Diana*, ed. A. Rallo, Madrid: Cátedra, 1991).

Petrarchan quest for authorial immortality as a cultural commonplace in the opening years of the 1580s:

> Damas que soys del mundo vn paraýso,
> . . .
> Por vosotras la fama es leuantada
> de los que sabiamente os an amado
> y por mil siglos viue eternizada.
> Porque los raros versos que á cantado
> Petrarca, eternizando su memoria
> el ser hermosa Laura lo á causado.
> . . .
> Y a Padilla, que va dando señales
> de dexarlos a todos por el suelo,
> mostrando fuerças más que naturales,
> quién pensáys que le haze dar tal buelo
> si no Siluia, vna dama más hermosa
> en la tierra, que Venus en el Cielo.
>
> (Ladies who are of the world a paradise
> . . .
> Because of you the fame is raised
> for those who wisely loved you,
> and lives eternal for a thousand centuries.
> Because the beautiful being, Laura,
> caused the rare verses that Petrarch sang,
> making his memory eternal.
> . . .
> And to Padilla, who is giving signs
> of leaving all [the poets] behind in the dust,
> showing supernatural forces,
> who do you think makes him take such flight
> if it is not Silvia?, a lady more beautiful
> on earth than Venus in Heaven.)[14]

It was commonplace for poets to see both themselves and their beloveds as sempiternal beings who overflowed the particularities of individual events and experiences, and transformed the inherited forms and tropes by which they understood themselves and one another. The poeticization of experience into the space of lyric discourse developed the sempiternal figurations of the erotic self. But it was the fictional narrativization of an otherwise figural poetic space as a form of emplotment contingent on the *novedades*

[14] (Padilla, *Églogas pastoriles*, 2010, 51).

of poetic life which created novelistic fiction. As the young Lope de Vega insisted in the prologue to his own *Arcadia* of 1598, the pastoral prosimetrum was as much a masked collection of the poet's lyric verse as it was a fully developed narrative which gave shape to the poet's private *vita* within his public life, a transformation of interior experience into exterior content (from the qualitative to the quantitative).[15] This gave to prose fiction the novelistic drive: a form of emplotment attuned to the exterior effects of lyric interiority as perennially contingent (both historically and allegorically).

This chapter studies the force of lyric subjectivity (uttered, constructed, and constructed as utterance) as the source and drive of novelistic emplotment in the practice of pastoral poetics in 1580s Madrid, with particular attention to Lauso (of the *Galatea*) whose tangential lyric plot broke from the standard unwanted marriage plot of the pastoral. The convergence of lyric and narrative in the *roman à clef* imbued Spanish poetics with a unique form of novelistic immediacy. At the confluence of allegory and history, verse and prose, lyric and narrative, the poet's subjectivity became the source of a new, perennially yet-to-be-written form of narrative fiction. Subsequent to the *Galatea*, Cervantes narrativized the lyric drive of the *figura of the poet* in the character of AQ/dQ in the *DQ*.[16] In fact, in the *DQ* Cervantes' lyric sense of character interiority as a determining factor of plot is so strong that even his narrators take on an interior life of their own. Because the practice of disguising interior experience within inherited literary models had been common cultural practice since at least the reign of Isabel de Valois, the *novedad* in 1580s poetic practice lay in the increasing presence of contemporary poetic personalities within the shared tropological fabric of poetic conventions transposed to prose fiction. This caused emplotment to be refashioned in the narrative "aftermath" of the lyric drive: plot as poiesis.

[15] "Si alguno no advirtiese que a vueltas de los ajenos he llorado los míos, tal en efecto como fui quise honrarme de escribirlos, pues era imposible honrarlos, acomodando a mis soledades materia triste, como quien tan lejos vive de cosa alegre" (Lope de Vega, *Arcadia*, 2012, 149). In the same edition, Sánchez Jiménez footnotes the same: "El autor también invita a buscar en la *Arcadia* alusiones a la vida personal de Lope, cuyos amores narran mezclados con *los ajenos* de los nobles. La auto-representación del poeta como sujeto perennemente triste por sus amores desgraciados es típica del género pastoril y conecta con la elegía clásica ..." (in Lope de Vega, *Arcadia*, 2012, 149–150).

[16] In the *Persiles y Sigismunda*, the lyrical qualities of the protagonists have been more fully integrated into their characters such that the author, by this time, has nearly eliminated the use of lyric verse. But the coordination of lyric temporality for both protagonists is still the structuring principle of the work.

Since Roland Barthes' "Death of the Author" and Michel Foucault's "What is an Author?," scholars have tended to seek out authorial distance in early modern authors as a signal of a prescient modernity shared with our present day. Ruth El Saffar's *Distance and Control in* Don Quixote*: A Study in Narrative Technique* reoriented critical focus to the various narrative frames that Cervantes employed in his masterwork.[17] In conjunction with this tendency, Felipe Valencia and Marsha Collins have recently called for a reading of poetic theory that emphasizes "the collapse of the fiction of sincerity" which would relegate Cervantes' most autobiographically explicit character, Lauso, to a "symbolic function as the embodiment of the poet."[18] This trend for reading Cervantes and the pastoral strictly as symbolic allegory, in conjunction with the twentieth-century theoretical insistence on an exaggerated and constructed divide between the life of the poet and the body of work, obscures as much as it illuminates this unique moment in the history of poetics by taking up one side of the lyric dynamic as if it were illustrative of the whole process and practice at that time. This chapter proposes a more complicated picture of the way in which 1580s poetic practice developed novelistic plots out of lyric subjectivity by accounting for the (self-conscious) role of an autobiographical literature of immediacy within the elaborate conventions of a highly allegorical mode of poetic discourse. Narrative distance was complementary (not contradictory) to biographical immediacy, just as allegorical commonplaces were transformative for contemporary (historicizable) experience. The closer the pastoral prosimetrum drew to the life of its author and his contemporaries, the more elaborate the constructions of the pastoral veil.[19] In prose fiction, the ordering into a causal narrative of these unifications of history and allegory produced the novelistic plot.

While the *Galatea* has frequently been dismissed in scholarship as a partially formed and immature work, or reinterpreted through standard approaches to the *DQ*, this chapter takes seriously the rich lyric stakes of Cervantes' first prosimetric novel.[20] In the *Galatea* – a sophisticated meditation on the nature of love and subjectivity inherent to Pastoral Petrarchism – the literary character was more fully developed as the *figura*

[17] (El Saffar, *Distance and Control*). This approach was further complicated by Carroll B. Johnson's late and incomplete work, *Transliterating a Culture*.

[18] (Valencia, "No se puede reducir"); (Collins, "Lauso, a Portrait").

[19] This paradox has also been observed in the many-layered telling of the "Captain's Tale" (*DQ I*) and its relevance to the life of the author.

[20] (El Saffar, "*La Galatea*: The Integrity"); (Polchow, "The Embryonic Manifestation"); (Collins, "Lauso, a Portrait").

of the poet through Cervantes' use of himself and contemporary poets as novel source material. While it is right to observe that the first part of the *Galatea* was by definition incomplete – Cervantes was still promising the second part on his deathbed – this does not justify repeated dismissals of the incompleteness of the first part which can be read as a total work in its own right. As is known, there is an exegetical tradition of taking the *DQ I* and *II* as two separate prefigurative works.[21] The *Galatea* arose out of shared poetic practices which lent novelistic immediacy to the timeless retreat of the pastoral and the repeated tropes and forms of Petrarchism through the transformation of the literary character (developed by events from the exterior to the interior in the genres of the Romance and the Chronicle) into the *figura of the contemporary poet* (developed by way of lyrically determined action from the interior to the exterior). This movement from the interior to the exterior was also a shift in temporality from the sempiternal to the chronological.

The re-scripting of the literary character through the *figura of the poet* introduced lyric sempiternity into a timeless landscape concerned with lived experience. This allotted unprecedented attention to subjective temporalities which dramatically affected the *chronotope* of the text. Of the *chronotope*, Bakhtin writes:

> We will give the name *chronotope* (literally, 'time space') to the intrinsic connectedness of temporal and spatial relationships that are artistically expressed in literature. The term (space-time) is employed in mathematics, and was introduced as part of Einstein's Theory of Relativity. The special meaning it has in relativity theory is not important for our purposes; we are borrowing it for literary criticism almost as a metaphor (almost, but not entirely). What counts for us is the fact that it expresses the inseparability of space and time (time as the fourth dimension of space). . . . In the literary artistic chronotope, spatial and temporal indicators are fused into one carefully thought-out, concrete whole. Time, as it were, thickens, takes on flesh, becomes artistically visible; likewise, space becomes charged and responsive to the movements of time, plot, and history. This intersection of axes and fusion of indicators characterizes the artistic chronotope. . . . in literature the primary category of the chronotope is time. The chronotope as a formally constitutive category determines to a significant degree the image of [hu]man in literature as well. The image of [hu]man is always intrinsically chronotopic.[22]

[21] (J. Casalduero, *Sentido y forma del Quijote: (1605–1615)*, Madrid: Insula, 1970).

[22] (Bakhtin, "Forms of Time," in *Dialogic Imagination*, 84–85, square brackets mine). While Bakhtin's concept of the chronotope is useful here, the present chapter does not share Bakhtin's understanding of poetry or lyric as oppositional to heteroglossia. By way of the constant play with inherited forms of

Where Bakhtin finds legitimacy in the chronotope as unity, in novelistic practice the pairing of these two categories was unstable and productive. The pastoral prosimetrum allowed characters, as lyric poets, to introduce multiple chrono-specificities into a single narrative topography through the use of lyric verse. As lyric time travelers, the shepherds of the *Galatea* interpolated lyric verse into the plot such that the chronotopic image of the human was multiplied, fractured, reproduced, and transformed, as will be seen in the example of Lauso discussed below. This novel introduction of characters whose temporal/spatial situation was repeatedly reconfigured through the sempiternity of lyric verse produced a new motor of genesis for the creation (poiesis) of narrative. These "stories" did not accord to predetermined allegories or pre-scripted histories; novelistic plot emerged as narrative from the impact of the sempiternal interior as a causal determination of exterior words and actions. This interiority was not simply a question of thoughts and desires; it was a form of lyric discourse whose temporality (sempiternity) was non-narrative. This introduction of the human interior as a creative determinant (poiesis) in the genesis of plot was distinct from divine, moral, chance, and historical orders of meaning.[23] As sempiternity, the lyric is the place of poiesis. The sophisticated narrative architecture of an author whose capacity to juggle multiple lyric temporalities within a single and "timeless" narrative landscape (what Cervantes calls a *tercia realidad*) has heretofore been underestimated. This tapestry of narrativized lyric subjectivity was necessary to the conception of the first modern novel. It was foundational for AQ's rupture from his temporally grounded village in the form of his discursive anachronisms.[24] In the *Galatea*, the chronotopic dynamism of the shepherd-poet Lauso narrativized lyric time in the poetic treatment of his own jealousy and erotic captivity. It gave the "untimely" concepts of the interior narrative consequence.

While the introduction of lyric temporalities into narrative prose did not begin in the 1580s, during this decade the boundaries between verse and prose became increasingly indistinguishable. Sannazaro's *Arcadia*, Garcilaso's *Églogas*, and Montemayor's *Diana* (and its continuations) all set a precedent for the elision of lyric and narrative. Francisco de Figueroa, Luis Gálvez de Montalvo, Pedro de Padilla, Pedro Laínez, Gómez de

poetic discourse, particularly Petrarchism, drawn from several linguistic cultures, sixteenth-century lyric culture was essentially heteroglot. It was for this reason that the appeal to ineffability frequently recurred as a singularity in contrast to the rich heteroglossia of lyric utterance. The only monoglot was silence.

23 In the *DQ*, this special quality of the lyric drive is at the heart of a narrative about AQ's lyrical life as dQ.

24 (Spitzer, "Linguistic Perspectivism"). See Coda for discussion.

Tapia, Cervantes, Lope de Vega, and many others all undertook writing which wove together seemingly distinct elements of lyric conceits and narrative plots into a single literary pastoral. Aware of the novelties involved in these sorts of transformations, in the "segunda parte" of his *Romancero* (*Églogas pastoriles*, 1582), Pedro de Padilla remarked:

> he querido poner en manos de discretos esta segunda parte de mis obras, con título tan humilde como lo es su dueño, son Églogas Pastoriles de diferentes sujetos y composturas, donde con versos sueltos, en lugar de Prosa van ligados los demás, que a diversos propósitos se hicieron
>
> (I have wanted to put in the hands of *discretos* this second part of my works, with a title as humble as that of its owner, they are Pastoral Eclogues of different subjects and compositions, where individual verses, in place of Prose go tied up with one another, which were made for various purposes)[25]

Padilla's self-conscious comment was in dialogue with Laínez's judgment that Padilla had been the first to enrich the Castilian language in this new way, as he stated in the approbation.[26] Padilla's versification of the voice of the narrator, whilst reminiscent of the bard or troubadour, introduced versified exposition into the eclogue and pushed the eclogue, as a genre, toward the novelistic qualities of narrative fiction. The concept of a "pastoral novel" written entirely in verse was still a novelty in the 1580s. Padilla's collection of thirteen eclogues, which together formed a single cohesive narrative, employed several novelistic techniques, such as exposition and dialogue – in addition to lyrics – all composed entirely in verse. Each of the first five eclogues undertook dialogues between two unique shepherds, but the sixth eclogue brought together six of the characters from the previous eclogues in order to reprise, develop, and emplot their lyrical positions.[27] That Padilla acknowledged the novelty of narrative interlacing in free verse anticipated Cervantes' subsequent reference to his own pastoral prosimetrum as an eclogue in the prologue to the same. This use of character or lyric-driven narrative, rather than thematic structuring devices, further pushed the eclogue from symbol to story. Padilla, Laínez, and Cervantes observed the distinction between lyric and narrative as separate but indispensable components (and temporalities) of pastoral poetry whether its execution was versified, prosified, or prosimetric. As

[25] (Padilla, *Églogas pastoriles*, 2010, 50 [iiv]).

[26] (Laínez in Padilla, *Églogas pastoriles*, 2010, 50[ii]).

[27] "Las dos primeras églogas vienen a ser el prólogo de la novela pastoril que hilvanan las restantes piezas del libro" (Labrador Herraiz and DiFranco in Padilla, *Églogas pastoriles*, 2010, 31).

José J. Labrador Herraiz and Ralph A. DiFranco have observed in the preliminary study to the 2010 edition of Padilla's *Églogas*,

> La 'invención' era enlazar el discurso sublime con el discurso humilde, y buscar la forma de diferenciarse del resto de los escritores intentando hacer una 'novela pastoril toda en verso'.
>
> (The "invention" was to interlace sublime and humble discourse, and to seek out the form in which to differentiate himself from the rest of the writers [by] intending to create a "pastoral novel entirely in verse.")[28]

Padilla's shift from prosified to versified fiction was further complicated by the introduction of another genre within the totality of the work. In the thirteenth and final eclogue, Padilla's text transitioned into philosophical dialogue in prose (in the preceding eclogues the characters dialogue in verse), forcing the reader to understand an internal logic which could not be wholly differentiated by virtue of the metrics or genre.

The prose of the thirteenth eclogue introduced the genre of the philosophical dialogue with one of the pastoral's favorite themes, glossed by Vélez de Guevara in the *Menosprecio de corte y alabanza del aldea* (1539), and later reprised by Cervantes in the *Galatea* with Damón's recitation of the "Canción de Lauso."[29] Consistent with the preceding twelve, the eclogue opened with an omniscient narrator speaking in unrhymed hendecasyllables. Only the discourse itself, bookended by versified narration, took place in prose. Much like the dialogue between Philo and Sophia in Abravanel's *Dialoghi d'amore*, in this closing dialogue the query of the shepherd, Alipino, was answered by the lectures of Miseno, who disambiguated the many Petrarchan allegories that he repurposed for the illustration of the *engañosa* life at court (instead of the *engaño de amor*). This shift into prose was not happenstance: it underscored that many of the dialogic aspects of pastoral fiction were of a philosophical rather than theatrical nature. Because the eclogue was traditionally sung as a dialogue amongst shepherds on a single theme or concept, it had retained a latent tie to philosophical discourse. The formal precedent for philosophical Arcadia was found in the idyllic setting of Plato's *Phaedrus*. As discussed in Chapter 4, Abravanel's *Dialoghi* took place in a rural and idyllic setting.

28 (Padilla, *Églogas pastoriles*, 2010, 23). See also: Aurelio Valladares Reguero in the same edition: "se trata de composiciones articuladas sobre una base narrativa, que estructuralmente se acercan mucho, por tanto, a las novelas pastoriles tan en boga en la época" (Padilla, *Églogas pastoriles*, 2010, 13). See also: (P. Fanconi, "La narratividad en las *Églogas pastoriles* de Pedro de Padilla," *Dicenda, Cuadernos de Filología Hispánica*, 13, 1995, 131–141).

29 (Cervantes, *Galatea*, 1961, vol. II, 35–40).

In the same way Giordano Bruno's *Heroic Frenzies* (1585) was also set in the pastoral mode, and Sánchez de Lima's *El arte poétcia* (1580) was presented as a dialogue amongst shepherds.[30] But the proximity was not only of setting: the lyric and the philosophical dialogue shared the ideal space of the conceit and the concept, respectively. This confluence of lyric sempiternity and the timeless state of philosophical inquiry wed immediacy and eternity in character development and gave conceptual formulations to the stories that arose there.[31]

The introduction of prosified philosophical dialogue into the final eclogue was not the only example of generic dynamism in Padilla's hybrid text. This transformation of versified and prosified arenas into a narratively cohesive story was further complicated when Padilla blurred the distinction between his authorship of the text as totality and his authorship as a lyric poet under the pseudonym Silvano. The full title, *Églogas pastoriles de Pedro de Padilla y juntamente con ellas algunos sonetos del mismo autor* (Pastoral eclogues by Pedro de Padilla and together with them some sonnets by the same author), indicated that author and poet were one and the same. As Labrador Herraiz and Di Franco observe,

> Esta vez prefirió reunirlos, para crear un cancionerito-epílogo y cerrar de esta manera con los veinticinco sonetos la historia de amor de Silvano y Silvia. Son sonetos que bien pudiera firmar Silvano. El eco de la primera parte del libro se escucha en todos ellos (menos en uno). Diez de ellos están dirigidos a Silvia. Hay uno, sin embargo, que no es una confesión de amor humano sino un acto de arrepentimiento, una confesión religiosa en toda regla dirigida a Dios, sentimiento religioso absolutamente nuevo en todo el libro.
>
> (This time he preferred to unite them, in order to create a *cancionerito*-epilogue and to close in this manner the history of the love of Silvano and Silvia with the twenty-five sonnets. They are sonnets that Silvano very well could have signed. The echo with the first part of the book is heard in all of them (except for one). Ten of them are addressed to Silvia. There is one, nonetheless, that is not a confession of human love but an act of repentance, a proper religious confession addressed to God, a religious sentiment absolutely new in the book.)[32]

Of course, in the tradition of Pastoral Petrarchism, even Padilla's late religious turn retained the pattern of Petrarch's *Canzoniere*: from Laura to the Virgin Mary. It blended Silvano's Pastoral Petrarchism with that of

[30] (M. Sánchez de Lima, *El arte poética en romance castellano*, Alcalá: Juan Iñiguez de Lequerica, 1580).
[31] (García-Bryce, A., "Conceptismo," in *Princeton Encyclopedia of Poetry and Poetics*, ed. Roland Greene, Princeton University Press, 2012, 289–292).
[32] (Labrador Herraiz and DiFranco in Padilla, *Églogas Pastoriles*, 2010, 40).

the author, Padilla, into a single Petrarchan *figura of the poet*. As much in his biography as in the final sonnet, and his subsequent *Jardín espiritual* (1585), Padilla produced a new *imitatio* of the *figura of the poet*, Petrarch, current in sixteenth-century Spain. The opening sonnet found in the epilogue of the *Églogas* was explicit enough to leave little ambiguity about his primary model:

> Petrarca celebró su Laura bella
> con ingenio y estilo leuantado,
> y hizo al mundo eterno su cuydado
> y la rara belleza que vio en ella.
> Biuen hoy imbidiosas muchas della
> porqu'es digno de ser muy inbidiado
> vn bien tan alto, y tan dichoso estado,
> que nunca pueda el tiempo contra ella.
> Yo solo a ti, gallarda Siluia hermosa,
> a quien di el coraçón en sacrificio
> querría dexarte de la misma suerte.
> Que esta alma en adorarte venturosa,
> solo te puede hazer este seruicio:
> que no te offenda el tiempo ni la muerte.

> (Petrarch celebrated his beautiful Laura
> with lofty *ingenio* and style,
> and he made his thought, and the rare beauty
> he saw in her, eternal in the world.
> Today many live in envy of her
> because she is worthy of being envied,
> a good so lofty, and such a happy state,
> that time is incapable against her.
> I alone to you, gallant beautiful Silvia,
> to whom I gave my heart in sacrifice
> would like to leave you the same fortune.
> That this soul, happy in adoring you,
> can only do for you this service:
> that you are offended neither by time nor death.)[33]

The introduction of these closing sonnets in a voice that blurred the distinction between Siralvo, the pseudonymic poet, and Padilla, the author, rhymed with the tradition of the *roman à clef* whilst explicitly and intentionally narrowing the space of authorial distance between the author and the *figura of the poet*. This collapse of the timeless pastoral space

[33] (Padilla, *Églogas Pastoriles*, 2010, 351 [238v–239]).

into the immediate and chronological time of the author refigured the chronotopic dimensions of the text such that the sempiternal qualities of the lyric were made immanent within the particular circumstance of the speaking poet. Conversely, the speaking poet raised himself (and his beloved) to the sempiternal, conceptual, or symbolic dimensions of his art.[34] Collected within this text, the pastoral work as Petrarchan *Canzoniere*, the versified eclogue as narrative, the philosophical dialogue as actionable content, the sonnet as both lyric expression and narrative practice, and the *figura of the poet* as author, were assembled in a quasi-fictional whole.

Padilla was not the only poet to experiment with the narrative potential of versified eclogues during the early 1580s. It is fitting that Pedro Laínez authored the *censura* for Padilla's pastoral eclogues because Laínez too, in his *Engaños y desengaños de amor*, employed the novelistic techniques of versified exposition, dialogue, and reported speech, in addition to the power of the lyric apostrophe.

> Cerca de aquella dulce y clara fuente
> que, por medio de acueste verde prado,
> discurre tan suave y blandamente,
> a la sombra de un sauce recostado,
> me acuerdo ahora que estaba el primer día
> que fui de Galatea enamorado.
>
> (Close to that sweet and clear spring
> that, in the middle of this green meadow,
> runs so smoothly and gently,
> reclined in the shadow of a willow,
> I remember now that it was the first day
> that I fell in love with Galatea.)[35]

So began Pedro Laínez's unfinished and unedited eclogue *Engaños y Desengaños de Amor*, which brought Cervantes to Esquivias in 1584 for the purpose of seeing his mentor's work appear posthumously in print.[36] This trip also occasioned Cervantes' meeting with and marriage to Catalina de Salazar; however, this occurred after the completion of the *Galatea*. Laínez had died in early March 1584, after Lucas Gracián Dantisco had signed the *privilegio* for the *Galatea* on February 1, 1584. Laínez's eclogue, like Padilla's, demonstrated a strong interest in verse narration of the *figura of the poet* practiced by several *ingenios* in early 1580s Madrid. Laínez's

[34] My allusion to Hegel here is both playful and serious. See the "Lyric" in (*Hegel's Aesthetics, Lectures on Fine Art*, ed. and trans. T.M. Knox, Cambridge University Press, 1975, vol. II).

[35] (Laínez, *Obras*, 1951, vol. II, 272).

[36] (Laínez, *Obras*, 1951, vol. II, 272–325).

Engaños were also concerned with the elusive shepherdess Galatea (a character somewhat distinct from Cervantes' eponymous heroine), who narrates to Amaranta the occasion by which Montano fell in love with her. Within the construction of the text, this was a significant development in narrative technique because the work opened with Montano recalling the same incident from his point of view. Both the perspective of Montano and that of Galatea on the same event were given over the course of the eclogue such that the plot arose out of the confluence of both lyric temporalities into a narrative whole.[37] Moreover, Galatea went on to directly recite the verses that Montano had sung to her and so resituated Montano's lyric time within her own chronotopic situation. More than literary artifact, Montano's verses also influenced Galatea's own lyric state within the narrative.

Cervantes readily employed this use of reported speech in the eclogue throughout the *Galatea*, amongst both the shepherds of the Tajo and those of the interpolated tales. The practice of having shepherds recite the lyric poetry of other shepherds introduced unprecedented temporal complexities into the fabric of the text. Because the poet's interiority, as expressed in lyric verse, was already abstracted into the sempiternity of literary figures and tropes, the "un-timed" experience of lyric verse as utterance disrupted the narrative with the temporality of the speaker's interior. It was for this reason that meetings of several shepherds in the *Galatea* frequently took on the guise of the "chronotope of the road," in which various temporalities converged at a single location, a location whose time/space specificity was shattered by the lyrical expositions of the interlocutors.[38] (Cervantes repurposed this device with the roadside inn and the palace of the duke and duchess in the first and second parts of the *DQ*.[39]) Once uttered or sung, the lyric as recitable became a linguistic and narrative artifact that introduced further dimensions into the time/space of the novel, depending on when, where, and how it was deployed. While this chronotopic dynamism was apparent in the work of Padilla and Laínez, it was Cervantes who would bring this novelistic element to its potential in the *Galatea*.

In the *Galatea*, the author's beloved did not take the eponymous title of the work, as had been the case in the work of Montemayor and Gálvez de Montalvo. Cervantes shifted the narrative focus away from himself (Lauso) and his beloved (Silena) to the amorous intrigue of Elicio and Galatea. This alteration in the architecture of the narrative was one of two

[37] (Laínez, *Obras*, 1951, vol. II, 272 and 296). [38] (Bakhtin, *Dialogic Imagination*, 98).

[39] Here, when AQ as dQ battles with the wineskins in his dream, the reader encounters a dream within a dream which pushes the lyric actuality of Quijano's poetic persona (dQ) toward novelistic realization.

major structural choices that Cervantes made for his pastoral prosimetrum. The other major decision was the choice to laud poets instead of noblewomen in the "Canto de Calíope" (the precedent for which can be found in Gil Polo's continuation of the *Diana*). With these changes Cervantes twice redirected the focus of the pastoral novel away from court gossip and toward the living art of poetic practice within his own milieu. In this view, Galatea's name was at once a nominal veil and literary symbol. The beloved of Pygmalion, in the Ovidian myth, Galatea was the beloved sculpture that Venus brought to life at the request of the artist. From a symbolic point of view, the young poets Elicio and Erastro were in pursuit of the muse herself, a muse who was the product of the poet's own poiesis. The details of the plot between Elicio, Erastro, and Galatea (speculatively, Lope de Vega, Liñán de Riaza, and Elena Osorio) developed the central drama as a new transformation of the unwanted-marriage plot as both a history and an allegory of poetic pursuits in the early 1580s. But it was the tangential story of Lauso and his beloved Silena that fully developed the chronotopic dynamism of the narrativized *figura of the poet* in the text.[40]

Whether Cervantes was in fact in love with a woman with the pseudonym of Silena, or whether the representation of Lauso's love for Silena offered Cervantes the opportunity to work through some of his own thoughts on the erotic philosophy and practices of the day, does not matter as much as the fact that Cervantes chose to represent himself to his contemporaries as a lyric lover with his own unique take on their shared poetic discourse.[41] Lauso's story introduced a novelistic tale of jealousy, resolution, and reversal which depended on lyric verse and the chronotopic dynamism of the human interior for the telling. By positing Silena as the "lady of his thoughts," Lauso's own poetic exteriorization of his interior development set a precedent in Cervantes' prose fiction for AQ's transformation of his interior into dQ, dedicated to Dulcinea (Aldonza Lorenzo), the "lady of his thoughts." In the *Galatea*, Lauso's trajectory took up the question of lyric sempiternity, identity, and narrative fragmentation, once native to Petrarch's *Canzoniere*, as novelistic plot. Nowhere in the *Galatea* did the *figura of the poet* come nearer to modern novelistic protagonist than it did in the case of Lauso.

[40] The unwanted marriage plot is reprised as the *bodas del camacho* in *DQ II*, which also shares a parallel with the wedding of Dardanio and Silveria in Book III of the *Galatea*.

[41] "[A] narrative cannot be divorced from the contexts of its utterance without substantially altering the narrative itself" (B. Richardson, "General Introduction," in ed. B. Richardson, *Narrative Dynamics: Essays on Time, Plot, Closure, and Frames*, Ohio State University Press, 2002, 1–7; 1).

Lauso's narrative arc occupied a curious structural position in the architecture of the novel. The central chronotope of the text was set on the banks of the river Tajo and revolved around the love of Elicio and Erastro for Galatea. This was populated by the shepherds of the Tajo, such as Florisa, Lenio, Dardanio, Silveria, Mileno, and Gelasia, as well as those that came from the Henares, such as Tirsi and Damón. In addition to the main story, several other tales or *novelas* were interpolated and interwoven into the text (Lisandro, Teolinda, Silerio, Rosaura, and their peers). These plots entered the central chronotope in *medias res,* and the protagonists often relied upon lyric verse and prose exposition in order to account for their appearance in the time/space of the story. Some of these plots were closed interpolations, as in the case of Lisandro in Book I, who appeared and then disappeared without continuing as part of the main plot or affecting it. Others, such as Teolinda of Book II and Silerio of Book III, saw their as-yet-incomplete tales evolve within the central chronotope. These interpolated characters were not all shepherds when they entered the story; they tended to be urban, bourgeois, or aristocratic. (Teolinda, as shepherdess of the Henares, is an exception.) In the case of Silerio, his transformation in the text from urban youth to pastoral hermit was one of the ways in which he blended with the central chronotope once his backstory had been partially recounted. In many ways, Lauso functioned similarly to an interpolated character. The drama of his narrative arc did not occur within the action of the novel. He appeared intermittently only to recount off-stage events which had already taken place. However, Lauso was not an interpolated character, but a shepherd of the Tajo who explicitly pertained to and was interwoven within the socio-poetic network of the central chronotope from the outset.

Like Petrarch's Laura, Lauso's Silena never enters the action of the text as an autonomous character. She is a mystery even to the other shepherds. The reader hears about her only by way of Lauso, who hardly discusses her in prose dialogue or exposition, but treats her almost singularly in the space of lyric verse. Lauso is also more distanced from the narrator than the other characters. While Cervantes has come to be known for his various narrators and their frames, Lauso's lyrical emplotment of his own narrative was unique within the omnisciently narrated text of the *Galatea.* The omniscient narrator hardly reveals this curious character from the authorial vantage point. Almost none of Lauso's lyric trajectory is given to the reader by the narrator; his backstory comes largely from the comments of other shepherds. The unanswered contours of Lauso's lyric plot (such as the true identity of Silena) evade narrative explication in an otherwise omnisciently ordered text. As such, Lauso's plot always refers back to the *figura of the poet*; lyric verse, lightly contextualized, remains the primary source for piecing together the narrative arc of this novel character.

Lauso's narrative sequence supplies a clear depiction of the way Lauso's lyric temporality disrupted symbolic and chronological plot expectations in the central chronotope. Lauso is first introduced as a character near the close of Book III, when he and Francenio enter into a friendly gloss competition of the *letra* "Huyendo va la esperanza / tenella con el deseo (Hope is fleeing / detain it with desire)" late in the marriage festivities for Dardanio and Silveria.[42] The reader first encounters him as a shepherd on the periphery of but party to the central chronotope. His narrative arc does not begin until Book IV, when he is overheard by Galatea, Florisa, and Teolinda while he sings the first of several poems ("Si yo dijere el bien del pensamiento"). Seated at the foot of a "verde sauce" (willow tree), Lauso remains unaware of the shepherdesses, who guess at the identity of his beloved Silena but who depart without his knowledge. The sparse explication of Lauso's identity is delivered through the disclosure of the thoughts of the shepherdesses. From their point of view, the reader learns that he has recently returned from abroad and that his amorous verses are a surprise since just the other day the *libre* Lauso had gone about in possession of his free will, mocking those who were unlucky enough to have fallen in love.[43] The shepherdesses wonder at the identity of his beloved Silena: "sin duda alguna creyeron que, con disfrazado nombre, celebraba alguna conocida pastora, a quien había hecho señora de sus pensamientos (without a doubt they believed that, with a disguised name, he celebrated some known shepherdess, whom he had made lady of his thoughts)."[44] Part shepherd of the Tajo and part interpolated character from his travels abroad, Lauso is also a contemporary poet of the 1580s who masks his beloved with a pastoral pseudonym: a pseudonym within a pseudonym.

The next the reader learns of Lauso also comes from the mouths of other shepherds. While Lauso is absent from the scene, Damón enters into a *plática* with visiting gentlemen over the high quality of pastoral life and the *menosprecio de corte* reprised in the thirteenth of Padilla's *Églogas*. As in the previous scene, the omniscient narrator refrains from speaking directly of Lauso, whose details are revealed to the gentlemen and the reader by way of Damón:

[42] Lauso's *glosa* (which does not form a part of his lyric plot) does in fact foreshadow the shape of his narrative: if hope is to be preserved with desire, then Lauso's final turn to disdain is the erasure of both hope and desire.

[43] (Cervantes, *Galatea*, 1585, 190v). [44] (Cervantes, *Galatea*, 1585, 190v).

> Cuán bien se conforma con tu opinión Darintho—dijo Damón—, la de un pastor amigo mío que Lauso se llama, el cual, después de haber gastado algunos años en cortesanos ejercicios, y algunos otros en los trabajosos del duro Marte, al fin se ha reducido a la pobreza de nuestra rústica vida, y antes que a ella viniese, mostró desearlo mucho, como parece por una canción que compuso, y envió al famoso Larsileo, que en los negocios de la corte tiene larga y ejercitada experiencia . . .
>
> ("How well does it conform with your opinion, Darintho," said Damón, "that of a shepherd friend of mine named Lauso, who after having spent some years in courtly exercises, and some years in work of hard Mars, in the end has reduced himself to the poverty of our rustic life: and before he came to this, he revealed his great desire for it, as appeared in a song that he composed and sent to the famous Larsileo, who has prolonged and practiced experience in the business of the court . . .")[45]

The omniscient narrator does not speak. The details of Lauso's place within the community of poets are given by Damón, who recalls Lauso's absence abroad (service to Acquaviva, Mediterranean military campaigns, captivity) and Lauso's *canción*, which the shepherd had sent to Larsileo before returning to the banks of the Tajo (the *Epístola a Mateo Vázquez* sent by Cervantes from Algiers). Without the narrator's intervention, the reader learns that Lauso is esteemed by the venerated Damón, who respects his poetry sufficiently to commit it to memory and recite it for the visiting gentlemen for the pleasure of all. In the following scene, the reader will learn that Lauso's reputation and friendship with Damón date to before his departure abroad (i.e. Cervantes' years in the court of Isabel de Valois) as the two have not seen each other since Lauso's return to the Tajo. Therefore, Damón committed Lauso's song to memory during his friend's absence, as perhaps the *Epístola a Mateo Vázquez* circulated within the court in the late 1570s, where Laínez was employed in the authorship of *aprobaciones* for printed works. Meanwhile, Lauso himself remains absent and embroiled in his own private erotic plot. He is not, for example, present for the famous debate on love between Tirsi and Lenio, itself a reprisal of Abravanel's *Dialoghi*.[46]

The next time the reader meets with Lauso, at the opening of Book V, his story picks up where it had left off in Book IV, with a poem for Silena, "Quién mi libre pensamiento," sung in solitude whilst a group of shepherds secretly listen. This second lyric appearance brings Lauso into closer dialogue with his companions of the central chronotope. After having sung

[45] (Cervantes, *Galatea*, 1961, vol. II, 34). [46] (López Estrada, "La influencia italiana").

his second poem, Lauso overhears the other shepherds and comes out to greet them, only to be reunited with his friend Damón, whom he has not seen since his time abroad (another indication that the novel treats Cervantes' return from Algiers in the early 1580s).[47] As Lauso converses with Damón ("su verdadero amigo"), details of his lyric plot spill into the text by way of his own narration.[48] He tells Damón that he had suffered a bout of jealousy which brought him to the point of *desesperación*, but that all had been remedied by speaking with his shepherdess, who had marked her reassurances with the gift of a ring.[49] In other words, this plot had developed out of an interior space (of jealousy) which motivated an exterior action (of reconciliation). This is a story concerned with the way in which the interior affects the exterior so as to create narrative consequence. It gives lyric interiority a causal role in the determination of outcomes.

Moreover, Lauso's scant summary is followed by an unfolding of events in lyric verse. The sonnet "Rica y dichosa prenda" that Lauso composed to commemorate Silena's reassurance (an apostrophe to the ring) introduces another lyric time into the narrative. The sonnet transports Lauso, Damón, and reader backwards into the time/space of Lauso's ecstatically renewed erotic faith in Silena, a lyric location wholly distinct from the poem of amorous longing that Lauso had been singing when the scene began. This temporal or chronotopic dynamism (a sort of early modern lyric flashback) is further complicated when Damón begs Lauso to recite another poem ("En tan notoria simpleza"), which transports shepherds and reader to even earlier lyric coordinates in Lauso's plot through its depiction of his desperate jealousy. Thus, while Lauso and Damón remain spatially

47 "con cuya compañía todos se holgaron, especialmente Damón, su verdadero amigo, con el cual se acompañó todo el camino que desde allí a la ermita había, razonando en diversos y varios acaecimientos que a los dos habían succedido después que dejaron de verse, que fue desde el tiempo que el valeroso y nombrado pastor Astraliano había dejado los cisalpinos pastos, por ir a reducir aquellos que del famoso hermano y de la verdadera religión se habían rebelado" (Cervantes, *Galatea*, 1961, vol. II, 93-94).

48 "y al cabo vinieron a reducir su razonamiento a tratar de los amores de Lauso, preguntándole ahincadamente Damón que le dijese quién era la pastora que con tanta facilidade la libre voluntad le había rendido. Y cuando esto no pudo saber de Lauso, le rogó que, a lo menos, le dijese en qué estado se hallaba, si era de temor o de esperanza, si le fatigaba ingratitud o si le atormentaban celos" (Cervantes, *Galatea*, 1961, vol. II, 94).

49 "A todo lo cual le satisfizo bien Lauso, contándole algunas cosas que con su pastora le habían sucedido, y entre otras le dijo como hallándose un día celoso y desfavorecido, había llegado a términos de desesperarse o de dar alguna muestra que en daño de su persona y en el del crédito y honra de su pastora redundase; pero que todo se remedió con haberla él hablado, y haberle ella asegurado ser falsa la sospecha que tenía, confirmando todo esto con darle un anillo de su mano, que fue parte para volver a mejor discurso su entendimiento y para solemnizar aquel favor con un soneto, que de algunos que le vieron fué por bueno estimado. Pidió entonces Damón a Lauso que le dijese"(Cervantes, *Galatea*, 1961, vol. II, 94).

situated within the central chronotope of the *Galatea* as they accompany the other shepherds to the hermitage of Silerio, the substitution of lyric verse for prosaic exposition repeatedly thrusts them and reader into various lyric temporalities which produce "fictive lyric events" in the unearthing of another plot.[50]

This chronotopic dynamism at work in the genesis of the narrative is further complicated by the fact that Lauso's plot is one of exterior action produced by interior upheaval. His experience of both longing and jealousy reorient the narrative emphasis to his interior state: thoughts, will, understanding, and madness (*pensamientos*, *voluntad/albedrío*, *entendimiento*, *locura*). Then, just as quickly as his lyric plot opened, Lauso's closes again and he disappears from the group with their arrival at the hermitage of Silerio, where Silerio's own interpolated tale is about to undergo further narrative and lyric complexity as it moves toward resolution. Later in Book V, the group of shepherds again overhear Lauso singing for his shepherdess ("Alzó la vista a la más noble parte"). With this poem Lauso's interior state returns to his present longing, but as an apostrophe to the divine beloved the lyric also wrests him from the bucolic scene into the sempiternity of his own erotic mysticism. More than exposition, the lyric, unlike storytelling, does not represent a new scene as artifact within the contours of the central chronotope; the lyric breaks open the central chronotope as a character's temporally dynamic interior verges on the sempiternity of the *figura of the poet*. This emphasis on interior space hijacks the scene and its temporal-spatial "ground."

The final stage of Lauso's inconclusive plot ensues later in Book V, when he reenters the narrative and becomes fully integrated into the central chronotope for the remainder of the text. This quasi-final reversal, or *volta*, of his amorous suffering frees the *libre* Lauso through the experience of *desdén*, for which he sings an encomiastic poem praising disdain for having liberated his will and understanding (*albedrío* and *entendimiento*) from the lady of his thoughts. From jealousy to longing to disdain, the lyrical plot of Lauso's interior develops a novelistic transformation of character enacted from within rather than from without. While Tirsi cautions against a freedom so quickly won, Lauso's lyric plot remains inconclusive at the close of the *Galatea* as the characters move toward the final day. But the import of this *imbroglio* lies not in a conclusion, but in the introduction of actions which are the consequence of lyric states. Following his liberation, Lauso remains a character within the central chronotope. Just as he had

[50] (Culler, *Pursuit of Signs*, 152–153). See also Chapter 2.

participated in the gloss competition for the wedding festivities of Dardanio and Silveria late in Book III, he also participates in the memorial eclogue for the deceased Meliso in Book VI, and in the other poetic games played by the shepherds during the progression of the central chronotope. In the closing scene, Lauso rallies the other shepherds to come to Elicio's aid in an intervention to prevent Galatea's unwanted marriage. But in novelistic terms, Lauso's plot concludes in Book V with his liberation from the lady of his thoughts. The narrative arc of this transformation, developed almost singularly through the lyric interior, became the building blocks for Cervantes' novelistic fiction and the divided modern figure of AQ/dQ, exterior/interior, poet/persona. This confluence, in which the lyric served at once as its own immediate expression and as a generator of narrative plot, situated the interiority of the fictional character at the heart of modern novelistic prose.

To borrow terms from Shklovsky, as *fabula* Lauso's poems may be reassembled into a chronological series of events. But as *syuzhet*, the disclosure of the movements of Lauso's interior are repositioned for the reader in a novelistic upending of traditional narrative expectations, such that a causally related series of actions and events becomes the consequence of the chronotopic dynamism of the lyric interior.[51]

Lauso's plot (fabula)

1. Poem of jealousy and desperation over Silena	3rd poem of Book V "En tan notoria simpleza"
2. Sonnet commemorating Silena's reassurance	2nd poem of Book V "Rica y dichosa prenda"
3. Love poem sung in private for Silena	1st poem of Book IV "Si yo dijere el bien del pensamiento"
4. Love poem sung in private for Silena	1st poem of Book V "¿Quién mi libre pensamiento"
5. Love poem for Silena	4th poem of Book V "Alzó la vista a la más noble parte"
6. Praise for "desdén," liberator from love	5th poem of Book V "Con las rodillas en el suelo hincadas"

While Lauso's narrative occurred adjacent to the central chronotope, it was integrated thematically. In Book III, the wedding eclogue of Orompo,

[51] (V. Shklovsky, *Theory of Prose*, trans. B. Sher, Normal: Dalkey Archive Press, 3rd printing, 1998).

Marsilio, Crysio, and Orfenio had been framed as a competition to determine the greatest form of amorous suffering. Damón had been the judge of this contest, in which he opined that jealousy was by far the worst, a judgment in which Damón used one of Cervantes' favorite phrases, a "curioso impertinente," to describe the disease of jealousy.[52] The plot of Lauso's own jealousy reprised and gave flesh to the judgment that Damón had earlier expounded; it carried this judgment beyond the theoretical into the novelistic. As a particular treatment of jealousy, Lauso's lyric plot introduced the content of the human interior as the subject of novelistic fiction. Lauso's lyrics were neither narrative ornament nor repositories for the author's poetic talent; they were essential and integrated components of Lauso's plot.

Lauso's lyrical plot is a ripe example of the chronotopic dynamism introduced to narrative storytelling in the pastoral prosimetrum. In this regard, it shares commonalities with the lyric poems of other shepherds in the *Galatea*, whose narratives are likewise generated through the causal relationship between interiority and exteriority. But Lauso, in particular, also embellished another key component of the chronotopic dynamism at work. Beginning with the opening of Book IV, when Teolinda, Galatea, and Florisa stop to eavesdrop on his verses, Lauso's lyric "Si yo dijere el bien del pensamiento" turns the literary character inside out by forcing prose fiction to attend to the sempiternity of the *figura of the poet*. Because the *Galatea* lacks a modern translation, I give this poem in its entirety.

Lauso

1 Si yo dijere el bien del pensamiento,
en mal se vuelva cuanto bien poseo,
que no es para decirse el bien que siento.

2 De mí mesmo se encubra mi deseo,
enmudezca la lengua en esta parte,
y en el silencio ponga su trofeo.

3 Pare aquí el artificio, cese el arte
de exagerar el gusto que en una alma
con mano liberal amor reparte.

4 Baste decir que en sosegada calma
paso el mar amoroso, confiado
de honesto triunfo y vencedora palma.

[52] (Cervantes, *Galatea*, 1961, vol. I, 230).

5 Sin saberse la causa, lo causado
se sepa, que es un bien tan sin medida,
que sólo para el alma es reservado.

6 Ya tengo nuevo ser, ya tengo vida,
ya puedo cobrar nombre en todo el suelo
de ilustre y clara fama conocida,

7 que el limpio intento, el amoroso celo
que encierra el pecho enamorado mío,
alzarme puede al más subido cielo.

8 En ti, Silena, espero; en ti confío,
Silena, gloria de mi pensamiento,
norte por quien se rige mi albedrío.

9 Espero que el sin par entendimiento
tuyo levantes a entender que valgo
por fe lo que no está en merecimiento.

10 Confío que tendrás, pastora, en algo,
después de hacerte cierta la experiencia,
la sana voluntad de un pecho hidalgo.

11 ¿Qué bienes no asegura tu presencia?
¿Qué males no destierra? Y ¿quién sin ella
sufrirá un punto la terrible ausencia?

12 ¡Oh, más que la belleza misma bella,
más que la propia discreción discreta,
sol a mis ojos, y a mi mar estrella!

13 No la que fue de la nombrada Creta
robada por el falso hermoso toro
igualó a tu hermosura tan perfecta;

14 ni aquella que en sus faldas granos de oro
sintió llover, por quien después no pudo
guardar el virginal rico tesoro;

15 ni aquella que con brazo airado y crudo,
en la sangre castísima del pecho
tiñó el puñal, en su limpieza, agudo;

16 ni aquella que a furor movió y despecho
contra Troya los griegos corazones,
por quien fue el Ilion roto y deshecho;

17 ni la que los latinos escuadrones
hizo mover contra la teucra gente,
a quien Juno causó tantas pasiones;

18 ni menos la que tiene diferente
fama de la entereza y el trofeo
con que su honestidad guardó excelente:

19 digo de aquella que lloró a Sicheo,
del mantuano Títiro notada
de vano antojo y no cabal deseo;

20 no en cuantas tuvo hermosas la pasada
edad, ni la presente tiene agora,
ni en la de por venir será hallada

21 quien llegase ni llegue a mi pastora
en valor, en saber, en hermosura,
en merecer del mundo ser señora.

22 ¡Dichoso aquel que con firmeza pura
fuere de ti, Silena, bien querido,
sin gustar de los celos la amargura!

23 ¡Amor, que a tanta alteza me has subido,
no me derribes con pesada mano
a la bajeza escura del olvido!
¡Se conmigo señor, y no tirano!

1 (If I were to articulate the good of my thought,
as much good as I possess would turn bad,
for the good that I feel is not to be spoken of.

2 From me myself my desire is concealed,
the tongue is muted on this part,
and puts the trophy on being silent.

3 Artifice stops here, art ceases
to exaggerate the pleasure love doles out
with a liberal hand in my soul.

4 Enough to say that in tranquil calm
I pass the amorous sea, trusting
in an honest triumph and victorious palm.

5 Without knowing the cause, the caused
is known, that it is a good so beyond measure
that it is reserved only for the soul.

6 I already have a new being, already [a new] life,
already I am known in all the earth,
of illustrious and clearly recognized fame;

7 the clean intention, the amorous zeal
that encloses my enamored breast,
can lift me up to the highest heaven.

8 In you, Silena, I hope; in you I trust,[53]
Silena, glory of my thought,
north by whom my will [*albedrío*] is governed.

9 I hope that you raise that unmatched
understanding [*entendimiento*] to understand that through faith
I am worth that which I do not deserve.

10 I trust, shepherdess, after having made yourself certain
of the experience, you will make something of
the healthy will [*voluntad*] of a noble gentleman [*hidalgo*].

11 What goods are not assured by your presence?
What bads are not exiled? And, who without [you]
could suffer one point the terrible absence?

12 Oh more beautiful than Beauty itself,[54]
more discreet than the very discretion,
sun of my eyes, and star to my sea!

13 Not she that of famed Crete[55]
was robbed by the false pretty bull,
could equal your perfect beauty;[56]

14 nor she for whom grains of gold rained[57]
in her skirts from he from whom she could not
guard her virginal treasure;

[53] Compare to *Viaje del Parnaso*: "También, al par de Filis, mi Silena / resonó por las selvas, que escucharon / más de una y otra alegre cantilena, / y en dulces varias rimas se llevaron / mis esperanzas los ligeros vientos, / que en ellos y en la arena se sembraron. / Tuve, tengo y tendré los penasmientos, / merced al cielo que a tal bien me inclina, / de toda adulación libres y esentos" (Cervantes, *Poesías*, 2016, 323).

[54] I have capitalized "Beauty" to clarify the Neoplatonic valence of the "form of beauty," "pure beauty," "absolute beauty," as discussed in Plato's *Symposium* and *Phaedrus*, as well as, for example, in the *Enneads* of Plotinus and in the third of Abravanel's *Dialogues of Love*, which, among other things, treats the cognition of Beauty.

[55] Europa.

[56] I translate both "belleza" and "hermosura" as "beauty" in order to observe their mutual (Neoplatonic) use as synonyms for the "the good."

[57] Danaë.

15 nor she who, in her clean, quick wit,[58]
with severe and angry arm, stained
the dagger in the chaste blood of her breast;

16 nor she who moved to fury and dispatched[59]
Greek hearts against Troy,
by whom Ilion was broken and undone;

17 nor she that made the Latin squadrons[60]
move against the Trojan people,
to whom Juno caused so many passions;

18 nor less she who had two reputations
one for fortitude and the other for triumph
with which she excellently guarded her honesty:

19 I say she who cried to Sychaeus,[61]
by the Mantuan Titirus known
for vain whim and improper desire;

20 not in any of the beauties the past
age had, nor the present now has,
nor in the future will be found

21 one who arrives to [the heights of] my shepherdess
in valor, in knowledge, in beauty,
in deserving to be lady of the world.

22 Happy he that with firm purity
will be loved by you, Silena,
without tasting the bitterness of jealousy!

23 Love, who has raised me to such a height,
don't knock me down with heavy hand
to the lowly darkness of the forgotten!
Be a good lord with me, and not a tyrant!)[62]

In this play on thought and feeling ("pensamiento," "siento") for "the good" (which is the *summa belleza* and *summum bonum* of his shepherdess), Lauso sings, paradoxically, of being brought to a state of silence by the ineffability of his subject ("en el silencio ponga su trofeo," Stanza 2), a trope that Cervantes' had already employed in his 1567 sonnet for Isabel. Here the "pastoral paradox of natural art" comes to the fore in the shepherd's literary appeal to drop all art and artifice (Stanza 3). This turn to simple,

[58] Lucretia. [59] Helen. [60] Lavinia. [61] Dido.
[62] (Cervantes, *Galatea*, 1961, vol. II, 27–29).

unadorned nature, to the bald feeling of the soul, recovers the language of the mysterious "cause" at the origin of this erotic mysticism. Within "lo causado" of a measureless good, the poet's will is given over to the lady ("norte por quien se rige mi albedrío," Stanza 8). The elision of a timeless Arcadia with the sempiternity of the lyric is not only a Hellenization of the Edenic myth whereby the poet is given a *vita nuova* (Stanza 6); it throws the myth in reverse and restores the lover to the *locus amoenus* by way of the beloved (Stanzas 11 and 12). Fittingly, Lauso does not refer to himself as a shepherd, but as an "hidalgo," again blurring the distinction between poet and persona. After declaring his shepherdess more excellent than several figures of Classical literature (Europa, Danaë, Helen, etc.), the poet then conjures an infinite temporality, a sempiternity, in which his shepherdess is not only of a moment, but exceeds all of the past, present, and future. In keeping with the commonplaces of Pastoral Petrarchism, the poet's own posterity is bound up in this appeal to immorality (an appeal for love to save him from "la bajeza escura del olvido," which indicates both the memory of the beloved and of posterity; Stanza 23). This first lyric (third in the text; #3 in the table) sets the stage for Lauso's subsequent lyric apostrophe (#4 in the table) "Quién mi libre pensamiento," in which the shepherd-poet fully develops the new sempiternal potential of lyric as narrative action.

In Lauso's first poem of Book V, the sempiternal features of erotic experience produce a lyric subjectivity that struggles to grasp itself temporally and linguistically. The lyric voice as poetic action thrusts forward into the space of narrative, whilst character-as-temporality disintegrates within character-as-spatiality.

1 ¿Quién mi libre pensamiento
me le vino a sujetar?
¿Quién pudo en flaco cimiento
sin ventura fabricar
tan altas torres de viento?
¿Quién rindió mi libertad,
estando en seguridad
de mi vida satisfecho?
¿Quién abrió y rompió mi pecho,
Y robó mi voluntad?[63]

[63] It should be noted that here Cervantes uses the word "voluntad" (rather than "libre albedrío") which was the "will" pertaining to the three faculties of the soul, which included "memoria" (memory) and

2 ¿Dónde está la fantasía
de mi esquiva condición?
¿Do el alma que ya fue mía,
y dónde mi corazón,
que no está donde solía?
Mas yo todo ¿dónde estoy,
dónde vengo, o adónde voy?
A dicha, ¿se yo de mí?
¿Soy, por ventura, el que fui,
o nunca he sido el que soy?

3 Estrecha cuenta me pido,
sin poder averigualla,
pues a tal punto he venido,
que aquello que en mí se halla,
es sombra de lo que he sido.
No me entiendo de entenderme,
ni me valgo por valerme,
y, en tan ciega confusión,
cierta está mi perdición,
y no pienso de perderme.

4 La fuerza de mi cuidado,
y el amor que lo consiente,
me tienen en tal estado,
que adoro el tiempo presente,
y lloro por el pasado.
Véome en éste morir,
y en el pasado, vivir;
y en éste adoro mi muerte,
y en el pasado, la suerte,
que ya no puede venir.

5 En tan extraña agonía,
el sentido tengo ciego,[64]
pues, viendo que amor porfía
y que estoy dentro del fuego,
aborrezco el agua fría,
que si no es la de mis ojos,

"entendimiento" (understanding). As Covarrubias writes, "VOLUNTAD. Del nombre latino VOLUNTAS, TIS. [No consider que dice San Ambrosio, lib. I, *Officiorum*,que por ley de naturaleza la voluntad está sujeta a la razón. Es potencia ciega. ¿Qué se puede esperar de un hombre que tiene más respeto a lo que su voluntad inclina, que a lo que la ley de Dios le obligue. . . ." (Covarrubias, *Tesoro*, 1995, 971-972, underline mine).

64 The use of "sentido" here invokes both connotations: the bodily senses, and the sense or meaning. See (Covarrubias, *Tesoro*, 1995, 890).

que el fuego augmenta y despojos,
en esta amorosa fragua,
no quiero ni busco otra agua
ni otro alivio a mis enojos.

6 Todo mi bien comenzara
todo mi mal feneciera,
si mi ventura ordenara
que de ser mi fe sincera
Silena se asegurara.
Sospiros, aseguralda;
ojos míos, enteralda,
llorando en esta verdad;
pluma, lengua, voluntad:
en tal razón confirmalda.

1 (Who came to subjugate
my free thought?
Who could with such a weak foundation,
in want of fortune,
fabricate such high windmills?
Who conquered my liberty
being satisfied
in the security of my life?
Who broke open my breast
and stole my will [*voluntad*]?

2 Where is the fantasy
of my aloof condition?
Where is the soul that once was mine,
and where is my heart,
which is not in its usual place?
But all of myself, where am I?
From whence do I come? Or to where am I going?
By chance, do I know myself?
Am I, by chance, he that I was?
Or have I never been he that I am?

3 A precise account I ask of myself,
unable to figure it out,
since I have come to such a point
that what is found in me
is a shadow of what I have been.
I don't trust myself to understand myself,
nor do I esteem myself to value myself,
and in such blind confusion,
my perdition is certain,
and I don't think to lose myself.

4 The force of my thought[65]
and the love which consents to it,
have me in such a state,
that I adore the present [tense]
and cry for the past.
I see myself in this [present] to die,
and in the past, to live;
and in this [present] I adore my death,
and in the past, my luck,
that already [presently] cannot come.

5 In such extraordinary agony
my senses have gone blind,[66]
well, seeing that love strives,
and that I am inside of that fire,
I abhor the cold water.
Unless it is she of my eyes
that augments the fire and debris
of this amorous forge,
I don't want or seek other water
nor any other relief for my vexations.[67]

6 All of my good will begin,
all of my bad will pass away,
if my fortune ordains
that Silena will be secured
by my sincere faith.
Sighs, secure her;
mine eyes, weeping
in this truth, inform her;
quill, tongue, and will,
in such reason confirm her.)[68]

[65] (Covarrubias, *Tesoro*, 1995, 382).

[66] "This caused me to take leave of my perception of what is outside me. . . . 'Ecstasy,' or we can name it 'alienation,' caused by loving meditation, which is more than half-death . . .. Sleep is more likely to cause life than to destroy it. And loving ecstasy does not do this . . . the alienation caused by loving meditation happens with sensory and motion deprivation, not naturally, but violently, and it brings neither rest to the senses nor refreshment to the body; on the contrary, it impedes digestion and the person becomes consumed" (Abravanel, *Dialogues*, 2009, 171–172).

[67] The 1585 edition reads, "En tan eftraña agonia / el fentido tengo ciego, / pues viendo que amor porfia / y que eftoy dentro del fuego / aborrezco el agua fria. / Que fino es la de mis ojos / qu'el fuego augméta y defpojos / en efta amorofa fragua / no quiero, ni bufco otro agua / ni otro aliuio a mis enojos." (Cervantes, *Galatea*, 1585, 239v). The period at the end of the fourth line seems to give a clearer indication of the syntactical structure of the stanza than that given in the 1961 edition. I have translated the stanza according to the 1585.

[68] (Cervantes, *Galatea*, 1961, vol. II, 92–93).

From the windmills ("tan altas torres de viento," Stanza 1) of an enamored mind to a subjectivity no longer in possession of itself ("Mas yo todo ¿dónde estoy, / dónde vengo, o adónde voy? / A dicha, ¿se yo de mí?," Stanza 2), to the disintegration of the lyric "I" as a temporal-spatial disunity pronounced in the conjugation of the verb *ser* ("to be"), the lyric temporality dismembers the chronotopic integrity of the speaking subject: "¿*Soy*, por ventura, el que *fui*, / o nunca *he sido* el que *soy*?" From simple present, to simple past, to a negated past perfect, back to present, the final two lines of Stanza 2 are bookended by the estrangement of "Soy" ("I am"). The spatial separation of "I am" in the text – a top to bottom, left to right diagonal cutting across the two lines – mimics the narratively temporary disintegration of an identity that is no longer one. Caught in this disintegration of the chronotopic self, in a nearly Sapphic affective overtaking of both sense and reason, within this Petrarchan paradox of fire and ice, the speaker of the poem enters into a state of becoming only by way of passing through the disintegration of a chronotopic "I" into the state of poiesis occupied by lyric subjectivity.[69] The Lauso of the poem ceases to be. In place of "he that I was," a lyric subjectivity emerges through language. At each conjugation of being he is a different traveler. As interior chronotope of the road, Bakhtin's concept becomes a metaphor for the passage of the self in sempiternal erotic experience. This is the true marvel of dQ's quest, that the "I" of the mad knight is always becoming, an interior journey that has been turned outward into AQ's poetic realization of interior time as public experience. Within the pages of the *Galatea*, this Petrarchan subjectivity is predicated upon the forfeiture of the poet's will to his beloved lady (Stanza 1). Like Petrarch, in Gordon Braden's words, "Thinking about her, he forgets the laurel."[70] "Quill, tongue, and will" (Stanza 6) have all been redirected to the beloved by the poem's close. This upending of the identity of the *libre* Lauso has narrative consequence in the unfolding of his plot. It singularly determines his subsequent actions. These ecstatic forays into erotic mysticism (a sort of early modern 'ego death'), drawn from the philosophy of Abravanel, were not singular representations of Lauso's amorous interior as a dynamic but ultimately unchanging state. They were coordinates in

[69] (Sappho, "31," in ed. and trans. Anne Carson, *If Not, Winter*, New York: Random House, 2003, 62–63); (Y. Prins, "Sappho's Afterlife in Translation," in ed. E. Greene, *Re-reading Sappho: Reception and Transmission*, University California Press, 1996, 36–67).

[70] (Braden, *Petrarchan Love*, 15).

a narrative trajectory determined by lyric interiority rather than by symbolic allegory or historical data.

There is no space here to explicate each of Lauso's lyric poems in full. But it is necessary to observe the way in which the series of causally determined events (the plot) that make up his narrative are all derived from the content of his lyric poetry. Following "¿Quién mi libre pensamiento . . .?," Damón requests the backstory for Lauso's current state. In answer, Lauso goes on to recall one of his earlier poems, which, unlike the previous two lyrics, does not appear as utterance but as recited text. This recitation thrusts the reader into an earlier interior state by way of a sonnet in which the closing tercet gives retrospectively the spiritual sovereignty that Silena exercises over Lauso. That is, the recited sonnet provides a narrative event precedent to "¿Quién mi libre pensamiento . . .?"[71] In the narrative event of the sonnet, Lauso delivers an apostrophe to the ring that Silena had given him in order to reassure him that there was no need for jealousy. Damón, like the other shepherds, becomes genuinely engaged in the question of jealousy unfolding through Lauso's narrative.[72] At his request, Lauso then returns to an even earlier event in his lyric trajectory with a poem which reanimates his experience of jealousy. That is, the lyric event of jealousy caused Silena's gifting of the ring (sonnet) which produced the spiritual sovereignty which eventually resulted in the lyric subjectivity and chronotopic dynamism of "¿Quién mi libre pensamiento . . .?"

1 En tan notoria simpleza,
nacida de intento sano,
el amor rige la mano,
y la intención tu belleza.

2 El amor y tu hermosura,
Silena, en esta ocasión

[71] "*Lauso* // ¡Rica y dichosa prenda que adornaste / el precioso marfil, la nieve pura! / ¡Prenda que de la muerte y sombra escura / a nueva luz y vida me tornaste! / El claro cielo de tu bien trocaste / con el infierno de mi desventura, / porque viviese en dulce paz segura / la esperanza que en mí resucitaste. / Sabes cuánto me cuestas, dulce prenda, / el alma, y aun no quedo satisfecho, / pues menos doy de aquello que recibo. / Más porque el mundo tu valor entienda, / sé tú mi alma, enciérrate en mi pecho; / verán cómo por ti sin alma vivo" (Cervantes, *La Galatea*, 1961, vol. II, 94–95).

[72] Again, the biographical underpinnings of the *roman à clef* rise to the surface of the allegorical veil. In response to Damón's pleasure with the sonnet, Lauso humbly asserts, "Eso será, Damón, por haberme sido tú maestro en ellos, y el deseo que tienes de ver lo que en mí aprovechaste, te hace desear oírlos" (Cervantes, *La Galatea*, 1961, vol. II, 95). Cervantes alludes to Laínez's poetic mentorship while the two were writing within the court of Isabel de Valois in the 1560s. These autobiographical asides complicated the symbolic potential of the shepherds by lending them the novelistic immediacy of particular human relationships that exceeded the allegorical function and referred directly to the time and context of the author and his peers.

juzgarán a discreción
lo que tendrás tú a locura.

3 Él me fuerza y ella mueve
a que te adore y escriba;
y como en los dos estriba
mi fe, la mano se atreve.

4 Y aunque en esta grave culpa
me amenaza tu rigor,
mi fe, tu hermosura, amor,
darán del yerro disculpa.

5 Pues con un arrimo tal,[73]
puesto que culpa me den,
bien podré decir el bien
que ha nacido de mi mal;

6 el cual bien, según yo siento,
no es otra cosa, Silena,
sino que tenga en la pena
un estraño sufrimiento.

7 Y no lo encarezco poco
este bien de ser sufrido,
que sino lo hubiera sido,
ya el mal me tuviera loco.

8 Mas mis sentidos, de acuerdo
todos, han dado en decir
que, ya que haya de morir,
que muera sufrido y cuerdo.[74]

9 Pero bien considerado,
mal podrá tener paciencia
en la amorosa dolencia
un celoso y desamado;

[73] "ARRIMAR. Es llegar una cosa a otra . . . 4. Arrimar a uno es destruirle y dejarle como muerto o desmayado, pegado a la pared . . ." (Covarrubias, *Tesoro*, 1995, 123).

[74] "CUERDA. *Latine* CHORDA, tiene varias significaciones. Una es la cuerda del instrumento músico; ésta es ordinariamente, o de tripa de carnero que son las que se gastan en las vihuelas y harpas, guitarras y otros instrumentos; otras son de arambre, que sirven a las cítaras, monacordios, clavicordios. Algunos destos instrumentos las tienen de plata, y si fuesen de oro pienso que harían más suave el sonido; aunque el que se hace tocando una pieza de a cuatro con otra, debe ser el major de todos para ablandar corazones, y llevarse el mundo tras sí, como otro Orfeo. . . 5. Cuerdo, el hombre de buen seso, *cordatus, a corde*. 'El loco por la pena es cuerdo'. 'Más sabe el necio en su casa que el cuerdo en la ajena" (Covarrubias, *Tesoro*, 1995, 375).

10 que en el mal de mis enojos,
todo mi bien desconcierta
tener la esperanza muerta
y el enemigo a los ojos.

11 Goces, pastora, mil años
el bien de tu pensamiento,
que yo no quiero contento
granjeado con tus daños.

12 Sigue tu gusto, señora,
pues te parece tan bueno,
que yo por el bien ajeno
no pienso llorar agora.

13 Porque fuera liviandad
entregar mi alma al alma
que tiene por gloria y palma
el no tener libertad.

14 Mas, ¡ay!, que fortuna quiere
y el amor que viene en ello,
que no pueda huir el cuello
del cuchillo que me hiere.

15 Conozco claro que voy
tras quien ha de condenarme,
y cuando pienso apartarme,
más quedo y más firme estoy.

16 ¿Qué lazos, qué redes tienen,
Silena, tus ojos bellos,
que cuanto más huigo dellos,
más me enlazan y detienen?

17 ¡Ay, ojos, de quien recelo
que si soy de vos mirado,
es por crecerme el cuidado
y por menguarme el consuelo!

18 Ser vuestras vistas fingidas
conmigo, es pura verdad,
pues pagan mi voluntad
con prendas aborrecidas.

19 ¡Qué recelos, qué temores
persiguen mi pensamiento,
y qué de contrarios siento
en mis secretos amores!

20 Déjame, aguda memoria;
olvídate, no te acuerdes
del bien ajeno, pues pierdes
en ello tu propria gloria.

21 Con tantas firmas afirmas
el amor que está en tu pecho,
Silena, que a mi despecho,
siempre mis males confirmas.

22 ¡Oh pérfido amor crüel!
¿Cuál ley tuya me condemna
que dé yo el alma a Silena
y que me niegue un papel?

23 No más, Silena, que toco
en puntos de tal porfía,
que el menor dellos podría
dejarme sin vida o loco.

24 No pase de aquí mi pluma,
pues tú la haces sentir
que no puede reducir
tanto mal a breve suma.

1 (In such famed simplicity,
born of a healthy intent,
love governs my hand,
and your beauty, my intention.

2 Love and your beauty,
on this occasion, Silena,
judged it to be discretion
what you will take to be madness.

3 He [love] forces me and she [your beauty] moves
me to adore you, and write,
and as my faith stems from both [love and beauty],
my hand[75] dares [to adore you and write].

4 And although in this serious fault [of the writing *ingenio*]
your icy severity threatens me,
my faith, your beauty, and love
will excuse the error.

[75] There is a play on the "palm" of the hand (of both lover and writer) and the "palm" of peace. Covarrubias' entry is capacious: (*Tesoro*, 1995, 797–798).

5 Well, with such a bond,[76]
given that they say it's my fault,
well could I speak of the good
that has been born of my bad.

6 That good, according to what I feel,
is nothing, Silena,
but that I have in this sorrow
a strange suffering.

7 And I don't exaggerate
the good of my suffering
without which it would have happened
already that the bad had driven me mad.

8 But my senses in agreement
have all been given to say
that since I have to die, better
I die suffering and sane.

9 But it's well considered
that a jealous and unrequited one
will poorly be able to have patience
in the amorous pain,

10 that in the bad of my frustrations,
all of my good is disconcerted
to have my hope dead
and the enemy before my eyes.

11 Enjoy for a thousand years, shepherdess,
the good of your thought.
I do not want contentment
reaped from damages to you.

12 Follow your pleasure, lady,
well, it seems so good to you
that I don't think to cry
for an alien good now.

13 Because it were a fickleness
to deliver my soul to the soul
that has for glory and palm
the lack of liberty.

[76] The play is on the Greek "rhuthmós" in the sense of linking or binding through rhyme in verse poetry: (Covarrubias, *Tesoro*, 1995, 123).

14 But there is what fortune wants
and the love that comes in it,
that neck cannot flee
the knife that wounds it.

15 I know clearly that I go
after she who must condemn me
and when I think to distance myself
the more I stay and the firmer I am.

16 What ties, what nets they have,
Silena, your beautiful eyes,
that the more I flee from them
the more they ensnare and detain me.

17 O eyes whom I distrust
that if I am looked at by you
it is in order to increase in me my thought
and diminish in me my consolation.

18 That your glances with me
are feigned, is plain truth,
well, they pay my will
with abhorred tokens.

19 What suspicions, what fears
pursue my thought,
and what contraries I feel
in my secret loves.

20 Leave me, sharp memory,
forget yourself, don't recall
the alien good, well, you lose
in it your own glory.

21 With so many signatures[77] you affirm
the love that is in your breast,
Silena, that to my spite,
you always confirm my troubles.

22 O perfidious cruel love,
what law of yours condemns me
that I give the soul to Silena
and that she denies me a [scrap of] paper?

[77] The implication relates to written notes, what Hurtado de Mendoza calls "hablar por cartapacio" in his *Sátira*.

23 No more, Silena, since I touch
upon points of such obstinacy
that the least of these could
leave me without life, or mad.

24 That my plume does not pass [further],
well, you make it feel
that it could not reduce
so much bad to a brief summary.[78]

As in Gálvez de Montalvo's poem to his book at the opening of *El pastor de Fílida*, and Grisóstomo's poem declaimed by his quill in the *DQ I*, Lauso's "plume" becomes an affected actor subject to Silena's influence. This poem, which marks the earliest event in Lauso's narrative, sets up the "pluma, lengua, voluntad" in the final stanza of "Quién mi libre pensamiento …?," which occurs three poems later in terms of plot. Lauso's inner vicissitudes, rather than exterior actions, become the impetus for the entirety of his narrative arc. A window in a window, the pastoral poetry functioned as a portal into the interior of human experience not otherwise expressed in socio-political or cultural contexts. Within this Arcadian space of interior life, which Lauso shares with the other shepherd-poets of the central chronotope, Lauso further extrapolated himself from the action of the story by transporting his fellow shepherds into the narrative trajectory of his own interior experience of erotic jealousy. Within this narrative arc, the lyric voice is not a representation of a static speaker, but rather one that recapitulates and vacillates within a space of confusion, contrariness, paradox, and defeat. As such the lyric stages the space of the interior as narrative fiction. It should be remembered that in the *DQ* I: 27, Cardenio enters the action of the text by way of two lyric poems (an *ovillejo* and a sonnet). If in the sixth stanza Lauso genuflects before his shepherdess, assuring her that he would not benefit from her derision (a gesture that recovers the genuflection of the closing of Cervantes' 1579 octaves for Veneziano), Lauso eventually succumbs to the unbridled negativity of his own jealous fantasies, in which even a look from his shepherdess becomes an "abhorred token" (Stanza 9). By Stanza 11 the speaker moves toward either death or madness, only to conclude, in the very renunciation of the possibility of any representation of his interior state, with a silence that itself represents the ineffability of his struggle.[79]

[78] (Cervantes, *Galatea*, 1961, vol. II, 95–97).

[79] As in Cervantes' 1567 sonnet to Isabel, the poem concludes in order to express the ineffable. In the case of jealousy, it is the poet's own interiority that exceeds articulation.

From the opening of Book IV through Lauso's encounter with Damón in Book V, the reader follows a temporally anarchic narrative from Lauso's amorous suffering of erotic longing (the first and second poems), to his previously renewed faith in Silena (the third poem), to his even earlier jealous ravings (the fourth poem). The sequence of the *syuzhet* concludes where the narrative arc begins. This is in contrast to the straightforward chronological movement of the central chronotope (the unfolding drama between Galatea and Elicio). Just as quickly as he had appeared for the other shepherds, Lauso departs from the group. When Lauso again meets with the group, following the happy reunion of Silerio, Timbrio, Nísida, and Blanca, the ensuing verses mark the third phase in the development of Lauso's amorous longing. Narratively, the interior location to which Lauso's story must return in order to continue onward after the chronotopic dynamism of his temporal tangent into the prior episode of jealousy must follow the second poem of longing given early in Book V. In fact, when Lauso again meets with the group, his third poem of longing reprises and develops the lexicon (Stanzas 1, 3, 6) of the first two poems of longing as narrative development over time. In the sequence of the narrative this next lyric event follows "¿Quién mi libre pensamiento . . .?"

> 1 Alzo la vista a la más noble parte
> que puede imaginar el pensamiento,
> donde miro el valor, admiro el arte
> que suspende el más alto entendimiento.
> Mas si queréis saber quién fue la parte
> que puso fiero yugo al cuello esento,[80]
> quién me entregó, quién lleva mis despojos
> mis ojos son, Silena, y son tus ojos.
>
> . . .
>
> 3 ¡Divinos ojos, bien del alma mía,
> término y fin de todo mi deseo;
> ojos que serenáis el turbio día,
> ojos por quien yo veo si algo veo!
> En vuestra luz mi pena y mi alegría
> ha puesto amor; en vos contemplo y leo
> la dulce, amarga, verdadera historia
> del cierto infierno, de mi incierta gloria.

80 "[EXENTO] Esento. El que es libre de alguna carga o servidumbre; *latine* EXEMPTUS, *a verbo eximo, is*. 2. Exento, lo que está escombrado y sin embarazos. 3. Exento, el que no tiene empacho, ni vergüenza. 4. Exento, el que está libre de la jurisdición ordinaria. Exento lugar, el que está descubierto, sin padrastro ni cosa que se le oponga delante" (Covarrubias, *Tesoro*, 1995, 527).

6 . . .
. . .
. . .
. . .
La gloria de tu vista he merecido
por mi inviolable fe; mas es locura
pensar que pueda merecerse aquello
que apenas puede contemplarse en ello.[81]

1 (The gaze raised to the most noble part
that the thought can imagine
where it saw valor, admired the art
that suspends the loftiest understanding.
But if you want to know who played the part
that put a fierce yolk on a neck exempt [from love],
to whom I deliver myself, who carries off my remains,
my eyes are [responsible], Silena, and they are your eyes.
. . .

3 Divine eyes, good of my soul,
end and aim of all my desire,
eyes that calm the turbulent day,
eyes for whom I see if I see anything [at all].
In your light, my sorrow and my happiness
have been placed by love, in you I contemplate and I read[82]
the sweet, bitter, true history[83]
of the certain hell, of my uncertain glory.

6 . . .
. . .
. . .
I have earned the glory of your gaze
by my inviolable faith, but it is madness
to think that it could be earned, that which
could hardly be contemplated within it [your glorious gaze].)[84]

In the first expression of longing given at the opening of Book IV ("Si yo dijere el bien del pensamiento"), Lauso's encomium for the divine Silena had raised him, as lover, to great heights, positioning the beloved lady as "glory of my thought / north by whom my will is governed." This relationship was further developed in the poem of amorous longing given near the opening of Book V

[81] (Cervantes, *Galatea*, 1961, vol. II, 124–125).
[82] Compare to (Garcilaso, "Soneto V" in *Poesía castellana*, 109).
[83] The notion of a "true history" intervenes here.
[84] (Cervantes, *Galatea*, 1961, vol. II, 124–125).

(¿Quién mi libre pensamiento . . .?), in which Lauso returned to the theme of erotic subjugation (itself a reprisal of the 1579 octavas for Veneziano). In this second treatment of the lady as spiritual compass, Lauso began to revolt against his amorous experience with the epimone of "who" throughout the first stanza. Playing on Silena's unknown identity, she became a mystery even to Lauso himself. In this poem Lauso lost himself to the windmills of an enamored mind, which reduce him to a shadow of what he once was. This chronotopic disintegration of "Soy" was precisely what made way for the emergence of lyric subjectivity. In spite of this Petrarchan unrest of contraries, the poem concluded on the object of faith and Lauso's erotic hope. In this third poem of longing, the lady as sovereign, captor, and protector of the poet's soul is conflated with the conceit of love through the gaze (as discussed by Abravanel in his *Dialoghi*). The play of the eyes is undergirded with the speaker's surrender to the lady. The concluding stanza recovers the concept of ineffability from the 1567 sonnet to Isabel and the lyrical event of his jealousy, and transforms this ineffability into the unthinkable. This third poem of longing not only repurposed several of Cervantes' known lyric conceits but also recovered the exalted apostrophe to the lady and carried it to new intensity and height. This is the narrative peak of Lauso's lyric plot. It is the poem in which the emergence of lyric subjectivity (in the previous lyric) results in an erotic event which occupies the climax of Lauso's interior arc. The rest is denouement.

Like all of the entrances and exits involved in Lauso's self-narrated plot, the *volta* of his lyric trajectory again interrupts the narrative later in Book V. This turn toward disdain restores him to his original identity as the *libre* Lauso, as he is known to the other shepherds when introduced into the narrative late in Book 3.[85] He has come full circle. By disdain, the light of Lauso's eyes (one and the same as Silena's eyes in the previous poem of longing) is returned to him. The loss of self which occurs in the second poem of longing ("¿Soy, por ventura, el que fui, / o nunca he sido el que soy?") is likewise restored ("y aun perdida / al ser primero ha vuelto que tenía"). In the same way the amorous *intento* recovers Lauso's earlier language as that same intention is redirected by disdain. It is disdain which does away with his madness and thus concludes the lyrical emplotment of his erotic experience as narrative. Where love had raised Lauso to great heights in his earlier poems of longing, disdain empowers Lauso's *ingenio* to raise itself and rid itself of the *desengaño de amor* (the "pesado sueño," which again recalls the "breve sogno" of Petrarch's "Voi ch'ascoltate"). Ultimately, disdain gives Lauso a *vita nuova* and tailors him in

[85] (Cervantes, *Galatea*, 1961, vol. II, 151–152).

a new habit (inverting Garcilaso's "os ha cortado a mi medida"). The final lyric coordinates of Lauso's plot, the poem to disdain, is much more than expression: it is an essential part of the narrative structure which undertakes development and transformation through the redeployment of the lexicon that Lauso's prior poems establish in the context of his plot. Cervantes' attunement to lexicon as development in character and plot would become one of the key features of his literary technique as a modern novelist. Indeed, it is attended to by both Spitzer (polyglossia) and Bakhtin (heteroglossia) in the *DQ*. In the context of the *Galatea*, Lauso is the first of shepherd-poets to be truly transformed into a novelistic character by way of his lyric interior as narrative genesis. It is Lauso as a quasi-*figura of the poet* who makes way for a representation of human experience which exceeds the bounds of both chronotopic specificity and the symbolic function. The introduction of Lauso's novel lyric plot, which is neither allegorical nor historical, introduces the landscape of the interior into the genesis of novel modern characters and their fictions. Significantly, it is in Lauso's speech that Cervantes first uses his language of a machine to discuss the human interior (as the *ingenio*), the same language that he will later use to describe AQ's madness in Chapter 1 of the *DQ*. Lauso:

> ya se han deshecho en mi sentido las encumbradas máquinas de pensamientos que desvanecido me traían; ya tornaré a la perdida conversación de mis amigos;
>
> (They have already been undone from my sense the lofty machines of thought which had me fainting; soon I will return to the lost conversation of my friends;)[86]

AQ:

> y asentósele de tal modo en la imaginación que era verdad toda aquella máquina de aquellas soñadas invenciones que leía, que para él no había otra historia más cierta en el mundo.
>
> (and it took a seat in such a manner in his imagination that the entirety of that machine of dreamed inventions that he read was true, that for him there was no truer history in the world.)[87]

[86] (Cervantes, *Galatea*, 1961, vol. II, 149).

[87] (Cervantes, *DQ*, 1999, I: 1, 39): "Yo tengo juicio ya libre y claro, sin las sombras caliginosas de la ignorancia que sobre él me pusieron mi amarga y continua leyenda de los detestables libros de las caballerías. Ya conozco sus disparates y sus embelecos, y no me pesa sino que este desengaño ha llegado tan tarde" (Cervantes, *DQ*, 1999, II: 74, 1217).

Both in the case of Lauso and of AQ, the *máquina* has to do with the way in which the lyric interior finds its own lexicon.

While the scope of the modern novel has typically been described as a linear trajectory, the makings of the *DQ* are already evident in the interpolation of this circular *imbroglio*. Lauso moves into a disordered state of jealousy, reaches the erotic heights of an ideal love, and suffers a *desengaño* which restores him to his former self. This is the plot of the *DQ*, from AQ's inspired madness to his lyrical poiesis as dQ, to his *desengaño* and return to himself. Lauso is the narrative model for AQ, with one major distinction. What separates them is death. In the *Galatea*, Tirsi warns that Lauso's *desengaño* may be merely temporary and that he may again find himself in the throes of love and jealousy, just as AQ slips in and out of dQ several times. Because he does not die, Lauso cannot fully achieve the *figura of the poet* through his sempiternal afterlife in letters. The same is not true of AQ or dQ. Through the finality of death, Cervantes gives to the *figura of the poet*, AQ/dQ, a literary afterlife to which the many narrators of his history testify.

CODA

Alonso Quijano's Lyric Subjectivity: Interior Lexicons and Exterior Lexicons in the Conception of the Modern Novel

> *"«La razón de la sinrazón que a mi razón se hace, de tal manera mi razón enflaquece, que con razón me quejo de la vuestra fermosura» … «Los altos cielos que de vuestra divinidad, divinamente con las estrellas os fortifican y os hacen merecedora del merecimiento que merece la vuestra grandeza … ». Con estas razones perdía el pobre caballero el juicio…"*
>
> – *DQ*, I: 1

To speak of the modern novel is implicitly to speak of the *modern subject*.[1] In the "post-historical" "Covid-era" of "posthuman" "cultural hyperspace," the nearly antiquated topic of the *modern subject* may register as

[1] The *subject* can be etymologically divided into two lines of inquiry: "One gives rise to a lineage of logico-grammatical and ontological-transcendental meanings, and the other to a lineage of juridical, political, and theological meanings" (E. Balibar, B. Cassin, A. de Libera, "Subject," in ed. B. Cassin, *Dictionary of Untranslatables: A Philosophical Lexicon*, trans. S. Rendall *et al.*, Princeton University Press, 2004, 1069–1091; 1078). The concerns of sixteenth-century Pastoral Petrarchism deal mainly with the former, but it must be said that the two "far from remaining independent of one another … have constantly overdetermined one another, because following Kant, the problematic articulation of 'subjectivity' and 'subjection' came to be defined as a theory of the constituent subject" (*ibid.*). Lacoue-Labarthe and Nancy have compared the German Romantic response via auto-poiesis to the Kantian "weakening of the subject" as generative of our present paradigm: "Whether it was situated as *arche* or as *telos*, within the divine or within the human (as either pure intellectual self-consciousness in Descartes or pure empirical sensibility in Hume), what had heretofore ensured the philosophical itself disappears. As a result, all that remains of the subject is the 'I' as an 'empty form' (a pure logical necessity said Kant; a grammatical exigency, Nietzsche will say) that 'accompanies my representations.' … The Kantian cogito is empty … in the absence of a subject whose self-presence is guaranteed by originary intuition and whose *mathesis* of this first evidence organizes the totality of knowledge and the world *more geometrico*, the system as such, although it is deeply desired by Kant … is continually lacking precisely where it is in greatest demand …. The entire movement, then, sets out to be an overcoming – which is also to say, a reversal – of Kant" (*The Literary Absolute*, 30–33). However the parallels between German Romanticism and Cervantes' novel may strike us (and the *DQ* was paramount for their thought), however compelling the appeal by Lacuoe-Labarthe and Nancy to understand the "literary absolute" of Romanticism as transhistorical, and however implicitly Romantic the gesture toward historicity, it must be understood that the *DQ* was born of pre-Cartesian poetics and the particular "aesthetics-avante la lettre" of Abravanel's *Dialoghi d'Amore*, and therefore cannot be sublated into a Romantic idea of the subject or of the literary absolute, but must be understood in all of its difference, a difference which, as this Coda argues, lies at the "heart" of the modern subject.

both parochial and quaint.[2] To speak of a single chronotopicity for which that subject would be relevant is likewise naïve.[3] In the words of Debjani Ganguly, the global novel, as an ekphrastic mode, makes "legible to our myriad virtual publics the melancholic, visually excessive remainders of our capitalistic deathworlds."[4] Or, as Amitav Ghosh suggests, integrated experience has moved beyond the contours of modern fiction's capacity for representation.[5] In the face of climate change, a global pandemic, increasing disparity of resources, and a radicalized hyperspace whose algorithmic narratives and their socio-political ramifications we are only beginning to understand, what could Cervantes' conception of the *modern subject* offer us?

Such a question retains the belief in a static figure, the *modern subject*, which has somehow survived its critiques if not also perished (in its totality) by them, a figure which has become all the more pervasive by virtue of its exile to the periphery, a figure which continues to ground self-understanding in a variety of discourses. If history is singular, chronological, and progressive, then such a figure is a vintage one (a metaphor Cervantes doubtless would have enjoyed). But if the present chronotopic dynamism of difference and futurity reveals the "end(s) of history" within us, where time itself is multiple and "periods" perennially available, then it should be clear that the *modern subject* continues to loom large in the present.[6] If it is the case that the contemporary global novel retains

[2] By "post-historical" I mean: "it is art after art history, constructed as the progressive, developmental narrative of art's self-definition" (N. Carroll, "The End of Art?," *History and Theory*, 37.4, 1998, 17–29; 20). The obvious reference is Frances Fukuyama, but the terms "post-historical" and the "end of history" cannot be treated here in their full theoretical depth and diversity.

For a cogent formulation of the modern subject via early modern authors: (Cascard, *Subject of Modernity*). While Bill Egginton's critique of the overuse of the term "subjectivity" is descriptively accurate, it is not the case that interrogations into subjectivity and the modern subject have lost their value: (W. Egginton, *How the World Became a Stage: Presence, Theatricality, and the Question of Modernity*, State University of New York Press, 2002, 123–124).

"It goes without saying that there can be no transformation without a corresponding resistance, but when transformative goals collapse, or when the dialectic of recognition and transformation ceases to have force, we move from the project of aesthetic liberalism to the potentially complicitous practices of the postmodern cultural hyperspace" (Cascardi, *Subject of Modernity*, 310).

[3] Insofar as Bakhtin borrows the chronotope from Einstein, it seems only appropriate that the use of the literary term "almost as a metaphor (almost, but not entirely)" not amount to a category error.

[4] (Debjani Ganguly, *This Thing Called the World: The Contemporary Novel as Global Form*, Duke University Press, 2015, 34).

[5] "The modern novel, unlike geology, has never been forced to confront the centrality of the improbable: the concealment of its scaffolding of events continues to be essential to its functioning . . .. It is certain in any case that these are not ordinary times: the events that mark them are not easily accommodated in the deliberately prosaic world of serious prose fiction" (Amitav Ghosh, *The Great Derangement: Climate Change and the Unthinkable*, University of Chicago Press, 2016, 23).

[6] See n.2 in this Coda. Again, my use of the "end(s) of history" should not be taken as an endorsement of Fukuyama's Western eschatology of political progress. On the contrary, the ironic allusion to

a nineteenth-century commitment to naturalism, then the worlds in which it will be forced to engage in the coming decades will doubtless defy the sove(reign)ty of the *modern subject.*[7] But if the modern novel is the product, not of mimesis, but of poiesis, then Cervantes' futurity retains its perennial prescience not as representation but as conception.[8]

Of course, the *modern subject* is anything but a totalizing concept, or totalizing only in its pluralities. The *modern subject*'s primary account of itself is one of autonomy and of division.[9] This takes shape largely in formulations of the Renaissance as the emergence of modernity (Michelet, Burkhardt, Pater, Cassirer), and in the advent of modern philosophy (Descartes and Kant) and its critique (Hegel, Nietzsche, Heidegger).[10] The postmodern account of the *modern subject* which grows out of those critiques is one of contingency and subjection (Greenblatt, Cascardi, Lyotard, Derrida, Foucault, Deleuze, et al.).[11] Modern *subjectivity* is no less opaque.[12] *Subjectivity* makes itself known, almost retrospectively, by

Fukuyama's phrase points instead toward a multiplicity of constellations (in Benjamin's sense) which reveal the fictional or constructed scaffolding of the "master narrative."

7 Ganguly astutely argues by way of Bakhtin and Lukács that the global novel goes beyond such a naïve realism: (Ganguly, *This Thing Called the World*, 21).

"Bataille . . . was probably the first of contemporary authors working in the French language to consciously exploit the possibility of inscribing a dialectical (or mystical) antimony at the heart of anthropology by defining the subject in terms of its 'sovereignty,' or in other words its non-subjection" (Balibar et al., 'Subject', 1080).

8 "Exemplifying a concern with the future, Renaissance and other futurities can be conceived as a willful projection into later times of a person's or a people's present and/or past cultural notions, modes, and materials . . .. Futurities may be also rediscovered retrospectively, when a later work such as a contemporary poem or painting, for example, may trigger echoes of earlier (Renaissance) works, leading to a rediscovery of their latent futurity . . .. By reversing the projection of futurities, we may discern new readings of older texts or artifacts of culture, moments where they echo their future and burst into later times as they seemingly challenge a linear historicity" (F.A. de Armas, "Futurities, Empire, and Censorship: Cervantes in Conversation with Ovid and Orwell," in eds. C. Villaseñor Black and M-T Álvarez, *Renaissance Futurities: Science, Art, Invention*, University of California Press, 2020, 65–82; 65–66).

9 "Whereas traditional thinking about the whole is characterized by a refusal to recognize its divisions . . . the philosophy of the subject represents a rejection of these principles in favor of an interpretation of the whole along dualistic lines. Modern philosophers define the whole in terms of the division of body and mind (Descartes), of faith and science (Pascal), or of the empirical and transcendental worlds, or formal and sensuous intuition (Kant). Insofar as the unity of these terms is to be reconstituted at some 'higher' level, they demand the creation of categories like Descartes's 'subject', Pascal's 'hidden God', or Kant's 'transcendental ego'. In response to these resolutions of the problem of dualism, Hegel seeks to reconcile the contradictions of subjectivity by redefining subject as Spirit" (Cascardi, *Subject of Modernity*, 277).

10 For the Hegelian critique: (Cascardi, *Subject of Modernity*, 278). For the Nietzschean critique: (eds. J. Constâncio, M.J. Mayer Branco, and B. Ryan, *Nietzsche and the Problem of Subjectivity*, De Gruyter, 2015). For the Heideggerian critique: (Egginton, *How the World*, 125–126).

11 (Cascardi, *Subject of Modernity*, 275–310, esp. 278 and 282).

12 "Subjectivity . . . rendered useless by its overdetermined vacuity" (Egginton, *How the World*, 123–124).

way of Nietzsche and Heidegger's critique of Descartes and Kant (and later Husserl). In that sense, *subjectivity* in its most basic theoretical usage indicates a destabilization in the *modern subject* which developed by way of critical engagements over the course of the late nineteenth and twentieth centuries, primarily but not exclusively within the discipline of philosophy. Part of that discourse involves a critique of the *modern subject* in political theory where the question of sovereignty concerns the subject of a state and the "individual whose self-consciousness is formed or produced through a sociocultural process of subjection to an anonymous power structure seeking to reproduce itself."[13] In casual terms, subjectivity is also a quality of perspectivism which reduces the *modern subject* to its particularity as a single and contingent vantage point within a whole which will never be entirely available to it. In literary terms, *lyric subjectivity* may refer to the nineteenth-century Romantic engagement with the *modern subject* through the "I" as a grammatical term and as the ground for the philo-poetic approach to the literary absolute.[14] For the present study, *lyric subjectivity* has been a useful way of discussing the conception of a poetic "I" through the use of the words *alma* and *ingenio*, and conjugations of the verb *ser* (to be) in lyrical poetic gestures toward sempiternity (atemporality) which found, defy, and generate the temporally particularized chronology of narrative as novelistic development. That is, *lyric subjectivity* as poiesis (in the strong sense) in the novel shares commonalities with, but cannot be sublated to, the nineteenth-century German Romantic understanding

[13] (Egginton, *How the World*, 123). See n.2 and n.7 in this Coda.

[14] In Shelley's *On Life*, "Rather than marking singular, discrete positions, the pronouns in Shelley's passage, including the 'I,' all seem to point to the 'one mind' with its different modifications, of what the writing subject is but a part. We are reminded, however, in an appositive clause, that the 'I' is the person who 'now writes and thinks. The one mind, with its inseparable modifications, goes on to rarefy itself beyond the limits of knowledge, and language, but this 'I' – 'the person who now write[s] and think[s]' – remains standing at the edge of an abyss, suspended between the impossibility of immanence within textuality and the prospect of absorption into non-differentiation and silence" (Z. Sng, "The Construction of Lyric Subjectivity in Shelley's 'Ozymandias'," *Studies in Romanticism*, 37.2, 1998, 217–233).

"The absolute of literature is not so much poetry (whose modern concept is also invented in *Athenaeum* fragment I 16) as it is *poiesy*, according to an etymological appeal that the romantics do not fail to make. The thought of the 'literary genre' is thus less concerned with the production of the literary thing than with *production*, absolutely speaking. Romantic poetry sets out to penetrate the essence of poiesy, in which the literary thing produces the truth of production in itself, and thus, as will be evident in all that follows, the truth of the production *of itself*, of autopoiesy. And if it is true (as Hegel will soon demonstrate, *entirely against* romanticism) that auto-production constitutes the ultimate instance and closure of the speculative absolute, then romantic thought involves not only the absolute of literature, but literature as the absolute. Romanticism is the inauguration of the *literary absolute*" (P. Lacou-Labarthe and J-L. Nancy, *The Literary Absolute*, 11–12). I do not share their conviction in the singular novelty of *Romantic* thought as pure invention, however apt the description of a singular moment self-consciously concerned with poiesis.

of *autopoiesy*, the fragment, and the novel.[15] These practices in sixteenth-century lyric poetry, characterized by an *erotic mysticism*, grew out of readings of Judah Abravanel's *Dialoghi d'amore*, which itself posits an "aesthetics-avante la lettre" which was taken up in poetic practice throughout the period.[16] Radically freed from religious valences through a reverse of the *contrafactum*, this lyric "I" was founded in the erotic, both corporally and "metaphysically," such that poiesis (the creator) and the lover became one.[17] It remains to be seen whether this *lyric subjectivity* has something to contribute to philosophical understandings of *subjectivity* at present (or whether such a category-hybridity – poiesis in the novel and poiesis in lived experience – would be permissible).[18]

What is evident is that the *DQ* as a modern novel, by virtue of its continued relevance for so many formulations of modernity, contains a consistently recognizable figuration of the *modern subject*, a subject which remains mysterious. Literally an inkblot, the *DQ* has passed through periods, languages, empires, and individuals like a Rorschach test. For the eighteenth-century English satirists it was a comic satire and a funny book; for the nineteenth-century German romantics it was the height of tragic irony.[19] By the early twentieth century, particularly in North America, Cervantes' modern novel had come to be regarded as a triumph of realism: the literary recapitulation of Enlightenment thought and its banishment of magic, superstition, and the fantastic. (These are curious demands for an author who uses the dust of a unicorn horn as a medicinal cure in at least one of his *novelas*.) In the late twentieth century, the Cervantine play of metalepsis crowned the novel a harbinger of postmodernity. For Ortega y Gasset, the *DQ* was *quijotismo*.[20] For a young Lukács, the modern rift between interiority and exteriority found its paradigm in dQ.[21] For Butler, dQ anticipates the folly of the Hegelian

[15] See n.14 in this Coda. The temptation here will be to understand the lyric (as the novel) in terms of the fragmentary exigency of Romanticism (Lacuoe-Labarthe and Nancy, *The Literary Absolute*, 39–58). The subtle differences and enlightening interplay between these two moments merit further study.

[16] For Abravanel: Chapter 4. For the discussion of Lauso's *soy* (I am): Chapter 6. Another paradigmatic example is Quevedo's sonnet "Desde la Torre" in which the speaker asserts, "Soy un fue, y un será, y un es cansado" (J. Olivares, "Soy un fue, y un será, y un es cansado: Text and Context," *Hispanic Review*, 63.3, 1995, 387–410; 395). For the emergence of *subjecto* and *sujeto* in early modern Spanish and its relevance for corporeality and intimacy in "certain contemporary philosophical usages" (Balibar et al., "Subject," 1088). Trenado de Ayllón's (ca. 1595) definitions for *anima* and *sujeto* or Covarrubias' (1611) definitions for *sujeto*, *sujetar*, and *sujeción* are likewise relevant.

[17] For poiesis, the poet, and the lover: (Plato, *Symposium*, 205c).

[18] This will have to be addressed in a future study.

[19] For reception history: (Close, *The Romantic 'DQ'*).

[20] (J. Ortega y Gasset, *Meditaciones del Quijote*, ed. J. Marías, Madrid: Cátedra, 9th ed., 2012, 84–85).

[21] (Cascardi, *Subject of Modernity*, 72–124).

subject.[22] Insofar as the *modern subject* has been not one but many things, the *DQ* has served its readers as a reliable mirror for modernity's divisions and transformations. But the figure which the text most immediately dramatizes, the *figura of the poet* as modern madman, rarely surfaces in theories of the modern novel or in modernity and postmodernity's most unforgiving and self-conscious critiques of the subject.[23] We remain on one side of an intractable divide: the division between reason and folly.[24] To occupy the space of unreason is to forfeit one's *subjectivity*, to cease to be a *modern subject*, or any other kind of *subject*, entirely. What Cervantes, a poet of futurity, shows us is that the modern madman is not outside of us but at our "center"; and that despite our deepest fears and wildest imaginings (the "mystique of madness"), that forbidden center, around which our poet has drawn the *cercle sacré* of madness, is no more nor less than the *figura of the poet.*[25] In this light, Cervantes' *modern subject* speaks from beyond an (interior) impasse which we ourselves have not yet consciously crossed, by way of poiesis as conception.

The Coda that follows engages prior theories of the novel which have unwittingly touched on *lyric subjectivity* as the motor of genesis in modern fiction qua the *DQ*. I return to Leo Spitzer's seminal article "Linguistic

[22] (J. Butler, *Subjects of Desire: Hegelian Reflections in Twentieth-Century France*, Columbia University Press, 1987, 23).

[23] The possible exceptions are Foucault on the figure of the poet in *History of Madness* and *The Order of Things*, and Derrida on madness and the subject in "Cogito and the History of Madness," in *Writing and Difference.*

[24] This was the source of a rift between Foucault and Derrida: "Foucault takes Descartes to be an exemplary witness of the current of thought that justified the expulsion of madness out of the unified field intended for reason alone, provoking its reclusion .... Madness must be discredited in order for reason to affirm its domination .... Once deprived of 'reason', they are relegated to reason's outside in the sense of a true extraterritoriality .... In the case of the mad, it is not that the mind functions poorly; rather, it has ceased functioning altogether .... For one cannot see how reason could possibly define itself other than devoid of unreason .... Classical thought thus has its dark side. But it has carefully set it aside .... Offering his own commentary on Descartes' text, Derrida's conclusions clearly deviate from, or even contradict those of Foucault ... the Cartesian cogito ... as the immediate self-grasping of thought ... 'is an experience which, at its furthest reaches, is perhaps no less adventurous, perilous, enigmatic, nocturnal, and pathetic than the experience of madness' ... reading Descartes between the lines to reveal a gap between ... what Descartes says, when affirming the purity of reason, and, on the other hand, what he does ... another twist of madness" (P. Macherey, "The Foucault-Derrida Debate on the Argument Concerning Madness and Dreams," in eds. Custer et al., *Foucault/Derrida*, 4–8).

[25] There is no space to treat this argument in full. But in the Q&A subsequent to Derrida's delivery of "Structure, Sign, and Play" at the 1966 Sciences of Man conference (Johns Hopkins University), Derrida does not (by his own account) do away with the "center'" of the subject; he suggests it is other than the identity (reason) previously afforded to it. Read in this way, postmodernism is not the rejection of modernity but its hyperbole.

Perspectivism in the *DQ*" (1948) in order to bring to light the underpinnings of Pastoral Petrarchism in Cervantes' modern novel. This negotiation of lexicons also invokes Mikhail Bakhtin's understanding of heteroglossia and polysemy in the *Dialogic Imagination* (1930s and 1940s, pub. 1975), and Gyorgy Lukács' understanding of a rift between interiority and exteriority as transcendental homelessness in the *Theory of the Novel* (1915).[26] While several of the insights found in their work hold true, their observations often unwittingly point toward the lyric, rather than epic, features of the novel as a modern literary genre. Their insights show that novelistic fiction is everywhere impossible without the *lyric subjectivity* at work in the practice of sixteenth-century Pastoral Petrarchism, in particular Cervantes' *Galatea*. In his conception of the modern novel, Cervantes preserves this *lyric subjectivity* through the transformation of the modern madman into the *figura of the poet*, and vice versa. In consonance with Postmodern, Postcolonial, and Posthuman critiques of the sov(reign)ty of the *modern subject* as the *subject of reason*, I consider the efficacy of the *subject of unreason* as an ethical and productive force within us.

~

A touchstone of novelists for roughly four centuries, the *DQ* has long held pride of place in literary forays associated with the modern novel. The result of this has been that the interpretations of the *DQ* and understandings of its novelistic features have tended to be derivative of the literary movements most marked by its influence. Inversely, this study has attempted to recover the literary tradition from which the *DQ* was conceived as an interpretive guide to Cervantes' "master" text, a literary tradition whose tastes, theoretical contours, and literary vocabularies were markedly different from those of subsequent centuries. This study has proposed that the novel as a genre was a mutation of literary prose fiction effected through the introduction of *lyric subjectivity* into the literary character, beginning with the poetic practices of the pastoral prosimetrum in mid- to late-sixteenth-century Spain. From the *figura of the poet*, novelistic characters began to emerge in pastoral fiction during the second half of the sixteenth century following the publication of Jorge de Montemayor's *Diana* in 1559. As a conventionalized literature of immediacy, pastoral fiction made possible the conception of the modern novel at the confluence of intimate contemporary history (*nouvelles, novedades*) and sophisticated poetic conventions attuned to allegorical representation

[26] That Luckács later distanced himself (1962) from this early work does not prejudice his contribution to theories of the novel.

drawn from classical Greek, Roman, and Renaissance literary topologies. In the *Galatea*, novelistic fiction emerged from a *lyric subjectivity* that organically produces its own narrative emplotment. In the *DQ*, the generic veil (a burlesque) was tailored from the romance of chivalry, but novelistic emplotment occurred as it had in the pastoral mode, by putting *lyric subjectivity* into narrative practice.[27]

In 1948, Leo Spitzer's "Linguistic Perspectivism" created a critical space soon fleshed out by work such as Joaquín Casalduero's *Sentido y forma del 'Quijote'* (1949), E.C. Riley's *Cervantes' Theory of the Novel* (1962), Bruce Wardropper's "'DQ': Story or History?" (1965), Alban Forcione's *Cervantes, Aristotle, and the Persiles* (1970), and Ruth El Saffar's *Distance and Control in DQ* (1974).[28] Because subsequent treatments of the *DQ*, during the final decades of the twentieth century and the early decades of the twenty-first, tended to focus on thematic or new historical content, Spitzer's assessment that "we are still far from understanding [the *DQ*] in its general plan and in its details" holds to this day.[29] Doubt in the value of a synecdochic reading (which grounds much of Spitzer's method) of the *DQ* has pervaded criticism, but the present study recognizes the role of linguistic perspectivism in the *DQ* as indicative of the pastoral prosimetrum at work beneath the surface of this lively burlesque. It takes seriously Spitzer's desire to see polyonomasia and polyetymologia as "paths toward the centre," but departs from Spitzer's notion of that "centre" as characterized by "the general attitude of the creator of the novel toward his characters."[30] This study contends that the nominal and etymological fluidity of the *DQ* extends beyond a single author, Cervantes (for whom Saavedra was a "pseudonym"), or text, the *Galatea* (a *roman à clef*), to the poetic practices of Pastoral Petrarchism, the *figura of the poet*, and a strong understanding of *lyric subjectivity* as poiesis.

In his article, Spitzer surmised that the polynomasia and polyetymologia found in the *DQ* reflected the various and changing ways that characters appeared to other characters, a form of perspectivism that extended beyond proper names and epithets to the vocabularies and lexicons of common things.[31] For Spitzer, the "relativistic attitude" of the author or "demiurge-poet" was ultimately subsumed in "the immovable, immutable principle of the divine."[32] This ladder from the fractured multiplicity of linguistic

[27] Where a lyric conceit is fully realized in novelistic practice, we may call it *praxis* (in the strong sense, as a union of theory and practice), in keeping with Marx and Aristotle.

[28] (B. Wardropper, "*DQ:* Story or History?," *Modern Philology*, 1965, vol. LXIII, 1–11).

[29] (Spitzer, "Linguistic Perspectivism," 164).

[30] (Spitzer, "Linguistic Perspectivism," 172).

[31] (Spitzer, "Linguistic Perspectivism," 163).

[32] (Spitzer, "Linguistic Perspectivism," 164).

perspectivism found in the characters, to the linguistically dexterous author, to the supralinguistic divinity (for whom meaning is understood in spite of language), readjusted the instability of linguistic perspectivism within a fiction ultimately governed by a presiding (and presumably reasonable) subject. This movement between linguistic relativity and a supralinguistc unity recalled Cervantes' own early poetic recourses to ineffability (for example, the 1567 sonnet to Isabel), as well as Abravanel's understanding of mythopoeia as both carrier and concealer of shards of truth, and his insights into allegory and the corporeality of language.[33] But it also belied the ways in which the *DQ* disperses perspectivism, not only amongst its characters but also amongst its many creators and narrators, so that discourse breaks down not through expansion but through temporal precision (the fractions of a second in which the "I," and so discourse, is lost entirely). Nonetheless, if the perspectivism of the novel indeed points to some totality beyond the text (and there is no reason to believe that it does), careful engagement with Cervantes' textual corpus indicates that such a unity refers to erotic love *as faith*, a lyric conceit, which immediately returns the reader to the chronotopic discursive perspectivism at work in the text. Through the practices of Pastoral Petrarchism, the text encodes a tension between the linguistic perspectives that characterized poets writing within shared poetic conventions and the conventions themselves as a perpetually transformed and transformative formal and tropological continuity. This was the unacknowledged source of the features of the novel with which Spitzer's observations are concerned; it was also the source of Bakhtin's *heteroglossia* and Lukács' *transcendental homelessness* in the modern novel. It will be helpful to see this, however cursory the brushstrokes, at work in the *DQ*.

The narrative structuring-device of the *DQ* was one that Cervantes took from Montemayor's *Diana* and effected in his own *Galatea*. This consisted in a gather-and-disperse movement, interwoven into a linear narrative, which allowed the author to emplot more than one *lyric subjectivity* (as an *imbroglio*) at once, something that David Quint has called, in the style of Ariosto, "narrative interlacing"; indeed, Calíope attributes the metaphor of weaving to Ariosto in the *Galatea*.[34] Because the solitary nature of the pastoral relied upon the reader's encounter with various isolated or

[33] "[H]ere, [Teresa Panza] is referring to the language of God, Who, as Sancho himself had already claimed, is the great Entendedor [Understander] of all kinds of speech . . . rather is Cervantes' God placed above the perspectives of language" (Spitzer, "Linguistic Perspectivism," 176 and 185).

[34] (D. Quint, *Cervantes' Novel of Modern Times: A New Reading of Don Quijote*, Princeton University Press, 2003).

seemingly isolated shepherds and shepherdesses, narrative cohesion depended on public gatherings as a way of mixing and resolving individual threads. In Montemayor's *Diana*, this occurred about midway through the narrative (in Book IV), when the many erotically troubled shepherd-poets came together at the Palace of the *sabia Felicia* (likely a *sobrenombre* for the then regent, Juana de Austria). Following the narrative gestation and transformation of several characters within this public and communal space, the characters are again sent out into the landscape, where they begin to disperse and are ultimately left *in medias res* in expectation of the novel's continuations (Alonso Pérez and Gaspar Gil Polo).[35] Cervantes employed this narrative structuring device in his *Galatea*, where various shepherds of the text are first brought together late in Book III for the wedding festivities of Dardanio and Silveria (reprised in the *Bodas del Camacho* of the *DQ II*). Throughout Books IV and V, the characters are again dispersed, only to be gathered together in Book VI for the memorial celebrations of the deceased shepherd-poet Meliso. Following these festivities, the various narrative threads are again scattered and left suspended in the expectation of a sequel (the "missing" second part).

In the first part of the *DQ*, Cervantes borrowed this structuring device with the third visit to the roadside inn, which functions as a thematic and narrative cluster in the don's second sally, wherein the emplotments of Cardenio, Dorotea, the Captain, and Zoraida, et al., are intertwined and developed. As in the *Diana* and the *Galatea*, this period of narrative gestation and transformation (which includes, in the style of the *Galatea*, the interpolated tale of the *Curioso impertinente*) is again followed by the dispersal of the various characters. In the *DQ I*, Cervantes underscored this mingling of lyric lexicons with the episode of the *basiyelmo* in order to remind readers that every lyric tale is in fact told in its own language. This structuring device is again repeated in the *DQ II* with the palace of the Duke and Duchess wherein Sancho's glimpse of the world as a mustard seed recalls the battle of the *basiyelmo* even as it tips the linguistic perspective of the squire in the way of the *yelmo* late in the second part.[36] However, in the *DQ* the weaving of trajectories in the polyvocal prosimetrum is retained but subsumed within the drama of AQ/dQ.

[35] (G. Correa, "El templo de Diana en la novela de Jorge de Montemayor," *Thesaurus*, 1961, vol. XVI, 59–76; 61).

[36] The structuring device is slightly less pronounced in the *DQ II* precisely because the inclusion of interpolated characters has minimized, and dQ's interest in Dulcinea amplified, in keeping with the fictional criticisms of the "first part of the history," as discussed in the text. For *clavileño*: (Cervantes, *DQ*, 1999, II: 41, 964).

Such interlacing, of course, was not unique to pastoral fiction. As I have said, the weaving device was characteristic of Ariosto, and can be traced to the tradition of the Byzantine Romance, such as Heliodorus' *Aethiopica* (Cervantes' model for the *Persiles y Sigismunda*). But *lyric subjectivity* marks this structuring device in the pastoral as generative of the *DQ*. As discussed in Chapter 6, in the pastoral prosimetrum the narrative trajectories which are dispersed and gathered arose organically out of the lyric interiors of the characters. Because pastoral fiction was prosimetric, it introduced lyric verse as the expression of a narrative drive. This meant that narrative emplotment was produced out of the force of the interior, rather than by virtue of exterior demands (as in the Romance and the Chronicle). The interpolated poems were not only decorative (as they had been in Sannazaro) but also interactive. Because narrative emplotment was produced by the lyric interiority of the character, it concretized the inherent instability of the subject as a dynamic and transformative figure for whom poiesis was not only linguistic but also existential. Cervantes used polynomasia (linguistic markers of the instability of the character as a subject) to mark *lyric subjectivity* in his emplotment of a character in action. As such, to speak of the *modern subject* AQ/dQ, we must also speak of the Knight of the Sorrowful Countenance (*Triste Figura*), the Knight of the Lions, Quijada, Quesada, and *el Bueno* (the final name in which this character is subsumed), etc. By way of the pastoral prosimetrum, Cervantes transformed "history" (the Romance and the Chronicle) through the role of *lyric subjectivity* in the conception of novel character and outcome.

But he also altered the indeterminate structuring device of the pastoral (its potential for serialization) in the conception of the *DQ* by introducing death as a finality, which contrasts with the sempiternity of *el Bueno's lyric subjectivity*. There is a reason, more compelling than Avellaneda's spurious continuation (1614), why Cervantes kills off AQ at the end of his second part. The *Galatea* "concludes" *in medias res* in the space of a "timeless" Arcadia, a *tercia naturaleza*. In the *DQ*, Cervantes privileges the emplotment of a single character in order to bring the sense of an ending to the *figura of the poet* in historical time. When AQ dies, not as Quejada or Quesada, but as *el Bueno*, dQ and Dulcinea achieve immortality in letters. This sense of an ending completes the realization of the Petrarchan project for the *figura of the poet*, anticipated by the apparition of dQ's history at the opening of the second part. And it is this sense of the posterity of a subject as arising out of the practice of *lyric subjectivity* that marks death as part of its futurity, and madness as its method. Insofar as the whole of dQ's actions are dedicated to Dulcinea, these *petits récits* are brought together like the *rime sparse* of the *Canzoniere*, the narrative fulfillment of a lyric life.[37] DQ is the *figura of the poet* at the heart of AQ. AQ, as a divided figure, marks the transformation of the *figura of the poet* qua Petrarch into the *figura of the poet* qua modern madman. Insofar as the whole of AQ's actions as dQ are subsumed in the totality of *el Bueno*, the summation of his character offers a figuration of the *modern subject* whose "center" is unreason. But AQ's actions as dQ are not only in service of the posterity of his own "story"; through poetic practice he alters the linguistic landscape (imperial, religiously fanatical, homogenized) through which he passes. Linguistic perspectivism is not a static field of demarcated differences within a single totalizing and homogenized discourse, but a dynamic flux of heteroglot forces which attain novel figurations by taking a historically anarchic view of language as plural and contingent. The means and the "essence" of AQ's transformation into dQ are his linguistic anachronism. By introducing a radically different lexicon into the landscape of an empire in decline, AQ as dQ becomes a revolutionary actor by demonstrating the very instability inherent in the illusion of hegemony. He not only alters the linguistic perspectivism of his peers, but also alters the lexicon of the romance of chivalry. He is a force of "futurity" and "posterity." If Cervantes repeatedly emphasizes that "la narración dél no salga un punto de la verdad (in its telling there is absolutely no deviation from the truth)," it is because the poiesis of dQ is no less true than the folly of AQ.[38]

If the *DQ* unfolds fractally inward – from AQ to dQ, their epithets, and *el Bueno*, it also unfolds fractally outward – from AQ to the archives of La Mancha, bushels of paper scraps, a *morisco* translator, Cide Hamete Benengeli, the unwieldy narrator, the narrator of the prologue, and finally to Cervantes-Saavedra (a pen name). That Cervantes introduces an Arab historian into the text by virtue of a scrap of manuscript marginal annotation which comments on an embodied Dulcinea points toward the inheritance of the Arabic tradition of erotic lyric poetry not only in medieval Iberia but also in Sicily and, it has been claimed, in the *fragmenta* of Petrarch.[39] In taking the author beyond Spain's "old Christians," Cide

[37] Again, it is here necessary to acknowledge the similarity with the later Romantic understanding of a fragmentary. See n.1 and n.14 in this Coda.

[38] (Cervantes, *DQ*, 1999, I: 1, 37); (Cervantes, *DQ*, 2003, 20). The ambiguity of this statement is insurmountable. I take the ironic mode as a deadpan of deadpan which amounts to aesthetic sincerity.

[39] (El Saffar, *Distance and Control*, esp. 115); (Mallette, *European Modernity*, 34–64); (Ponce-Hegenaur, "Lyric and Empire").

Hamete also recalls the transposition of religious faith with erotic faith which Cervantes enacts as early as the *Tratos de Argel*, either in Algiers or shortly after his return, a transposition consonant with the poetries of *erotic mysticism* which developed out of readings of Abravanel's *Dialoghi* (itself a synthesis of the multi-faithed eroticism of the *Convivencia*). The presence of Cide Hamete in the narrative framing likewise participates – alongside Zoraida/Maria, Ricote, and Ana Félix – in the dramatization of the exile of the *moriscos* in 1609, which was the culmination of oppressive policies that had begun with the taking of Granada in 1492 and which escalated with the brutal suppression of the uprising in the Alpujarras from 1568 to 1571.[40] But I would like to consider here the possibility that Cide Hamete Benengeli is not an Other from without, but another from within. In the style of Pastoral Petrarchism, Cide Hamete Benengeli is one of the many pseudonyms that the poet, Cervantes, employs for his own unstable linguistic perspectivism when he embeds the *figura of the poet* as the madman at the heart of the *modern novelistic subject*.[41] This pseudonym of the author's own invention could easily date to his time in Algiers if in fact the *baños* were the prison in which the book was conceived, a gesture which heightens the irony of the xenophobic expressions littered throughout the text.

While Spitzer related polynomasia to the way a given character appears to other characters (as in the case of Teresa Panza), he did not relate nominal fluidity to the way in which a character transforms within their own narrative trajectory (as in the case of Lisandro in the *Galatea*). For Spitzer the nominal fluidity of the text indicates the diverse but more or less static socio-cultural identities of the various characters: "In this way, 'soberana y alta señora' [sovereign and sublime lady] becomes 'alta y sobajada señora' [sublime and fondled lady] – which the barber connects to 'sobrehumana o soberana' [superhuman or sovereign]: for this single term of address we are presented with these versions, resulting in a polyonomasia, as in the case of proper names."[42] In the case of Dulcinea's poetic epithets, where each variation indicates the speaker's socio-linguistic identity, the barber ironically stumbles upon the most pastoral of these linguistic veils. But Cervantes' use of nominal fluidity does more than

40 For example: (L.A. Marchante-Aragón, "*DQ*'s Ana Félix: The Virile Morisca Maiden, and the Crisis of Imperial Masculinity," *Hispanófila*, 176, 2016, 3–18).

41 These personae can be traced beyond the *DQ* (and beyond dQ) to the character of Lauso in the *Galatea*, the speaker of the 1579 *octavas* to Veneziano, and even the 1567 sonnet to Isabel. Perhaps Cide Hamete, like Saavedra, is a *sobrenombre* which dates to the author's time in Algiers (the *DQ* was famously conceived in prison).

42 (Spitzer, "Linguistic Perspectivism," 180–181).

distinguish one character from another: changes of name and lexicon indicate internal transformations through the narrative emplotment of *lyric subjectivity*. Names reveal how characters relate to themselves. As discussed in Chapter 6, Cervantes' attention to the temporal discontinuity of the "I" appears in the *Galatea* when Lauso conjugates his own disintegration with the verb *ser* (to be).[43] The same is true of Cardenio's transformation from *el loco de la Sierra Morena* (author of the abandoned sonnet), Dorotea's quest as the Princess Micomicona, and Zoraida/María. The metonymic movement of linguistic perspectivism that Cervantes brings from the pastoral into the modern novel by way of the practice of *lyric subjectivity* is itself fluid. Insofar as this polynomisia preserves *lyric subjectivity* in all of his characters, nominal fluidity is part and parcel of their *heteroglossia*; it is also evidence of their *transcendental homelessness*.

Where Spitzer funnels the polyonomasia of names and things through the author-demiurge and toward a divinity for whom language is arbitrary to meaning, Bakhtin disperses the fiction of language as "lively play" for which there is no clear or central vantage point. This is closer to Cervantes' usage (the absence of a vantage point in fact legitimates the nominal fluidity). Bakhtin's analysis of discourse in the novel ultimately extends beyond the dichotomy of the *basiyelmo*, to the observation that "the development of the novel is a function of the deepening of dialogic essence, its increased scope and greater precision. Fewer and fewer neutral, hard elements ('rock bottom truths') remain that are not drawn into dialogue. Dialogue moves into the deepest molecular and, ultimately, subatomic levels."[44]

But Bakhtin curiously exiles poetry as monologic from the *heteroglossia* of competing forms of discourse. What I have tried to show in *Cervantes the Poet: The* Don Quijote, *Poetic Practice, and the Conception of the First Modern Novel* is that lyric discourse as it developed in poetic practices throughout the sixteenth century was not only accidentally *heteroglot* but also *heteroglossia* in practice. Additionally, what Cervantes reveals in the emplotment of *lyric subjectivity* is that the dialectic of reason/unreason resists the solidification of the *modern subject* as a static identity in whom

43 (Cervantes, *Galatea*, 1961, vol. II, 92–93).

44 "The orientation of the word amid the utterances and languages of others, and all the specific phenomena connected with this orientation, takes on *artistic* significance in novel style. Diversity of voices and heteroglossia enter the novel and organize themselves within it into a structured artistic system. This constitutes the distinguishing feature of the novel as a genre . . ." (Bakhtin, *Dialogic Imagination*, 300).

a monoglossia could take root (as long as unreason is acknowledged as a legitimate part of its "totality"). Before characters negotiate lexicons amongst themselves, faced with the ever-present possibility of silence as speech, Cervantes' protagonists must first negotiate between ineffability and articulation within their own interiors. Like the poets of Pastoral Petrarchism, these characters make their interiors legible through the difficult negotiation of a diverse, heterogeneous, and at times multifarious linguistic inheritance in which any sense of the "I" is continuously at stake. In so doing, that multifarious linguistic inheritance is resisted and transformed through repeated self-identification and recognition in speech. Where Bakhtin locates in poetry the dangers of monoglossia, the practice of Pastoral Petrarchism (and its traces in the *DQ*) reveal that *lyric subjectivity* in practice introduces novel fragmentation into any pretense of linguistic or discursive homogeneity. When Bakhtin writes, "the novel, after all, has no cannon of its own. It is, by its very nature, not canonic. It is plasticity itself. It is a genre that is ever questing, ever examining itself and subjecting its established forms to review,"[45] he implicitly invokes the *figura of the poet* and the dynamic multiplicity of language in the poetic practice of *lyric subjectivity* as narrative poiesis.

That such a subject is discursively at stake both within itself and within its social whole immediately invokes Lukács' formulation of *transcendental homelessness*.[46]

> What is the problem of the transcendental *locus* if not to determine how every impulse which springs from the innermost depths is coordinated with a form that it is ignorant of, but that has been assigned to it from eternity and that must envelop it in liberating symbols? When this is so, passion is the way, predetermined by reason, towards complete self-being and from madness come enigmatic yet decipherable messages of a transcendental power, otherwise condemned to silence. There is not yet any interiority, for there is not yet any exterior, any 'otherness' for the soul. The soul goes out to seek adventure; it lives through adventures, but it does not know the real torment of seeking and the real danger of finding; such a soul never stakes itself; it does not yet know that it can lose itself, it never thinks of having to look for itself. Such an age is the age of epic.[47]

[45] (Bakhtin, *Dialogic Imagination*, 39).
[46] For Lukács and the modern novel: (Cascardi, *Subject of Modernity*, 72–124).
[47] (Lukács, *Theory of the Novel: A historico-philosophical essay on the forms of great epic literature*, trans. Anna Bostock, Cambridge: MIT Press, 1987, 28–29).

The "loss" of the coordinated "age of epic," which Lukács observes in the *DQ*, is manifest in the lyric rift between interior and exterior, and the continual coming-into-language which is its process and by which it generates its own forms. The lyric, perhaps more acutely than any other genre, knows that it can lose itself. In epic, the hero's many conflicts never put at stake his own status as an exemplar within his own particular social order. When Odysseus goes to Hades, it is not the inner hell of Robert Lowell, but a collectively recognized underworld.[48] When dQ descends into the Cave of Montesinos, he goes alone as sole witness "to the other side."[49] In epic, the hero may be a negative or positive exemplar, but he is never peripheral. In lyric, the "I" of the speaker is only ever at stake. But where Lukács, and later Cascardi, lament this "loss," what Cervantes' *modern subject, the figura of the poet* as modern madman, reveals is that this *transcendental homelessness* is the condition of possibility for an ethical and productive actor, and that the practice of such an actor is necessarily *quixotic*.[50]

In the sixteenth-century practices of Pastoral Petrarchism, *lyric subjectivity* as erotic mysticism lacked a transcendental signified but it was not without a (sovereign) *logos* beyond itself.[51] The erotic has always occupied a curious position between interior and exterior, formal and sensuous, real and ideal.[52] It is the erotic nature of AQ/dQ's *lyric subjectivity* that renders

[48] (Lowell, "Skunk Hour," 82–83). Lowell, of course, is drawing on Milton's Satan, "Which way I fly is Hell; myself am Hell" (*Paradise Lost*, Book IV, line 75).

[49] As a lyric in prose, Joyce's *Ulysses* falls out of language.

[50] This departs from Ortega y Gasset's assertion that the *DQ* is *quijotismo*, whereas dQ is only mistaken as such. If the *DQ* is *quijotismo*, then its first author, Alonso Quijano, is too.

[51] On this problem in phenomenology: (D. Carr, "The 'Fifth Meditation' and Husserl's Cartesianism," *Philosophy and Phenomenological Research*, 34.1 (1973) 14–35; esp. 30).

[52] In a letter of September 4, 1872, a sixteen-year-old Sigmund Freud confided an early erotic experience to his friend Eduard Silberstein, with whom he had devised an epistolary exchange under the name of the *Academia Española* following their reading of Cervantes' *Coloquio de los perros*. As epistolary pseudonyms they took the names of Cervantes' talking dogs, Cipión and Braganza. The young Cipión (Freud) wrote, "I have soothed all my turbulent thoughts and only flinch slightly when her mother mentions Gisela's name at table. The affection appeared like a beautiful spring day, and only the nonsensical Hamlet in me, my diffidence, stood in the way of my finding it a refreshing pleasure to converse with the half-naïve, half-cultured young lady. One day I shall explain to you the difference between my affection and another passion at some length; for the moment let me just add that I did not suffer any conflict between ideal and reality, and that I am incapable of making fun of Gisela .... But I have strayed from the subject dear to me; it would seem that I have transferred my esteem for the mother to friendship for the daughter. I am, or consider myself to be, a keen observer; my life in a large family circle, in which so many characters develop, has sharpened my eye, and I am full of admiration for this woman [her mother] whom none of her children can fully match .... Gisela's image refused to budge from my mind. Carambi!" (ed. W. Boehlich, *The Letters of Sigmund Freud to Eduard Silberstein, 1871–1881*, trans. A.J. Pomerans, Harvard University Press, 1990, 16–19). Insofar as Freud suppresses this unity of the real and the ideal in his early erotic life, his work cannot be thought to grapple candidly with the erotic psyche.

this protagonist an embodied novelistic character, and saves him from the erasure of the "pure, absolute, and universal" concept or the "pre-scripted and stale" refurbished literary trope.[53] Like the *divinos ingenios* of sixteenth-century poetry – Garcilaso, Montemayor, Figueroa, Herrera – and their model, Francesco Petrarca, dQ seeks poetic immortality and everlasting fame through his many exalted and embodied apostrophes to the timeless lady of his thoughts.[54] But, unlike the characters of the romances of chivalry, Dulcinea is not, as Eric Auerbach would have her, a fiction.[55] Dulcinea is a pseudonym, the poetic immortalization of Aldonza Lorenzo, a woman from a nearby village whom AQ, it is said, had loved and to whom he had failed to make known his affections.[56] She is a *giovanile errore*; perhaps he saw her standing at a balcony once. "Transcendental" lady of his thoughts, she is the ground in which his linguistic perspectivism takes root. Aldonza Lorenzo/Dulcinea del Toboso (mimesis/poiesis) is the sovereign lady (the "*Celia*") of this *modern subject*. Aldonza Lorenzo (whoever she was) is the corporeal unreason (that which cannot be reasoned), the *summa belleza* at the "center" of *el Bueno*.[57] Not by way of mimesis, but by way of poiesis he roots himself beyond himself and yet within the "world," or at its limits. His foundation is not within reason, but beyond it.[58] As such, she marks and also facilitates his transitions between

[53] In the Romantic sense, he possesses organicity (Lacoue-Labarthe and Nancy, *The Literary Absolute*, 44).

[54] (Cervantes, *DQ*, 1999, I: 1 and II: 67).

[55] Writing on Sancho's attempt (Part II, Chapter 10) to convince dQ that an anonymous laborer is his Dulcinea, Auerbach remarked, "the scene is distinguished by the fact that here for the first time the roles appear exchanged. Until now it had been Don Quiojote who, encountering everyday phenomena, spontaneously saw and transformed them in terms of the romances of chivalry, while Sancho was generally in doubt and often tried to contradict and prevent his master's absurdities. Now it is the other way round . . ." (E. Auerbach, *Mimesis: The Representation of Reality in Western Literature*, NY: Doubleday Anchor Books, 1957, 339). Auerbach's insistence, like that of so many of Cervantes' critics, to treat the figure of Dulcinea as an invented object, interchangeable with windmills, barber's helmets, and roadside inns, is one of the great reading errors that Cervantes' work has suffered. If Dulcinea could enter the physical landscape that AQ and Sancho Panza share, she would come as the aging Aldonza Lorenzo. Outside of this possibility, dQ cannot project her into presence as he does with giants and the helmet of Mambrino, because she is not, by definition, of his making. Both Auerbach and Sancho Panzo fail to understand this discrete facet of AQ's madness.

[56] "¡Oh, cómo se holgó nuestro buen caballero cuando hubo hecho este discurso, y más cuando halló a quien dar nombre de su dama! Y fue, a lo que se cree, que en un lugar cerca del suyo había una moza labradora de muy buen parecer, de quien él un tiempo anduvo enamorado, aunque, según se entiende, ella jamás lo supo ni le dio cata dello). Llamábase Aldonza Lorenzo, y a esta le pareció ser bien darle título de señora de sus pensamientos . . ." (Cervantes, *DQ*, 1999, I: 1, 44). For my departure from the reading given by González Echevarría: (Ponce-Hegenauer, "La muerte de Aldonza Lorenzo").

[57] For the "*Celia*": Chapter 4. See n.53 in this Coda on organicity.

[58] Dulcinea is the point of recognition that lends sense to his madness, the order of meaning upon which all of his words and actions depend. His primary interlocutor, if he has an interlocutor at all, is

exterior lexicons and interior lexicons. This is the innermost unreason of the *modern subject*, and it is only once AQ's erotic psyche is transformed into dQ's erotic psyche – the fact that dQ has a psyche at all – that the burlesque becomes a novel.

The exterior madness of AQ is somewhat less complex. As a socio-political actor he is understood by his peers within the fiction and by the narrators who immortalize him (and by most readers of the *DQ*) as a figure of folly.[59] Because *lyric subjectivity* is at stake in its own articulation, it renders contingent the field of competing discourses into which it enters, and to the degree to which it makes itself anew, it also refashions those same discourses which it puts to use. As such, the lyric does not lack in individual "totality," but neither does it claim a "discourse of the whole."[60] Because the *lyric subject* is perennially at stake in these transformations, its position at the impasse between reason and folly (intelligibility and unintelligibility) is by no means assured. Its place between those who are fools and those who are not is perennially contingent. As a *petit récit*, a lyric conjures the lexicon necessary for its articulation and so produces a heterogeneous coincidence of form and substance from competing and contingent fields of discourse. It is transformative. But, in terms of social recognition, of existential status, the charge of folly and the "redemption" of reason are not left to the poet to decide because these are socially constructed judgments. Exterior madness is the product of the *lyric subject*'s unwillingness or inability to operate intelligibly or appropriately within the discursive "totality" of a given historical instant. This folly can be understood as the heterogeneous introduction of untimely and fantastic lexicons into the perceived "homogeneity" of a linguistic landscape, with a purposive eye to futurity. Such "mad" utterances articulated at the periphery of the perceived cultural "totality" are consonant with Foucault's understanding of folly, "where the values of another age, another art, another morality are put into question, and also, where all the forms, even the most distant, of the human imagination, are mixed up, troubled, and strangely compromised by one another in a common chimera."[61] Such madness, then, is always contingent on the degree to

Dulcinea, not Sancho Panza, as many have surmised. By interlocutor, I mean she is the place where language begins to happen for him. (Cervantes, *Trato de Argel*, 913 n.62).

59 Recall that the figure of folly invoked an inverted world in early-modern thought.

60 (Cascardi, *Subject of Modernity*, 124).

61 "Folie, où sont mises en question les valeurs d'un autre âge, d'un autre art, d'une autre morale, mais où se reflètent aussi, brouillées et troublées, étrangement compromises les unes par les autres dans une chimère commune, toutes les formes, même les plus distantes, de l'imagination humaine" (Foucault, *Histoire de la folie*, 57).

which the lexical persona of a *subject* differs from the discursive "totality" which that subject resists, seeks to transform, and in which it seeks its own social recognition. In this sense the impasse between reason and unreason is truly a line drawn in the sand (on a windy beach just before high tide); it is a sliding scale in which the speaker and the language of articulation are eternally contingent. What Cervantes' linguistic perspectivism ultimately reveals about the *modern subject* is that the discursive "totalities" in which we find ourselves, when faced with lyrical poiesis, turn out to be rather flimsy fictions, so long as we stake "ourselves" within them. This is the exterior unreason of Cervantes' quixotic *modern subject.*

But at the close of the *DQ*, weeping narrator and all, Cervantes is not finished. In the remaining year, prior to his death on April 22, 1616, he completed what he considered his *magnum opus*, a prose Romance meant to compete with Heliodorus' *Aethiopica*. In the *Persiles and Sigismunda*, Cervantes moves from the singular narratological structure of the novel – man and world – into the pluralistic narratological structure of the Byzantine Romance – lovers in the world.[62] The question of *lyric subjectivity* as an *erotic subjectivity*, posed in Lauso of the *Galatea* and only poetically realized in *el Bueno* of the *DQ*, is reprised and reconfigured in the ever-*ingenious* Persiles. Where the emplotment of a single *lyric subjectivity* finds the culmination of its practice in death, the practice of the intersubjective Romance (which, in this instance, is also romantic) realizes itself in union. Driven by an erotic subjectivity through an uncharted landscape, the *lyric subjectivity* of this Cervantine *ingenio* is matched by that of the very physical "lady of his thoughts" (she is only "transcendental" for the durations during which he is separated from her), Sigismunda, whose narrative emplotment moves in accordance with her own interior ideation of the beloved.[63] More than mere poetic figuration or mimetic memory (though neither lover dispenses with these "metaphysical" traveling compasses), she is a *divino ingenio* and a *modern subject* driven forth by her own *erotic subjectivity* – a lyric lover for whom religious tropes are

62 (D. de Armas Wilson, *Allegories of Love: Cervantes's Persiles and Sigismunda*, Princeton University Press, 1991, esp. xv).

63 "Yo – replicó Auristela – no sé que es amor, aunque sé lo que es querer bien" (Cervantes, *Los Trabajos de Persiles y Sigismunda*, ed. J. B. Avalle-Arce, 1969, III: 19, 401). For the risk of Tristan and Isolde, "Tristan, Isolde, Isolde, Tristan, in the boat carrying them to the black hole of betrayal and death. A facility of consciousness and passion, a redundancy of resonance and coupling" (G. Deleuze and F. Guattari, *A Thousand Plateaus: Capitalism and Schizophrenia*, ed. and trans. Brian Massumi, University of Minnesota Press, 1987, 174–191, esp. 184); (G. Deleuze and F. Guattari, *Capitalsime et Schizophrénie 2: Mille Plateaux*, Éditions de Minuit, 1980, 214–234, esp. 224). How Cervantes avoids this risk will have to be treated elsewhere.

appropriated and repurposed in the service of erotic outcomes.[64] Where AQ's return to his legal name is both his completion (*el Bueno*) and his *desengaño*, the return of Periandro and Auristela to their legal names constitutes their completion and fulfillment, a re-enchantment of the world. Perhaps it is this lyrical character of the intersubjective Romance which we are slowly building the conceptual tools to apprehend.

[64] In the infamous words of Madonna, "like a prayer."

Index